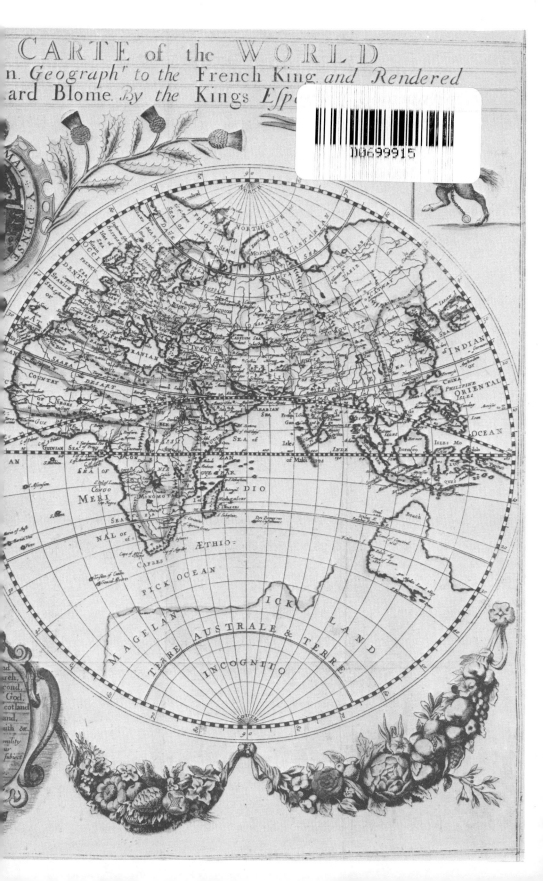

CARTE of the WORLD

n. Geograph.ᵉ to the French King. and Rendered

.ard Blome. By the Kings Esp

The
GREAT MAP
of
MANKIND

I have always thought with you, that we possess at this time very great advantages towards the knowledge of human Nature. We need no longer go to History to trace it in all its stages and periods. History from its comparative youth, is but a poor instructour . . . But now the Great Map of Mankind is unrolld at once; and there is no state or Gradation of barbarism, and no mode of refinement which we have not at the same instant under our View. The very different Civility of Europe and of China; The barbarism of Tartary, and of arabia. The Savage State of North America, and of New Zealand.

(Edmund Burke to William Robertson, 9 June 1777,
The Correspondence of Edmund Burke, III,
ed. George H. Guttridge, Cambridge, 1961, 350–1.)

The
GREAT MAP
of
MANKIND

British Perceptions of the World
in the Age of Enlightenment

P. J. Marshall
&
Glyndwr Williams

J. M. Dent & Sons Ltd
London Melbourne and Toronto

First published 1982
© P. J. Marshall and Glyndwr Williams 1982

This book is set in VIP Baskerville by
D. P. Media Limited, Hitchin, Hertfordshire

Printed in Great Britain by
Biddles Ltd, Guildford, Surrey
for
J. M. Dent & Sons Ltd
Aldine House, 33 Welbeck Street, London W1

British Library Cataloguing in Publication Data

Marshall, P. J.
    The great map of mankind.
    1. Discoveries (in geography)—European
    I. Title   II. Williams, Glyndwr
    910'.94   G80

    ISBN 0-460-04554-7

Contents

The maps on the endpapers are taken from Richard Blome, *A Geographical Description of the Four Parts of the World* (1670) and John Pinkerton's *Modern Atlas* (1812) and are reproduced by courtesy of the British Library.

Preface

We have written the Introduction, Chapters 1 and 2 and the Conclusion together. Chapters 3 to 6 are the work of P. J. Marshall, who wishes to thank the Royal Society of London, for permission to quote from the Society's MSS, and Dr Shirley Jones of the Department of French, University College, London, for much bibliographical advice. Chapters 7 to 9 are by Glyndwr Williams, who wishes to thank Dr Anthony J. Barker and Dr Michael Hoare for letting him consult their work before it was published.

In using quotations from contemporary sources we have modernized the use of capitals, but preserved the original spelling and punctuation. Titles of published works are given in full on the first occasion in each chapter when they are cited. The place of publication is London unless otherwise stated.

P.J.M.
G.W.

Introduction

Many books have been written about the 'attitudes' towards, or about the 'discovery' of, one society (usually a non-European one) by another (usually European) at some period in the past. Abundant material for such books can be gathered from contemporary accounts, letters or diaries; but the selection and focusing of this material raise serious problems. Whose attitudes are being examined and exactly what is being discovered? In some studies, those for example dealing with non-European influences on European art, music and literature, these questions can be answered with confidence. The attitudes of a limited number of authors, painters or musicians are in question and their discoveries and borrowings can be identified in their work. Other attempts are less well defined and more ambitious in their scope. This book falls into that category. In 1777 Edmund Burke congratulated William Robertson on his new *History of America*. Readers of such works, Burke wrote, would find that 'the Great Map of Mankind is unrolld at once' for their consideration. We shall be trying to describe what Burke, his immediate contemporaries, and also previous generations going back to the late seventeenth century, saw on this 'map' of non-European peoples that was being displayed to them. Thus both the peoples observed and the body of observers are potentially vast in extent. Practical limits are, however, forced upon us and we have reduced Burke's 'Mankind' to the peoples of Asia, North America, West Africa and the Pacific. In trying to assess the responses of a British 'public' we can only offer the vaguest conjectures about what, if anything, the great mass of the British population made of the world outside Europe in our period. This book is concerned almost entirely with the small group of individuals who committed their views to print.

The discoveries and claims of such men will be presented in their own terms. In other words this is a book about images and conceptions; only incidentally does it seek to chart the growth of objective knowledge. Such a growth certainly took place in our period. Maps became more comprehensive and accurate; linguistic expertise developed; there was a serious attempt to present the customs and manners of alien peoples as something more than a string of anecdotes. The great collections of travel accounts brought together at the end of the sixteenth century and the beginning of the seventeenth by Hakluyt and Purchas were supplemented by the ever-growing volume of new accounts and new collections, described in chapter 2. For certain areas the growth of knowledge was especially marked. The Pacific and its peoples took shape and came to life in the charts and observations of James Cook. Exploration began to penetrate beyond the slave coasts of West Africa. British travellers entered Tibet. By the end of the eighteenth century scholars in Britain were able to translate Sanskrit texts and a thirteen-year-old English boy had even spoken a few words of Chinese to the emperor in Peking.

Yet to point out that Englishmen by 1800 undoubtedly knew more than their predecessors had done about non-European peoples is not necessarily to claim that they understood these peoples any better. The frequency with which western experts in our own time have been confounded by developments in what has come to be known as the Third World is a sobering reminder of the limitations of knowledge.

When one society views another it seems inevitable that even those best informed will mix their knowledge with assumptions, preconceptions and prejudices. That is why we are concerned with the images created by this mixture in the minds of eighteenth-century Englishmen. Such images seem to us to be well worth studying for a number of reasons. In the first place, growing awareness of the outside world has long been recognized as an important aspect of the European Enlightenment. More than one new world was revealed to the scholars of our period; they came crowding in to excite and perplex the imagination. The rediscovery of antiquity was being matched by the revelation of existing races and peoples hitherto either little known or even completely unknown. Men were now able to seek explanations of their own society in a much wider continuum of time and space. To a greater degree than ever before Europe was compared to other societies. Such comparisons could stimulate revision of Europe's view of itself; much more commonly, however, they served to give greater weight to concepts already formed in Europe. The suggestion that 'One of the ways in which men are led to make most vividly manifest the values and habits of thought which underlie their own social attitudes is by contact with ways of life and thought which are alien to them' has much force.[1] Travel literature and assessments of travel literature in our period are some of the most trenchant statements of the Enlightenment's view of man.[2]

This new awareness of the wider world, this enlargement of mental horizons, did not take place in a vacuum. At the end of the seventeenth century England already possessed an empire in the Caribbean and North America, while her trade was spreading along the coast of West Africa and in maritime Asia. By 1800 Britain's global dominance, if not already in existence, would clearly be a matter of time. A vast, new, territorial empire was being created in India, bridgeheads had been established at Sierra Leone, New South Wales and the Cape of Good

Hope, and the instruments of nineteenth-century British supremacy – commercial dominance, naval power and missionary zeal – were already enfolding the world. Neither of us would wish to suggest that the climate of opinion which we are attempting to describe 'caused' British expansion in any direct or simple sense; yet action involving non-European peoples was inevitably influenced by preconceptions and supposed knowledge. And while we do not suggest that Englishmen in general during the eighteenth century thought that it was their destiny to rule over non-Europeans in a colossal empire, we can discern and trace a series of assumptions which by the end of our period indicated that non-European societies could be understood by Europeans and were markedly inferior to those of Europe, above all of Britain itself. Should it become Britain's fate to rule others, those assumptions would become important.

Our way of treating 'The World' reflects contemporary assumptions in Britain. When Gibbon surveyed his life in his *Autobiography* he reflected that he had avoided the fate of most of his fellow creatures, who had been born either under 'slavery' or under 'barbarism'. For eighteenth-century Englishmen, Asia was the continent of 'slavery', that is of civilizations once of considerable achievement but now atrophied under despotic systems of government. These features extended from the Hellespont to the China Sea. Throughout this huge area 'eastern' or 'oriental' peoples could be sharply distinguished from their neighbours in Europe. They shared many characteristics and it was possible to generalize about them. Accordingly, our sections on Asia treat the continent as a whole, however questionable this would seem to be now. By so doing we can illustrate eighteenth-century preoccupations much more clearly. Egypt, 'accessible only on the side of Asia, whose revolutions in almost every period of history, Egypt has humbly obeyed' (again to quote Gibbon)[3] is included in the Asian chapters. The world of 'barbarism' or of 'savagery', that is of people in an early stage of existence, appeared to contemporaries to be much more fragmented. 'Savages' were to be found in many parts of America and Africa, across Siberia, in the Pacific islands; but the differing pace of Europe's recognition of them, the varied nature of the contact when it was made, and the changing inhibitions of the observers, produced regional as well as chronological differences which point to separate chapters for the three areas of 'savagery' best known to the British in our period – North America, West Africa and the South Pacific.

Chronologically, the book covers what is by most conventions regarded as the period of the Enlightenment. It begins in the late seventeenth century, dealing with approximately the last quarter or so of it, and ends at about 1800, on the eve of 'Britain's imperial century'.

NOTES

1 J. W. Burrow, *Evolution and Society: A Study in Victorian Social Theory* (Cambridge, 1966), p. 2.
2 See the discussion in R. Pomeau, 'Voyages et lumières dans la littérature française du xviiie siècle', *Studies on Voltaire and the Eighteenth Century*, lvii (1967), 1269–89.
3 *Decline and Fall of the Roman Empire*, ed. J. B. Bury (1896–1900), i. 25.

PART I

1

Images of the World

Both writing about one's own travels and reading what other people have recorded about strange lands are very ancient human activities; but in western Europe towards the end of the seventeenth century there was a marked growth in the output of travel books and in the amount of critical attention devoted to them. Reports about the peoples of the world were acquiring a new value as the raw material for the attempts to analyse man and nature that came to be known as the European Enlightenment. This chapter will try to indicate what informed Englishmen could have been expected to know about the world, or those areas of it examined in this book, in the years of quickening interest and increasing information in the last quarter of the seventeenth century.

Asia

In forming their views of Asia, late seventeenth-century Englishmen were in fact the heirs to several different images of it. In spite of the flow of new information, Asia for most Europeans of education was still the Asia portrayed in the two most revered sources of knowledge: the Bible and the writings of Greek and Roman antiquity. Asia was first of all the Asia of the children of Israel, the land of Canaan and its immediate neighbours, such as Egypt, together with the great empires of the Assyrians and the Babylonians. Asia was also the Asia of Troy, the Greek colonies, the menace of Persia and of Alexander's world empire. Biblical and classical traditions later merged when Asia became the eastern province of the Roman empire, the setting for Christ's ministry, and the home of the early Christian churches. The Bible, or the writings of Herodotus, Pliny, Strabo and Ptolemy remained authorities on Asia which, for many, needed little if any revising or supplementing until the nineteenth century. The formidable scholar bishop, William Warburton, still believed in the mid-eighteenth century that 'the learned reader acquiesces in antiquity; the sensible reader prefers the evidence of a contemporary writer to the conjecture of a modern traveller'.[1] At the end of the century the distinguished naturalist and geographer Thomas Pennant thought 'HOLY WRIT our safest guide on all occasions' for Asian history.[2]

Medieval writers had embellished, refashioned and christianized classical traditions about Asia, while assimilating to them, often in a highly fanciful way, new information gained from the ebb and flow of contact between Europe and Asia, such as that brought back by the friars and merchants who had travelled in eastern Asia during the so-called Mongol peace of the fourteenth century. Accounts of such journeys extended the bounds of Asia well beyond those accepted in the Biblical or classical versions. For some areas, especially the huge mass of central Asia commonly called Tartary, medieval descriptions were not to be superseded until the eighteenth century. Medieval Europe had also faced an Asian phenomenon in the rise of Islam, on which neither the Bible nor the ancient world could give it any direct guidance. Here, too, medieval approaches continued to exercise a powerful influence throughout the seventeenth century. Indeed for Asia as a whole, medieval views, fabulous stories and all, have been described as still 'firmly embedded in all forms of literature' throughout northern Europe, including England, at the beginning of the century.[3] The most famous compendium of such views had an even longer life. The fourteenth-century compilation called *The Travels of Sir John Mandeville* was reprinted ten times in England in the late seventeenth and early eighteenth centuries.[4] At the very end of the eighteenth century Pennant could still describe Mandeville as 'the greatest traveller of his or any other age', even if he was willing to concede that Mandeville had been 'shamefully falsified by the monks'.[5]

During the sixteenth and seventeenth centuries contact between Europe and Asia took place on a greatly increased scale. Voyages round the Cape of Good Hope multiplied, especially with the establishment of the English and Dutch East India Companies in the early seventeenth century. At the same time permanent diplomatic and commercial contacts were built up with the Ottoman empire, and the Russians developed their great drive into Siberia. A much larger range of contacts meant a much greater flow of information coming out of Asia to Europe. More and more men returned to Europe to tell of their experiences in Asia, to bring Asian objects with them, and in some instances to write books describing what they had seen in Asia. By the end of the seventeenth century a considerable body of writing on Asia, either originally published in English or translated from other languages, was available to English readers.

The amount of knowledge which this literature conveyed to the

curious varied greatly according to the part of the continent in question. Late seventeenth-century maps of Asia were fundamentally different from sixteenth-century ones, which had still largely been based
on the theories which Ptolemy had expounded in the second century
AD. Portuguese knowledge began to appear on European printed maps
of Asia during the second half of the sixteenth century. During the
seventeenth century increasingly accurate calculations of longitude on
land enabled more realistic outlines to be given to the coasts visited by
European shipping. Inland, however, much remained uncertain.
Arabia, for instance, was still thought to harbour the 'Arabia Felix' of
classical geography. This was a land known for the 'fruitfulness and
richness of the soil, which produces plenty of corn, wine, fruits, odifer-
ous spices, great increase of cattle, also abounding in gold, pearls,
balsom, myrrhe, frankinsence, several sorts of drugs'.[6] Even maps of
areas as frequently visited as northern India contained striking errors.
The course of the Ganges was shown to be due south on most maps.
Mainland south-east Asia was still usually called 'India Extra
Gangem'. The names of its main states were known in some form or
other, but the extent of their territory was unclear. Beyond the frontiers
of India or China there was almost total obscurity. Heylyn's *Cosmography* in its 1682 edition assumed that there was still a Great Cham ruling
over Cathay from a city called 'Cambalu', although it admitted that
nothing had been heard of him for over a hundred years.[7] Virtually
nothing was as yet known in England of what the Russians had found in
Siberia. Maps did not make it clear what lay north of Cathay or
Tartary. One of a series of questions which the Royal Society hoped
would be resolved by travellers was whether Japan was or was not an
island.[8] A land of Jesso was usually located somewhere in north-eastern
Asia, but opinion varied as to where.

The part of the map of Asia likely to be etched most firmly upon the
minds of educated Europeans by the end of the seventeenth century
was the Levant. A considerable body of material about the Near East
was available in English. This relative abundance reflects geographical
proximity and ease of access; but it is also a clear indication that the
Levant was the part of Asia that seventeenth-century Englishmen most
wanted to know about. In the age of Gibbon and Voltaire Englishmen
interested in the Near East might be concerned, if superficially, with
such things as the arts and literature of the Arabs, the Turks and the
Persians or the character of Muhammad. For most of the seventeenth
century, however, priorities were very different. Knowledge of Islamic
civilization came almost as a by-product of a number of other preoccupations.

As was stressed at the beginning of this chapter, Asia was still largely envisaged in terms of the Bible, or of Greek, Roman or early Christian history. Those who travelled in the Near East did so with the Bible, Homer or Herodotus in hand. Many of them were more concerned with traces of antiquity than with any civilizations they actually saw. In their journeyings they tried to pinpoint ancient sites and to produce maps of the Middle East which would illustrate the Bible or classical history. For them Greek or Roman coins, inscriptions or statues were the great prizes. The value of Middle Eastern languages was directly related to their supposed age. For instance, Arabic was learnt as much for its value for the study of the Old Testament as for any understanding of the history or literature of the Arabs. The customs of the people of the Near East were of some interest because they were the same people who had lived in the area in Biblical times and it was assumed that Asian peoples did not change their mode of life. Even Sir John Chardin, the famous 'philosophical' traveller, had a 'favourite design' to prepare 'notes upon very many passages of the Holy Scriptures, whereof the explication depends on the knowledge of the custom of the eastern countries'.[9] Others went even further. 'Knowledg of the customs of the Indians' was said to be 'in no ways useful itself' but should only be acquired 'to justify what is told us of the ancients'.[10] Even the study of the plants and animals of the Near East could help to illuminate the Bible. Such priorities remained throughout the eighteenth century. In 1746 Thomas Shaw explained that his 'chief study and endeavour' in writing two books of *Travels, or Observations Relating to several Parts of Barbary and the Levant* had been 'to illustrate such portions of the sacred writings, as any way regarded the civil or natural history of those countries, that are there described'.[11]

Those who hoped that travel in the Levant would throw new light on the world of the Old Testament or on the history of Greece or Rome must in general have been disappointed by the end of the seventeenth century, and indeed were to continue disappointed for most of the eighteenth. Sites could be visited, but in the absence of archaeological techniques little could be found out about them that carried much conviction. Egyptian antiquities proved to be particularly frustrating. More and more English travellers went to Lower Egypt during the seventeenth century. They poked about sites, getting inside the pyramids and being lowered into mummy pits. Descriptions were written, measurements taken and things that could be conveniently purloined were carried home. As a result Englishmen could join in European debates about the age of Egyptian civilization, the meaning of the hieroglyphs and the purpose of the pyramids, but sober men recognized that such questions were still far from settled.[12] Inscriptions that were not in Greek or Latin could not be read. Travellers reported that they had found the site of Babylon and even of the Tower of Babel, although it was 'mightily ruined and low'.[13] Some spectacular sites largely new to Europeans were investigated – Baalbec, Palmyra and above all Persepolis. English merchants from Aleppo claimed to be the first explorers of Baalbec in 1691.[14] Readers of Chardin and of the Belgian traveller Le Bruin[15] were given dramatic illustrations depicting Persepolis as well as long descriptions of it. Remarkable as all three sites seemed to be, there was virtually no sure knowledge as to their history or use. Persepolis aroused as much disagreement as any Egyptian site. Even Troy kept its secrets. There was no agreement as to precisely where the city had been.[16]

Seventeenth- and eighteenth-century travellers, for all their ingenuity, could add little that served to elucidate the ancient Near East and therefore, as was universally assumed, the early history of man. So scholars remained tied to their traditional sources, the Bible and the Greek historians. Elaborate speculations, usually based on etymological guesses about unknown languages, were offered to bridge the chasms where evidence was lacking. Speculative theories of this kind were often the life's work of deeply learned men, but critics began to show a certain impatience with what seemed to be ultimately fruitless exercises.

At the very end of the seventeenth century the learned world was, however, given one addition to its knowledge of ancient peoples. This came as the result of the study in England of material sent back by travellers in Asia. The material was in Arabic and what was claimed to be ancient Persian. From it what were said to be the sacred writings and history of the Persians, the followers of Zoroaster and the religion of the Magi, were presented to Europe for the first time by Thomas Hyde, Professor of Arabic and Hebrew at Oxford University. A people of great antiquity, only previously known through what the Greeks or the Jews had said about them, could now be studied through their own writings.

Hyde, who had learnt Persian through his work on the Polyglot Bible, had gained his knowledge of ancient Iran partly from Arabic sources at Oxford and partly from material acquired from the Parsis of western India. Like a number of other Europeans, Hyde had come to appreciate that the Parsis were a people displaced from Iran. Apparently by what he later called 'a little bribing of one of their priests with a little money' and 'telling him it is for me who is a great lover of their religion',[17] Hyde's correspondents were able to persuade Parsis to part with copies of some of their scriptures. What Hyde obtained, or at least what he could read, was not apparently as antique as he supposed. But in 1700 he was able to publish an enormous book in Latin called *Historia Religionis Veterum Persarum*. When it appeared, the book sold badly. Hyde became discouraged and is said to have 'boil'd his tea kettle with the greatest part of the impression'.[18] His reputation grew after his death, however, and his work came to be accepted throughout Europe as definitive until the nineteenth century. It is totally dominated by the religious preoccupations of its own time and will be examined in that context in a later chapter, but modern scholars of Zoroastrianism still have some respect for Hyde's book.

Hyde's discoveries about the ancient Persians were an offshoot of the fostering of oriental languages at the universities largely by clerical patronage. Archbishop Laud had been the great benefactor of such studies at Oxford in the seventeenth century. He endowed an Arabic Chair, built up a great collection of manuscripts which ultimately passed to the Bodleian and took an active interest in the career of Edward Pococke, the first and probably the most distinguished Professor of Arabic. The motives of Laud and other churchmen in encouraging the study of eastern languages beyond Hebrew were largely theological. Islam was not regarded as an object worthy of study in its own right. A knowledge of Arabic was thought to be an important aid to the understanding of the Hebrew text of certain books of the Old Testament, as well as being the means of communicating with Christians in the Levant and possibly even of converting Muslims. But secular considerations also had some weight, at least in the establishment of the Cambridge Chair of Arabic, whose benefactor spoke of 'good literature' and 'much knowledge' which would become accessible through Arabic, as well as the growth of 'our commerce with those easterne nations'.[19] At Oxford Pococke marked out a programme of studies in his inaugural lecture which included Arabic literature, history and science.[20] By the end of the seventeenth century theological objectives were certainly not neglected, but the study of the by now abundant Arabic material available in Britain was beginning to make scholars increasingly aware of what had been the primary concerns of the authors so assiduously collected, their own history, literature, scientific knowledge, and inevitably their own religion. Scholarship began to leave the ancient world to grapple with Islamic civilization.[21]

So, too, did the travellers in the Levant, even if many of them, like the scholars at home, had often in the first instance been more interested in matters relating to the Bible or the classics. Many of those who worked on Arabic at the universities had been to the Levant, often as chaplains, but a rough division of labour did develop between scholars and travellers in the study of Islamic civilization and of Islam itself. The scholars produced editions of texts and studies of the origins of Islam and of its early expansion; travellers recorded their impressions of life in Islamic countries.

By the seventeenth century there was a considerable history of European attempts to come to some understanding of Islam. At certain times in the Middle Ages scholars, hoping to reconcile Muslims to Christianity or to convert them, had studied Islam in some depth. But by the sixteenth century there was little more than hostility and denunciation.[22] Much of this survived into the late seventeenth century and well beyond. Muhammad was still portrayed in the terms used by his Christian detractors for centuries as a power-crazed fanatic, or to some as an instrument of the devil, who had carefully manufactured a set of religious beliefs from Jewish and Christian doctrines communicated to him by renegades. He was a man of deplorable moral standards, but by cunning, including the forging of miracles and offers to his followers of sensual gratification both on earth and in heaven, he had deluded the Arabs into accepting his divine mission. The Arabs had then exploited the weakness and divisions of their neighbours, including the Eastern Christians, to extend their empire. For his inscrutable purposes God had chosen the Muslims to be the punishment for the sins of Christians. For the same reason he still allowed the great Islamic empires of Turkey, Persia and Mughal India to continue in being. They remained, in the words of Humphrey Prideaux's *Life of Mahomet* of 1697, 'a scourge unto us Christians, who, having received so holy and so excellent a religion through His mercy to us in Jesus Christ our Lord, will not yet conform ourselves to live worthy of it'.[23] Christians should amend their lives and wait patiently until God chose to bring down the infidel empires which he had raised up. In the meanwhile, the study of Islam was hardly a way in which it was profitable for them to pass their time. In popular publications the Koran was dismissed as the fabrication of a depraved and ignorant man, 'a thing so full of *tautologies*, incohaerencies, and such gross absurdities of so impure and carnal mixture, that he must lay aside the use of his natural reason, who is taken in by it'.[24]

Yet during the seventeenth century greater knowledge of Arabic and increased access to texts did lead to serious study of Islam in a number of European countries. Versions of the Koran were produced in various languages, including an English translation from a French version.[25] To one of his editions of an historical text, the *Specimen Historiae Arabum* of 1649, Pococke added three hundred pages of notes, containing 'a large account of the true opinions of the Mahometans', taking care 'upon proper occasions, to do them justice, by vindicating them from such things as have been fasten'd upon them without sufficient ground'.[26] Others were prepared to go further. An anonymous manuscript 'Account of the rise and progress of Mahometanism with the life of Mahomet and the vindication of him and his religion from the calumnies of Christians' achieved some circulation. It has been identified as the work of Henry Stubbe who died in 1676. Stubbe stressed that the teaching of Muhammad was not necessarily 'contrary to the dictates of reason and common sense'.[27] Orthodoxy among scholars was asserted by Prideaux at the end of the century. His book was both a biography of Muhammad and an exposition of the doctrines of Islam, based on some Arabic sources, usually in translation. It was entirely out of sympathy with its subject. Muhammad was an 'illiterate barbarian', 'very licentious and wicked in his ways',[28] while Prideaux found 'Mahometan divinity' to be 'the oddest stuff you ever saw in your life'.[29]

Traditional European assumptions about religious practices in Muslim countries were that non-Muslims were ruthlessly persecuted, while the faithful took part in meaningless rituals in public and lived licentiously in private. Closer observation of Muslim societies in the Levant did something to soften this picture. Most travellers shared the contemporary European aversion to Muhammad and believed that Islamic theology was worthless, but they often found things to admire in the piety and personal conduct of Muslims. The Levant Company chaplain, Thomas Smith, an austere Anglican, dismissed Islam as a concoction of 'folly and imposture and gross absurdities', but grudgingly accepted that Muslims were 'generally pious at prayer', and that some of them were 'hearty and sincere' in their devotions.[30] Another chaplain, Henry Maundrell, denounced Turkish 'lust, arrogance, covetousness, and the most exquisite hypocrisy', yet he could admire 'the profound respect they pay to religion and to every thing relating to it' and 'their great temperance and frugality'.[31] Thomas Hyde received at Oxford a 'Turkish liturgy' which was to be published after his death. He pointed out its 'nonsense and folly', but added that 'many of the Mahometans excel in the love of God. . . . Moreover, many of them are shining examples for alms, justice and other moral and theological virtues.'[32] Such comments were in line with what foreign travellers were also reporting. 'In Christendom', Thévenot wrote, 'many think that the Turks are devils, barbarous and men of no faith and honesty, but such as know and have conversed with them, have a far different opinion. . . . They are very devout and charitable; very zealous for their religion.'[33]

Whatever legends might hold to the contrary, all travellers reported that non-Muslims were not forcibly converted to Islam and that other religions were not proscribed. Assessments of the practical disabilities imposed on Christians varied. The Levant merchant, Sir Dudley North, thought that Christians enjoyed 'all freedom in performing their

ceremonies, that possibly can be allowed them'.[34] The consul Sir Paul
Rycaut, on the other hand, believed that everything possible was done
'to render them contemptible, to make them poor, and their lives
uncomfortable'.[35] The foreign merchant and diplomatic communities
were able to practise their religion freely. Relations between them and
Muslims seem usually to have been marked by indifference or disdain,
but contact of a warmer kind was occasionally made. Sir Thomas
Baines, a physician on his travels, encountered 'Vani Effendi, the great
preacher amongst the Turks'. Sir Thomas told him that: 'He believed a
Mussulman, living up to the height of his law, may be undoubtedly
saved. He thought himself obliged . . . not to touch a hair of a Mussulman's head for his difference in religion, but rather to help, assist,
relieve, and cherish them in every good office that he was able to do
them.' At which Vani Effendi 'wept and said he could not believe any
Christian came so near true Mussulmen, but that they had all been
idolaters'.[36]

Travellers' accounts also revealed something of the diversity of
Islam. Explaining that 'the diversity of opinions in Turkey is almost
infinite and more numerous than in England',[37] Rycaut provided one
of the several guides available to 'the sects and heresies' of the Turks.
He stated that free thinking and even atheism existed in Islam as well as
in Christian countries. Indeed, Thomas Smith thought that 'the greatest part of the Cadyes' were atheists, 'sensible of the idle fopperies of the
Alcoran and of the imposture of Mahomet'.[38]

Scholars working on the great collections of manuscripts accumulated in England rediscovered the learning of the Arabs that had so
impressed medieval Europe. Most of the Arabic professors became
advocates of the continuing value for the West of Arab medicine,
astronomy and geography. Practitioners of these subjects were not
always so impressed, but medical treatises and astronomical tables did
arouse interest. Translations of both were sometimes published.
Travellers in the Levant were more concerned with the arts and sciences as they were actually being practised in the seventeenth century.
Here the verdicts were almost unanimously unfavourable. Whatever
the Arabs may have been, the Turks were crude philistines. To their
sterner critics they were a 'people generally of the grossest apprehension, and knowing few other pleasures, but such sensualities as are
equally common both to man and beast'.[39] To those more lenient they
'improve not sciences much, and it is enough for them to read and
write'.[40] Arab astronomy had degenerated into Turkish astrology. The
Arabs had been famous geographers; a Turkish admiral told Thomas
Smith that he did not know where England was.[41] 'For other sciences as
logick, physick, metaphysick, mathematicks and other our university

learning, they are wholly ignorant'.[42] In a letter from Aleppo, Robert Huntington summed up the views of his contemporaries: 'The country is miserably decay'd and hath lost the reputation of its name, and the mighty stock of credit it once had for eastern wisdome and learning: it hath followed the motion of the sun, and is universally gone westward.'[43] Europe now had nothing to learn from the Levant.

Yet she still had something to fear. The Ottoman empire was still intact at the end of the seventeenth century. Analysis of Ottoman strengths and weaknesses was a major preoccupation of those who wrote about the Near East. In the manner of contemporary political writers they tried to identify the 'spirit' which kept the whole together. There was little doubt that fierce and rigid discipline provided the spirit of the Ottoman empire. Sir William Temple called the Turkish system 'the fiercest . . . in the world'.[44] The Sultan was an absolute ruler, sustained by ministers who were slaves rather than by an hereditary aristocracy. They owed their appointment to his whim and might lose their lives at his slightest displeasure. The core of the army was the slave regiments of janissaries and spahis. There were no titles or offices or indeed property of any kind which could stand against the power of the Sultan. From highest to lowest obedience was enforced by cruelty and terror. No one enjoyed security. The end result might be an all-powerful Sultan, but the price was poverty and devastation. A population constantly pillaged by the government had no incentive to produce beyond its barest wants. All commentators believed that lands which had once been prosperous and fertile in Biblical and classical times were now wretchedly impoverished by Turkish rule. François Bernier, who claimed that he had 'travelled through nearly every part of the empire', reported that it was 'lamentably . . . ruined and depopulated'.[45]

This simple picture of a streamlined despotism holding itself in power by ruthless discipline was in fact being contested in details by observers who had actually witnessed Turkish government in action. For instance, Dudley North agreed that Turkish government was in theory 'tyranny in the highest degree', but described his own experiences in Turkish courts where he found that a fixed law was applied by judges who could be relied on to 'determine according to right'.[46] Nevertheless, the stereotype was not seriously questioned until the eighteenth century. Indeed, acceptance of it provided increasing grounds for optimism. Even before their great defeats at the hands of the Austrians in the 1680s, signs of Turkish decline were being noted. The spirit was sagging; discipline was being relaxed and thus the empire must be in danger. Sultans were proving unworthy and were allowing ministers to become corrupt and the army to pass out of control. Early in the seventeenth century Sandys had scented corruption and decay.[47] To Thomas Smith the 'decay of discipline' was a good omen, since 'empires are kept and preserved by the same arts wherewith they were first establisht, which ceasing they begin to moulder into pieces'.[48] Rycaut diagnosed the Turkish government as becoming 'factious, and yet slothful'.[49] But if there were encouraging portents, few hazarded a guess as to when the end might come.

Iran, seen by late seventeenth-century Englishmen largely through the eyes of French travellers, offered a prospect in some ways similar to the Ottoman empire. It, too, was an Islamic society and it, too, was taken to be a despotism. A number of differences were, however, suggested, and in general the Iranians were presented in a more favourable light than the Turks. By contrast with the brutal, boorish Turks, Chardin, the universally acknowledged authority on Iran, described a people whose 'natural parts' are as 'beautiful as their bodies'. They were tolerant, hospitable, sweet-tempered, 'the most civiliz'd people of the East. . . . The polite men amongst them are upon a level with the politest men of Europe'.[50] The English surgeon, Fryer, believed that 'their natural ingenuity . . . exceeds all the eastern people, both for facetiousness of wit, civil behaviour, gallantry in appearance. . . . The very plebeans . . . are here affable and kind, not rude or unmannerly'.[51] Extravagance, idleness and excessive pride were also noted with disapproval; but Heylyn summed up contemporary opinions when he described the Persians as 'For the most part addicted to *hospitality*, magnificent in expence, lordly in their compliments, fantastical in their apparel, maintainers of *nobility* and desirous of peace'.[52]

Iranian learning was also thought to be superior to that of the Turks. Chardin considered them to be the most erudite of all non-European peoples, not excluding the Chinese. Like other writers he noted their enthusiasm for knowledge and found that they were acquainted with the full range of Greek and Arab learning. But Europeans were disappointed to find little progress beyond the classics. Chardin found them ignorant of all the more recent achievements of Europe. Instead of progressing they were becoming more and more involved in 'occult philosophy', 'necromantick problems' and soothsaying.[53] Chardin could only wonder at this blindness in men otherwise so intelligent.[54]

Iranians were not only thought to be more learned than the Turks, but they were also considered by Europeans to be an artistically creative people, which the Turks were certainly not. Their fondness for poetry was noted. Major translations of Persian poetry were not attempted until the eighteenth century, but fragments of Hafiz and Sadi were put into Latin by Thomas Hyde and into French by Chardin.[55] Persian miniatures were praised for their colouring,[56] and

Thévenot described the maidan at Isfahan as 'not only the lovliest' but also 'the greatest and finest' piazza in the world.[57]

To all Europeans the seventeenth-century Persian monarchy was a tyrannical despotism. Commentators were, however, inclined to find it less atrocious than the rule of the Sultan. Chardin thought that Shah Abbas I had built up the most powerful state in the world from any ruler's point of view. The King had a sanction which the Sultan did not. But except when they chose to eliminate potential enemies, Persian Kings behaved in a more regular way than did other Muslim rulers. The mass of the population suffered much less from them than did the subjects of the Sultan. Individual rights to land were recognized and were rarely disturbed. The Persian peasantry held their lands on reasonable terms and were not overtaxed. Indeed Chardin thought that their condition might be better than that of many peasants in Europe.[58] Under an able ruler like Abbas I the Persian monarchy might work tolerably well, but oriental despotisms were thought to be thoroughly unstable. A vicious or a weak ruler could bring all to ruin. In the second half of the seventeenth century Persia seemed to be on the way to ruin. During a residence of more than ten years Chardin believed that its wealth had fallen by a half.[59]

European observers found the Mughal empire, at its fullest territorial extent under Aurangzeb at the end of the seventeenth century, yet another example of Muslim despotism. Edward Terry, who accompanied an embassy early in the seventeenth century, and John Ovington, who wrote of his visit in 1689, used almost identical words. Terry believed that the Emperor 'makes his will his guide and therefore any thing lawfull that likes him'. His government was 'arbitrary, illimited, tyrannical'.[60] According to Ovington, 'The whole kingdom of Indoston is intirely in the possession of the Mogul's, who appoints himself heir to all his subjects. . . . His will likewise is the law, and his word incontestably decides all controversies among them'.[61] François Bernier, who had practised medicine at the Mughal court and travelled very widely throughout the empire, was the international authority on Mughal India. He was also one of the most outspoken exponents of the theory of oriental despotism which he saw as the blight that lay on the Ottoman empire, Persia and Mughal India. Security of property created prosperity, but 'Actuated by a blind and wicked ambition to be more absolute than is warranted by the laws of God and of nature, the kings of Asia grasp at every thing, until at length they lose every thing.' Although India was a fertile country with a favourable balance of trade, Mughal government produced poverty and lands went uncultivated.[62]

Europeans who had read about the Ottoman and Persian empires seem to have felt that closer study of the Mughals would tell them little that they did not already know. India was, however, the home of a vast population who were not Muslims. Yet in spite of nearly a hundred years of continuous trading contact with India, English readers who were curious about the Hindus at the end of the seventeenth century would have found little of substance in their own language. Seventeenth-century Europeans approached Hinduism with expectations based on the classics and on the Bible. There was a small corpus of Greek writing on India, most of it said to have originated in Alexander's expedition, which had been much glossed by later writers. According to these texts the Greeks had encountered sects of 'Brachmanes' or 'Gymnosophists' who cultivated recondite learning and lived austere lives. Valiant attempts were made to establish links between modern Brahmins and the Greeks. Transmigration in Hinduism and Buddhism was thought to be the origin of Pythagorean doctrines. Sir William Temple believed that Democritus and Lycurgus as well as Pythagoras had been taught by the Indians.[63] According to Henry Lord, Plato and Pythagoras still enjoyed 'an honoured mention amongst the people'.[64] Those who looked a little more closely at the complexities of Hinduism usually confessed, however, that Greek learning was now not easy to detect. They generally concluded that modern Brahmins had degenerated and forgotten their ancient wisdom. Terry found them 'a very silly, sottish, and an ignorant sort of people who are so inconstant in their principles, as they scarce know the particulars are which they hold'.[65] The other line of the pedigree foisted on the Hindus was rather easier to sustain. An ancient Asian people who had not been converted to Islam presumably kept alive the heathen doctrines of the gentiles against whom the Jews of the Old Testament had battled. The idolatry which had fascinated and appalled the Jews seemed to be preserved in the Hindu pantheon so luxuriously portrayed in temples. An early seventeenth-century traveller saw Hindus as 'naturally discended from the Gentiles'.[66] To a later writer they were 'indeed the antient Gentiles, . . . the seed of those who revolted from Moses, forgetting God to worship a molten calfe'.[67] The common term for Hindu remained Gentile or sometimes Gentoo.

English readers who wanted more solid fare could with some difficulty find it in translations from European sources. A genuine Hindu text had been presented in a book by the Dutch pastor Abraham Roger. His translation of the so-called Sentences of Bhartrihari was rendered into English by John Ogilby with accounts of the incarnations of Vishnu and similar matter.[68] Bernier disliked Hinduism, but a man of his intelligence who had lived several years in India could at least give his readers some genuine information.

Europeans, whose experience during the seventeenth century was largely confined to the trading and weaving communities on the Indian coasts, agreed that Hindus were submissive, frugal, industrious people. They were thought to be intensely conservative and to adhere rigidly to ancient custom. Much was written about caste. A popular geography summed up conventional knowledge:

> They are of strong quick apprehension, ready wit and good fancy, ingenious in all manner of fine manufactory. They are civil to strangers, profoundly submissive to their governors, timorous, and cowardly to their enemies, and mean spirited in their common actions. They are divided into many TRIBES, who constantly herd together and marry in their own clans.[69]

Although Portuguese, Dutch and English settlements had existed throughout south-east Asia for most of the seventeenth century, the mainland (or 'India Extra Gangem') was in 1682 still said to be 'not so well discovered at the present' so that only a 'lame' account could be given of it.[70] At the very end of the century the situation was to change somewhat. A great deal of publicity was to be directed at Siam as the consequence of a new policy being pursued by its ruler Phra Narai and his Greek minister, Phaulkon. The new policy was one of close relations with France. Thai embassies went to Europe and French missionaries and ambassadors were received cordially in Siam. In 1688 Phra Narai was overthrown and his French commitments abandoned. But during the short period of contact Europe was given a great deal about Siam from missionaries and above all from one of the ambassadors, La Loubère, whose book, translated in 1693 into English as *A New Historical Relation of the Kingdom of Siam*, was widely acclaimed. In 1699 William Dampier published a volume of voyages, which contained a full account of a period spent in Tonking. An ex-buccaneer who had sailed all over the world and already published a most attractive book of his adventures,[71] Dampier was assured of a large audience.

Readers of La Loubère and Dampier would learn yet more about Asian despotism. The mass of the population were poor, and oppression by uncontrolled governments was the direct cause of their poverty. Perceptive readers of La Loubère would also find in his book one of the fullest of the early European descriptions of Buddhism, even though it was not clearly identified as such.[72]

In spite of some trading contacts, English accounts had contributed virtually nothing to European knowledge of China by the end of the seventeenth century. During the sixteenth century information had been provided by the Portuguese. Throughout the seventeenth century there had been an ever-increasing volume of reports from the very cosmopolitan Jesuit mission working in China. Some material from other religious orders was also published, as were accounts of those who had accompanied Dutch and Russian embassies to Peking. English readers took a keen interest in China and from the late sixteenth century were provided with many translations. A recent authority suggests that even by 1600 the Chinese had become a 'real and accomplished people for the English'.[73] During the seventeenth century English translations were made of most of the significant work on China appearing in print. The first of the great Jesuit books, Trigault's account based on the papers of Ricci, the mission's pioneer, remained accessible only in Latin, but other Jesuit books were issued in English, such as Semmedo's *History of that Great and Renowned Monarchy of China* (1655), *The New History of China* written by Gabriel Magaillans (1688) and various editions of the highly controversial *Memoirs and Observations . . . made in a late Journey through the Empire of China* by Louis Le Comte. A compilation of Jesuit translations from Confucius which had originally appeared in French was rendered into English as *The Morals of Confucius* in 1691. One of the Dutch accounts of their mission to Peking, by Nieuhoff, was also made available in translation as *An Embassy from the East-India Company . . . to the Grand Tartar Cham Emperour of China* (1669).

By the end of the seventeenth century interpretations of China were becoming highly controversial in Catholic circles. The slant given to accounts varied between missionary orders and even among the Jesuits themselves. But little of this would as yet have been apparent to English readers. Nothing had been translated from the Dominicans who were usually critical of Jesuit interpretations. The translations that were available generally agreed on certain salient points. China was shown to be a colossus both in area and in population. Millions of people were tightly packed on the land and into innumerable towns and great cities. This huge population was thought to be subject to a quite extraordinary degree of centralized control which imposed an astonishing uniformity on them. The Emperor's will was believed to operate evenly and without check or obstacle over the whole of his vast country. The Chinese reverence for authority was the explanation for this. Chinese children unhesitatingly obeyed their parents and adults unhesitatingly obeyed the government. Thus China was governed like one large family. The Emperor was father of all. Chinese government was of course absolute, but it was a regulated absolutism, quite unlike the capricious despotism of the Muslim regimes in Turkey, Persia or India. The Emperor was brought up to put the welfare of his subjects before all other considerations and he never wavered in this. Emperors were open to advice and criticism. Most important of all, they exercised power not by personal whim carried out by slave ministers who went in peril of their lives, but through regular hierarchies of mandarin officials chosen for learning and virtue by public examination. All decisions had to be taken through the appropriate official channels. So whatever might happen to individual Emperors or dynasties (Europeans had recently witnessed the overthrow of the Ming and the Manchu conquest), the system of government survived unchanged and eternally constant. It had clamped the Chinese into a mould which had kept them the same from age to age back into a very remote past.

All accounts agreed that Chinese society was indeed very old. From the classical Chinese histories Jesuits reported certain dates for the founding of the monarchy of which the most often cited was 2952 BC. Such dating involved the Society in controversies about the age of the earth according to Christian traditions which will be examined in a subsequent chapter. The conciliatory approach to Chinese chronology was characteristic of the Jesuits' interpretation of Chinese religion as a whole. This interpretation was open to many objections. What was the precise nature of Confucian beliefs was the central issue in the debates within the Catholic Church about the Chinese Rites. But even Protestants accepted that an ancient set of beliefs worthy of respect survived in China. According to Nieuhoff:

> Of all the heathen sects which are come into the knowledge of those in Europe, we have not read of any who are fallen into fewer errours than the Chineses, ever since the first ages; for in their books we read that these people have worshipp'd the highest and one God-head.[74]

Some English readers were inclined to accept Jesuit claims about the age of Chinese civilization and the virtues of Confucius. In an essay of 1678 called *The Antiquity of China* John Webb accepted that China had been inhabited since 3000 BC and that 'never were pagans who less offended'.[75] Sir William Temple thought that Chinese government 'is known to have continued for several thousand years'.[76]

Although the Chinese system of government was said to depend on formal educational qualifications and the acquisition of learning, seventeenth-century accounts are full of doubts about the quality of what was learnt. The Chinese like the Persians had been left behind by the advance of knowledge in Europe. They were conceited, reluctant to abandon outmoded ideas, and incapable of 'that spirit of penetration and exactness which is so necessary to those who addict themselves to the search of nature'.[77] Like so many other Asian peoples, they applied much of their energy to following the blind alley of astrology. Missionaries who had been given official appointments on the Board of Astronomy found serious deficiencies in Chinese mathematics.

The portrayal of China available to readers at the end of the seventeenth century was largely the work of Jesuits. It was not, as is sometimes supposed, an unalloyed panegyric. Chinese xenophobia and overweening pride were frequently noted. The mass of the people were superstitious and idolatrous. Many of the educated were cynical atheists. Justice was often corrupted in practice, offices were sold, and officials were extortionate, however admirable the institutions of the empire might be. While some Jesuits wrote of plenty, others saw the mass of the people living in grinding poverty, subject to famine and driven to infanticide and even rebellion. Yet overall, China was held up for admiration. A totally stable government of immense antiquity administering wise laws through an élite of philosophers and keeping a strict public peace by deference rather than by terror was a wonderful phenomenon. Peace and order enabled a huge population to develop agriculture, manufacturing and trade to very high levels. China was a vast human ant heap of industry.

In the eighteenth century this picture was to be subjected to very close scrutiny. It was to become apparent that the missionaries did not agree among themselves, their accuracy was to be questioned and others, ultimately including Englishmen, were to make their contributions. But in the late seventeenth century readers had little alternative to accepting the broadly favourable consensus that was offered them. English readers generally seem to have done so. England produced an early Sinophile in Sir William Temple, who thought: 'It were endless to enumerate all the excellent orders of this state, which seem contrived by a reach of sense and wisdom, beyond what we meet with in any other government of the world'.[78] John Webb agreed that 'if ever any monarchy in the world was constituted according to political principle, and dictates of right reason, it may be boldly said that of the Chinois is'.[79] The Royal Society expected 'an empire of learning, . . . a new Indian mine and treasure' from closer acquaintance with China.[80] To the compiler of the *Compleat Geographer* the first reports of 'so polite a nation' seemed 'more like romances than truths', but the missionary accounts 'all agree to assure us, that 'tis the true state, which otherwise I must confess might be doubted, since in so many cases it seems hyperbolical'.[81]

By the end of the seventeenth century Western contact with Japan was on a very restricted basis indeed. In the 1640s the 'Christian Century' had come to a bloody end. Europeans had been expelled and only the Dutch were permitted to maintain a trading post at Deshima at Nagasaki in conditions of almost complete isolation, apart from the annual summonses for Dutch delegations to attend at the Shogun's capital at Edo. The expulsion of the Christian missions of course ended the supply of missionary accounts which had been Europe's staple source of information about Japan. In the second half of the

seventeenth century the Dutch did not add much to the older missionary descriptions of Japan. Two Dutch publications were translated into
English: the brief *True Description of the Mighty Kingdomes of Japan and
Siam* by François Caron[82] and a collection by Arnoldus Montanus
called *Atlas Japannensis* (1670). There was a famous early seventeenth-
century English account by William Adams which was frequently to be
reprinted in the eighteenth century.

From these rather fragmentary sources compilers of geographies
put together a picture of the Japanese which was generally favourable
to them. They were said to be very industrious and frugal, so much so
that they resembled the 'old English Puritan, opposite to the Papists
in things fit and decent'.[83] They were, however, cruel and warlike.
Inevitably their government was despotic. Their religion was deeply
puzzling.

At the end of the seventeenth century the long period of European
ignorance about central Asia and Siberia was being brought to an end
by Russian expeditions and by Jesuits travelling into Chinese Tartary
from Peking. The history of the Mongols and other peoples was beginning to be studied from sources in Arabic and Persian. But very little of
this new knowledge was as yet available in print in English, apart from
Jesuit accounts, including one of Tibet.[84] Maps remained highly
speculative and geographers' descriptions were in essentials still drawn
from Marco Polo and other medieval sources. The area was said to be
inhabited by Tartars, some of whom were cannibals.[85]

It was customary to begin sections of seventeenth-century geographies
with florid invocations of the continents. Asia was normally described
in glowing terms. It was vast in size, rich in products, the seat of great
monarchies and the cradle of the arts and the sciences. Cicero's 'Asia
vero tam opima est ac fertilis . . . facile omnibus terris antecellat' was
quoted or paraphrased over and over again. It was said to be 'the
common suffrage of other writers'.[86] But above all this, Asia was the
setting for the Garden of Eden and it was in Asia that Christ was born.
By the end of the seventeenth century, however, a new note was being
sounded. After reciting the conventional praises of Asia, the compiler of
the *Compleat Geographer* added: 'But much of its ancient glory is lost' and
went on to make specific criticisms. 'The inhabitants are reckoned to be
of effeminate nature'; 'the mighty power of the princes has always kept
them in slavery'; and 'in religion they are very stupid'.[87] Such opinions
were by no means unique to him.

The modern scholar, Donald F. Lach, concluded his masterly
survey of European responses to Asia in the sixteenth century by
suggesting that by 1600 'a representative group' of European intellec-

tuals recognized that they had 'much to learn' from Asia, and had lost their 'robust confidence in European secular ideals, ideas, institutions and arts'.[88] If this confidence had indeed ever been lost, it had been regained by the end of the seventeenth century in England and, in as far as the sources considered in this chapter reflect wider European views, in Europe as a whole. Increased knowledge of Asia had prompted comparisons at many levels. The terms of the comparisons were of course set by Europeans; but within their own terms few Europeans doubted that they excelled Asians. To a Europe whose culture was overwhelmingly Christian the fact that there were few Christians in Asia was the clearest possible mark of European superiority. Even where Christian fundamentalism was being diluted for a few intellectuals by rationalism, Asian religions with the possible exception of Confucianism were several degrees less rational than Christianity. In secular terms Asia failed test after test devised by Europeans. Despotism was diagnosed everywhere, except in Arabia where wild Arabs were thought to be ungovernable. Only in China were the effects of despotism moderated in practice. For all its potential wealth, Asia was poorly cultivated, except in China and parts of India, and its people were generally poor by European standards. In science and technology Europeans believed that they were making progress while Asians were at best standing still. It was generally supposed that the sciences and the arts of civilized life had originated in Asia; Egypt was the usual source, but China and India were also suggested. But for the last two hundred years or so Europe had forged ahead by methods of rational inquiry, experiment and observation which seemed to be quite alien to Asia. 'The knowledge of the Asiaticks is so restrained', wrote Chardin, 'that it consists only in learning and repeating what is contained in the books of the ancients'.[89] Astrology consumed such originality as they were capable of applying. Although astrology in fact remained a preoccupation of educated Europeans for much of the seventeenth century, those who wrote about Asia fiercely denounced it. Bernier concluded that most Asian peoples were 'infatuated' with astrology, while in Europe, 'where the sciences flourish, professors in astrology are considered little better than cheats or jugglers'.[90]

Writers of books about the contact of peoples often seem to be searching for lost ages of innocence when men esteemed one another more or less as equals. Eighteenth-century Englishmen had little innocence to lose about Asia. They acquired new knowledge and asked new questions, but they started with comfortable assumptions of superiority.

North America

The first English concepts of America were faint reflections of the Spanish reaction to the New World. They formed an undistinguished part of the general European response to the intellectual problem presented by the discovery of America. A massive new double continent had been unexpectedly revealed, known neither to classical geographers nor to scriptural authority. It was separated by wide oceans to its east and west from the ancient cradles of civilization in the Old World. Its very existence posed disturbing questions, summed up by the Florentine historian Guicciardini in the 1530s when he noted that 'not only has this navigation confounded many affirmations of former writers about terrestrial things, but it has also given some anxiety to the interpreters of the Holy Scriptures.'[91] Much of its flora and fauna was distinctive, and so perhaps were its human inhabitants. But if America had developed in isolation, what then of Biblical explanations of the origin and spread of mankind from a single source?

Discussions of this and other issues were at first dominated by Spanish writers, whose narratives describing the conquest were soon translated into English and French. The Aztec empire, in particular, made a profound impact, both on those Spaniards who witnessed it even as it crumbled, and on the Europeans at home who wrestled with the implications of the extraordinary societies which the accounts laid before them.[92] The conquest prompted the first debate in Europe on the nature of the American, a polemic associated with the struggle between Las Casas and his antagonists, but which went far beyond the immediate matter of the treatment of the subjected peoples; for in the end it raised the more fundamental problem of the humanity, or lack of humanity, of the American. Efforts to relegate him to a sub-human category were for the most part resisted, and an elaborate process of migration and diffusion was postulated to explain his appearance in the New World.[93] Even so, by the late sixteenth century the majority of Spanish writers accepted a derogatory stereotype of the 'Indian' as naturally inferior to the European. Discussion might be couched in terms of theological scholarship, but behind these lay urgent practical considerations – as one Spaniard explained in 1600, 'the Indians can be said to be slaves of the Spaniards . . . And for this reason Nature specially proportioned their bodies, so that they should have the strength for personal service'.[94] The Spanish American empire could not have prospered, perhaps not even survived, without a docile work force whose duties rather than rights were stressed by the authorities.

Outside Spain the debate continued and spread, for in the seventeenth century it was influenced by the surge of overseas expansion from the nations of north-west Europe into the Americas. In North America, despite early Dutch footholds, the contest for supremacy lay between England and France. Before it was resolved in 1760 two-thirds of the continent had been revealed, together with a host of Indian peoples unknown to the early Spaniards: Abenaki, Montagnais, Huron, Iroquois, Cree, Chipewyan, Natchez, Susquehannah, Illinois, Sioux and many more. The diversity of language, custom, appearance and environment made the task of generalization difficult enough. It was made even more hazardous by the difference in outlook among the European reporters, for in this context the term 'European' has as much and as little meaning as the term 'Indian'. It implies certain broad cultural similarities, but obscures the endless variety of outlook which influenced the observers' perceptions.[95] By the end of the seventeenth century the English colonies were comparatively prosperous and well-populated, but they were confined to the Atlantic seaboard, and contact with the Indians was usually of a frontier nature. The French, by contrast, were few in number, but among them were men who had roamed over vast stretches of the continent. Fur traders and missionaries had reached the Great Lakes and beyond, and had followed the Mississippi down to the Gulf of Mexico. Frenchmen lived among Indians, sharing their hardships and often their customs, in a fashion which would have horrified most Englishmen; and the experiences, attitudes and reporting in North America of the nationals from the two countries differed radically for most of the period.

The English image of North America and its indigenous inhabitants was coloured by settler experiences as well as by those preconceptions which grew out of an awareness that across the Atlantic dwelt people without, it seemed, recognizable religion, government or even social structure. The image was the product of an uneasy and sometimes violent relationship which came to dominate the published accounts. It took time to develop, and was never uniform; it was not evident at the beginning, for the first abortive attempts to settle 'Virginia' in the 1580s saw friendly if cautious contacts established between Englishmen and Indians. It was lack of support from home, and ineptitude on the spot, that led to the colony's mysterious and tragic end, rather than hostility from the Indians.[96] One of the legacies of these forlorn attempts was the superb Indian pictures of John White, painted in 1587. As engraved and published by Theodor De Bry, these had an extraordinary circulation in Europe, and can be found in one guise or another well into the eighteenth century. They also helped in the creation of a noble primitive, for a comparison of White's watercolours with the engravings shows that the Indians of the originals had been 'smoothed' and Europeanized, with more than a suggestion of

27

classical parallels.[97] They could be taken as visual representations of the savages that the French essayist, Montaigne, had described in his sketch *Of the Cannibales*, for though he was writing about Brazilian Indians in the second half of the sixteenth century his remarks were later applied to primitive peoples elsewhere. They formed a classic statement on the simplicity of man living outside civilized society, and a plea that he should not be judged by conventional European standards:

> We all call barbarism that which does not fit in with our usages . . .
> Those people are wild in the sense which we call wild the fruits that
> Nature has produced by herself and her ordinary progress; whereas in
> truth it is those we have altered artificially and diverted from the
> common order, that we should rather call wild. In the first we still see,
> in full life and vigour, the genuine and most natural and useful virtues
> and properties, which we have bastardized in the latter, and only
> adapted to please our corrupt taste . . . Those nations, then, appear to
> us so far barbarous in this sense, that their minds have been formed to
> a very slight degree, and that they are still very close to their original
> simplicity. They are still ruled by the laws of nature, and very little
> corrupted by ours.[98]

To Montaigne both states, the civilized and the natural, had their merits. If the Brazilians had no knowledge of letters and numbers, neither did they possess slaves. They ate human flesh on occasion, but displayed in their warfare none of the relentless ingenuity of the Europeans. If they had no wealth, they had little poverty. Because they lacked Europe's obsession with property, political power and the rest, so were 'the very words denoting falsehood, treachery, dissimulation, avarice, detraction, pardon, unheard of.'

Montaigne's *Essayes* were first translated into English in 1603, at a time when new efforts were being made to found colonies in North America. Settlements were established in Chesapeake Bay, Virginia, and further north along the coasts of New England. Interest in these infant colonies was considerable and was reflected in the published accounts. To Thomas Harriot's earlier *Briefe and true report of the new found land of Virginia* (1588) were now added John Smith's *Map of Virginia* (a narrative as well as a map, 1612), and above all his celebrated *Generall historie of Virginia* (1624). Various volumes of De Bry's *America* contained illustrations spanning the first twenty years of the colony's existence, and gave graphic representation to episodes which were to linger long in the English memory, notably the saving of John Smith's life by Pocahontas, and the Indian massacre of settlers in 1622. The Puritan-dominated ventures to New England, which reached a peak in the 1630s, were described and sanctified by a number of narratives, not all of which were published at the time. In the accounts generally of early English settlement in North America two contrasting features were prominent: the potentialities of the New World, and its hardships. One scholar has put forward an intriguing comparison between Ireland and America in so far as their impact on English opinion was concerned. Both had 'savages' to be conciliated or subdued, and sufferings to be endured; both also, or so it is claimed, gave rise to a stream of returning soldiers, sailors and settlers bearing tales of misery and misfortune.[99] To balance this, another commentator has noticed a significant difference of attitude between the accounts of eyewitnesses in Virginia, who saw the Indians surviving and even flourishing in an environment which the first settlers found harsh and hostile, and the descriptions of compilers in England.[100] Among the considerations which affected the selections of the latter, and long outlived the early contact period, was the popularity of sensational accounts of Indian treachery and cruelty. 'Indian barbarism attracted the reading public, sold books, and might be used to justify displacement.'[101] Certainly the Virginia massacre of 1622, when three hundred settlers were killed, lost nothing in the telling and retelling. After that horror, wrote Samuel Purchas, the Indians could only be considered 'so bad people, having little of humanitie but shape, ignorant of civilitie, of arts, of religion; more brutish than the beasts they hunt.'[102]

There had been signs of tension and distrust earlier. Between the Indians and the land-hungry settlers, often short of food, there could be little understanding or compromise. The same process had taken place more than a century earlier when the first friendly if bewildered contacts between the Spaniards and the Arawaks had turned to brutal violence once material interests were involved and in conflict. From the newcomers' viewpoint the happiest solution was that reported in 1670 by Daniel Denton from the newly-acquired colony of New York: 'Where the English come to settle, a Divine hand makes way for them, by removing or cutting off the Indians, either by wars one with the other, or by some raging mortal disease.'[103] Farther north the competition for land in New England was given a keener edge by the unbending religious attitude of the colonial governments, and by the destruction of the Indian wars which broke out twice during the century. From being suppliers of food, guides and helpers, the Indians were transformed into a menace which seemed to threaten the existence of the young settlements. The New England Puritans used the printing press as other Europeans did cannon, so there is no shortage of information during the course of the century, much of it put out with polemic or justificatory intent. Puritan writings from William Bradford and John Winthrop onwards are heavy with detail about the Indians, but their main concern was to show God's 'Wonder-Working Providence' in the New World.[104]

To look for details of the contact between the English and the

Indians in the general works published in England is an unrewarding task because of the time-lag which afflicted the compilers of the geographies and cosmographies now becoming fashionable. In 1652 Peter Heylyn published a 1000-page world geography, *Cosmographie in four bookes*, which was reprinted eight times before the end of the century. Heylyn's materials mostly dated from the previous century, and one result of this was that only ninety pages were devoted to the Americas, a mere six of them to English activities there. The fact was that the Spanish experience in the New World still dominated the literature.[105] The fourth volume of Samuel Purchas's *Hakluytus Posthumus, or Purchas His Pilgrimes*, the great English collection of voyages published in 1625, and second only to Hakluyt's compilations in importance, included the second English edition of Las Casas' *Brevisima relacion* and other writings, together with selections from Acosta's *Historia natural y moral de las Indias*, and Garcilaso de la Vega's *Comentarios reales de los Incas*. No English work on the Americas approached the majestic scale of these Spanish surveys, which continued to be read throughout Europe for the revelation of the American empires they described. Most English readers probably shared Acosta's insistence that, although the Indians of Mexico and Peru were ethnologically inferior to the literate 'barbarians' of the East, they were superior to the 'savages' who lived in other areas of the Americas, and who seemed not to have any semblance of settled life and formal institutions. Certainly when Thomas Hobbes wrote his celebrated description of man in a state of nature in *Leviathan* (1651) he took it for granted that if evidence were needed of that miserable condition, then America was the place to find it: 'For the savage people in many places of America, except the government of small families, the concord whereof dependeth on natural lust, have no government at all; and live at this day in that brutish manner. . . .'[106]

The same regional emphasis was shown in the imaginative literature of the period. The ready availability of source material, and the dramatic pathos of the events, sent most writers to the story of the Spanish conquest and its aftermath. One of the earliest plays with an Aztec theme was Marin le Roy's *Polexandre*, translated into English in 1647, and the inspiration for Dryden's *The Indian queene* of 1664. The text of Dryden's sequel, *The Indian emperour*, a sympathetic if wildly inaccurate account of Montezuma's last days, went through ten editions between 1667 and 1703. It was Almanzor in another of Dryden's plays on the same theme, *The Conquest of Granada*, who declaimed from the London stage in 1664

> I am as free as Nature first made man,
> Ere the base laws of servitude began,
> When wild in woods the noble savage ran.[107]

This was the first known use of a term which summarized and popular-
ized an important dimension in the English perception of the American
Indian – from the mid-seventeenth century increasingly the North
American Indian. It was a dimension which obscured rather than
illuminated the Indian, who tended to become 'a surrogate for the
white man's better self'[108] rather than a member of a society with a
culture which had evolved in tune with a natural environment very
different from that of Western Europe in the seventeenth and eighteenth centuries. Whereas the relationship between the Spaniards and
their Aztec or Inca victims had a recognizable quality which appealed
to writers, the North American Indian remained an anonymous, indis-
tinct figure. He did not appear on the English stage, for example, until
John Dennis's *Liberty Asserted*, a play first performed in 1704. Indians 'in
the flesh' visited England from time to time, the first ones whose names
survive in 1584. But the degree and scope of the contact were limited,
and the only Indian visitors who caught the English imagination as
individuals were Pocahontas in the early seventeenth century and the
Mohawk chief Thayendanegeo (better known in England as Joseph
Brant) in the American revolutionary period. The same lack of recognition of any individual personality was largely true even of the more
intensive French contact. In the first volume of the *Dictionary of Canadian
Biography*, covering the period before 1700, out of 594 biographies only
65 are of Indians. 'For almost all of them', the editors comment, 'the information is fragmentary. Like fireflies, they glimmer for a moment before
disappearing again into the dark forest of unrecorded history.'[109]

   If there was no English equivalent of the great Spanish surveys,
neither did the English in America produce the detailed and comprehensive studies of the Indian that the French managed in the
seventeenth century. Since French settlement was sparse, there was not
the natural antipathy between French and Indian which so often
existed beween English and Indian. To the fur-trader, the missionary,
the soldier, the Indians of New France were suppliers of furs,
neophytes, potential allies; and a voluminous mass of descriptive material was provided on the Indians which the English could not match.
Samuel de Champlain's accounts of his exploits, and especially his
Voyages of 1632, contained lengthy observations on the Hurons, allies of
the French. Champlain was a leader, an organizer, an empire-builder,
and his approach to the Indians was the same as that of John Smith in
Virginia, revolving around the issue of how much they might help or
hinder the activities of his countrymen in North America. Written from
a different viewpoint was Marc Lescarbot's *Histoire de la Nouvelle-France*,
first published in 1609 and twice translated into English. Lescarbot's
Indians were virtuous, they had many similarities with the peoples of

classical antiquity, and lacked only the benefits of the Christian religion. Another favourable impression was given by Gabriel Sagard, a lay brother in the mendicant order, the Recollets, pioneers of Catholic missionary enterprise in Canada. In *Le Grand Voyage du Pays des Hurons*, published in Paris in 1632, Sagard gave a stern account of the hardships of Indian life, but he displayed considerable admiration for the Hurons' form of government, their fortitude, and the potential of their fertile land. John Locke was among those Englishmen, a small group one suspects, who had read Sagard.

Dwarfing these accounts in scale and significance were the *Jesuit Relations*, published in France each year from 1632 to 1673. They were works of propaganda, appeals for support and funds, but above all they were vast repositories of knowledge about the Indians. The information collected by the individual Jesuit missionaries was not easy to assimilate or summarize, and Du Creux's brave attempt to do this in his *Historia Canadensis* of 1664 was deprived of a wider circulation by the fact that it was written in Latin. Nor is there evidence that the Jesuit observations reached England in any significant way in the seventeenth century. The *Relations* were not translated into English,[110] and the English writers who made use of them did so mainly in the next century, and then through the compilations of Du Creux, Lafitau and Charlevoix. Set against the vitality and learning of the Jesuit missionaries, with their expressed determination to master the necessary Indian languages, was a mere handful of Englishmen, and notably John Eliot. Working for the small New England Company, oldest of the English Protestant missionary societies, Eliot produced in 1663 a Bible in Algonkian, and later an English grammar. Magnificent though this achievement was, it remained an isolated one in a region where the missions were to be overwhelmed by the Indian-settler warfare of the 1670s. The Company remained, but its efforts to bring the Indians into supervised settlements produced only feeble results. 'If converts were few', the historian of the Company has written, 'so were those who attempted to make them: a few missionaries practising what so many propagandists had preached.'[111]

English readers had to wait until 1671 before they could turn to a general work which did any sort of justice to the English mainland settlements in America. In that year John Ogilby's *America* was published, based on a Dutch work, and unusually well illustrated. Even now, less than one hundred of its 674 pages were devoted to North America, for the Spanish accounts still dominated. New France received short shrift, nine pages in all, but the sections on the Indians of the English colonies were fuller than normal. The year before, for example, Richard Blome's *Geographical Description of the four parts of the*

World, based largely on the French of Sanson, had given only a most generalized description of the Indians – 'very barbarous, having neither religion, nor learning . . . they eat sometimes the flesh of their enemies . . . they use bows and arrows', and so on.[112] Ogilby at least tried to distinguish between the various Indian nations. The Mohawks, for example, were described in lowering terms as vicious man-eaters, so strong that they had been known to kill a dog with a flick of the finger. In contrast were the attractive 'Aberginian' Indians north-west of New England, handsome, long-lived, with little in the way of property or laws to bother them. 'In a word, take them when the blood skips in their veins, when the flesh is on their backs, and marrow in their bones, when they frolick in their antique deportments and Indian postures, they are more amiable to behold (though onely in Adam's livery) than many a trim gallant in the newest mode.'[113] The southern Indians were treated in less detail, but in a generally balanced way. So, although the Indian massacre in Virginia was mentioned, so was the Indians' first helpfulness on the arrival of the English. Likewise, the hostilities between the Carolina Indians and the French and Spaniards were blamed on the Europeans. Although Ogilby, like any compiler, was dependent on his sources, he made a spirited attempt to depict the Indians of the eastern seaboard from a variety of viewpoints. His work, however, does little to remove the impression that after seventy years of contact the information on the Indians collected by the English compared poorly both in detail and perception with that published in France.

West Africa

The same lack of detailed information and of comprehensive general accounts also held good of English knowledge of West Africa in the seventeenth century. It is true that the educated Englishman of the Jacobean period could dip into classical, Biblical and medieval writings and find material on Africa and its inhabitants. He would emerge with a confusing mixture of references to Ethiopia and Prester John; to accounts of Egypt and Libya by Herodotus, Pliny and Ptolemy; to Arab descriptions of the western Sudan; to more recent Portuguese journals of seaborne ventures to the Guinea coast.[114] They would leave him with a mystifying impression of different races, colours, religions and customs. In the way of precise, ascertainable knowledge he would have gathered very little. If he were willing to limit his reading to those coastal regions of West Africa where the English were developing commercial contacts, then he had Hakluyt, whose *Principall Navigations* in its fullest version of 1600 served as text-book, merchants' guide and leisure reading to generations of Englishmen. The amount of information in Hakluyt on Africa did not approach that on America and Asia, and what there was tended to dwell, as the 1554 account by Richard Eden of John Lok's pioneer voyage to Guinea put it, on 'the wonders and monstrous things that are engendred in Africke'. The narrative gave readers an early glimpse of the physical environment of the West African coast – 'smothering hote, with hote showres of raine also, and somewhere such scorching windes that what by one meanes and other, they seeme at certaine times to live as it were in fornaces, and in maner already halfe way in purgatorie or hell.'[115] Even the moon at night, Lok's crew complained, gave out heat. Across the landscape moved monstrous, incredible creatures: elephants, rhinoceri, hippopotami, crocodiles. Lok's men brought an elephant skull back with them, and Londoners were able to scrutinize its massive size, five hundredweight of it according to Eden. Docile except when attacked by a serpent which 'windeth his taile (being of exceeding length) about the hinder legs of the elephant, & so staying him, thrusteth his head into his tronke, and exhausteth his breath', the great mammal seemed preferable to the human inhabitants of the region. They, wrote Eden, were 'Negroes, a people of beastly living, without a God, lawe, religion, or common wealthe, and so scorched and vexed with the heat of the sunne, that in many places, they curse it when it riseth.' The fact that Lok brought back some Negro slaves whose behaviour seemed reassuringly normal – they took European food and drink, but proved susceptible to the damp and cold of England – did not seem to disturb Eden in his fantasizing about their homeland. Early on, then, a pattern began to take shape by which the image of the Negro in books was formed by accounts of his existence in Africa, and remained undisturbed by the evidence of men's own eyes of the black presence in England.

The impact of the black African on the English was more sudden, and possibly more disturbing, than it was for the Spanish or Portuguese, whose contact with North Africa and its inhabitants was of long standing. Englishmen's first encounters with Africans in their homeland was likely to come on a direct voyage to the Guinea coast 'where men were not merely dark but almost literally black: one of the fairest-skinned nations suddenly came face to face with one of the darkest peoples on earth.'[116] The fact was that the African, instead of being white and clothed, was black and naked, an initial impression summed up in the ribald verses of Robert Baker who was on the coast in the 1560s.

> And entering in [a river], we see
> a number of black soules,
> Whose likeliness seem'd men to be,
> but all as blacke as coles.

> Their Captain comes to me
> as naked as my naile,
> Not having witte or honestie
> to cover once his taile.[117]

How and when the Negro became black was a question which was to exercise and trouble scholars. It was not a subject which could be discussed without constraint, for the possible theological consequences were portentous. The Bible, from the Book of Genesis onwards, was quite unequivocal: there had been a single act of creation from which all men descended. Monogenesis was a fundamental part of the Christian belief, not to be lightly challenged. There was in the Bible a simple climatic explanation for the blackness of the Negro, neatly expressed in the Song of Solomon, 'I am black, because the sun hath looked upon me.' As early as the mid-sixteenth century this explanation seemed less than convincing to some Englishmen. Eden's account in Hakluyt noted that American Indians living roughly in the same latitude as the African Negroes were 'neither blacke, nor with curlde and short wooll on their heads, as they of Africke have, but of the colour of an olive, with long and blacke heare on their heads.'[118] In 1578 George Best took the matter further: 'I myselfe have seen an Ethiopian [sic] as blacke as a cole brought into England, who taking an English wife, begat a sonne in all respects as blacke as the father was, although England were his native country, and an English woman his mother; whereby it seemeth that blackness proceedeth rather of some natural infection of that man.'[119] Best advanced an alternative explanation with Biblical authority, the curse of Noah upon Ham, so that 'all its posteritie after him should be so blacke and lothsome, that it might. remaine a spectacle of disobedience to all the world.' But however convenient an explanation this might be to pro-slavery apologists, it seemed at odds both with Christian charity and with scientific probability. It was a confession of failure rather than a reasoned explanation when Peter Heylyn wrote of the Negro's blackness that 'we must wholy refer it to Gods peculiar will and ordinance'.[120]

Yet the issue was not simply the preoccupation of distant voyagers or of philosophers and theologians. The growing number of black servants, free Negroes, and slaves, in England during the seventeenth century was a constant reminder to the populace of London and the sea ports in particular of the physical character of the African.[121] In other ways the imagery of Africa found a prominent place in the English language – from the significant linking of blackness and sexuality in Shakespeare's *Othello* to the commonplace expressions of many lesser writers. 'Many dramatists who never created a single African character referred to the gold of Barbary or to the tears of the crocodile, the monsters of Africa, or merely used the terms Moor, Negro or Ethiop in a simile of blackness, cruelty, jealousy, lustfulness or some other quality commonly credited to the African.'[122] The *Oxford English Dictionary* has columns of relevant entries, many of them dating back to the sixteenth century, or earlier: black for mourning, the black box (coffin), the black fiend, black looks, black-hearted, to blacken a character, the black arts, black magic. There is no need to labour the point: when white Englishmen first encountered black Africans preconceptions of distaste, even repulsion, already existed. The Negro – black, naked or semi-naked – was deviant in appearance, and there would be no great surprise if he should turn out to be deviant in behaviour and custom.

In the early seventeenth century more detailed accounts of West Africa became available to English readers, notably in the 1625 edition of the *Pilgrimes* of Samuel Purchas. Unable to match Hakluyt either in editorial skill or in the strength of his appeal to patriotic fervour, Purchas nevertheless rescued or reprinted many accounts of value, and his sections on Africa were fuller and more informative than those of the *Principall Navigations*. They included the extensive first-hand description of North Africa, the Sahara and the western Sudan by Leo Africanus, first published in 1550, and issued in English as *A History of Africa* in 1600; the English translation of Pigafetta's account of the Congo; Jesuit letters from Upper Guinea; Jobson's remarks on the Gambia; and the first of the Dutch narratives from the Guinea coast. The intention of these accounts, Purchas reminded his readers, was to enable them 'to travell thorow that least knowne part of the Elder-knowne world'.[123]

Leo Africanus's section on 'the Land of the Negros' was limited to those areas of West Africa – Kano, Bornu, Timbuktu – under Muslim influence and approachable from the north. The detail on the coastal regions missing in his work was partly supplied in the lengthy 'Description and historicall declaration of the golden Kingdome of Guinea', translated from the Dutch of Pieter de Maries. In one sense this account of the West African coastal regions where the Dutch were active seemed to be a series of contradictions, but underneath the inconsistencies of detail was a more serious dilemma which lay open to view by the end of the journal. The inhabitants of the Gold Coast were idolatrous and polygamous, persistent liars and thieves, though physically well-formed and 'very upright, ingenious to learne any thing, and readie to conceive it'.[124] Above all the narrative showed that there existed in the coastal areas a commercially-minded society, familiar with the use of gold as a currency, with markets and manufactures, a varied agriculture, and a settled way of life under elective rulers. This had been achieved 'although they are altogether wild, rough, and uncivill, having neither scripture nor bookes, nor any notable lawes that might be set downe'. Even more puzzling were African religious beliefs, probably past understanding and certainly beneath contempt, centred as they were on fetishism. In matters religious, the theological and linguistic gap was too wide to be bridged – 'When the Netherlanders saw them use such vaine toyes, which were so foolish and laught and jested at them, they were ashamed, and durst make no more Fetissos in our presence, but were ashamed of their owne apishnesse.' Later the gulf opened again, when the narrator puzzled over the Africans' simple but effective form of justice, 'so that although they bee wild men, and without any civilitie or good behaviour; yet there in they use a very good and laudible custome'. We are back here to a medieval use of the term 'wild', implying 'everything that eluded Christian norms and the established framework of Christian society, referring to what was uncanny, unruly, raw, unpredictable, foreign, uncultured, and uncultivated'.[125]

The problem was a stark one, and had been posed in the early years of contact when Hakluyt recorded a note from a trading venture to 'Guinie' in 1566 that 'although the people were blacke and naked, yet they were civill'.[126] Conventional assumptions pointed to the essential presence of religious observance in a Christian manner, a written language, and a formal legal code, as minimum requirements for an orderly society. Here on the West African coast none of these existed, yet the inhabitants lived in a peaceful and regulated fashion. Implicit throughout the narrative was the only assumption which could resolve these difficulties. Africans were in an early stage of social existence out of which they had the potential to move in imitation of European ways. A few were already christianized, some had a glimmering of an afterlife, others had a smattering of Dutch or Portuguese, many more were getting used to European manufactures and utensils. In brief, the civilization of the African was to be judged by the alacrity with which he conformed to European standards and European behaviour; on the merits or otherwise of this process there was little discussion. In most of the accounts attitudes of condescension and superiority were self-evident, and in England these attitudes were to be strengthened by the nation's increasing participation in the African slave-trade in the seventeenth century and by the position of dominance which it attained in the trade during the eighteenth century.

The Pacific

Least known to seventeenth-century Englishmen of all four areas examined in this survey was the Pacific. From Magellan onwards

Europeans of several nations – Spaniards, French, Dutch, English – had ventured into, and sometimes across, the Pacific; but their explorations tended to be both inconclusive and little-known. Not until the publication in 1756 of the first large-scale collection of voyages devoted exclusively to the Pacific, *Histoire des Navigations aux Terres Australes* by Charles de Brosses (followed by its English version, John Callender's *Terra Australis Cognita*) were accounts of the main voyages brought together in accessible form.[127] Although Hakluyt and Purchas printed detail on some of the Spanish voyages, it was the circumnavigations of Drake and Cavendish, spectacular in intention but meagre in geographical information, which seized the limelight. As the title-page of the *Principall Navigations* announced, they were 'the two renowned and prosperous voyages . . . round about the circumference of the whole earth.' When English interest in the Pacific revived in the last thirty years of the seventeenth century the motives remained the same as those which had prompted the Elizabethans: trade and plunder. The Pacific caught the English imagination not as an immense, trackless ocean but as the western rim of Spain's American empire. The 'South Sea' which now began to exercise its fascination over distant enterprises was confined, for most practical purposes, to the waters which lapped the shores of Chile, Peru and Mexico.

The voyages, from Narborough's of 1669–71 to Anson's of 1740–44, produced some useful information of course.[128] Narborough's Peruvian venture was a failure in most respects, but it resulted in the publication of a map of the Strait of Magellan which long remained a standard authority. Better received in England than Narborough's obscure and disappointing ventures were the activities of the buccaneers who pillaged and burned along the Pacific coasts, and whose exploits proved of unending interest to the reading public. Among the ranks of the buccaneers were men with literary skills. There was Basil Ringrose, who had enough classical learning to negotiate with the Spaniards in Latin, and whose book, 'Containing the dangerous Voyage, and bold Assaults of Captain Bartholomew Sharp, and others, performed in the South Sea', became the supplement to the 1684 English edition of Esquemeling's *Bucaniers of America*. Above all, there was William Dampier, a man of immeasurable zest and curiosity who waded through the rivers of Darien with his journal secured inside a length of bamboo cane, and whose books were to become classics of travel and adventure. Reports of the buccaneers' exploits whetted public and mercantile interest in the South Sea. After more than twenty years Narborough's journal was printed in 1694; alongside it, more importantly, was an account of Tasman's voyage to Australia and New Zealand in 1642. Dampier's first and best book, *A New Voyage round the*

World, was published in 1697. The title-page showed the extent of Dampier's peregrinations:

> Describing particularly, the Isthmus of America, several Coasts and Islands in the West Indies, the Isles of Cape Verd, the Passage by Terra del Fuego, the South Sea Coasts of Chili, Peru, and Mexico; the Isle of Guam one of the Ladrones, Mindanao, and other Philippine and East-India islands near Cambodia, China, Formosa, Luconia, Celebes, &c. New Holland, Sumatra, Nicobar Islands; the Cape of Good Hope, and Santa Hellena. Their Soil, Rivers, Harbours, Plants, Fruits, Animals, and Inhabitants. Their Customs, Religion, Government, Trade, &c.

With what Dampier described as its 'mixt relation of places and actions', the book was an instant success, and by 1699 was in its fourth edition. The same year saw the publication of Lionel Wafer's *New Voyage* and William Hack's *Collection of Original Voyages*, which included another Narborough journal, and Cowley's voyage round the world in 1683–86. The popularity of Dampier's book led to further volumes from his ready pen: *A Supplement* to the *Voyage round the World* in 1699, *A Voyage to New Holland* in 1703, and his *Continuation of the New Voyage* in 1709. Dampier's *Voyages*, as they became collectively known, were finally published together as a four-volume edition in 1729, and extracts from them featured in most of the compilations of voyages and travels for the rest of the century.[129]

A wanderer rather than an explorer, Dampier had a good eye for detail, particularly in matters of natural history. Spanish America and the East Indies saw most of him, but in the north Pacific he had touched at Guam, under rather tenuous Spanish control, and had stayed for six months at Mindanao in the southern Philippines, a Muslim country placed uneasily between the Dutch and Spanish spheres of influence. At Mindanao an English trader redeemed an islander from the southeast, Jeoly, 'the painted Prince', and then reached a business arrangement with Dampier by which the native was to be taken to England. When Dampier returned home in 1691 shortage of funds compelled him to sell his interest in Jeoly, who was exhibited at side-shows before dying of small-pox at Oxford. He must have made a spectacular if bizarre impression on the onlookers. Jeoly's decoration had been applied by one of his five wives, according to Dampier's account. 'He was painted all down the breasts, between his shoulders behind; on his thighs (mostly) before; and in the form of several broad rings, or bracelets round his arms and legs. I cannot liken the drawings to any figure of animals, or the like; but they were very curious, full of great variety of lines, flourishes, chequered-work, &c. keeping a very graceful proportion . . .'[130] Although Dampier had hoped to use 'the prince' in opening trade contacts with his homeland, in England there seems to have been no serious interest in the unfortunate being. His value as a freakish exhibit was heightened by reports that his beautiful sister had been taken from slavery by the Sultan of Mindanao, who fell in love with her; 'but these', Dampier noted, 'were stories indeed', as were the tales circulating about the magical properties of Jeoly's body-paint.

Of Dampier's ventures into areas outside European control, and indeed on the very periphery of Europe's knowledge, most notable were his brief visits to the western coasts of Australia in 1688 and 1699. His descriptions of the Australian Aborigines were the first recorded by any Englishman, and their effect was to be long-lasting. More than seventy years later, when Cook and Banks reached the east coast of Australia in the *Endeavour*, it was Dampier's account which they had with them and which influenced their first encounters: 'the miserablest people in the world . . . setting aside their humane shape, they differ but little from brutes . . . their eyelids are always half closed, to keep the flies out of their eyes . . . they have great bottle-noses, pretty full lips, and wide mouths . . . Their hair is black, short and curl'd, like that of the Negroes . . . the colour of their skins, both of their faces and the rest of their body, is coal-black . . . they all of them have the most unpleasant looks and the worst features of any people that I ever saw, tho I have seen a great variety of savages.'[131]

In one way the published journals of Dampier and his contemporaries marked the beginning of the vogue for 'voyages and travels' which was to reach such enthusiastic proportions in the eighteenth century; in another they helped to fuel an obsessive British interest in the South Sea which was to fade only with the abrupt disillusionment of the South Sea Bubble in 1720. The excitements and the ambitions of the years between, the tales of voyagers, the entrancing maps and alluring pamphlets, brought the South Sea to the attention of the literate public. The seas beyond Cape Horn were not only the realms of privateers and adventurers; they provided the setting for some of the most popular fiction and satire of the period. Gulliver's travels took him to the Pacific, where Lilliput was situated north of Van Diemen's Land, and Brobdingnag somewhere east of Japan. Defoe's *Robinson Crusoe* owed much to the story related by the privateer Woodes Rogers of the marooning of Alexander Selkirk on Juan Fernandez. The interest had its limits, as we have seen, of region as well as of subject. Not until the second half of the eighteenth century did British interest in the Pacific become truly oceanic, attention turn to unknown islands rather than settled coasts, and the quest for knowledge become a motive as important as material considerations.

NOTES

1 *Works of William Warburton* (1788), ii. 689.
2 *Outlines of the Globe* (1798–1800), i. 4.
3 D. F. Lach, *Asia in the Making of Europe* (Chicago, 1965–), ii. 325.
4 C.W.R.D. Moseley, 'The Availability of Mandeville's Travels in England 1356–1750', *The Library*, 5th ser., xxx (1975), 125–33.
5 *Outlines of the Globe*, iii. 112.
6 R. Blome, *A Geographical Description of the World* (1680), p. 247.
7 *Cosmography*, pt. iii. 169–70, 180.
8 *General Heads for the Natural History of a Country* (1692), p. 92.
9 Preface to *Travels of Sir John Chardin into Persia and the East Indies* (1686), pt. i. Chardin was a French Protestant who had settled in England after many years of travelling in the Middle East. The 1686 version of his memoirs was to be supplemented by a fuller edition in 1724 (a translation of a new French edition of 1711). The fullest version appeared in 4 vols as *Voyages en Perse* (Amsterdam, 1735). This was never translated into English.
10 *The Agreement of the Customs of the East-Indians with those of the Jews and other Ancient Peoples* (1705), p. viii.
11 *A Supplement to a Book entitled Travels, or Observations* . . . (Oxford, 1746), p. xi.
12 E. Iversen, *The Myth of Egypt and its Hieroglyphs in European Tradition* (Copenhagen, 1961); J. D. Wortham, *British Egyptology 1549–1906* (Newton Abbot, 1971).
13 'Leonhart Rauwolf's Itinerary', *A Collection of Curious Travels and Voyages*, ed. J. Ray (1693), pt. i. 175.
14 H. Maundrell, *A Journey from Aleppo to Jerusalem at Easter 1697*, 10th edn. (1810), pp. 181–7). See *Philosophical Transactions of the Royal Society*, xix (1695–7), 84–110, 129–75 for early accounts of Palmyra.
15 *Travels into Muscovy, Persia and Part of the East Indies* (1737), ii. 9ff.
16 T. J. B. Spencer, 'Robert Wood and the Problem of Troy in the Eighteenth century', *Journal of the Warburg and Courtauld Institute*, xx (1957), 75–105.
17 Letter to T. Bowrey, 13 April 1701, India Office Library, MS Eur. E. 192, no. 15.
18 *Navigantium atque Itinerantium Bibliotheca*, ed. J. Harris (1764 edn.), ii. 890.
19 Cited in A. J. Arberry, *Oriental Essays* (1960), p. 12.
20 P. M. Holt, 'An Oxford Arabist: Edward Pococke', *Studies in the History of the Near East* (1973), pp. 16–17.
21 For the history of Arabic scholarship, see Holt, *Studies*; S. N. Khairallah, 'Arabic Studies in England in the late seventeenth and early eighteenth centuries', London Ph.D thesis (1972).
22 R. W. Southern, *Western Views of Islam in the Middle Ages* (Cambridge, Mass., 1962); N. Daniel, *Islam and the West: the Making of an Image* (Edinburgh, 1958).
23 *The True Nature of Imposture fully display'd in the life of Mahomet*, 10th edn. (1808), p. 93.
24 Heylyn, *Cosmography* (1682 edn.), pt. iii. 105.
25 Alexander Ross, *The Alcoran of Mahomet* (1649).
26 L. Twells, *The Theological Works of the Learned Dr Pocock* (1740), i. 35.
27 P. M. Holt, *A seventeenth-century defender of Islam: Henry Stubbe and his Book* (1972), p. 21.
28 *Life of Mahomet*, pp. 9, 26.
29 Khairallah, 'Arabic Studies', p. 144.
30 *Remarks Upon the Manners, Religion and Government of the Turks* (1677), pp. 27, 51–2, 60.
31 *A Journey from Aleppo*, p. 198.
32 *Four Treatises concerning the Doctrines, Discipline and Worship of the Mahometans* (1712), pp. 107–8.

33 *Travels of Monsieur de Thévenot into the Levant* (1686), pt. i. 58.
34 Roger North, *Life of the Hon. Sir Dudley North* (1744), p. 30.
35 *The Present State of the Ottoman Empire* (1668 edn.), p. 103.
36 *Early Voyages and Travels in the Levant*, ed. J. T. Bent (1893), p. 271.
37 *State of Ottoman Empire*, p. 127.
38 *Remarks Upon Turks*, pp. 114–15.
39 Maundrell, *Journey from Aleppo*, p. 53.
40 Thévenot, *Travels*, pt. i. 57.
41 'Historical Observations relating to Constantinople' in *Travels*, ed. Ray, pt. ii. 60.
42 Rycaut, *Ottoman Empire*, p. 32.
43 *Correspondence of John Locke*, ed. E. S. De Beer (Oxford, 1976–), i. 353.
44 *Works of Sir William Temple* (1814), iii. 390.
45 *Travels in the Mogul Empire*, ed. A. Constable, revised V. Smith (1914), p. 234.
46 *Life of North*, pp. 30, 45.
47 *Travels, containing an history of the Original and present state of the Turkish Empire*, 7th edn. (1673), pp. 39–40.
48 *Remarks Upon·Turks*, pp. 123–4.
49 *Ottoman Empire*, p. 170.
50 *A New and Accurate Description of Persia* (1724), ii. 120–30.
51 *A New Account of East India and Persia*, ed. W. Crooke (1909–15), iii. 36, 143.
52 *Cosmography* (1682 edn.), pt. iii. 138.
53 Fryer, *New Account of East India*, iii. 87.
54 *Voyages en Perse* (Amsterdam, 1735), iii. 130–2, 162–5.
55 R. W. Ferrier, 'British–Persian Relations in the Seventeenth Century', Cambridge Ph.D thesis (1970), p. 435; Chardin, *Voyages*, iii. 261–73.
56 Le Bruin, *Travels into Muscovy and Persia*, i. 130.
57 *Travels*, pt. ii. 79.
58 *Voyages en Perse*, iii. 293–6, 339–44, 368–9.
59 *A New Description of Persia*, ii. 31.
60 *A Voyage to East India* (1655), p. 370.
61 *A Voyage to Suratt in the Year 1689* (1696), p. 197.
62 *Travels in the Mogul Empire*, p. 231.
63 Temple, *Works*, iii. 456–7.
64 *A Display of Two Forraigne Sects in the East Indies* (1630), p. 51.
65 *Voyage to East India*, p. 346.
66 R. Coverte, *A True and Most Incredible Report* (1612), p. 45.
67 T. Bowrey, *A Geographical Account of Countries round the Bay of Bengal*, ed. R. C. Temple (1905), p. 25.
68 *Asia the First Part* (1673), pp. 134–43.
69 *The Compleat Geographer*, 3rd edn. (1709), pt. ii. 91.
70 Heylyn, *Cosmography*, pt. iii. 211.
71 See below, pp. 38–9.
72 See below, pp. 110–12.
73 Lach, *Asia in the Making of Europe*, ii. 388.
74 *Embassy from the East-India Company*, p. 216.
75 *The Antiquity of China*, pp. 47, 87.
76 *Works*, iii. 456.
77 L. Le Comte, *A Compleat History of the Empire of China* (1739 edn.), p. 213.
78 *Works*, iii. 340. Temple's interest in China is analysed in W. W. Appleton, *A Cycle of Cathay* (New York, 1951), pp. 42–7.
79 *Antiquity of China*, p. 92.
80 *Philosophical Transactions*, xvi. (1686–7), 37.
81 1709 edn., pt. ii. 137.
82 There is a modern edition by C. R. Boxer (1935).

83 Heylyn, *Cosmography*, pt. iii. 219.
84 *China and France; or Two Treatises* (1676), pp. 4–5, 95–111.
85 *Compleat Geographer* (1709 edn.), pt. ii. 79.
86 Ogilby, *Asia*, preface.
87 1709 edn., pt. ii. 1–2.
88 *Asia in the Making of Europe*, ii, 563–6.
89 *A New Description of Persia*, ii. 257.
90 *Travels in the Mogul Empire*, pp. 161–2.
91 Quoted Hugh Honour, *The New Golden Land: European Images of America* (New York, 1975), p. 84.
92 See Benjamin Keen, *The Aztec Image in Western Thought* (New Jersey, 1971).
93 See L. E. Huddleston, *Origin of the American Indians: European Concepts 1492–1729* (Austin, 1967).
94 J. H. Elliott, *The Old World and the New 1492–1650* (Cambridge, 1970), p. 44; see also Elliott's Raleigh Lecture at the British Academy, 'The Discovery of America and the Discovery of Man', *Proceedings of the British Academy* (1972).
95 See Robert F. Berkhofer, Jnr., *The White Man's Indian: Images of the American Indian from Columbus to the Present* (New York, 1978), p. 3 and elsewhere.
96 Although see D. B. Quinn, *England and the Discovery of America, 1481–1620* (1974), Ch. 17.
97 See Stephen Lorant, *The New World: The First Pictures of America* (New York, 1946); for a different view see William N. Fenton, *American Indian and White Relations to 1830* (Chapel Hill, 1974), pp. 26–7.
98 *The Essays of Montaigne*, trans. E. J. Trechman (1935), i. 204–5.
99 H. M. Jones, *O Strange New World* (1965), p. 173.
100 Karen O. Kupperman, *Settling with the Indians: the Meeting of English and Indian Cultures in America, 1580–1640* (1980), p. 106.
101 Loren E. Pennington, 'The Amerindian in English promotional literature, 1575–1625', in K. R. Andrews *et al.*, *The Westward Expansion: English Activities in Ireland, the Atlantic, and America, 1480–1650* (Liverpool, 1978), p. 178.
102 Samuel Purchas, *Hakluytus Posthumus, or Purchas his Pilgrimes* (Glasgow, 1906 reprint), xix. 231; quoted, with much other material, in R. H. Pearce, *The Savages of America: A Study of the Indian and the Idea of Civilization* (Baltimore, 1953), p. 7. For recent work on the Virginia massacre and its aftermath see Kupperman, *Settling with the Indians*, pp. 176–8; H. C. Porter, *The Inconstant Savage: England and the North American Indian 1500–1660* (1979), Ch. 24; Bernard W. Sheehan, *Savagism and Civility: Indians and Englishmen in Colonial Virginia* (Cambridge, 1980), Ch. 6.
103 Daniel Denton, *A Brief Description of New-York* . . . (1670), p. 7.
104 See Alden T. Vaughan, *New England Frontier: Puritans and Indians 1620–1675* (Boston, 1965), p. vi.
105 See Colin Steele, *English Interpreters of the Iberian New World from Purchas to Stevens: A Bibliographical Study 1603–1726* (Oxford, 1975), p. 69; Richard S. Dunn, 'Seventeenth-Century English Historians of America', in *Seventeenth-Century America: Essays in Colonial History*, ed. J. M. Smith (Chapel Hill, 1959), pp. 207–8.
106 Thomas Hobbes, *Leviathan*, ed. Michael Oakeshott (Oxford, 1955), p. 83.
107 H. N. Fairchild, *The Noble Savage: A Study in Romantic Naturalism* (New York, 1928), p. 29; see also Steele, *English Interpreters*, pp. 76–7.
108 Bernard Sheehan's phrase in *Savagism and Civility*, p. 89.
109 *Dictionary of Canadian Biography*, i (Toronto, 1966), 5.
110 Or at least not until the monumental 73-volume edition by Reuben G. Thwaites, which has the original text and English translation on facing pages, *The Jesuit Relations and Allied Documents*. . . . (Cleveland, 1896–1901).

111 William Kellaway, *The New England Company 1649–1776: Missionary Society to the American Indians* (1961), p. 276.
112 Richard Blome, *Geographical Description of the four parts of the World* (1670), pt. iv. 9.
113 John Ogilby, *America* . . . (1671), p. 151.
114 For a good general discussion see Robin Hallett, *The Penetration of Africa . . . Volume 1 to 1815* (1965), pp. 3–103.
115 Richard Hakluyt, *The Principal Navigations of the English Nation* (Glasgow reprint, 1903–5), vi. 170, 165, 167 (in order of citation).
116 Winthrop D. Jordan, *White over Black: American Attitudes towards the Negro 1550–1812* (Norton Library edition, New York, 1977), p. 6.
117 *Ibid.*, pp. 4–5.
118 Hakluyt, *Principal Navigations*, vi. 176.
119 *Ibid.*, vii. 262.
120 Jordan, *White over Black*, p. 20.
121 See James Walvin, *Black and White: the Negro in English Society, 1555–1945* (1973).
122 Eldred Jones, *Othello's Countrymen: the African in English Renaissance Drama* (1965), p. 126.
123 Purchas, *Hakluytus Posthumus*, v. 303.
124 *Ibid.*, 263, 289, 294, 312 (in order of citation).
125 Richard Bernheimer, *Wild Men in the Middle Ages: A Study in Art, Sentiment, and Demonology* (Cambridge, Mass., 1952), p. 19.
126 Hakluyt, *Principal Navigations*, vi. 270.
127 See below, pp. 260–4.
128 Much of the information in the remainder of this section is taken from Glyndwr Williams, ' "The Inexhaustible Fountains of Gold": English Projects and Ventures in the South Seas, 1670–1750', in John E. Flint and Glyndwr Williams, *Perspectives of Empire* (1973), pp. 27–53.
129 On the various editions of Dampier see N. M. Penzer's bibliographical note to the edition of *A New Voyage Round the World by William Dampier* published by the Argonaut Press (1927), pp. v–viii.
130 *Ibid.*, p. 344.
131 *Ibid.*, pp. 312–13; also William Dampier, *A Voyage to New Holland*, ed. J. A. Williamson (1939), pp. 102–3. See below, p. 273.
132 See Bryan Little, *Crusoe's Captain* (1960), Ch. 12.

2

The Diffusion of Knowledge

The increased activity of Englishmen overseas during the seventeenth century was reflected in a widening stream of publications on travel and on distant regions by the end of the century. At times during the next century it was to reach flood-tide proportions. Many individual accounts will be discussed later; the concern of this chapter is with the dissemination of knowledge about the wider world in more general terms.

Works of travel came off the press in many forms: published journals, reprints, translations, abridgements and compilations. They did not conform to a common pattern, though advice on this score was not lacking. During the seventeenth century those going abroad were repeatedly enjoined to keep records of what they saw and experienced, and various models were suggested as to how this should be done. Bacon, in his essay 'Of Travaile', advised on 'the things to be seene and observed'. Bernard Varen in his *Geographica generalis* of 1650 presented travellers with ten categories into which they should arrange their observations:

> Stature, shape, skin color, food, habits
> Occupation and arts
> Virtues, vices, learning, wit
> Marriage, birth, burial, name giving
> Speech and language
> State and government
> Religion
> Cities and renowned places
> History
> Famous men, inventions and innovations[1]

Elaborate instructions were also issued by Robert Boyle in 1666 in the *Philosophical Transactions* of the Royal Society, later published separately as *General Heads for the Natural History of a Country ... for the use of Travellers and Navigators*. More comprehensive and exacting was the 'Advice to Travellers' published in 1704. They should take notes on:

> Climate, government, power, places of strength, cities of note, religion, language, coins, trade, manufactures, wealth, bishoprics,

universities, antiquities, libraries, collections of rarities, arts and artists, publick structures, roads, bridges, woods, mountains, customs, habits, laws, privileges, strange adventures, surprising accidents, rarities both natural and artificial, the soil, plants, animals and whatsoever may be curious, diverting or profitable.[2]

Even if he took a more relaxed view of what was expected of him, a traveller with a sharp eye and a modicum of literary capacity could hope to gain money and reputation by publishing a book on his return. The preface to the English edition of one of the most highly esteemed French accounts of Asia suggested in 1686 that 'It would be needless without doubt, by any preliminary discourse, to recommend the relations of TRAVELS to publick perusal; since the universal approbation they meet with in the world, and the eagerness wherewith they are sought after by all people, is an argument convincing enough that they are delightful at least, if not also profitable.'[3] 'Delightful' and 'profitable' was probably as far as the ambition of most works of travel went. The advice of armchair scholars on the scope and variety of travellers' accounts was honoured more in the breach than in the observance. Polymath travellers there were – Johann Reinhold Forster, for example – but they were few and far between. Lack of any form of scientific training or linguistic expertise, the distraction of arduous, often dangerous circumstances, and not least the juggling and rewriting of an author's material at the behest of publishers anxious not to bore the reading public, produced many works of haphazard arrangement and doubtful reliability. As late as 1774 Cornelius de Pauw complained in his *Défense des recherches philosophiques* that only ten out of a hundred travel accounts contained authentic or useful information. 'The scholar', he continued, 'was in the position of a botanist who, in order to find a particular plant, had to search forests, rocks and cliffs – sometimes indeed a whole land – before he found what he was looking for.'[4]

Although the acquisition and interpretation of knowledge about the world had become a major intellectual preoccupation of educated Englishmen, there was little of the central direction to the gathering of information that emerged in late seventeenth-century France with its formidable apparatus of royal patronage and state-sponsored academies. It is true that the Royal Society regarded knowledge of the world and its peoples as a branch of science which it was proper for it to promote. It hoped that 'there will scarce a ship come up the Thames, that does not make some return of experiments, as well as merchandise'.[5] In addition to providing instructions for travellers it received many communications from them, some of which were published in its *Philosophical Transactions*. John Ray edited *A Collection of Curious Travels and Voyages* which was published under the Society's imprimatur in

1693; and a few years later another pot-pourri of papers presented to the Society was published as *Miscellanea Curiosa, Containing a Collection of Curious Travels, Voyages and Natural Histories of Countries*.

There were also on the market in the late seventeenth century increasing numbers of 'geographies', a term used to describe a compilation of extracts and summaries from travel books. As a distinct discipline, seventeenth-century geography was generally interpreted in a rather narrow fashion to be what would now be regarded as cartography, that is the fixing of places. The voyages of the sixteenth and seventeenth centuries, together with better methods of calculating latitude and longitude had led to much publishing of new maps and atlases. Many publishers of collections of maps wished to include material other than the usual dissertation on the mathematical principles of map-making. As the cartographer Herman Moll put it, 'topography' might be 'the better part of what every body desires to know in geography', but 'geography alone is dry and jejeune and makes but small impression on the memory'. He therefore added 'the history of nature with descriptions of countries' to his *System of Geography* published in 1701. In doing this he was following a well-beaten track. The mixture of physical and human geography was becoming increasingly common. The best-known exponents of this genre earlier in the century had been Peter Heylyn and Nathanael Carpenter. Originally published in 1621 and 1625 respectively, their books went through several editions. After 1652 Heylyn's was entitled *Cosmographie*, meaning a mixture of 'natural and civil story . . . for it hath from natural history or geography the regions themselves, together with their sites and several commodities; from civil history, habitations, governments and manners; and from mathematicks, the climates and configurations of the heavens'. The result was a sort of gazetteer in which the continents were described country by country. This model had many imitators. *Systems, Manuals, Dictionaries* or *Grammars* of geography were published in profusion.[6] If 'geography' is the term which contemporaries most frequently used to describe such books, and if it is a title which it still seems appropriate to use, since they were usually written around maps, they were also collections of information about history, religion, and what were taken to be social customs. They were repositories for myths and observations of all kinds. In short, the compiler was supposed to have some of the versatility expected of the traveller who provided him with the information.

Some of these compact geographies were very popular indeed. Patrick Gordon's *Geography anatomiz'd or the geographical grammar* was first published in 1693, and went through twenty editions by 1754. The year 1695 saw the appearance of the *Thesaurus geographicus* which managed to deal with America in fourteen pages; it was this book which was later reshaped by Herman Moll into the much superior *System of Geography* of 1701, which was superseded in turn by enlarged editions in 1709 and 1723. A tiny, much compressed example of the type was Laurence Eachard's *A most Compleat Compendium of Geography* of 1691. Its perky introduction made a virtue of its microscopic dimensions as it addressed its compilers:

> So you great volumes rack, to find what's true,
> And in a method most concise, yet new,
> Lay out those treasures to a publick view,
> Drake's ship tho' bigger than this little spot,
> Yet never past more seas, more knowledge got.

An analysis of the travel literature from the 1690s onwards indicates that, like many of the voyages which it described, it owed less to institutional encouragement than to motives of commercial profit, at times strengthened by patriotic fervour. The renewed popularity of travel accounts was marked first by the South Sea narratives and collections discussed in the previous chapter, but of more consequence and magnitude were two general collections of voyages which appeared in 1704 and 1705: *A Collection of Voyages and Travels* published by the booksellers Awnsham and John Churchill, and *Navigantium atque Itinerantium Bibliotheca*, edited by John Harris (soon to become Secretary to the Royal Society) for a syndicate of booksellers. The Churchill collection was contained in four folio volumes, the Harris collection in two; both were ambitious undertakings in an intellectual as well as a financial sense, and had been several years in the preparation. The Churchills took advice from Hans Sloane of the Royal Society, and from John Locke, to whom Awnsham felt 'particularly oblig'd for your assistance about my collection of voyages'.[7] It included a long, preliminary 'Catalogue and Character' of travel books in Latin, Italian, Spanish, French and English (possibly contributed by Edmund Halley), and an editorial preface which concluded in resounding fashion with the assertion:

> The Empire of Europe is now extended to the utmost bounds of the earth, where several of its nations have conquests and colonies. These and many more are the advantages drawn from the labours of those, who expose themselves to the dangers of the vast ocean, and of unknown nations; which those who sit at home abundantly reap in every kind: and the relation of the traveller is an incentive to stir up another to imitate him, while the rest of mankind, in their accounts without stirring a foot, compass the earth and seas, visit all countries, and converse with all nations.

The 1,600 folio pages of the Churchill collection were mostly devoted to accounts not previously available to English readers. There had been nothing like it since the heroic collections of Hakluyt and Purchas, neither of whom provided material for the Churchill volumes. Instead, there were translations from seven European languages, and many journals in English which had previously existed only in manuscript form. Volumes V and VI were added to the collection when it was reprinted in 1732 (volume V containing the valuable Barbot journal of Guinea from the 1680s), and further additions came in 1747. The arrangement of the collection was idiosyncratic, but the amount of new material published was impressive.

John Harris's rival collection was equally erratic in presentation, and its first volume was heavily dependent on Hakluyt and Purchas. The second volume, too, showed little of the originality of the Churchill collection, most of its selections already being available in English in some form or other. In the 1740s it was revised, enlarged and reissued under the editorship of John Campbell. It was, in effect, a new collection both in subject-matter and arrangement. Campbell had consulted, he claimed, more than 600 volumes in putting together his work. It was intended both for 'Pleasure and Improvement', but what was implicit in the other collections was now made explicit. Campbell's avowed purpose was to encourage trade to all parts of the world 'as the surest means of making us a great, wealthy, powerful and happy people', and the collection of texts was interspersed with explanations and exhortations designed to open up new branches of commerce and revive old ones. His work, Campbell hoped, would help to dispel 'that supine indolence, which for many years has locked up our faculties, with respect to discoveries, while other nations that we seem to despise have crept so fast into naval power, as already to tread upon our heels'.[8] Its 2,000 pages of small print, in double columns, its massive proportions and weight, clearly restricted the number of bound editions of the collection. It is significant, perhaps, that it ends abruptly in Asia, without the promised section on Africa. If this hints at financial problems, then presumably the device of offering the collection to the public in instalments, thus limiting the expense to small weekly or monthly payments, had not been altogether successful. This method of increasing sales was of long standing. It seems to have been applied to collections of voyages for the first time in 1708 when a group of booksellers headed by John Knapton issued a collection of translations edited by John Stevens called *A View of the Universe*. The monthly parts cost only 1s. or 1s. 6d.[9] A more lavish production, the *Atlas Geographus*, which also began publication in 1708, in turn became available in instalments, the 800 pages of Volume V on the Americas taking the best part of four years (1715–18) to reach completion. The getting together of booksellers, such as the Stevens group, to finance jointly the publication of large-scale works of travel had been tried as early as the 1680s, when a translation of Garcilaso de la Vega's *Comentarios reales de los Incas* was undertaken by a combination of booksellers.[10]

Just as Churchill and Harris had offered rival collections in the early years of the century, so Campbell's revision of Harris had its competitors. In 1743 the bookseller Thomas Astley launched an ambitious project – *A New General Collection of Voyages and Travels*, which was issued in 1745–7 under the editorship of the cartographer John Green (alias Bradock Mead). It, too, was offered in instalments, although it could also be bought in four large, bound volumes. Astley was able to attract well over 1000 subscribers, but even so the enterprise closed prematurely. Astley himself was arrested in connection with another, more political, matter, while Green complained that he had suffered from 'the violent aspersions' and almost united opposition of his rivals.[11] This sort of rivalry was common, and was reflected in the newspaper advertisements of the period which extolled the virtues of one work and denigrated the qualities of a competitor. In other ways, the Astley collection was a good example of the development of these vast compilations. It included some material appearing for the first time in English, but most of its selections were already available, some since Hakluyt and Purchas, others of a more recent date – Francis Moore's *Travels into the Inland Parts of Africa* (1738), the translation of Peter Kolben's *Present State of the Cape of Good Hope* (1731) and of Du Halde's *Description of the Empire of China* (1738–41). The aim of the editor was not so much to rescue unknown accounts languishing in manuscript form or in inaccessible languages as to bring together what he judged to be the most reliable descriptions of a region – to produce, in his own words, 'a system of modern geography and history, as well as a body of voyages and travels'.

Set against Campbell and Astley, the final volumes VII and VIII added to the Churchill collection in 1747 (usually known by the name of the bookseller and publisher, Thomas Osborne), wore an old-fashioned look. The two volumes were compiled from sixteenth- and seventeenth-century printed texts in the Harleian library, bought by Osborne in 1742. The texts were printed without editing, and the work was 'frankly a miscellany of rare and interesting narratives'.[12] Osborne's volumes completed an ambitious programme of rival publishing activity on the grand scale: Campbell's enlargement of Harris (1744–48), the third edition of Churchill (1744–46) and its supplementation by the Osborne volumes (1747), and the Astley collection (1745–47). In their valuable survey of this literature, G. R. Crone and

R. A. Skelton point to a change in the nature of the subscribers. There are fewer clergy on the subscription lists, and increasing numbers of merchants, for 'the literature of travel now found a public, not only among dilettanti who read for amusement, but also among merchants and brokers who had invested money in commercial ventures to Africa, Asia and the Pacific'.[13]

If the folio volumes of the great collections made the most imposing show, the attempt by publishers to exploit a lower section of the market continued throughout the eighteenth century. The book-buying public was wooed with cheap, handy-sized editions, carefully pruned of matter that the general reader might find dull. Ever since Purchas, even the largest collections had resorted to the mutilation of texts, to remove routine details of journeys and to highlight the accounts of strange places and peoples. This process was now carried much further. The 'size and price of a folio' were 'sufficient to intimidate the ordinary reader', John Knox claimed in introducing his collection in seven small volumes in 1767. He would leave out 'too minute and disgustingly dry' descriptions, as well as technical matter that 'none but mere pilots or seafaring people can read without disgust'.[14] He aimed to 'catch the fancy' while he 'improved the understanding'. 'We live in an age of levity and caprice that can relish little besides works of fancy', wrote Tobias Smollett. His *Compendium of Authentic and Entertaining Voyages* would suit the taste of such an age. He would convey 'instruction . . . under the pleasing form of entertainment . . . polish the stile, strengthen the connexion of incidents, and animate the narration, wherever it seemed to languish'. In 1796 William Mavor issued twenty volumes of his *General Collection of Voyages and Travels* which would 'satisfy without fatiguing, and convey the most requisite information at a price too limited to be regarded'. His volumes would be 'worthy a place in the pocket, the parlour, or the library'. 'Youthful innocence and female delicacy' had nothing to fear from them.

Anthologies of travel accounts which had been rigorously pruned shaded easily into obvious works of synthesis. The seventeenth-century 'geographies' were the prototypes of such books. The model established by Heylyn was still imitated without any radical departures. Two major geographical works appearing at the end of the eighteenth century, which included much new information, but still presented it in a stereotyped form, were Thomas Pennant's *Outlines of the Globe* in four volumes (1798–1800), and Pinkerton's *Modern Geography* (1802) in two. Less ambitious single-volume gazetteers of the world proliferated. A successful book might have a very long life indeed, going through many slightly modified editions. William Guthrie's *Geographical Grammar* almost equalled the earlier record of Gordon's *Geography anatomiz'd* by reaching twenty-one editions in 1801. Rigid distinctions were not made between 'geography' and what was called 'modern history'. A major practitioner of the latter was Thomas Salmon, a credit to Grub Street about whom it would be interesting to know more. Commercially he seems to have been very successful. His best-known book, *Modern History; or, the Present State of all Nations*, began as a serial in 1724. Subscribers collected it for fourteen years, and a number of bound editions were later published. At least on Asia, Salmon's *Modern History* retailed worthwhile information, for he appears to have been to the East himself, and had gathered first-hand accounts from 'Governors, Consuls and merchants'.[15] Salmon was also marketed in single-volume form, such as *The Modern Gazeteer: or, a Short View of the Several Nations of the World* and his *New Geographical and Historical Grammar*.

Travel literature also contributed to more scholarly works of synthesis. The *Universal History* was an immense project, resulting in the publication of sixty-five volumes between 1747 and 1765 by many different authors. There was some Asian material in the first or 'ancient' series of the *History*, with four volumes devoted to Asia and two to Africa in the second, *The Modern Part*. Readers were presented with the findings of those working on Arabic manuscripts, of the Jesuits on the history of the Chinese, of French, Dutch and English accounts of West African societies. Those who wished to know more about non-Christian religions could consult two English versions of a compilation originally published in French. One of the translations, *The Ceremonies and Religious Customs of the Various Nations of the Known World*, appeared in serial form and in seven bound volumes between 1733 and 1739.

The expanding world of periodicals and newspapers was much concerned with voyages and travels. The Royal Society continued to act as patron of travellers, receiving communications from them and publishing those of sufficient interest in its *Philosophical Transactions*. Its Copley Gold Medal might be awarded to an explorer for the best paper published in the *Transactions* in a particular year; it went to Christopher Middleton in 1742 for an account of Hudson Bay, and to the more celebrated James Cook in 1776. Other scholarly periodicals covered specific aspects of the overseas world. For example, *Archaeologia*, published from 1770, included pieces on Asian antiquities. Material on Asia, America and the Pacific also appeared in the *Annual Register*, sixty-five pages of extracts from Hawkesworth's *Voyages* in 1773, for example. It was, though, the more popular periodicals such as the pioneer *Gentleman's Magazine* and the *London Magazine*, both founded in the 1730s, which carried most information about exotic regions. Extracts from new books were a staple part of their output, and travel books were among the foremost from which extracts were quarried, often to make up long serials. A book might well achieve a wider circulation in extracts than it did in its full form. It was also common practice to include long extracts from a book as part of a review. In the second half of the eighteenth century a number of specialized literary journals were established, such as the *Monthly Review*, the *English Review*, and the *Critical Review*, which enabled their readers to gain some acquaintance with the contents of a wide range of books, both English and foreign. A sampling of the *London Magazine* between 1773 and 1778 shows reviews of, or commentaries from the English translation of Bougainville's voyage; Hawkesworth's *Voyages*; Bruce's travels; an account of Russian exploration in the north Pacific; Adair's *History of the American Indians*; and the accounts by James Cook and George Forster of Cook's second circumnavigation.

Readers of imaginative literature would also be instructed about distant lands. The boundary between travellers' factual accounts and fictional 'voyages' was not absolute. Even the most obvious work of fiction, such as *Gulliver's Travels*, made references to current knowledge, shown graphically in the maps which accompanied many editions. Goldsmith's *Citizen of the World* had elaborate footnotes referring to travel books, and it reflected many contemporary assumptions about Siberia and China in particular. Some of Defoe's writing was likely to leave readers in doubt whether they were perusing fact or fiction. His *Farther Travels of Robinson Crusoe* closely followed recent writing on Asia, and in a *New Voyage round the World* in 1724 he used geographical settings which were as exact as he could make them. Sometimes the confusion was total. The *Monthly Miscellany or Memoirs for the Curious*, a short-lived periodical edited by James Petiver, printed in 1708 a preposterous 'Letter from Admiral Bartholomew de Fonte, then Admiral of New Spain and Peru, and now Prince of Chili', describing an imaginary voyage through a Northwest Passage. The *Monthly Miscellany* soon disappeared from view, but Fonte's letter survived, to be reprinted a dozen times during the course of the century as part of a serious debate about the geography of north-west America. Even more noteworthy is that the Royal Society accepted, and printed in its *Philosophical Transactions* for 1767, a letter from a young midshipman solemnly describing the 'giants' of Patagonia encountered on Byron's discovery voyage of 1764–66: 'there was hardly a man less than eight feet, most of them considerably more'.[16] The most famous hoax of all was probably that perpetrated by George Psalmanazar, who passed himself off as a Formosan, writing a *History of Formosa* in 1704 and inventing his own language.

If readers of fictitious accounts and hoax articles sometimes imagined that they were fact, so the reverse might happen. The account by Lahontan of North America in the late seventeenth century, issued in its first English edition in 1703, is a case in point. Suspicion about Lahontan's 'Long River' flowing towards the Pacific, and about his Indian informant and disputant, Adario, grew until the whole work was in danger of being discredited. Harris had printed selections from Lahontan without comment in 1705; but when Campbell revised the *Bibliotheca* in the 1740s he noted, 'As to the accounts of Lahontan . . . they have formerly been much admired, yet we are now very well satisfied that they are rather romances than relations'.[17] Nor was this scepticism simply an expression of Francophobia, for in France the process of disbelief reached such a stage that in the 1750s the author of the *Encyclopédie* article on 'Canadiens (Philosophie des)' was beginning to doubt the existence not only of the voluble Adario but of Lahontan himself.[18] Suspicion of the veracity of travel accounts was rife. Chardin summed it up when he complained that 'I have passed my life in reading the accounts that travellers give, and I have not met with two that have given me the same idea of the same people.'[19] This, no doubt, was part of their attraction.

At the bottom end of the market, writers who aimed at supposedly simple readers felt no need to keep abreast of current knowledge. Stereotypes of great antiquity survived tenaciously. In chap-books, short illustrated books in simple language which sold cheaply, the peoples of the Near East were portrayed as Turks and Saracens to be fought by the heroes of the medieval romances which remained an important element in such books throughout the eighteenth century.[20] For instance, the hero of *The Famous History of the Valiant London Prentice* was apprenticed to the Levant Company (a concession to modernity), but once in Turkey he fought the Turkish chivalry in full armour, killing Grodam, 'the son-in-law of the Great Turk'.[21] Further east, versions of Sir John Mandeville inevitably sufficed. In a short account of his *Foreign Travels*, readers could learn about the King of Java's golden palace, about an island where men and women had heads like hounds and worshipped the ox, of the great Caan of Catha, of speaking trees and of Prester John, whose lands were so full of precious stones that they were made into cups and dishes.[22]

Travel literature was an important prop of the eighteenth-century book trade, and authors were not the only people whose interests were involved. Booksellers, who acted as publishers, were often playing for sizeable stakes, while the public's appetite for travel accounts provided employment for editors, translators, and other literary oddjobmen. One of the most successful books of its kind, *A Voyage round the World . . . by George Anson*, can serve as an example. It was published in May 1748 as a handsome quarto volume, the work almost certainly of two editors, and was followed before the end of the year by four further editions. By 1776 no fewer than fifteen editions, mostly in the cheaper octavo or duodecimo format, had appeared; this was in Britain alone, and on the continent the account was translated into French, Dutch, German and Italian. Extracts from the book were given in serial form in the newspapers and periodicals of the day, the fullest in the *Gentleman's Magazine*, where extracts appeared in five consecutive monthly issues. In addition, abridged versions were included in several of the collections of voyages published in the second half of the century. The plates for this kind of book kept artists and engravers busy. The Anson volume was accompanied by forty-two full page plates, available separately at 7s. the set, and these also were widely copied and pirated.

How the rewards of all this literary effort were divided was a matter for controversy. Even admired authors did not necessarily do well. Some critics thought that Robert Orme's *History of the Military Transactions of the British Nation in Indostan* was one of the outstanding historical achievements of its time. Yet four years after the publication of the first volume in 1763 Orme complained that his return from the sale of 1,000 copies had not paid for the books that he needed to write it.[23] Most translators and compilers seem to have been paid little. Samuel Johnson's first literary earnings were five pounds for translating a book on Abyssinia.[24] A lesser-known Johnson, Richard, described as 'a printer who took to hack writing', was paid six guineas a volume in 1783 for editing *The Polite Traveller or British Navigator*.[25] Those who felt inadequately rewarded often seemed to have assumed that booksellers were making excessive profits out of their labours. But John Lockman came to the booksellers' defence. Although admitting that translators and editors were badly paid, he insisted that 'the fate' of voyages was 'so very precarious, that often 'tis not in the power of a book seller to pay a writer suitably'.[26] On the other hand, men of established literary reputation often did very well. Tobias Smollett agreed to produce seven volumes of edited 'voyages' in 1753 at a guinea and a half for each sheet. Since it was assumed that the volumes would be about one hundred sheets each, he could expect to make about £160 a volume.[27] Still more striking was the case of John Hawkesworth's editing of Cook's first voyage in his three-volume *Account of the Voyages undertaken by the Order of His Present Majesty for making Discoveries in the Southern Hemisphere*, published in 1773. This created such a stir that it became something of a *cause célèbre* which, it was widely thought, led to Hawkesworth's death within the year. In his second and third volume, Hawkesworth fused the journals of Cook and Banks to make a single account which, whatever its literary merits, made nonsense of much of what they had actually said. Hawkesworth had felt free, he pointed out in the preface, to insert 'such sentiments and observations as my subject should suggest'. For this he was reputed to have collected the sum, astonishing by eighteenth-century standards, of £6,000.[28]

To quantify the popularity of the books of voyages and travel is impossible. Conclusions are bound to be impressionistic, and may be misleading. There are almost too many prefaces of the sort attached to Anders Sparrman's *Voyage to the Cape of Good Hope* (1785) to carry total conviction. 'Relations of voyages and travels have at all times, and in all ages, since the invention of letters, been favourably received by the public; but, perhaps, in no age as well as in the present; writings of this kind being bought up with avidity and read with eagerness, more especially in this island.' Is this the expression of plain, unadorned fact, or is it a case of a publisher whistling to keep his spirits up? One takes for granted the importance and popularity of the accounts of Cook's voyages – Hawkesworth's £6,000 sticks in the mind – but the publishing history of the third voyage is instructive. When the official account was published in June 1784 at £4 14s. 6d. a set, it sold well. The *Monthly Review* became quite excited by it all: 'We remember not a circumstance like what has happened on this occasion. On the third day after publication, a copy was not to be met with in the hands of the bookseller; and, to our certain knowledge, six, seven, eight, and even ten guineas, have since been offered for a sett.'[29] To meet this demand a second edition was issued in 1785, which presumably also sold well, because a third edition came out before the end of the year. But in 1801 there was still left, the publisher reported, 'a great number' of that edition, and little profit had been made on the whole thing.[30] It may be, of course, that the cheap, pirated editions had spoilt the market. One also remembers, though, that there were still copies left of the Churchill collection, published in 1704, at the time of Awnsham Churchill's death, twenty-four years later. The market for travel accounts was not insatiable, particularly when prices were high, and cheaper equivalents available.

The accessibility and circulation of travel books, as of other printed works, was greatly increased by the growth of libraries of every kind in this period: commercial circulating libraries, non-profit subscription libraries, local book clubs, and community libraries. Multi-volume and expensive editions of the standard accounts might be obtained in this way – the Churchill collection or the *Universal History*, for example, or even (at the London Library Service) the fourteen-volume Paris edition of 1781 of the Jesuit *Lettres édifiantes et curieuses*.[31] Library holdings and library borrowings do not necessarily coincide, but Paul Kaufman's researches have directed a narrow but revealing beam of light on the latter. His use of the (unique) records of the Bristol Library provides firm evidence of the popularity of voyages and travels in the years from 1773 to 1784, at least as far as Bristol readers were concerned. Hawkesworth comes top of the list, with more than two hundred individual borrowings. Parkinson's posthumous account of the first Cook voyage, the English edition of Bougainville, Cook's account of his second voyage and the two separate books on it by J. R. Forster and his son George, Edward Long's history of Jamaica, and Charlevoix's North American travels, also show up well. Of the books which do not quite fall within the category of voyages, but which have close associations, Robertson's *History of America* was borrowed more than a hundred times, and Raynal's *Philosophical History of the East and West Indies* a remarkable one hundred and seventy times if the French and English editions are both taken into account.[32]

The impact of the travel accounts was strengthened by the increasing number of illustrations which publishers included to depict exotic scenes and people. During the century generally the demand was for new and striking illustrations which conformed to artistic fashions and current moral standards – sometimes with disturbing results to accuracy – until towards the end of the century no seaborne discovery expedition was complete without its contingent of amateur or professional artists. Many of these made creditable drawings, but artists of real quality were rare. Mark Catesby and William Bartram made superb sketches and paintings of the flora and fauna of the southern American colonies, and William Hodges and John Webber brought back impressive records of Cook's explorations, but some of their best work was never published. When it was, there could be problems. Earlier accounts had suffered from hack artists and engravers, working with a textual description before them, but little else. The difficulties this could cause were shown in the English edition of Lahontan's *New Voyages* of 1703, where the author grumbled that he had been forced to correct 'almost all the cuts of the Holland impression, for the Dutch gravers had murder'd 'em, by not understanding their explications, which were all in French. They have grav'd women for men, and men for women; naked persons for those that are cloath'd, and è contra.' Even when the artists used were of high reputation, the results of their retouching work on the primary record could be insidious and damaging. Bernard Smith has shown how the ministrations of the artist Giovanni Cipriani and the engraver Francesco Bartolozzi to a drawing of the Fuegans by Alexander Buchan on Cook's first voyage 'transformed the state of miserable wretchedness depicted by Buchan into the state of primitive elegance imagined by Hawkesworth'.[33] In the same way some of Hodges' paintings on the second voyage, when engraved in neo-classical style for the published account, were radically changed. George Forster, who was on the voyage, pointed out of one of them: 'The connoisseur will find Greek contours and features in this picture, which have never existed in the South Sea. He will admire an elegant flowing robe which involves the whole head and body, in an island where the women rarely cover the shoulders and breast; and he will be struck with awe and delight by the figure of a divine old man, with a long white beard, though all the people of Ea-oowhe shave themselves with muscle-shells.'[34]

If the artists' vision was often clouded once it was transferred to print, then a more accurate if static representation of what the explorers had seen might be found in the 'specimens' they collected. As Swift showed when he made Gulliver bring back from Brobdingnag the corn from the toe of a maid of honour, and a footman's tooth, travellers were expected to collect 'rarities' and 'curiosities' of all kinds, whose attractions were not necessarily aesthetic. Sir Hans Sloane, for example, Secretary and later President of the Royal Society, was presented with 'a pebble stone, with a picture supposed to be done with the urine of a land tortoise' on it.[35] What conclusions Sloane was supposed to draw from it are not clear, but other objects more obviously informative came to the Society, such as the yoke and plough from Tonking presented by Captain Knox.[36] Sloane's own collection of botanical, geological and ethnographical specimens, as well as his books and manuscripts, formed after his death the basis for the British Museum, established by Act of Parliament in 1753, and first opened to the public six years later. It included about 350 ethnographical items, roughly half from North America (if we include Eskimo); interestingly, there were only twenty-nine items from Africa.[37] The Museum's establishment is indicative of the fact that the eighteenth century was the period of the great institutionalized collections, though many had begun as the personal collection of an individual. So England's first public museum, the Ashmolean in Oxford, was founded in the 1680 when the collector Elias Ashmole presented the University with 'twelve cartloads of curiosities', many of them from Virginia. In the eighteenth century, among much else, it was to acquire some of the ethnographic specimens brought back by J. R. Forster from Cook's second voyage. Other museums remained private ones, for example Sir Ashton Lever's which moved from Manchester to Leicester Square, London, in 1775, and included many items from Cook's voyages. Extending over seventeen rooms, the Museum contained an 'Otaheite Room' and, after Cook's third voyage, a 'Sandwich Island Room' which displayed 'the magnificent dresses, helmets, idols, ornaments, instruments, utensils etc. etc. of those Islands never before discovered, which proved so fatal to that able navigator Captain Cook'.[38] When, after a change of ownership, the contents of the Museum were sold by auction in 1806, almost 8,000 items were dispersed into museums and private possession throughout Europe.

The break-up of the Leverian collection was symptomatic of the lack of interest in England in many of the ethnographic items brought back. John Douglas, the editor of the account of Cook's third voyage, was before his time in directing attention to the ethnographic collections of the British Museum and the Leverian on the grounds that 'the novelties of the Society or Sandwich Islands seem better calculated to engage the attention of the studious in our times, than the antiquities, which exhibit proofs of Roman magnificence'.[39] Whereas great care was lavished on the preservation, drawing and cataloguing of the natural history specimens, the so-called 'artificial curiosities' or ethnographic items were neglected – at the British Museum, for example, buried in 'the rag-and-bone Department'. The scholar who has pieced together the evidence of dispersal, loss and survival, has written: 'The British Museum, although truly excited about their newly acquired collections of natural curiosities from Cook's voyages, relegated the artificial curiosities to near obscurity. The collection of ethnographic artefacts – terms which did not even exist at the time – was only incidental to Cook's voyages.'[40] Equally obscure was the fate of many collections presented to museums outside London: of a splendid collection of 'curiosities' from Hudson Bay presented to the Royal Society of Edinburgh in 1787, no trace remains except, frustratingly, a manuscript list of the items drawn up by the donor.[41] Even where they were preserved, little systematic study was made of them; to the learned of eighteenth-century England they remained, quite simply, 'curiosities', evocative of remote lands and strange peoples, but no more. They were in the category of mementoes brought home by George Townshend, commander of the British army at Quebec after Wolfe's death in 1759 – a grim little collection with which to thrill his guests of 'scalps & some Indian arms & utensils'.[42]

Artefacts of Asian civilizations had an additional attraction over those found in the primitive world since they appealed not only to the collector of 'curiosities' but also to the connoisseur of works of art. Since the sixteenth-century European travellers had shown little compunction in carrying off Egyptian objects that could conveniently be removed. Specimens of hieroglyphs were particularly valued by scholars who hoped to be able to deduce their hidden meaning by study in their own country. Early in the eighteenth century Edward Wortley Montagu, Lady Mary's husband, was a particularly zealous collector of Egyptiana. A good part of what had been gathered by private enterprise eventually found its way into public collections. The British

Museum had Egyptian exhibits from its opening. These were soon augmented, the most spectacular acquisition being the great spoil taken from the French in 1801, when a considerable part of what the savants accompanying the 1798 expedition had garnered was surrendered to the victorious British. By this time the appeal of Egyptian objects had definitely become aesthetic as well as antiquarian; Egyptian figures became motifs for neo-classical architects rather than symbols of occult wisdom.[43]

Only a few pieces of Hindu sculpture came to Britain during the eighteenth century. There are, however, indications that they were arousing serious interest. Notable collectors such as Charles Townley and Ashton Lever had one or two pieces, which caught the attention of aesthetes like Richard Payne Knight. By the end of the century the publication of drawings made on sites and in temples in India was reinforcing the impression created by these few objects and raising hopes that Indian art would become 'a field of taste and speculation'.[44]

Though the study of man as a science was still in its infancy, the appeal of works of travel was widespread and pervasive. Scholars, theologians, seamen and merchants, casual readers after a good yarn, might all be attracted. Many examples of the use made of travel literature by political philosophers from Locke to Millar will be found in the following chapters. Here, it is enough to suggest that the availability of travel accounts in unprecedented quantity during the eighteenth century gave a new dimension to the mental horizons of the literate Englishman. For some, it probably amounted to little more than an enlargement of the Grand Tour by proxy. Men could now pass in their imagination through the great cities of Asia or the forests of North America as easily as they could read of Venice or Rome. So Defoe's *Compleat English Gentleman* could 'make the tour of the world in books, he may make himself master of the geography of the universe in the maps, atlasses, and measurements of our mathematicians. He may travell by land with the historians, by sea with the navigators. He may go round the globe with Dampier and Rogers, and kno' a thousand times more in doing it than all those illiterate sailors.'[45]

For a few, the prospect of distant lands and their peoples brought an uplifting of the spirit which was almost mystical. Thomas Traherne, the Restoration poet, wrote: 'When I heard of any new kingdom beyond the seas, the light and glory of it pleased me immediately, it rose up with me, and I was enlarged wonderfully. I entered into it, I saw its commodities, rarities, springs, meadows, riches, inhabitants, and became possessor of that new room, as if it had been prepared for me, so much was I magnified and delighted in it.'[46] For others, simple escapism might fit the bill better. By the end of the eighteenth century only a few hundred Englishmen had visited Tahiti, but the spell cast by the islands was already strong. Cook's first biographer, Andrew Kippis, wrote in 1788 that his voyages had 'opened new scenes for a poetical fancy to range in'. Tahiti, perhaps, was unique, but the mixture of liberty and exoticism which it represented could be found elsewhere. Lahontan wrote ecstatically of the joys and freedom of wilderness life, and even Father Charlevoix, a steadier member of society altogether, wrote with nostalgic pleasure of his journey between Lakes Erie and Huron. 'In every place where I landed, I was inchanted with the beauty and variety of a landscape, bounded by the finest forest in the world . . . If one always travelled, as I did then, with a clear sky, and a charming climate, on a water as bright as the finest fountain, and were to meet every where with safe and pleasant encampings, where one might find all manner of game at little cost, breathing at one's ease a pure air, and enjoying the sight of the finest countries, one would be tempted to travel all one's life.'[47]

Travel literature became more serious, more respectable during the course of the century. Specialists might complain still of the unscholarly nature of the observations, but there was more perception and less melodrama about most of the accounts. As Sparrman wrote, 'Men with one foot, indeed, Cyclops, Syrens, Troglodytes, and such like imaginary beings, have almost entirely disappeared in this enlightened age.'[48] Above all, there was now a general consensus that there was much to learn from knowledge of the world outside Europe. In his *Advice to an Author* (1710) the 3rd Earl of Shaftesbury had referred to travel books as 'the chief materials to furnish out a library . . . These are in our present days what books of chivalry were in those of our forefathers.' He continued, rather sourly, 'Histories of Incas or Iroquois, written by friars and missionaries, pirates and renegades, sea-captains and trusty travellers, pass for authentic records and are canonical with the virtuosi of this sort . . . They have far more pleasure in hearing the monstrous accounts of monstrous men and manners than the politest and best narrations of the affairs, the governments, and lives of the wisest and most polished people.'[49] By the end of the eighteenth century Englishmen had been long accustomed to turning overseas for accounts of peoples both 'monstrous' and 'polished'.

NOTES

1 Annemarie De Waal Malefit, *Images of Man: A History of Anthropological Thought* (New York, 1974), p. 45.
2 *A Collection of Voyages and Travels* comp. A. and J. Churchill (1704), I, p. lxxi.
3 *Travels of Monsieur de Thévenot into the Levant* (1686), Pt. I, preface.
4 Michèle Duchet, *Anthropologie et histoire au siècle des lumières* (Paris, 1971), pp. 97, 99.
5 Thomas Sprat, *History of the Royal Society* (1667), p. 86.
6 Many are listed in the useful bibliography in A. J. Barker, *The African Link: British Attitudes to the Negro in the Era of the Atlantic Slave Trade, 1550–1807* (1978), especially pp. 236–40.
7 Letters of 17 Nov. 1701, 4 Nov. 1702: Bodleian Library, MS Locke, C.5, pp. 156, 201.
8 *Navigantium atque Itinerantium Bibliotheca: or, a compleat Collection of Voyages and Travels, rev. and enlarged by John Campbell* (1744–48), II, 1011.
9 R. M. Wiles, *Serial Publication in England before 1750* (Cambridge, 1957), pp. 87–8.
10 Colin Steele, *English Interpreters of the Iberian New World from Purchas to Stevens: A Bibliographical Study 1603–1726* (Oxford, 1975), p. 92.
11 See Wiles, *Serial Publication*, pp. 229–30.
12 G. R. Crone and R. A. Skelton, 'English Collections of Voyages and Travels, 1625–1846', in *Richard Hakluyt and his Successors*, ed. Edward Lynam (The Hakluyt Society, 1946), p. 87.
13 *Ibid.*, pp. 88–9.
14 *A New Collection of Voyages, Discoveries and Travels* 1767), I, pp. iv–xi.
15 Thomas Salmon, *Modern History. . . .* (3rd edn., 1744–6), I, pp. vi, viii; see also Wiles, *Serial Publication*, pp. 92, 136.
16 On this, and the 'giants' generally, see Helen Wallis, 'The Patagonian Giants' in *Byron's Journal of his Circumnavigation 1764–66* (Cambridge, The Hakluyt Society, 1964), pp. 185–213.
17 Campbell, *Bibliotheca*, II, 350.
18 Duchet, *Anthropologie et histoire*, p. 101.
19 Percy G. Adams, *Travelers and Travel Liars 1660–1800* (Berkeley and Los Angeles, 1962), p. 232.
20 V. E. Neuberg, *Popular Education in Eighteenth-Century England* (1971), p. 117.
21 J. Ashton, *Chap-books of the Eighteenth Century* (1882), pp. 228–9.
22 *Ibid.*, pp. 405–16; M. Letts, *Sir John Mandeville: The Man and his Book* (1949), pp. 125, 179.
23 Orme to Robert Clive, 25 Jan. 1767: India Office Library, MS Eur. G 37, Box 44.
24 W. J. Bate, *Samuel Johnson* (1978), pp. 137–40.
25 M. J. P. Weedon, 'Richard Johnson and the Successors to John Newbery', *The Library*, 5th ser., IV (1949), 28.
26 John Lockman, *Travels of the Jesuits* (1743), I, p. xxii.
27 *Letters of Tobias Smollett*, ed. E. S. Noyes (Cambridge, Mass., 1926), pp. 23–4.
28 On all this see *The Journals of Captain James Cook: The Voyage of the Endeavour 1768–1771*, ed. J. C. Beaglehole (Cambridge, The Hakluyt Society, 1955), pp. ccxlii–ccliii.
29 *The Monthly Review*, LXX (1784), 474.
30 See *The Journals of Captain James Cook: The Voyage of the Resolution and Discovery 1776–1780*, ed. J. C. Beaglehole (Cambridge, The Hakluyt Society, 1967), p. cciv.
31 See Paul Kaufman, *Libraries and their Users: Collected Papers in Library History* (1969).
32 See Paul Kaufman, *Borrowings from the Bristol Library 1773–1784* (Charlottesville, Va., 1960).
33 Bernard Smith, *European Vision and the South Pacific 1768–1850* (1960), p. 23.

34 *Ibid.*, p. 53.
35 *A Journey from St Petersburg to Pekin 1719–22 by John Bell of Antermony* ed. J. L. Stevenson (Edinburgh, 1965), p. 3.
36 Royal Society MSS, Journal Book, VI, 21 Nov. 1683.
37 H. J. Braunholtz, *Sir Hans Sloane and Ethnology* (1970), p. 20.
38 Quoted Rüdiger Joppien, 'Philippe Jacques de Loutherbourg's Pantomime "Omai" . . .', in *Captain Cook and the South Pacific* (British Museum Yearbook 3, 1979), p. 112 *n.*79.
39 James Cook and James King, *A Voyage to the Pacific Ocean.* . . . (1784), I, p. lxix.
40 Adrienne L. Kaeppler, 'Tracing the History of Hawaiian Cook Voyage Artefacts in the Museum of Mankind', in *Captain Cook and South Pacific*, p. 168.
41 *Andrew Graham's Observations on Hudson's Bay 1767–91*, ed. Glyndwr Williams (Hudson's Bay Record Society, XXVII, 1969), pp. 7*n*, 386–7.
42 Hugh Honour, *The New Golden Land: European Images of America* (New York, 1975), p. 128.
43 E. Iversen, *The Myth of Egypt and its Hieroglyphs in European Tradition* (Copenhagen, 1961), p. 114.
44 Comment by Thomas Pennant, *Outlines of the Globe* (1789–1800), II, 137–8. On interest in Indian sculpture see P. Mitter's valuable *Much Maligned Monsters* (Oxford, 1977).
45 Quoted Peter Earle, *The World of Defoe* (1976), p. 47.
46 Thomas Traherne, *Centuries* (1969 edn.), p. 122.
47 P. F. X. de Charlevoix, *A Voyage to North-America* (Dublin, 1766), II, 2.
48 'Andrew' Sparrman, *A Voyage to the Cape of Good Hope* (1785), p. xv.
49 Quoted R. W. Frantz, *The English Traveller and the Movement of Ideas 1660–1732* (reprinted New York, 1968), p. 8.

PART II

PART II

3

Asia: Growing Awareness and Changing Perspectives in the Eighteenth Century

During the seventeenth century Englishmen in Asia had been thinly spread over a number of areas, the greatest concentration probably being in the Levant, which was also the area about which information was most readily available in Britain. By 1800 the situation was entirely different. The British now ruled a huge territorial empire in India, thousands of Englishmen had been there, and a huge body of very miscellaneous information about India was in print for those who cared to read it. 'Asia' for most seventeenth-century Englishmen had probably been synonymous with the Asia of the Bible and of the ancient world, that is with the Near East; by the end of the eighteenth century it had become almost a synonym for India.

Even if English concerns in the Levant were eclipsed during the eighteenth century by the growth of those in India, there was still an important British connection with the Near East and the public was evidently still keen to read about it. For most of the eighteenth century the kind of Englishmen who went to the Levant seem to have been very similar to those who had gone there during the previous hundred years: they were either members of the Levant Company or travellers of various sorts.

The Levant Company conducted its operations at Aleppo, its main centre until late in the century, Smyrna, Constantinople, where an ambassador to the Porte lived, and Tripoli and Acre, the sites of small factories.[1] Where there was a British community, its members consorted very closely with one another, sometimes living under the same roof, or with other Europeans. Contact with the peoples of the Middle East, outside business, was generally desired by neither side. As one of the Company's chaplains at Aleppo put it, all they wanted from the Turks was to be able to live 'in quiet and safety . . . their conversation being not the least entertaining. Our delights are among ourselves'.[2] Few seem to have made any serious study of Turkish or Arabic. There were, however, some exceptions in the seventeenth century. A number of the Company's chaplains, such as Edward Pococke, Robert Huntington or Thomas Smith, were skilled linguists and notable scholars.

The eighteenth-century Levant Company merchants apparently lived even more self-contained lives than their predecessors. The habit of wearing Turkish dress declined.[3] No more great Arabic scholars served the Company but some of its members were still men of high intellectual quality. One of its surgeons, Alexander Russell, produced a widely admired *Natural History of Aleppo*. One of the ambassadors, Sir James Porter, wrote a book of *Observations on the Religion, Law, Government, and Manners of the Turks*.[4] Another ambassador brought with him a famous wife, Lady Mary Wortley Montagu. Lady Mary, who was already a notable literary figure, spent the years 1716 to 1718 in Turkey. Her letters, which were in fact carefully written up in England after her return and are 'partially fiction',[5] were not published until 1763. They show that she at least did not live solely within the European community. She established cordial relations with a Turkish official in Belgrade on her way to Constantinople. Once there, she 'rambled' incognito in 'feringée and asmack', frequently went to Turkish houses and cultivated friendships with Turkish ladies.[6]

The number of private travellers going to the Levant seems to have increased during the eighteenth century. They were usually wealthy young men with serious interests in 'antiquities'. Some were capable of sustained investigation. Richard Pococke gave Europe a much fuller account of Upper Egypt than any yet existing in his *Description of the East* of 1743. Another learned traveller, Robert Wood, undertook an elaborate expedition between 1749 and 1751 in which he and his friend James Dawkins made full surveys of Baalbek and Palmyra, later published to much acclaim. In 1764 the Society of Dilettanti dispatched an architect and a draughtsman under the direction of the scholar Richard Chandler 'to some parts of the East, in order to collect information and to make observations relative to the ancient state of these countries, and to such monuments of antiquity as are still remaining'.[7] Other travellers with similar interests followed them.

Parts of the Middle East not previously known to Englishmen were explored. In the years 1737–8 Pococke went up the Nile to sites beyond Aswan. This encouraged others to venture further, culminating in James Bruce's journeys which took him far up the Nile and across the Sudan desert on his way to and from Abyssinia in 1768 and 1772. Several chapters in the first volume of his *Travels to Discover the Source of the Nile* (1790) dealt with sites in Upper Egypt; the fourth volume described Nubia. Arabia and the Red Sea came to be better known as Englishmen sought quicker ways of getting to and from India. A number of travellers used the Red Sea and the overland crossing through Egypt to and from Suez. One of them, Eyles Irwin, left a vivid account of his journey in his *Series of Adventures in the Course of a Voyage up the Red Sea* (1780). Journeys on camels across the desert from Aleppo to Baghdad and then by river boat or by camel down to Basra before taking ship to India became commonplace. Several descriptions of such journeys were published.[8] Closer acquaintance with Arabia led to mounting cynicism both about the traditions of a fertile 'Arabia Felix' and about the good qualities of the Arabs of the desert. The whole area was said to be 'a lonesome desolate wilderness',[9] inhabited by 'an ignorant, brutish, low-lived sort of people'.[10]

There seems to have been a lively public demand for books on the Near East. Books of no great merit about the Turks, such as Aaron Hill's *Present State of the Ottoman Empire* or *The Present State of the Turkish Empire. Collected from the best Authors by the Rev. Mr Purbeck*, were offered to the public in serial numbers by booksellers in the first half of the eighteenth century.[11] Seventy separate titles of books in English about the Levant have been identified for the years 1775 to 1825.[12] Yet it would be hard to name any eighteenth-century English travel account which made a contribution to the understanding of the contemporary Near East in any way comparable to that of the French travellers of the later seventeenth century or even of Sir Paul Rycaut. Sir James Porter, who himself made a serious study of the Turks, could complain with some justice that 'we have not yet extant, an exact genuine account of the customs, manners, practices of these people or really of these countries'.[13]

The lack of such accounts from travellers in the eighteenth century is in part attributable to the fact that, with conspicuous exceptions like Lady Mary Wortley Montagu, most of them were not primarily interested in the contemporary Levant. Like their seventeenth-century predecessors, they were still trying to reconstruct the geography of the Holy Land, speculating on Egyptian remains, or hunting for the site of Troy. Indeed, the neo-classical movement of the later eighteenth century brought heightened interest in the Levant's classical past. The conventional book of travels was usually a journal describing sites visited, sumptuously illustrated with views, plans and elevations. Incidental remarks were often added about the beastliness of the Turks, the depravity of the modern Egyptians and the tendency of the Arabs to steal from strangers, while the author lamented the debilitating effects of despotism and the decline of the countries he was visiting from their ancient splendour. Richard Pococke, for example, found the Egyptians 'malicious' and 'envious' as well as being 'slothful'.[14] Robert Wood was outraged by the 'shameless venality' of Turkish public life.[15]

No foreign traveller during the eighteenth century achieved the status in English eyes of Chardin and his contemporaries. Some of the most informative accounts, like Benoît de Maillet's *Description de l'Egypte* (1735), were never translated at all. By the end of the century, however, English readers were perhaps becoming aware of new trends in investigating the Middle East in European countries that were superseding very amateur English efforts. The 'philosophical' travellers of the past were losing some of their prestige by the second half of the eighteenth century. Individual polymaths capable of fitting their observations into universal theories about human nature were not as fashionable as they had once been. The new breed of travellers were likely to be specialist members of an expedition working as a team: botanists, surveyors, epigraphers. Precise empirical knowledge, such as measurements, statistics, thermometer readings, botanical and zoological specimens, or exact plans, was more valuable than profound reflections.[16] Cook's expeditions to the Pacific were prime examples of this trend in Britain. Russell's *Natural History of Aleppo* was a book in the new genre. But the application of 'scientific' principles to reporting on the Middle East during the eighteenth century was to come in the first instance from Denmark and then from France, rather than from Britain. A Danish expedition of 'observation and discovery', including a botanist, an engraver, a philologist, a surveyor and a professor of medicine, arrived in Egypt in 1761 and went on to Arabia. All its members perished, except for one, Carsten Niebuhr. A considerable part of his book was translated into English in 1792.[17] In the 1780s two formidable young French savants conducted studies which have been seen as laying the groundwork for the dispatch of the great body of scholars who accompanied the 1798 invasion of Egypt. Both the books which they produced, Savary's *Lettres sur l'Egypte* (1785) and Volney's *Voyages en Syrie et en Egypte* (1787), were quickly rendered into English. The 1798 expedition set entirely new standards of precise investigation and its achievements included the long-awaited first decyphering of hieroglyphs. When translations of the French findings began to appear in English in 1803, they aroused very great public interest.

English knowledge of the Middle East did not depend solely on the reports of travellers. The study of oriental languages, not merely Hebrew but Arabic and Persian as well in some cases, had become established academic disciplines in the seventeenth century in universities, in some Dissenting Academies, and even in schools like Westminster. At first even Arabic and Persian were studied for the contribution they could make to the understanding of the Bible. Men like Edward Pococke had, however, made very important contributions to European knowledge of Islam and its civilization and they had followers even if Arabic learning does not seem to have been in very robust health in British universities during the eighteenth century. At Oxford Thomas Hyde had lamented that 'lectures (though we must attend upon them) will do but little good, hearers being scarce and practicers more so'.[18] In 1699 the government paid Hyde £100 a year to enable him to train up 'young students . . . in the modern Arabick and Turkish languages' who would be able to translate diplomatic correspondence with Muslim states. But this endowment had ultimately been used to finance another Chair in Arabic rather than more students.[19] Nevertheless, scholars working at home on the great collections of manuscripts in British libraries were to achieve considerably more in adding to knowledge about the Middle East during the eighteenth century than did British travellers.

The outstanding scholarly contribution made in England was the publication in 1734 of an English version of the Koran by George Sale, which was quickly accepted as the best available in any European language. Voltaire was among its many admirers. Sale is a man about whom disappointingly little is known. He did not hold a post at a university, and was apparently drawn to the study of Arabic by a project launched by the Society for Promoting Christian Knowledge for publishing Gospels in Arabic for the use of Christians in the Levant. He was taught by a Syrian.[20] Sale added extensive notes to his text, some of them drawn from Muslim commentators, and published with it a long Preliminary Discourse, which was of itself an important contribution to debates about Islam.

Interest in the Koran and in Muhammad led to interest in his historical setting and in the expansion of Islam. Seventeenth-century scholars like Edward Pococke had been attracted by the history of the Arabs and had published Latin translations of historical texts with notes and commentary. Early in the eighteenth century, Simon Ockley, professor at Cambridge, published a narrative *History of the Saracens* from Arabic sources,[21] vividly written in English. Ockley made a powerful case for studying the history of a non-European people. The Arabs, he wrote, had 'rendered themselves so very considerable, both for their arms and learning, that the understanding of their affairs seems no less, if not more necessary than the being acquainted with the history of any people whatsoever, who have flourish'd since the declension of the Roman empire'.[22] Ockley had a number of followers. The author of a long treatment of the Arabs in the multi-volume *Modern Part of the Universal History*, who was probably John Swinton of Oxford, claimed that he had 'completed the plan Mr Ockley chalked out' and had been able to give English readers a full history of the Arabs down to the fall of the Caliphate.[23] The history of Asian peoples written from Asian sources was readily accepted as a legitimate form of history by the learned in the eighteenth century. The young Gibbon was much influenced by Ockley, whom he called 'an original in every sense',[24] and gave the Arabs a very prominent place in the *Decline and Fall of the Roman Empire*.

Seventeenth-century scholars had been well aware of the rich resources of Arabic and Persian literature in the manuscript collections accumulated in Britain. But until public taste showed some liking for apparently exotic offerings there was little incentive to publish translations. It was in fact a French Arabist, Antoine Galland, who first aroused popular enthusiasm for what was thought to be oriental literature. He edited and freely translated from Arabic into French the collection to be known in English as *The Arabian Nights Entertainments: Consisting of One Thousand and one Stories*.[25] The first of very many English editions appeared between 1704 and 1712. Galland's example was followed by François Pétis de La Croix, another French oriental scholar. His *Persian and Turkish Tales* or *The Thousand and One Days* began to appear in English translations from 1714. Again there were many editions. English translators then turned to other French collections, giving them titles like *Mogul Tales*, *Chinese Tales* and *Tartarian Tales*. Whereas Galland and Pétis de La Croix had made genuine translations, if very free ones, from originals in Asian languages, the later collections were works of pure fiction written in what was presumed to be an oriental manner.

The success of translations from the French stimulated an outpouring of English work written in an oriental style . The 'tale' in the manner of the *Arabian Nights* was the supposed eastern form most widely used.[26] It provided a vehicle for Addison, Steele, Johnson and many lesser men to demonstrate moral precepts and to criticize current *mores*. The oriental tale was also a weapon for political satire, as for instance in Lord Lyttelton's attacks on Walpole in *Letters from a Persian in England to his friend in Ispahan* (1735) or by Horace Walpole in 1757 on the case of Admiral Byng in his *Letter from Xo-Ho, a Chinese Philosopher in London, to his friend Lien Chi at Peking*. What were thought to be Asian settings and Asian diction were liberally used. Characters were given more or less improbable Asian names. Plots were set in harems or pagodas, in 'Bagdat' or 'Tauris'. 'Sublime' sententiousness and 'wild' metaphors were thought appropriate. Verse as well as prose was affected by this. William Collins's *Persian Eclogues*, said to have been inspired by reading the appropriate section of Thomas Salmon's *Modern History*, is conventionally regarded as the best of such works. One 'oriental' work seems, however, to stand head and shoulders above the other pastiches and parodies, both for its imaginative qualities and for what has been called an almost miraculous re-creation of what is genuinely Asian in spirit.[27] This is William Beckford's 'Arabian tale', *Vathek*, published in 1786 in an English version of what Beckford had originally written in French. *Vathek* was in no sense a translation, but the young Beckford had made serious attempts to learn Arabic and Persian.[28]

Genuine translations of Asian literature by English scholars began to appear in the second half of the eighteenth century. Those of William Jones attracted most public attention. Jones had come up to Oxford in 1764 with the reputation of a schoolboy prodigy. He learnt Arabic and Persian at Oxford, publishing his first translation, from a piece of modern Persian, in 1770. In 1771 he produced a Persian grammar and in 1772 the most famous of his early works, *Poems, Consisting chiefly of Translations from the Asiatick Languages*. In all his writings at this period Jones insisted that Asian poetry, if sensitively translated and edited, could be judged by normal critical standards and that by such standards it would not be found wanting. The *Shah-nama* had 'the spirit of our Dryden and the sweetness of Pope'.[29] They might not be able to approach the excellence of the Greek and Latin classics, but Asian poets could provide Europe with a new range of 'images and similitudes', showing a liveliness of fancy and a richness of invention that would refresh European poetry.[30] Jones had quickly built up a reputation as a man of taste and polish as well as of great learning. Some of his translations, such as a 'Persian Song of Hafiz' with its invocation of 'all Bocara's vaunted gold' and 'all the gems of Samarcand', achieved great popularity.

Jones's success was gained in the face of considerable misgivings. Critics of discrimination remained sceptical about the merits of oriental literature. The exotic qualities, which had made the collections of tales so popular and which had been imitated in the parodies, were the very things they disliked. Thomas Warton characterized Arabic poetry as being full of 'extravagant and romantic conceptions'.[31] For Horace Walpole the ultimate praise for the *Arabian Nights* was that it did not seem to be 'oriental' at all.[32] Gibbon considered that eastern authors lacked 'the temperate dignity of style, the graceful proportions of art, the forms of visible and intellectual beauty', among other virtues of the classics. He hoped that Jones would moderate 'the fervent, and even partial, praise which he has bestowed on the Orientals'.[33] To later generations, however, Jones's enthusiasm was much more congenial. He has been judged to have left a deep imprint on nineteenth-century literature.

While Jones had translated poetry in Arabic and Turkish, his greatest successes had been from the Persian. Other authors were also offering Persian translations. In 1774 *A Specimen of Persian Poetry: or Odes of Hafiz* was published by John Richardson, an accomplished Arabic and Persian scholar educated at Edinburgh, who had moved to Oxford.

Richardson was also responsible for a Persian dictionary. Probably in 1768, Warren Hastings drew up proposals for endowing a new Professorship of Persian at Oxford.[34] Nothing came of it, but Joseph White, Professor of Arabic at Oxford, announced in the press some years later that he was willing to give lectures on Persian in London.[35]

Rising interest in Britain in the Persian language in the second half of the eighteenth century was not a reflection of increased British contact with Iran itself. Following the Afghan invasion of 1720, political stability in Iran broke down for long periods. English trade with the Persian Gulf region declined. The East India Company abandoned its factory at Isfahan and even for a time withdrew from Gombroon, the traditional centre for its Gulf trade. Merchants from the Russia Company tried a different route, coming into northern Persia round the Caspian Sea. The trade was ultimately unsuccessful, although it did lead to the writing of what was to be the most substantial English book about Iran until the last years of the century, Jonas Hanway's *An Historical Account of British Trade over the Caspian Sea* in four volumes (1753). In the 1790s two interesting accounts of Iran were published by intrepid young men who travelled alone on foot from India, passing themselves off as Muslims for much of the time.[36] Otherwise, Chardin remained the standard authority. Persia was no longer of any great interest to English readers. Oliver Goldsmith dismissed it as 'a land of tyrants, and a den of slaves'.[37] Persian, on the other hand, was the diplomatic and official language of India, and India was very much in the forefront of British minds. It was for use in India, not in Iran, that efforts were made to promote the study of Persian in Britain.

The scale and scope of British involvement with India grew out of all recognition in the second half of the eighteenth century. Provinces populated by millions of people came under British rule, direct in the case of Bengal and indirect, but increasingly real, in south-eastern India. By the end of the century effective British influence also stretched up the Ganges valley almost to Delhi, and the enclaves of territory on the west coast were growing in size. British people of many kinds were drawn to this expanding empire. Most went as soldiers or sailors, serving either the East India Company or the crown. Ordinary soldiers and sailors are not likely to have had much formal education and their opportunities for seeing India outside cantonments or ships may not have been very great. On the other hand, those that survived and went home were likely to spread tidings of India by word of mouth to sections of the population who might not be readers of travel writing. One view of India from the other ranks was committed to print by a footman called John Macdonald. It is a most attractive document.

Macdonald appears to have been very happy in India and to have liked both Indians and their country. It would be pleasant, but probably unrealistic, to suppose that many others in situations similar to his felt like him.[38]

The upper reaches of the Company's civil and to a lesser extent its military service were very much an intellectual élite, offering ample opportunities for travel and observation. By the 1770s the so-called civil service in Bengal had grown to over two hundred. The Governor General, Warren Hastings, thought that it contained men of 'cultivated talents' and 'liberal knowledge'. Its younger members recognized that, with the new responsibilities being imposed on them by the expansion of British territorial empire, 'a classical education' and 'a talent for writing' were now the keys to a successful career.[39] These generally well educated young men were much more closely involved with Indian society than would have been the case for the old-style servants of the East India Company in its purely commercial phase, who had lived as largely isolated self-contained communities in Indian ports, much in the manner of the Levant merchants, from early in the seventeenth century until the mid-eighteenth century.

From the 1750s officers in the East India Company's army began to command large forces of Indian sepoys, whose dispositions had to be studied with care. Diplomacy with Indian rulers was conducted by ambassadors or 'residents' who had to understand the workings of Indian states and courts. The administration of the new British provinces required the mastery of what was called 'revenue' procedure. Revenue was a system of taxation levied from the produce of the land. Successful collection entailed considerable knowledge. To know who ought to be paying how much, it was necessary to understand Indian land tenure and agricultural methods. A British official concerned with revenue had also to be able to interrogate his underlings and to comprehend arcane accounts kept in Indian languages. The administration of justice was the other main function of government. This inevitably meant that the British magistrate or judge was given some insights into Indian life. He must master the Hindu or Muslim law appropriate to his cases. Both judges and revenue officials began from the late 1760s to move out of the coastal cities and to take up residence in provincial towns or the countryside.

Indian administration required some linguistic knowledge. 'Moors', Hindustani or Urdu, was the language of the army and of much else in northern India. Persian was the official language of Mughal India. This was very widely studied by Europeans. Some tried to learn the regional language appropriate to where they were stationed, such as Bengali, Telugu, Tamil or Marathi. A very select few with great linguistic gifts and much determination began to study Sanskrit, the classical language of Hindu India. The needs of administration stimulated the acquisition of other kinds of knowledge. Surveys were carried out and maps published. Statistics were compiled to aid revenue assessment. Laws had to be investigated and codified. Historical inquiries were conducted to elucidate (usually in fact to obfuscate) vexed questions of land tenure.

The boundary between collecting knowledge as an aid to administration and seeking to know more about India as an end in itself was a narrow one and easily crossed. To enable men to learn languages, dictionaries and grammars were compiled, thus laying the foundation for the study of literature and for editions of texts. The first of the legal codes produced for the use of the Company's courts, the *Code of Gentoo Laws* of 1776, was the work of Nathaniel Halhed, who had been to Oxford. He provided a Preface for his code in which he discussed Hindu history, Sanskrit poetry and other matters not related to the law.[40] Warren Hastings very much encouraged such activities, for he felt that Englishmen in India should certainly not limit their inquiries to what would be useful for administrative purposes. At his most ambitious he hoped systematically to educate an English public to what he regarded as a proper appreciation of things Indian. 'Every instance which brings their real character home to observation will impress us with a more generous sense of feeling for their natural rights and teach us to estimate them by the measure of our own.' The researches of the Company's servants would be the means of educating the public at home.[41] Hastings was directly responsible for giving the ablest linguist among the servants of his time the leisure and opportunities for the mastery of Sanskrit. Charles Wilkins, who achieved this extremely difficult feat, was the first European to have done so for several generations. In 1785 the first fruit of his prodigious talent appeared in print, an English translation of the *Bhagavad Gita*, which has generally proved the most accessible of all Hindu scriptures for western readers.[42] The extent of scholarly interests among the British community in India was made apparent with the setting up in 1784 in Calcutta of a learned body called the Asiatic Society, the prototype of similar societies in Europe. The society published volumes of proceedings called *Asiatic Researches*. These attracted a wide European readership. They were reissued and translated into French and German. Much of their attraction derived from the fact that they became the vehicle for William Jones's second career as an orientalist. Jones had left Oxford for the law, and in 1783 he obtained an appointment as one of the judges of the royal court in Calcutta. There he became proficient in Sanskrit and added translations from it and studies of India to what he had already achieved in

Arabic and Persian. In his essays in *Asiatic Researches* he summed up existing knowledge on many different Asian civilizations as well as presenting challenging new findings on Hindu India in an easily assimilable form.

Men like Halhed, Wilkins or Jones would have been able to accomplish very little without the co-operation of learned Indians. Before the 1770s Europeans had made virtually no contact with such people. Brahmin pundits in particular had a reputation for being extremely secretive. Relations of confidence were gradually established. Much of the credit was clearly due to Hastings who assiduously cultivated and rewarded pundits and learned Muslims. Wilkins gained acceptance in Benares, the centre of Hindu scholarship in northern India. Jones, too, was able to persuade a number of pundits to work with him. Such relationships may have been somewhat one-sided, but perhaps only in the best days of the Jesuit missions at Peking had a similar partnership been established between European and Asian scholars.

By the end of the eighteenth century an English reader with a serious curiosity about India could, as the historian William Robertson showed,[43] acquire a fair amount of specialized knowledge. A major piece of Hindu sacred writing, the *Gita*, had been translated. So too had a Sanskrit play, *Sakuntala*, by Jones, and a book of fables, *Hitopadesha*, by Wilkins. In a *Memoir of a Map of Hindoostan* Major James Rennell had produced a set of maps and a full geographical commentary. Mughal history had been written from Persian sources in the way that Ockley had written Arab history.[44] The *Asiatic Researches* of the Calcutta Asiatic Society carried a great deal of miscellaneous information.

Readers who were not as serious-minded or as assiduous as Robertson could content themselves with numerous conventional travel books. At certain times their newspapers would contain accounts of battles and the progress of British arms in India. Snippets of news from India, mostly about the doings of the British community, were also published in the press. Polemical articles and pamphlets appeared about disputed events in India and readers were invited to take sides for or against controversial figures like Clive, Warren Hastings or Lord Pigot. From even the crudest polemics an ignorant reader could learn something of the Indian setting. Some of the pamphlets written by experienced Company servants, such as Luke Scrafton, William Bolts, Harry Verelst, Philip Francis or Warren Hastings's supporters were very informative even if they were sharply slanted to one side or the other in a dispute. Although there were no British missions operating in India, those who received the *Annual Accounts* of the Society for Promoting Christian Knowledge could read descriptions of the activities of the German Lutherans whom the Society subsidized.[45]

With the growth of empire in India some members of the British public had to show rather more than idle curiosity about it. Intervention by parliament or the national government in Indian matters was slow and uncertain, but men concerned with public affairs could not afford to ignore it completely. Parliamentary inquiries took place in 1767, 1772–3 and from 1781 to 1783. Those who took part sifted huge masses of documents and examined men who had served in India. During one particularly wide-ranging inquiry into the nature of law in India in 1781 they even examined an Indian, the emissary of a Maratha claimant, who had been befriended by Edmund Burke and gave evidence 'concerning the usage and religion of the Hindoos'.[46] Much parliamentary time was taken up with the impeachment of Warren Hastings when issues like the nature of political authority and the rights of subjects in Indian history were argued at length. It is doubtful whether more than one or two British political figures found it necessary to acquire anything more than the most superficial knowledge of India; but Burke was one for whom India did become intensely vivid. His reading of books, records and letters had been encyclopedic and he had talked to many who had been to India. What he had learnt may or may not have accorded with reality, but it had given him a deeply-felt sympathy for a society entirely alien to him.

The Maratha envoy who came to Britain was a rarity in the eighteenth century. Few Indians did so, except for seamen, some of whom ended up 'shivering and starving' in the streets of London in the 1780s.[47] But if the British public had little opportunity for seeing Indians in the flesh, they were given some visual images of them by the numerous British painters who were attracted to India late in the eighteenth century and exhibited their work on their return or sold engravings of it. Most of them were portrait painters seeking commissions from rich Englishmen, but Indian courts also provided opulent patrons. John Zoffany did much of his work at the court of the Wazir of Oudh at Lucknow. He and Arthur William Devis also took a keen interest in portraying ordinary scenes of Indian life.[48] So too did William Hodges, a landscape painter who had already been to the Pacific with Cook.[49] Hodges believed that it was one of the duties of a painter 'faithfully' to 'represent the manners of mankind'. His *Travels in India* of 1793 was profusely illustrated with engravings which included studies of Indian types and occupations.

The East India Company's direct involvement in south-east Asia during the eighteenth century was on a limited scale. Until the settling of Penang in Malaya in 1786, the only official post on the mainland was a short-lived one in Burma. In the Archipelago the English were permanently established at Benkulen in Sumatra, where they acquired some responsibility for the administration of people. At certain periods they had factories at Balambangan and Bandjarmasin in Borneo. Two men who had served at Benkulen and Bandjarmasin respectively produced books which won them deserved recognition. In 1783 William Marsden published his *History of Sumatra*, a study very much in the mould that had become fashionable in the late eighteenth century, full of careful observations and precise detail about men and nature. Daniel Beeckman published a very interesting *Voyage To and From the Island of Borneo* in 1718. It is the record of a man who had tried with some success to establish close relations with the people of the island whom he had encountered. In the second half of the eighteenth century Alexander Dalrymple, a servant of the East India Company at Madras, and from 1779 their official hydrographer in London, built up a very extensive knowledge of the Archipelago, partly from his own voyages around the islands in the 1760s and partly from assiduously collecting charts, maps and journals, many of which he published.[50]

Dalrymple apart, it was freelance, private, so-called 'country' captains who travelled most widely through the Archipelago in their own ships, usually from Indian ports. Such men became experts on the geography of the area and on its peoples. Far from being unlettered seamen, some of them wrote books of considerable sophistication. In the course of his various enterprises William Dampier came several times into the south-east Asian Archipelago. He wrote a good deal about it in his famous books, which suggest that he was not only an accurate observer, but that he also had genuine gifts for establishing a rapport with the peoples of the islands. Alexander Hamilton wrote of south-east Asia in his two-volume *New Account of the East Indies*, published in 1727. Much later, Thomas Forrest, another sharp observer with a talent for human relations, produced *A Voyage to New Guinea and the Moluccas in 1774–6* (1779).

Although there had been a trickle of books, Michael Symes could write at the end of the eighteenth century that there were 'no countries of the habitable globe, where the arts of civilisation are understood, of which we have so limited a knowledge, as of those that lie between the British possessions in India and the empire of China'. He himself did something to remedy that lack of knowledge by producing a long book on Burma. This was *An Account of an Embassy to the Kingdom of Ava* (1800), the outcome of a mission sent by the East India Company's government in Bengal to establish contact with their neighbours in 1795.

Foreign accounts did little to fill up the gaps left by British ones. After the blaze of publicity in the late seventeenth century, French, and indeed any other European, contact with Thailand languished. La

Loubère's was still said to be the best account over one hundred years after it had appeared.[51] Dutch publications were not very frequent, and very few of them were translated. The early eighteenth-century classic, *Oud en Nieuw Oost Indien* by François Valentijn, was, for instance, never put into English.

With an accelerating demand in Britain for tea, and with the establishment of a generally assured if uneasy access to China through the port of Canton, Britain's China trade grew very rapidly in the eighteenth century. In the 1720s up to four of the East India Company's own ships were calling at Canton in any trading season. Private British ships from Indian ports were also coming in increasing numbers. By the end of the eighteenth century twenty or thirty ships a year could be expected from Britain and at least that number of Indian ships. Thus considerable numbers of Englishmen were at least setting foot on Chinese soil.

Although increased trade brought increased contact with China, for the most part it was contact of the most superficial and transitory kind, giving very few opportunities for the acquisition of knowledge. Canton and the Portuguese settlement at Macao became the only places open to Europeans. In theory even the main city of Canton was out of bounds. Europeans were confined to a very limited area which they were officially required to leave after the trading season was over. Within this small portion of the city European contacts were largely restricted to their servants, the licensed Hong merchants who engaged in foreign trade and the keepers of numerous shops, many of them 'after the English manner' with signs 'in English characters or adapted to English orthography'.[52] Foreigners were allowed no dealings with the Chinese government; all representations had to be made through the Hong merchants.

The Chinese authorities officially discouraged foreigners from learning Chinese. Communication was made through 'linguist' interpreters or by 'pidgin'. A striking example of pidgin, on, of all surprising subjects, the abolition of the slave trade, was committed to print by one traveller. A Chinese shopkeeper told him: 'Aye, aye, black man in English country, have got one first chop, good mandarin Willforce, that have done much good for allau blackie man . . . Merchant-man tinkee for catch money, no tinkee for poor blackie man: Josh, no like so fashion.'[53] A few Englishmen did, however, learn Chinese and acquire at least a limited proficiency. The Directors of the East India Company gave such endeavours their encouragement. In 1736 a boy called James Flint was sent to Canton with a salary from the Company in order to learn the language. In course of time he apparently learnt to speak well, although he still required help with writing. In 1759, however, he put his skill to a use which ended in his being confined to Macao and then deported, while the regulations which controlled the activities of Europeans were tightened up appreciably as a consequence. Flint drafted a petition directly to the imperial court, asking for redress for malpractices commited on the English by the authorities at Canton. Such disregard of the proper channels of communication was regarded as intolerable.[54] In spite of this setback, another English interpreter continued to work in Canton until 1780 and the regular training of young men by Chinese instructors began in the 1790s.[55]

Trade, however large its volume, under so many discouragements and restrictions obviously did not stimulate much awareness of China. But regulations could be evaded, more or less permanent residence at Canton becoming common late in the eighteenth century, and a few individuals did take the opportunity of acquiring knowledge as well as wealth. Some Chinese books were brought back to Britain. A private merchant early in the eighteenth century learnt some Chinese and acquired a copy of a Chinese play, which he began to translate. The translation eventually found its way to the distinguished scholar, Thomas Percy, by whom it was edited and published, with very extensive notes and supporting pieces, as *Hau Kiou Choaan; or, The Pleasing History* in 1761. In the 1740s a young Scot called William Chambers twice sailed to Canton as an officer on a Swedish ship. Architecture was already Chambers's real interest in life and he used his time in Canton to make drawings and take notes. Some years later Chambers was prompted by his patrons in England to publish a book of *Designs of Chinese Buildings, Furniture, Dresses, Machines and Utensils* (1757). Assumptions that Chambers had embellished his original notes with material from Jesuit accounts of Chinese buildings and gardens and from his own imagination[56] seem to be confirmed by the comments of one Mr Brown who had seen the gardens of many of the rich merchants of Canton. He found little resembling the plates in Chambers's book or in his later *Dissertation on Oriental Gardening* (1772). Brown reported that the Chinese were fond of water and summer houses in gardens, but 'The water is always stagnated, exceeding muddy of a nasty yellow colour . . . , and the summer houses, sheds, and railings put together in a very clumsy manner, and without the least proportion'.[57] Another piece of English writing arising out of a visit to Canton in the 1740s also attracted international attention. This was a portion of an immensely popular account of the voyage made round the world by the ships of the Royal Navy under Anson between 1740 and 1744. After crossing the Pacific, Anson put into Canton to refit his ship. By doing so he violated official Chinese regulations prohibiting warships. The Chinese authorities were very obstructive during his stay, and the author of his

Voyage Round the World, about whose identity there is some uncertainty,[58] took his revenge. He wrote with venom of the way in which Anson had been treated, and went on to make some very hostile comments on Chinese civilization in general. The Canton trade allowed a few Chinese to come to Europe. At least three of them became objects of curiosity to London society and seem to have adapted themselves well to it.[59]

Canton was capable of handling a very large volume of trade, but by the end of the eighteenth century the restrictions imposed on foreigners and the lack of any alternative access to China were increasingly resented. The British government hoped that the Chinese might be persuaded to ease their regulations if the emperor himself could be confronted at Peking by a British ambassador. An elaborately planned expedition reached China in 1793. Its main business was to negotiate commercial concessions, but every opportunity to accumulate information about China was also to be taken. Lord Macartney, the ambassador, travelled with a small train of savants in the manner of the expeditions going to the Pacific. He had with him a 'natural philosopher', an 'experimental scientist', a botanist, a painter and a 'draughtsman'. He himself was a man of wide intellectual interests, as was his secretary, Sir George Staunton, and the Comptroller of the expedition, John Barrow. Formally the embassy accomplished very little. The Chinese were not in any way inclined to make the sort of concessions required; they seem to have conceived of the embassy as the representatives from a barbarian state who were bringing tribute and seeking benediction. But at least the embassy had given a number of educated Englishmen opportunities to observe China which were entirely new. The expedition went from the coast to Peking, and was received both in the imperial palace at Peking and in the summer palace at Jehol in southern Manchuria. It then travelled right through China by the great canal system to rejoin the ships at Canton.

As was to be expected, many journals and memoranda were written, while William Alexander, the 'draughtsman', recorded many scenes. His drawings have been described as showing 'real men and women in authentic settings' rather than 'romantic visions of "Cathay" '.[60] Once the expedition got home, the booksellers appear to have raced one another to get some of this material before the public in print. Macartney's valet, a man called Aeneas Anderson, was first off the mark with a *Narrative of the British Embassy to China* in 1795. In 1797 a sumptuous *Authentic Account of an Embassy* by Staunton in two volumes with a volume of plates from Alexander was issued at four guineas; an abridged version published in instalments at half a guinea was also to be had.[61] One of the soldiers of the escort produced *The Journal of Mr*

Samuel Holmes in 1798. Finally, Barrow offered the public his *Travels in China* in 1804 with a second edition two years later. Macartney himself remained silent. He kept a journal, which is an attractive document, the record of a tolerant, humane man with a wide range of learning at his command. The journal was used by Staunton, but a full version of it has only recently been printed.[62] The members of the Macartney embassy were not the first British subjects to go to Peking or even to write about it. That honour belongs to a Scot, John Bell, who made an overland journey right across Siberia to China as surgeon to a Russian embassy from 1719 to 1722. His memoirs were published in 1763.[63] Superficial as books like Staunton's and Barrow's may now seem, as a result of the Macartney mission, for the first time the English saw themselves as authorities on China.

Before the publications following the Macartney embassy began to appear, English readers had depended almost entirely on Continental sources for their knowledge of China. These were very plentiful and a considerable selection were translated. As a previous chapter showed, seventeenth-century English views of China had largely been formed by accounts by the Catholic missions, especially the Jesuits. During the eighteenth century Jesuits continued to publicize their missionary enterprises with skill and perseverance. The essential Jesuit source was the series of volumes of *Lettres édifiantes et curieuses*, published beteen 1702 and 1773 with many subsequent editions. The letters which appeared in print had been subjected to careful editing with the interests of the Society firmly in mind. A much more drastic process of selection and editing took place when translators produced English collections of the letters: one was issued in two volumes in 1707–9, [64] a single volume in 1714,[65] followed by the selection with the widest circulation, *Travels of the Jesuits into various parts of the world*, edited by that very prolific man of letters, John Lockman. His first edition appeared in two volumes in 1743 with a second one in 1762.

In 1735 the Society of Jesus produced a digest of both printed and unpublished letters on China together with some remarkable maps and some extracts of translations from Chinese literature. The whole was called *Description de l'Empire de la Chine*. It was edited, again with Jesuit points of view very much in mind,[66] by Father Du Halde. The appearance of the book aroused much interest in England. Two translations of it eventually competed against one another. The bookseller John Watts got his out first in 1736 in four volumes, costing £1. 4s. It presumably did well, since it went into three editions quite quickly. Edward Cave, the publisher of the *Gentleman's Magazine*, set himself against Watts, claiming that Watts's version was incomplete. Cave proposed to publish his version in monthly or two-weekly instalments, the whole eventually not to cost the subscriber more than three guineas. To make the project worthwhile, he hoped for at least a thousand subscribers, but he apparently had some difficulty in raising support and it was generally supposed that he lost money.[67] Whether it was read in Watts's four volumes or in Cave's two volumes (the form in which it could be bought by those who had not subscribed to the parts), Du Halde became the standard authority on matters Chinese for much of the eighteenth century.

For a considerable length of time during the middle of the eighteenth century the Royal Society maintained direct contact in a rather desultory way with the Jesuits in China. The connection seems to have originated with the son of one of the Fellows, who had been in China with the East India Company. Astronomical observations made in Peking were delivered through him.[68] In the 1750s the Society received more observations, maps, plans and books, including a 'Notitia' or Gazetteer of China in 24 volumes.[69] Two Jesuits were made Associates of the Royal Society and correspondence continued into the 1760s, the Jesuits being asked to pronounce on a famous controversy, whether lettering found on an Egyptian bust at Turin was in any way similar to Chinese lettering.[70] By the middle of the eighteenth century, however, the Jesuits' position in China was very much weaker than it had been. For at least part of the long reign of K'ang-hsi, which ended in 1722, they had received some imperial patronage. Now they were no longer countenanced and were on occasions actively persecuted. In Europe the Society came under attack and was formally dissolved in 1773. But the flow of Jesuit publications on China continued: seventeen volumes of *Mémoires* beginning in 1776 and a new *Histoire générale de la Chine* in twelve volumes between 1777 and 1785 (part of this appeared in English as a two-volume *General Description of China* (1788) edited by the Abbé Grosier). Anthologies of Jesuit pieces also continued to be published in translation.[71]

Modern scholars appear to find considerable merit in the late Jesuit writing about China, but by the end of the eighteenth century much less interest was being taken in them in Britain. The Society of Jesus was, of course, an equivocal and even a sinister body to Anglo-Saxons. Those, like Lockman, who made translations of the Chinese letters, usually conceded that on strictly religious matters the Jesuits could not be trusted to tell the truth. Their letters were full of 'miracles' and 'conversions' which would appear 'insipid or ridiculous to most English readers; and indeed to all persons of understanding and taste'. So he had simply left them out. But in other respects he was willing to 'reverence the Jesuits . . . for their knowledge in the arts and sciences, and the discoveries they make in them', in spite of their 'hypocrisy and cunning'.[72] The proposition that the Jesuits were sound observers and could be trusted, except on matters strictly religious, appears to have been generally acceptable. In 1775 an editor could still write: 'We have no reason to distrust the fidelity of the above-named authors, except where religion or particular interest of the Jesuits order is concerned.'[73] To a modern reader the last point is the crucial one. The Chinese Rites controversy, whose outlines will be discussed in the following chapter, was forcing the Jesuits to present a particularly tendentious interpretation of certain aspects of Chinese society, history and above all religion. There is, however, little direct evidence suggesting that many English readers were aware of the implications of the Rites controversy.

When confidence in the Jesuits began to wane in Britain, the cause seems to have been doubt about the Jesuits' competence as observers rather than concern for their religious bias. Their writing represented an old-fashioned approach to the study of man: too 'high-flown' and 'rhetorical' and 'much beyond the life' with too little precise observation.[74] An astronomer writing to the Royal Society in 1746 doubted whether the Jesuits were 'sufficiently versed in European or Chinese learning, or both, to give us proper information'.[75] A compiler of a collected edition of 'voyages' complained that they were 'generally superficial and full of gross mistakes'.[76] Adam Smith regretted that readers had to rely too much on 'stupid and lying missionaries' instead of 'more intelligent eyes'.[77] John Barrow evidently believed that books like his, which had come out of the Macartney embassy, had now superseded the Jesuits. 'The voluminous communications of the missionaries are by no means satisfactory'; they were 'tinsel' and 'tawdry varnish'.[78] A more 'scientific' approach was required.

Whether they were convinced or sceptical, English readers still had to rely very heavily throughout the eighteenth century on the Jesuits as interpreters of China. Yet in spite of this continuing dependence on a single source, there was scope for a wider range of English interpretation of China than had been the case earlier. In the first place, for all the care taken by Du Halde and others in their editing, the Jesuits still spoke with many different voices. Belief that they were mere apologists for all things Chinese will not survive even the most superficial acquaintance with their writings. Secondly, material from other sources was becoming increasingly accessible in English. The *Collection of Voyages and Travels*, published by the Churchills in 1704, contained a translation of an account of China written by a Dominican, Domingo Fernandez Navarrete. His views, especially on Chinese religion, were very different from those of most Jesuits.[79] A year later another collection, the *Navigantium atque Itinerantium Bibliotheca*, edited by John Harris, included a translation of the record of an overland journey from Moscow to China by Isbrant Ides, a Dane in Russian service. Ides made a number of comments on Chinese 'barbarity'. In 1733 an English translation was made of a work which had originally appeared in French, *Ancient Accounts of India and China by Two Mohammedan Travellers*, whose editor, Eusèbe Renaudot, put in much material derogatory to the Chinese with his translation. Anson's *Voyage* appeared in 1748. Non-Jesuit sources available to those only able to read English multiplied in the second half of the eighteenth century. Two volumes of Swedish accounts were published in 1771,[80] and the French physiocrat Pierre Poivre's *Travels of a Philosopher* appeared in two separate translations in 1769. Poivre's panegyric on Chinese agriculture and on the government's care for the welfare of the mass of the population is an illustration of why any division of books on China into sympathetic Jesuit accounts and hostile non-Jesuit ones would be inadequate. Diversity of sources helped to produce a very wide range of interpretations among which English readers could pick and choose in reaching their verdicts.

The verdicts of many Englishmen were likely to be influenced by objects which they had seen as well as by what they had read. Chinese porcelain, lacquer work, wall-papers, silk cloth, painting on glass and carvings could all be decorated with landscapes and figures. In 1664 John Evelyn recorded having seen

> prints of landskips, of their idols, saints, pagoods, of most ougly, serpentine, monstrous and hideous shapes to which they paie devotion: pictures of men, and countries, rarely painted on a sort of gumm'd *calico* transparant as glasse; also flowers, trees, beasts, birds &c; excellently wrought on a kind of sleve-silk very naturall.[81]

Chinese objects circulated more widely in the eighteenth century. Until late in the century the East India Company shipped up to 1,000,000 pieces of Chinaware a year, usually chosen without very much discrimination to ballast the tea on its ships.[82] Objects for connoisseurs were generally left to the private trade of the crew of the ships which were going to China in ever increasing numbers.

Chinese objects stimulated imitation, parody and pastiche, just as stories or poetry in Arabic and Persian were doing. 'Chinoiserie', that is designs or figures supposed to be Chinese, was applied in England to silver, earthenware and later porcelain, English lacquer work or 'Japan', wall-paper, and to furniture.[83] Chinese styles were not thought suitable for English houses, but a number of Chinese summer houses, pavilions, temples, pagodas and bridges were built, mostly in the 1740s and 1750s, as ornaments to parks.[84] There was much speculation on the nature of Chinese gardens and debates continued throughout the century as to whether what were considered to be Chinese principles of gardening could be applied in Britain.

Whatever their limitations as a vehicle for conveying information about another society, it might be supposed that objects at least were not contaminated, as travel books were, by the preconceptions of foreigners. This was rarely so for items imported from China. Some works of art acceptable to Chinese connoisseurs found their way to Europe, but the great bulk of imports were what is known as 'export art', items specifically made for the European market by Chinese craftsmen.[85] Porcelain especially was made in very large quantities for sale to the foreigners at Canton. Much of what Europeans believed to be typically Chinese in the form, colouring or decoration of objects they bought was in fact due to the skill of the Chinese in providing what was expected of them. Even early in the seventeenth century, patterns of 'Chinese' motifs were being sent eastwards from Europe to be imitated.[86] If eighteenth-century Englishmen envisaged China as a willow-pattern world of quaint figures crossing little bridges, they were envisaging what was essentially a construct of Europe's own imagination.

Englishmen had no direct contact with Japan in the eighteenth century. For new information they and other Europeans had to rely on what was provided by the Dutch at Deshima. In general little came from this source. The intellectual quality of the staff of the Deshima factory was not usually very high.[87] One work of great importance did, however, emerge from Deshima. This was the memoirs of Englebert Kaempfer, a German in Dutch service. Hans Sloane, President of the Royal Society, bought Kaempfer's papers and specimens for the Society and commissioned a translation of his memoirs, which appeared in two volumes in 1728 as the *History of Japan*. Kaempfer's work was highly respected, being said by its admirers to rival 'the Britannia of Camden in minuteness and precision'.[88] In the 1780s Isaac Titsingh, another learned servant of the Dutch East India Company, spent some years at Deshima. His findings did not appear in English until very much later, but William Jones, who got to know him in Bengal where he served after leaving Japan, prophesied that Titsingh would displace Kaempfer as Europe's main authority on Japan.[89]

Central Asia and Siberia was the part of the world, at least until the systematic exploration of the Pacific, of which European geographical knowledge underwent the most dramatic improvement in the eighteenth century. The British contribution to this was very small. Cook's third expedition searched for a north-west passage in the seas off eastern Siberia and other British ships followed late in the century.

John Bell crossed Siberia with his Russian employers, publishing a full account of it in 1763. After 1774 the British could claim to be authorities on Tibet. Warren Hastings responded to the invitation of the Panchen Lama, who was subordinate to but also to some extent the rival of the Dalai Lama at Lhasa, to send a mission. He deputed a young Scot called George Bogle to represent the East India Company. Bogle was briefed to gather as much information as possible about an area with which the only previous European contact had been occasional visits by Jesuit or Capuchin missions. Bogle spent some months in Tibet, but little of what he recorded ever appeared in print. A paper based on his findings was published in the *Philosophical Transactions of the Royal Society* for 1777,[90] and he himself died two years later. In 1783 another envoy was sent from India to Tibet, accompanied by a 'draftsman and surveyor'. The new envoy was not allowed to go to Lhasa, which had also been forbidden to Bogle. He did, however, publish a book complete with engravings.[91]

Foreign accounts of central Asia were much more substantial. They seem to have been read with interest by the British public. To many in the eighteenth century 'Tartary' was part of the ancient Scythia, home of the Goths who had later migrated into Europe.[92] So the ancestors of the modern northern Europeans might still be visible on the plains of Asia. The British were told to remember that 'we are no other than a colony of Tatars'.[93] The Tartars were thought to preserve 'several traces of Gothic government . . . the ruder draughts of states general, of parliaments, of juries'.[94] The conquerors Cingis Khan and Timur (Tamerlane) also attracted much interest. The Tartars were a people who had made 'more extensive conquests and destroyed more men, than any other nation known in history'.[95]

The picture that emerged during the eighteenth century was somewhat prosaic. A previously vaguely delineated Tartary or Cathay, thought to be ruled over by a Great Cham, was now divided with a fair degree of precision into distinct peoples (although there was no agreement about nomenclature or spelling). The whereabouts of these peoples and the extension of the power of the Russians and the Chinese were plotted on maps. There were three main sources of information: accounts of Russian expeditions, mostly overland but some by sea to eastern Siberia, the letters of the missionaries who had gone into the western and northern territories of the Chinese empire, and the authors of histories based on Arabic, Turkish or Persian sources in western libraries.

The Russian conquest of Siberia was spectacularly quick; they had reached the sea at the extremity of Asia by 1648. Information about these feats, as indeed about Russia itself, reached Britain rather slowly.[96] Some material about the peoples of Central Asia and Siberia appeared in 1693 in *Travels into Divers Parts of Europe and Asia*, a translation of a book by a Jesuit, Father Avril, who had tried to open an overland route to Peking. He had not gone beyond Moscow, but had been able to gather information about what would have lain ahead. The book that came to be regarded as the beginning of sound western knowledge of the region was published in translation in 1736 as *An Histori-Geographical Description of the North and Eastern Part of Europe and Asia*, including a very full map of 'Tartariae Magnae', by von Strahlenberg. He was a Swedish officer, captured by Peter the Great and sent to Siberia, where he was able to travel very widely and to collect much material which he brought back with him at the end of the war. During the reign of Catherine the Great the Russians themselves promoted expeditions to survey their new empire and to investigate its peoples and natural history. Peter Pallas, a German naturalist, was the best known of these travellers. He had a number of British contacts, corresponding with the naturalist Thomas Pennant and giving permisison to the scholarly clergyman, William Coxe, who had travelled in Russia, to make translations from the German version of his journals.[97] Large extracts, presumably from these translations, appeared in three volumes of a compilation called *The Habitable World Displayed* produced by John Trusler in 1788. Trusler chose to omit what was 'dry and uninteresting', concentrating on descriptions of 'people, their manners and customs'. Coxe was also responsible for editing and translating accounts of Russian voyages by sea, of which Bering's were the most famous, to eastern Siberia.[98] A further selection was produced by Johann Reinhold Forster.[99] Such accounts contained some material about the peoples of coastal regions like Kamchatka, but for a comprehensive account of the peoples of Russia's Asian empire English readers would have been best served by William Tooke's translations in four volumes of J. G. Georgi's *Russia: or a Compleat Historical Account of All the Nations which compose that Empire* (1780–3).

The westward expansion of the Chinese empire from the end of the seventeenth century may not have been as spectacular as that of the Russians, but much territory was absorbed and the Russians themselves were forced off the Amur river. Chinese expansion continued in the eighteenth century. Their influence was effectively exerted over Mongolia, Tibet and large parts of Turkestan. Jesuits had good opportunities for seeing the newly acquired territories. The peripatetic K'ang-hsi often took his European mathematicians and astronomers with him on his journeys to the marches of his empire. He also used Jesuits as cartographers. Long letters describing what they had seen were reprinted in English and a great deal of space was given to

'Tartary' in Du Halde's *General History of China*, which included splendid new maps of it.

The Arabic, Persian and Turkish histories acquired in the Middle
East by European collectors not only permitted men like Ockley to
write about the Arabs but gave others scope to study the history of the
Mongols and their conquests. François Pétis de La Croix the elder,
father of the translator of the *Persian and Turkish Tales*, was the
leading exponent of Mongol history. His biography of Cingis Khan was
translated into English as *The History of Genghizcan the Great* in 1722. Von
Strahlenberg brought back from Russia what was regarded as the first
history of the Mongols by a 'Tartarian writer', Abu'l Ghazi. The
French translation was put into English in 1730 as *A General History of
the Turks, Moguls, and Tatars with a full account of the present state of Central
Asia* in two volumes. The only original English contribution to the
history of the Mongols was made by an East India Company officer and
one of the Arabic Professors at Oxford,[100] who published together
Institutes Political and Military . . . By the Great Timour (1783) from a text
held by some contemporaries to be of dubious authenticity.

Eighteenth-century Mongol history generally presented a highly
flattering picture both of the people and of their leaders in the past.
'The empire of the Moguls . . . is one of the surprizing phaenomena
which has appeared on the theatre of this world; and what deserves
more than any other to attract the reader's admiration.' Those who
thought that the English and the Tartars might be related were no
doubt pleased to note that at the time of Cingis Khan the Mongols were
deists with an ancient constitution, including a 'dyet' for the approval
of laws.[101] The actual state of the peoples of central Asia as revealed by
the Jesuits or the Russians proved to be a sad anti-climax. The peoples
were very fragmented. 'The vague name of Tartary is nearly discarded
from our maps.'[102] Terms like 'Mongol' or 'Tartar' could hardly be
used. A series of petty despotisms were incapable of resisting the
Russians or the Chinese. Natural deism had given way to Islam or what
was coming to be identified as Buddhist Lamaism. In Siberia the
Russians were revealing the existence of peoples previously unknown to
Europe, but shown to be backward and ignorant. John Bell dismissed
them as 'poor savage tribes'.[103]

Whatever its quality may have been, information about Asia was being
made available during the eighteenth century in some abundance to
English readers. For most of them no doubt it was matter to be dipped
into in a desultory way for amusement or to satisfy a not very exacting
curiosity. Some, however, studied it with more serious intent and in a
more systematic way. The approaches adopted by such people to new

knowledge of Asia can crudely be divided into one that was traditional and one that was more recent. The concerns of the traditionalists were historical and textual – they hoped for new material from Asia to supplement existing textual authorities, the Bible and the classics of Greece and Rome, and thus to provide a fuller picture of the early history of man – and central to such preoccupations was the belief that human history could be traced from a single point of origin. There had been a single act of creation and therefore religious inspiration, civilized life and learning, and language all originated in one place before spreading outwards across the world from people to people. Polygenesis or even the independent development of religion and language in separate places was hardly countenanced. The task of scholars was therefore to trace the sequence of diffusion from its point of origin, where the Bible had not already made this clear. It was hoped that new knowledge about Asia would provide a much fuller picture, but in fact it generally raised as many problems as it solved. Were the Egyptians an older people than the Indians or the Chinese? Who had colonized whom? Was Hebrew the original language taught by God directly to men? If so, what was its connection with other languages? Were Egyptian hieroglyphs and Chinese characters descended from one another? If so, which was the older? Did Hinduism and Confucian beliefs contain elements of the original religion of the patriarchs? Who had taught whom?

Although most of the questions could not be conclusively answered, this kind of scholarship retained much of its vitality during the eighteenth century. It was not even a Christian monopoly. Critics of Christianity also postulated historical patterns of diffusion, although they were of course different from those in the Biblical version, and they set the authority of Chinese, Egyptian or Indian texts against the authority of the Bible. Perhaps the most remarkable monument to the old scholarship in England was Jacob Bryant's *A New System, or, an Analysis of Ancient Mythology* of 1774, in which Bryant traced the history of the world from Babel. He believed that he was able to give irrefutable proof of the truth of Biblical history by showing that every literate people in the known world acknowledged Noah in some form as their first ruler.[104] New material about India or China was slotted into this framework.

Even in the seventeenth century there had been critics of this mode of scholarship. French travellers in the Middle East, especially Chardin and Bernier, won an international reputation for themselves as a new kind of 'philosophical' traveller. Bernier, in particular, contrasted his interest in nature and in the customs and politics of the countries he visited with what he called the pedantry of the old scholars, obsessed with the remote past and with musty texts.[105] Thomas Hyde, a fine scholar of the old school, was warned that his great book on the old Persians was 'not so agreeable to the studies of experimental philosophy, mathematicks, and natural history' of the members of the Royal Society, who were unlikely to subscribe to it.[106] In the eighteenth century criticism became more strident. Bolingbroke felt a

> thorough contempt for the whole business of these learned lives . . . They have supposed, they have guessed, they have joined disjointed passages of different authors, and broken traditions of uncertain originals, of various peoples, and of countries remote from one another as well as from ours. In short, that they might leave no liberty untaken, even a wild similitude of sounds has served to prop up a system.[107]

The alternative to antiquarian inquiries was what was most commonly called the study of 'the natural history of man'. The concept of 'natural history' was usually traced back to Bacon. For him it involved 'the most comprehensive collection of experiments and observations gathered over the whole field of nature'.[108] To apply this technique to man himself considered as a part of nature and therefore to study 'the natural history of man' became increasingly common. The term was particularly associated with the great French naturalist, Buffon, and it accurately describes the interests of those who studied man and society at Edinburgh or Glasgow under the influence of Adam Smith, David Hume or Adam Ferguson. Lord Kames, a leading figure in the Scottish Enlightenment, commented on how 'natural history, that of man especially, is of late years much ripened'.[109] In his *History of Sumatra* of 1783 William Marsden described how 'those philosophers, whose labours have been directed to the history of man', should go about their task. They must have

> facts to serve as *data* in their reasonings, which are too often rendered nugatory, and not seldom ridiculous, by assuming as truths, the misconceptions, or wilful impositions of travellers. The study of our own species is doubtless the most interesting and important that can claim the attention of mankind; and this science, like all others, it is impossible to improve by abstract speculation, merely. A regular series of authenticated facts is what alone can enable us to rise towards a perfect knowledge in it.[110]

For the natural historians of man the diversity of humanity was not to be explained and brought to order by explorations of common origins through piecing together inadequate and unreliable fragments of a remote past. This could best be done by studying the present state of man throughout the world. As William Warburton put it, it was

> an old inveterate error, that a similitude of customs and manners amongst the various tribes of mankind most remote from one another,

must arise from some communication. Whereas human nature, without any other help, will in the same circumstances, always exhibit the same appearances.[111]

William Robertson, historian and Principal of Edinburgh University, who will feature in much of this book through his interest in India and America, made the same point: '. . . the human mind, whenever it is placed in the same situation, will, in ages the most distant, assume the same form and be distinguished by the same manners'.[112] If human nature was constant, differences among men would be revealed by the study of what Warburton called their 'circumstances' and Robertson their 'situation', that is climate, physical environment, forms of government or modes of production. To understand man's early history, it was better to study the present state of man in certain parts of the world than to waste time with texts. 'Savages' or 'primitive' peoples at the present time were the best possible evidence of what early man in general had been like. What came to be called 'conjectural history', that is extrapolation from the present backwards into the past, was far superior to efforts to reconstruct the past with imperfect texts. Edmund Burke made this point in a letter to Robertson:

> I have always thought with you, that we possess at this time very great advantages towards the knowledge of human nature. We need no longer go to history to trace it in all its stages and periods. History from its comparative youth, is but a poor instructour . . . But now the great map of mankind is unrolld at once; and there is no state or gradation of barbarism, and no mode of refinement which we have not at the same instant under our view.[113]

Asia provided a huge field of study for the natural historians of man. Men could be found living there in many different situations and circumstances: in the snowy wastes in Siberia, the deserts of Arabia, the steppes of Central Asia, the fertile river valleys of China and India, or on tropical islands. Asians lived under many forms of government, but especially under the great 'despotic' empires, which seemed to be so alien to western Europe. From the tribes of the Arabs to the centralized bureaucracy of China, Asia offered many different stages of social development. Its history was worth studying, not because it might supplement the Bible, but because it showed the rise and fall of empires in more recent times.

As the travellers produced their versions of Asia, the natural historians of man began to assimilate them into their work. The self-confessed natural historian of religion, David Hume, used Islam to illustrate his theories. He also made references to Asia in the essays in which he tried to construct a 'science of politics'. Asian examples featured in two other of the most important Scottish inquiries into social development, John Millar's *Origin of the Distinction of Ranks* and Adam Ferguson's *History of Civil Society*. China and India were discussed in the supreme achievement of the Scottish Enlightenment, *The Wealth of Nations*. Knowledge of Asian languages, especially William Jones's theories about Sanskrit,[114] played a decisive role in the study of language in general. Scholars gradually ceased their search for a single original language, be it Hebrew or another contender, and turned to comparing the structure of existing languages. Modern philology has been traced from this.[115]

Asia thus offered much to interest eighteenth-century scholars, whether they were primarily searching through Hyde's supposed ancient Persian scriptures, the Jesuits' Chinese annals or Jones's findings in Sanskrit for light on the early history of man, or whether they were collecting specimens of his present state. Of the many problems raised for scholars by the new material being offered them on Asia, two seem to have intrigued them most: the diversity of Asian religion and how Asia was to be fitted into what were coming to be regarded as normal concepts of social development. Interest in these particular problems seems indeed to have gone far beyond scholars. The two stereotypes which were perhaps to be most persistent about Asia down to relatively modern times appear to have taken root in the eighteenth century: Asia was a continent of bizarre religions fanatically adhered to and it was a continent whose peoples changed very little.

NOTES

1 R. Davis, *Aleppo and Devonshire Square* (1967), pp. 35–7.
2 H. Maundrell, *A Journey from Aleppo to Jerusalem*, 10th edn. (1810), p. 198.
3 A. Russell, *The Natural History of Aleppo* (1756), pp. 134–5.
4 Published 1768, 2nd edn. 1771.
5 R. Halsband, *The Life of Lady Mary Wortley Montagu* (Oxford, 1956), p. 59.
6 The embassy letters are reprinted in vol. i of *The Complete Letters of Lady Mary Wortley Montagu*, ed. R. Halsband (Oxford, 1965–7).
7 R. Chandler, *Travels in Asia Minor* (Oxford, 1775), pp. vii–xii.
8 A number were edited by D. Carruthers in *The Desert Route to India* (1929).
9 Thomas Salmon, *Modern History: or, The Present State of All Nations*, 3rd edn. (1744–6), i. 398.
10 B. Plaisted in Carruthers, *The Desert Route*, p. 94.
11 R. M. Wiles, *Serial Publication in England Before 1750* (Cambridge 1957), pp. 48, 329.
12 W. C. Brown, 'The Popularity of English Travel Books about the Near East 1775–1825', *Philological Quarterly*, xv (1936), 77.

13 *Philosophical Transactions of the Royal Society*, xlix (1755), 102.

14 *Description of the East*, i. 177.

15 *The Ruins of Balbeck* (1757), p. 4.

16 See S. Moravia, 'Philosophie et géographie à la fin du xviiie siècle', *Studies in Voltaire and the Eighteenth Century*, lvii (1967), 937–1011; M. Duchet, *Anthropologie et histoire au siècle des lumières* (Paris, 1971), pp. 107–8.

17 *Travels through Arabia and other Countries in the East*, 2 vols (Edinburgh, 1792).

18 W. D. Macray, *Annals of the Bodleian Library* (Oxford, 1868), p. 120.

19 H. Hall, 'The Origins of the Lord Almoner's Professorship of Arabic', *The Athenaeum*, 16 Nov. 1889.

20 The fullest account of him is in S. N. Khairallah, 'Arabic Studies in England in the late seventeenth and early eighteenth centuries', London Ph.D (1972).

21 2 vols, 1708, 1718.

22 *History of Saracens*, i, p. ix.

23 *Op. cit.*, xvi (1765), p. iii. The sections on the Arabs appeared in vols i and ii, published in 1759.

24 *Memoirs of My Life*, ed. G. A. Bonnard (1966), p. 43.

25 Mohamed Abdel-Halim, *Antoine Galland: sa vie et son oeuvre* (Paris, 1964), pp. 259 ff.

26 For a list of such works, see M. Conant, *The Oriental Tale in England in the eighteenth century* (New York, 1908), pp. 267–93; for a recent assessment of them, see A. J. Weitzman, 'The Oriental tale in the eighteenth century: a reconsideration', *Studies in Voltaire and the Eighteenth Century*, lviii (1967), 1841 ff.

27 A. Parreaux, *William Beckford: Auteur de Vathek* (Paris, 1960), p. 324.

28 There is a helpful edition of *Vathek* by R. Lonsdale (1970).

29 *Works of Sir William Jones* (1806), ii. 313.

30 *Ibid.*, iv. 547–8.

31 *History of English Poetry*, ed. W. C. Hazlitt (1871), i. 188.

32 *The Yale Edition of Horace Walpole's Correspondence*, ed. W. S. Lewis (New Haven, 1937–), xi. 20–1.

33 *Decline and Fall of the Roman Empire*, ed. J. B. Bury (1896–1900), vi. 51.

34 P. J. Marshall, 'Warren Hastings as Scholar and Patron', *Statesmen, Scholars and Merchants*, ed. A. Whiteman, J. S. Bromley, P. Dickson (Oxford, 1973), pp. 245–6.

35 *Morning Chronicle*, 8 Jan. 1782.

36 William Francklin, *Observations made on a Tour from Bengal to Persia* (1790); George Forster, *A Journey from Bengal to England*, 2 vols (1798).

37 *Citizen of the World*, Everyman edn. (1934), p. 98.

38 *Memoirs of an Eighteenth-century Footman. John Macdonald's Travels*, ed. J. Beresford (1927), pp. 111–70.

39 Cited in P. J. Marshall, *East Indian Fortunes: The British in Bengal in the Eighteenth Century* (Oxford, 1976), p. 207.

40 Reproduced in P. J. Marshall, *The British Discovery of Hinduism in the Eighteenth Century* (Cambridge, 1970), pp. 140–83.

41 Cited in Marshall, 'Hastings as Scholar', *Statesmen, Scholars and Merchants*, p. 256.

42 For him, see Mary Lloyd, 'Sir Charles Wilkins, 1749–1836' *India Office Library and Records Report for the Year 1978* (1979), pp. 9–39.

43 Robertson's notes to his *Historical Disquisition concerning the Knowledge which the Ancients had of India* of 1791 show a wide range of up-to-date sources.

44 Described in J. S. Grewal, *Muslim Rule in India: the Assessments of British Historians* (Calcutta, 1970).

45 See below, p. 122.

46 *The Correspondence of Edmund Burke*, iv, ed. J. A. Woods (Cambridge, 1963), 368; *Reports from Committees of the House of Commons* (1803–6), v. 39–40.

47 A. J. Barker, *The African Link* (1978), p. 31.

48 M. Archer, *India and British Portraiture 1770–1825* (1979).
49 See below, pp. 276, 281.
50 See H. T. Fry, *Alexander Dalrymple and the Expansion of British Trade* (1970).
51 J. Pinkerton, *Modern Geography* (1802), ii. 209.
52 A. Anderson, *A Narrative of the British Embassy to China*, 2nd edn. (1795), p. 383.
53 *Ibid.*, p. 404.
54 E. L. Farmer, 'James Flint versus the Canton Interest', *Papers on China from Seminars at Harvard University*, xvii (1963), 38–66.
55 S. R. Stifler, 'The Language Students of the East India Company's Canton Factory', *Journal of the North China Branch of the Royal Asiatic Society*, lxviii (1937).
56 See the discussion by Eileen Harris in J. Harris, *Sir William Chambers* (1970), pp. 144–8.
57 Letter of 20 Nov. 1773, India Office Library, MS Eur.F.129/1, ff. 121–2.
58 Discussed in G. Williams's edn. of *Voyage* (1974), pp. xxi–v.
59 W. W. Appleton, *A Cycle of Cathay* (New York, 1951), pp. 132–6.
60 M. Archer, 'Works by William Alexander and James Wales', *The Royal Asiatic Society: Its History and Treasures*, ed. S. Simmonds and S. Digby (Leiden, 1979), p. 119.
61 *An Historical Account of the Embassy to the Emperor of China* (1797).
62 *An Embassy to China*, ed. J. L. Cranmer-Byng (1962).
63 There is a modern edition by J. L. Stevenson (Edinburgh, 1965) entitled *A Journey from St Petersburg to Pekin*.
64 *Edifying and Curious Letters of . . . the Society of Jesus.*
65 *Travels of Several Learned Missionaries of the Society of Jesus.*
66 V. Pinot, *La Chine et la formation de l'esprit philosophique en France, 1640–1740* (Paris, 1932), pp. 161–81.
67 J. Nichols, *Literary Anecdotes of the eighteenth century* (1812–16), v. 44–7; Wiles, *Serial Publication*, pp. 184–5.
68 Royal Society MSS, Journal Book, xviii. 19, 23.
69 *Ibid.*, xx. 338, 559; xxi. 281–2, 361–4, 401; *Le P. Antoine Gaubil S. J. Correspondance de Pékin* (Geneva, 1970); *Philosophical Transactions*, xlviii (1753), 253 ff., 309–13.
70 *Ibid.*, lix (1769), 489 ff.
71 *Miscellaneous Pieces Relating to the Chinese*, 2 vols (1762); *The Chinese Traveller*, 2 vols (1775).
72 Lockman, *Travels* (1762 edn.), i, pp. vi, xvi–xvii.
73 *The Chinese Traveller*, i, p. iv.
74 *Navigantium atque Itinerantium Bibliotheca*, ed. J. Harris (1764 edn.), ii. 975.
75 Letter of G. Costard, *Philosophical Transactions*, xliv (1746–7), 477.
76 *A New General Collection of Voyages and Travels*, T. Astley (1745–7), iii. 513.
77 *Wealth of Nations*, ed. R. Campbell, A. Skinner, W. B. Todd (Oxford, 1976), ii. 729.
78 *Travels in China* (2nd edn., 1806), p. 3.
79 See J. S. Cummins, Introduction to *The Travels and Controversies of Friar Domingo Navarrete* (Cambridge, 1962), vol. i.
80 *A Voyage to China and the East-Indies by Peter Osbeck*, trans. J. R. Forster (1771).
81 *The Diary of John Evelyn*, ed. E. S. De Beer (Oxford, 1955), iii. 373–4.
82 K. N. Chaudhuri, *The Trading World of Asia and the English East India Company 1660–1760* (Cambridge, 1978), pp. 406–10, 519–20.
83 H. Honour, *Chinoiserie* (1961); O. B. Impey, *Chinoiserie* (1977).
84 Described by E. Harris in J. Harris, *Sir William Chambers*, p. 147.
85 M. Jourdain and R. S. Jenyns, *Chinese Export Art in the Eighteenth Century* (1967).
86 J. Irwin, 'Origins of the Oriental Style in English Decorative Art', *Burlington Magazine*, xcvii (1955), 106–14.
87 C. R. Boxer, *Jan Compagnie in Japan* (reprint, Tokyo, 1970), p. 140.
88 Pinkerton, *Modern Geography*, ii. 152.

89 Jones, *Works*, i. 108–9.
90 Vol. xlvii, 465–92.
91 S. Turner, *An Account of an Embassy to the Court of the Teshoo Lama in Tibet* (1800).
92 S. Kliger, *The Goths in England* (Cambridge, Mass., 1952), pp. 213–17.
93 *A General History of the Turks, Moguls and Tatars* (1730), i, p. iii.
94 J. Richardson, *Dissertation on the Languages, Literature and Manners of Eastern Nations*, 2nd edn. (Oxford, 1778), p. 163.
95 Lord Kames, *Sketches of the History of Man* (1788 edn.), i. 109.
96 M. S. Anderson, *Britain's Discovery of Russia 1553–1815* (1958).
97 C. Urness, ed., *A Naturalist in Russia. Letters from Peter Simon Pallas to Thomas Pennant* (Minneapolis, 1967), p. 47.
98 *Account of the Russian Discoveries* (1780).
99 *History of the Voyages and Discoveries made in the North* (1786).
100 William Davy and Joseph White, see Grewal, *Muslim Rule in India*, pp. 32–3.
101 *Modern Part of the Universal History*, ii. 264, 331.
102 Pinkerton, *Modern Geography*, ii. 55.
103 *Travels from St Petersburg in Russia to diverse parts of Asia* (Glasgow, 1763), ii. 146.
104 Vol. i, p. xiii.
105 *Les Correspondants de François Bernier*, ed. L. de Lens (Angers, 1872), p. 43.
106 *Syntagma Dissertationum . . . Thomas Hyde*, ed. G. Sharpe (Oxford, 1767), ii. 489.
107 *Letters on the Study and Use of History* (1752), pt. i. 6–7.
108 R. F. Jones, *Ancients and Moderns* (St Louis, 1936), p. 56.
109 *Sketches of the History of Man* (1788 edn.), i. 70.
110 *History of Sumatra*, pp. vii–viii.
111 *Works of William Warburton* (1788), ii. 671.
112 *The Progress of Society in Europe*, ed. F. Gilbert (Chicago, 1972), p. 154. For similar statements in his *History of America*, see below, pp. 219–20.
113 *The Correspondence of Edmund Burke*, iii, ed. G. H. Guttridge (Cambridge, 1961), 350–1.
114 See below, p. 136.
115 H. Aarsleff, *The Study of Language in England 1780–1860* (Princeton, 1967).

4

The Religions of Asia

The oceanic expansion of the sixteenth century had made Europeans aware of religious diversity on an entirely new scale. Whatever may have been hoped for them in the past, the peoples of Asia proved not to be Christian in any large numbers; when they were put into the balance, Christians had to admit that they themselves were only a minority of the world's population. What these Asian religions were and how they fitted into a view of the world, which for nearly all Englishmen remained an essentially Christian one, were still topics of absorbing interest for those who concerned themselves with Asia in the eighteenth century.

When studying other systems of belief eighteenth-century Englishmen applied to them assumptions which they held about Christianity. They believed that Asia was clearly divided between adherents of distinct 'religions', which in time they were to classify as 'Hinduism', 'Buddhism', 'Taoism', or under some other name. Each 'religion' had, as Christianity was thought to have, a fixed body of doctrine stated in sacred writings. The expounding of these doctrines and the performance of rites were entrusted to a priesthood. Asian religions were also thought to have historical traditions akin to the Judaic-Christian one. Biblical history was still literally interpreted by the vast majority in eighteenth-century Britain. It was the record of how God had acted at specific points in the past through chosen men, Abraham, Moses or the Apostles. Non-Christian religions had purely human founders, whose historical existence was not seriously doubted. Scriptures had been written and patterns of worship devised by a Muhammad, a Zoroaster, a Confucius or an historical Brahma.

Assumptions that Asian religions had distinct identities, formal structures and historical traditions akin to Christianity, even if there was a huge gulf between them and it in all matters of substance, provided a framework for comparisons. From the sixteenth century more and more books appeared in Europe describing 'new' religions and comparing them with one another and ultimately with Christianity.[1]

Educated Englishmen by the end of the seventeenth century could have been in no doubt that the pattern of religion in Asia was very diverse indeed. Islam dominated the Near East and Iran. In India Muslims ruled over a huge population of 'gentiles', sometimes referred to as Brahmins or Banians. Dr Thomas Hyde had shown that one of the communities of western India still practised the religion of ancient Persia. In Ceylon and in Siam and other parts of south-east Asia more 'gentiles' were to be found. Whether they were different from one another and from the gentiles of India was hard to determine. The missionary accounts had shown that there were many different sects among the educated Chinese, but it seemed that in some form or other they all accepted the beliefs of ancient China as restated by Confucius. Other Chinese cults had deviated completely from the original model, especially the adherents of 'Laokin' (Taoists) or Fo (Buddhists). The religions of the Japanese appeared to be totally confusing. There were said to be 'twelve sects in all' in Japan.[2] Richard Baxter's response to the puzzling medley of Asian religions was no doubt that of many Christians; within a Christian framework he made comparisons:

> The literate in China excel in many things, but besides abundance of ignorance of philosophy they destroy all by denying the immortality of the soul and affirming rewards and punishments to be only in this life. . . . The Siammenses, who seem the best of all, and meant for Christians, have many fopperies and worship the devil for feare as they do God for love. The Indian Bramenses, or Banians, also have Pythagoras errors and place their piety in redeeming bruits.[3]

By the end of the eighteenth century considerably more knowledge was available about certain Asian religions. Hinduism had been studied to some effect. Serious students could at least identify Buddhism and draw connections between different manifestations of it in different parts of Asia. The Koran and the historical origins of Islam had been investigated, although little had been done to study religious life in Muslim countries. The missionary interpretations of Chinese religion, formulated in the seventeenth century, still held the field. Where new knowledge had been acquired about Asian religions it was fitted into a framework that changed hardly at all in the eighteenth century. Religions were still seen as formal structures, defined by their founders' intentions in laying down doctrines and forms of worship.

The important role which scholars working on texts lodged in British libraries played in interpreting Islam reinforced the strongly historical slant to the study of religion: great importance was attached to knowledge of the founder and of his doctrine, of Muhammad and the Koran. The traditions and current religious life of Islam were of little interest.

Seventeenth-century portrayal of Muhammad and the Koran had

drawn heavily on medieval polemic. Muhammad was described as a depraved and wicked man who owed his success either because God had chosen him as an appropriate instrument of vengeance on a great part of mankind, or because he had allied with the devil. So long as the rise and spread of Islam was explained in other than human terms, Muhammad could be reviled as debauched and ignorant, in the words of Humphrey Prideaux's life of him published in 1697, 'an illiterate barbarian'.[4] But in the studies of Arab history by men like Pococke and Ockley the providential element in Islamic history was given much less emphasis. God no doubt directed the destinies of the world, but he worked out his purposes through human agents whose successes must be explained in human terms. Deplorable as the success might be, in worldly terms Muhammad had been extraordinarily successful. So the career and character of Muhammad and those aspects of Islam that had won it acceptance needed to be reassessed. A pamphlet called *Historical and Critical Reflections upon Mahometanism and Socinianism* of 1712 admitted that 'the false prophet had very fine natural talents', adding: 'As to what concerns his mind, 'tis easy to conclude that he was a man of extraordinary genius.'[5] A compilation of *Four Treatises Concerning the Doctrine, Discipline and Worship of the Mahometans*, also of 1712, included a piece on the 'Life and Actions of Mahomet', which concluded: 'It is agreed on all hands, that he was a man of very ready and piercing wit, and undaunted courage.'[6] Ockley did not write directly about Muhammad's life, but Jean Gagnier, one of the Oxford Arabic Professors, did produce histories of him in Latin and later in French.[7] Gagnier had no hesitation in condemning Muhammad as a supreme criminal who had denied the divinity of Christ and destroyed many Christian churches, but he said that he would not make unfair accusations against him as a man.[8] Sale went further than Gagnier in the Dedication and Preliminary Discourse attached to his translation of the Koran. Muhammad had played a great historical role and must be regarded with 'equal respect, tho' not with Moses or Jesus Christ . . . yet with Minos or Numa'.[9] This verdict was repeated by the popularizers, like Thomas Salmon in his *Modern History: or, the Present State of All Nations*: 'The pretended prophet . . . wanted neither parts nor judgment.'[10]

If Muhammad was to be raised from the status of an ignorant, crafty trickster to that of a kind of pagan hero of antiquity, leader of his people in war and their law-giver, verdicts on his supposed doctrine also required reassessment. The establishment of Islam probably owed something to the qualities of what was propounded as well as to Muhammad's skill. Even before Sale's version made it generally accessible, it was becoming difficult to maintain convincingly that the

Koran was no more than absurdity garnished with promises of sensual pleasures to come. By standards other than strictly Christian ones, merit could be found in it. The Dutch Arabist Reland pointed out that a 'religion which hath largely spread itself over Asia, Africa, and even Europe, commends its self to men by a great appearance of truth'.[11] The Koran was said to have 'beauty and majesty'.[12] Sale thought Muhammad had given the Arabs 'the best religion he could', and that the Koran was 'generally beautiful and fluent . . . and in many places, especially when the majesty and attributes of God are described, sublime and magnificent'.[13] A writer in the *Gentleman's Magazine* in 1753 considered that it, 'in point of morality, is second to no book upon earth, except the holy Scripture'.[14] Such opinions were widely held, although it was probably true that the majority of those who had any acquaintance with the Koran could not find much merit in it. Not only was this the case with orthodox Christians but also with unbelievers like Hume.[15] Nevertheless, there seems to have been a general willingness not to condemn it out of hand but to relate it to the times and the peoples for whom it had been designed. It might be unattractive to eighteenth-century Europeans, but it was usually conceded that the Koran was well suited to seventh-century Arabs.

Greater knowledge of Muhammad and the Koran gradually drove many of the medieval traditions about Islam out of circulation. Stories of pigeons used to impersonate the Holy Ghost or of the influence of renegade Jews and Christians featured rather less. One medieval tradition, however, abated very little, and may even have gained in strength. That was the tradition of Muhammad as imposter, the deliberate fabricator of false doctrines. If Muhammad was shown to be a man of ability and resolution and the Koran to be a work of genuine attractiveness for those to whom it was first preached, then the imposture was a high-class one, but it was still an imposture. Indeed, the common assumption that religions were the work of founders, who devised their doctrines, made any other conclusion difficult to accept. Some French free thinkers doubted whether the Koran was a conscious fabrication, Voltaire ultimately coming to believe that Muhammad deceived himself while deceiving others.[16] Sale was prepared to leave the issue open, as was Gibbon, who hedged his bets between 'fraud' and 'enthusiasm'.[17] But imposture remained the standard explanation in Britain. Even William Jones, who ranked Muhammad as one of the most able rhetoricians and finest of poets, called the Prophet an imposter.[18]

While the Islamic past attracted much interest, less was written about the present state of Islam. The verdict of the very scholarly Danish traveller, Carsten Niebuhr, that 'the doctrines and rites of the

Mussulman religion are in general sufficiently known'[19] seems to have been typical. Eighteenth-century commentators usually agreed with their seventeenth-century predecessors that although there was much for a Christian to condemn in the religious life of Islam, extreme accusations of hypocrisy and cruelty could not be sustained. This was the point of view of Joseph Pitts, who wrote the most circumstantial and certainly the most vivid of the early eighteenth-century accounts. Pitts was a seaman who had been captured by the Algerines and had lived as a slave in Muslim housholds, even going on the Haj. His book first appeared in 1704 and was frequently reprinted, Pitts being told that 'there was a great demand for it (especially in London) and that it was the best account of the Mahometan religion we have extant in our language'.[20] It was even serialized in the London press.[21] Whatever else might be held against Muslims, Pitts thought they were at least sincere in their religious devotions. There were some who dissented from this. Lady Mary Wortley Montagu believed that 'plain deism' was 'the secret of the effendis'.[22] George Forster, who travelled incognito on a long journey from India to the Caspian Sea, came to the conclusion that there was a deep hypocrisy between the professions and the actual lives of the ordinary Muslims whom he encountered.[23] Nowhere is any sense conveyed of Islam as a dynamic and developing faith. To Europeans it seemed at best to be static, keeping its hold on an ignorant population by suppressing all questioning and intellectual endeavour. Its fate seemed to be bound up with that of the great empires who were thought to enforce it, the Ottomans, the Persians and the Mughals. By the end of the eighteenth century with the Turks in retreat before the Russians and the Austrians, the Persian monarchy in disorder and the Mughal empire virtually extinct, some even began to suppose that Muslims might be won back in time to Christianity.[24]

Throughout the eighteenth century western knowledge of Zoroastrianism was almost entirely dependent on a single book, Thomas Hyde's *Historia Religionis Veterum Persarum* of 1700.[25] Hyde's interpretation of Zoroastrianism was highly favourable by western criteria and shows remarkable similarities to Jesuit interpretations of Confucianism.[26] The conventional accusations against 'the Magi' had been that they were idolatrous worshippers of the sun and of fire, and moreover that they were Manicheans, who believed in the equality of God and Satan. Hyde insisted that these were merely the outer trappings of an inner religion that was in essence monotheism. The great reformer, Zoroaster, built on this foundation, restoring his people's beliefs to their original purity. From his contact with the Jews he was able to include their prophecies in his writings and he was even able to foretell the coming of Christ. Hyde concluded that Zoroaster was a false prophet, but that God had permitted him to find out divine truths.

In 1771 a book published in France, called *Zend-Avesta, ouvrage de Zoroastre*, levelled certain criticisms at Hyde, pointing out that he had not been able to read any script of genuine antiquity and offering, in place of Hyde's authorities, Zoroastrian texts which were much less easy to assimilate to western ideas. This book was by a young Frenchman, Anquetil Duperron, who had been working on manuscripts which he had acquired in western India. Duperron passed through Britain in 1762, creating great ill-feeling on a visit to Oxford by the bluntness with which he exposed English errors. Within a generation Duperron's work was to win recognition. It is perhaps the most remarkable single achievement of the eighteenth century in the understanding of Asian religion.[27] But at the time, his conclusions were rejected both in Britain and in France. His texts seemed to be too inconsequential for the wisdom of the Magi. William Jones told Duperron that they could not be the work of the philosopher and man of genius that Zoroaster was known to have been.[28] So Hyde survived the assault for the time being. An English bishop in 1790 still believed that since Hyde had shown that Zoroaster had received 'communications from heaven concerning the future saviour of the world', it was reasonable to expect that the modern Parsis might be easily converted to Christianity.[29]

A feat in many ways comparable to Anquetil Duperron's *Zend-Avesta* was Charles Wilkins's *The Bhagvat-Geeta, or Dialogues of Kreeshna and Arjoon*, which on its appearance in 1785 was the first major translation of a Hindu Sanskrit text into a European language. But unlike Duperron, Wilkins was not a solitary individual struggling single-handed against the hazards of an Asian journey and against disbelief and rejection in Europe. Wilkins was one of a number of men who were being actively encouraged by patrons such as Warren Hastings in India and even by a generous policy towards scholarship shown by the Directors of the East India Company at home. Until the rise of academic Indology in Germany and France in the nineteenth century, Englishmen actually serving the East India Company in India became the leading interpreters of Hinduism to Europe.

In the seventeenth century, although some more penetrating studies were available, Hindus had usually been depicted either as idolatrous gentiles in the manner of the Old Testament or as proto-Pythagoreans as in Greek and Roman geography. In the early eighteenth century little of substance came directly from English sources, but English readers could obtain some quite full accounts of Hinduism in translations of reports from the Indian missions of the Jesuits or from the German–Danish Lutherans working on the Coromandel Coast.[30]

Some of these found their way into Salmon's *Modern History*. Such accounts tended to make a distinction, frequently to be repeated in descriptions of other religious systems, between the beliefs of an élite and the cults of the masses. The élite were depicted as being the guardians of esoteric doctrines of great antiquity, which were deposited in closely guarded sacred texts, usually called 'Wedams' or 'Veds'. These doctrines did indeed include, as the Greeks had reported, the transmigration of the soul from body to body, which was a concept repellent to Christians. On the other hand, there was undoubtedly also some kind of belief in a supreme being as a single entity and in rewards and punishments in a future state, although ultimate felicity took the profoundly unchristian form of 'being entirely reunited to the *being of beings*'.[31] For learned Hindus, the pantheon of deities, of which many lurid accounts were available, were apparently no more than symbolic representations of the attributes of the supreme being. The religion of the masses was another matter altogether. This was rank polytheism and idolatry, deliberately manufactured by the 'priestcraft' of the unscrupulous Brahmins to enable them to impose their will on a deluded populace.

Following the great expansion of British military and political power in India in the mid-eighteenth century, a number of English accounts of Hinduism began to appear. These claimed to be based on Hindu scripture and to have an authenticity which previous versions had lacked. In fact early British accounts, such as those of J. Z. Holwell and Alexander Dow, which were well received in Europe by Voltaire among others, were based on texts of very dubious authenticity indeed.[32] It was not until Wilkins and Jones had achieved a working knowledge of Sanskrit that English contributions became indispensable. Wilkins's translations and Jones's essays in *Asiatic Researches* set standards that were not to be matched for a generation, and were to create an awareness of Hinduism in Goethe and some of his contemporaries.

Wilkins and Jones tended to reinforce the distinction made in earlier accounts between the doctrines of the élite and the 'superstitions' of the mass. The élite were certainly not polytheists; they believed in a single supreme being, even if much of what they appeared to believe seemed to Europeans educated in the classics to be more easily assimilable to Greek philosophy than to Christian theologies. 'The most learned Brahmans of the present time are unitarians', wrote Wilkins. 'They believe but in one God, an universal spirit'.[33] Jones described the beliefs of 'the *Vedantis*, unable to form a distinct idea of brute matter independent of mind', who 'imagine that the deity is ever present to his work'.[34] Robertson, the historian, found in the *Gita* 'descriptions of the Supreme Being entitled to equal praise with those of the Greek philosophers'.[35] The scientist, Joseph Priestley, thought that the idea of raising the soul through meditation 'to a state of union with God' was similar to 'the practices of the Christian monks, who in fact only copied the heathen Platonists'.[36]

But the profusion of cults and images, caste divisions and rituals of all kinds, including the much-publicized widow burning, remained the staple of travel books and required explanation. To most Europeans they were signs of degeneration. The élite doctrines were the ancient truths, but the mass of the people, encouraged by self-interested priests, had been no more able than the masses elsewhere to maintain intellectual austerity. The best that could be said for the popular cults was that they were allegories of inner truths. The most ingenious interpretation of this kind was undertaken by William Jones in an essay to explore similarities between the pantheons of the Hindus and of the Greeks and Romans. He concluded that 'the whole crowd of gods and goddesses in ancient Rome and modern Varanes [Benares], mean only the powers of nature and principally those of the sun, expressed in a variety of ways and by a multitude of fanciful names'.[37] Other writers at least commended the social effects of 'popular' Hinduism. Hindus appeared to be sincerely pious after their fashion and to live harmless, frugal lives. They were called 'a meek, superstitious, charitable people'.[38] They were 'mild, laborious, and naturally virtuous in their dispositions. All who have opportunities of observing the lives of the Hindoos, admire their patience, probity, and benevolence.'[39] Caste produced social stability, based on a division of labour, which had 'effects the most happy in themselves, and powerfully operative in uniting the leading bonds of society'.[40] Burke concluded that 'wherever the Hindu religion has been established, that country has been flourishing'.[41]

By the end of the eighteenth century there was a tendency in British writing on Hinduism to stress the relative purity by European standards of its 'inner' doctrines and at least to be restrained in comments on the mass cults. But very different interpretations were possible. To Priestley the degradations inflicted by the caste system were without parallel in any other human society anywhere.[42] The geographer, Pinkerton, thought that Hindus were 'the puerile slaves of a capricious imagination. . . . If we judge from the fanatic penances, suicides and other superstitious frenzies, no where on earth is the mind so much disordered'.[43] The material had already been accumulated which was to be deployed early in the nineteenth century by those who felt on both religious and secular grounds that the British should use the power which empire had given them to bring about changes in a backward and unhappy society.

Eighteenth-century interpretations of religion usually involved not only establishing its doctrines, preferably through its sacred texts, but also identifying its founder and explaining its origins. For Hinduism these were extremely difficult tasks. It had long been known that Hindus claimed a great antiquity. Access to pundits and texts made it clear that such claims were very extensive indeed. The world was said to be 6,000,000 or 7,000,000 years old.[44] Indians were obviously candidates with the Egyptians, Chinese or Chaldeans for the title of most ancient people on earth. Much ingenuity was devoted to pointing out similarities between ancient peoples and to trying to deduce from them which was the parent and which was the offspring. In particular, arguments began in France and were taken up in Britain as to whether the Egyptians had taught the Indians or the Indians had taught the Egyptians. Such arguments proved very little to those who were not participants. The search for a founder for Hinduism proved equally inconclusive. Since it was assumed that gods were often deified men, there was speculation about an historic Brahma. To some Jesuits he was in fact Abraham.[45] English writers were wary of such identifications, merely assuming that he was 'one of those great geniuses', like Zoroaster or Confucius, who had devised a system of religion and law for their people.[46] Jones and his contemporaries abandoned the hunt for an historic founder of Hinduism. The Hindus were assumed to be a very ancient people indeed, about whose origins little could be discovered. Jones did, however, believe that he could dispose of their more provocative claims to antiquity. In an essay 'On the Chronology of the Hindus', he argued that the Hindus' 'historical age cannot be carried back further than about two thousand years before Christ'. It could therefore be no real threat to the Biblical dating of the world's history. India had no doubt been settled soon after the dispersion of the peoples following the Deluge, but claims that went beyond that could be safely ignored. Indeed Jones thought that the Hindu view of creation showed distinct intimations of the Biblical one.[47]

Thus Hinduism as presented to Europe by English writers at the end of the eighteenth century conformed fairly closely to what Europeans expected a religion to be. It had an ancient set of beliefs about the existence of a supreme being, which were confined to an intellectual élite. The masses were fed on polytheism and ritual.

With the conquest of Bengal the British acquired responsibility for a huge Muslim population. The attention given to Islam was, however, very small by comparison with that lavished on Hinduism. Hastings commissioned translations of legal books, was the patron of a *Madrasa* college in Calcutta and encouraged the writing of Mughal history.[48]

His approach to Islam in India seems to have been that of the majority of his contemporaries: Indian Muslims were an alien ruling minority. They were often described as Tartars, whose vigour the soft, enervating climate of Bengal had sapped. 'Perfidy and sensuality' were now their distinguishing features.[49] Very little account seems to have been taken of the vast Bengali population of the east who were Muslims. Two very experienced Company servants, the geographer James Rennell and the former Governor Harry Verelst, when asked to estimate the proportion of Muslims to Hindus, both made the same surprising reply: about one-fifth.[50] But even if Englishmen had been aware of the size and nature of the Muslim community of Bengal, it is still doubtful whether it would have attracted much attention: Islam was thought to be well known; Hinduism was a novelty.

While the British were able to establish themselves as the leading European experts on Hinduism, they were entirely dependent on the expertise of others for knowledge of Chinese religion. Great importance was attached in the eighteenth century to canonical texts, yet it is doubtful whether any Englishman could read a Chinese text. Copies of some of the Confucian classics were sent to England from Canton,[51] presumably to remain unread. The Jesuits were recognized to be the guardians of Chinese texts, thought to be five books 'correspondent with the Mosaical history' and 'esteemed by them the source of all science and morality'.[52] English readers depended on such translations as the Jesuits published, and indeed on their interpretations of Chinese religion as a whole.

Essential to the Jesuit interpretation was a three-fold division between 'the learned' Confucianists and the Taoists and Buddhists. All their attention was concentrated on the learned, the practitioners of the state cult whose classics provided the official ideology of the empire and the body of learning which its bureaucracy was required to master. If conversions were to be made at the higher levels of Chinese society, Christianity must be presented in terms which minimized conflict with Confucianism. Wherever possible the Confucian tradition should be assimilated to the Christian one and Confucian cults should be tolerated. Accommodations between Christianity and Confucianism, however, required not only the willingness of the Chinese to be accommodated, but also the assent of the ecclesiastical authorities in Europe. This the Jesuits were ultimately unable to attain. Members of other missionary orders working in China had rejected their tactics and complained about them. This set off the so-called Chinese Rites controversy in Europe. The Papacy eventually decided against most of the accommodations proposed by the Jesuits. But the controversy influenced much that the Jesuits wrote about Chinese religion. They hoped to create a picture of it in Europe that would gain support for their interpretations.

An extreme statement of the Jesuit point of view on Confucianism contained in a book by Louis Le Comte was freely available in Britain, three editions appearing between 1697 and 1699 with new versions in 1737 and 1739;[53] but Du Halde, in what was regarded as the standard Jesuit version,[54] was more moderate in his assessment of what were the most controversial points of interpretation, the age of some of the Confucian doctrines and whether they were or were not theistic. Of the various dates for the founding of their dynasties and of their religion given in the classical Chinese histories and repeated by Jesuit scholars, Du Halde was inclined to accept that attached to the personage whom Europeans called 'Fo Hi', the first emperor. This would mean that China had enjoyed settled government for some 4,000 years. That the Chinese had been sophisticated enough to be able to record an eclipse in 2155 BC appeared to be additional evidence of the great antiquity of their civilization. Such claims conflicted with the normal Biblical dating of the world; but by using the Septuagint dating the origins of China could be safely put some two hundred years after the Flood. Although support for Chinese claims to antiquity risked accusations of heterodoxy about dating, they helped to provide Confucianism with an extremely respectable pedigree. It could be traced back to the Biblical patriarchs. Du Halde described how, relatively soon after the floods abated and the Ark came to rest, 'the sons of Noah' moved into China and settled down there. 'Instructed by tradition, concerning the grandeur and power of the Supreme Being, they taught their children, and thro' them their numerous posterity, to fear and honour the sovereign Lord of the Universe, and to live according to the principles of the law of nature written in their hearts.'[55]

Questions of chronology fascinated eighteenth-century scholars. A number of English authors commented on the material provided by the Jesuits. In his *Sacred and Prophane History of the World* of 1728 Samuel Shuckford suggested that Fo Hi might not be just a close relation of Noah; he probably was Noah himself.[56] This idea was enthusiastically taken up by the author of a section of *The Modern Part of the Universal History*. After a 'two hundred years peregrination' Noah had settled in China. The excellence of Chinese institutions could be attributed to their founder. 'The religion, laws, government, policy, morality, philosophy etc of the Chinese' are 'every way worthy of so divine a patriarch and lawgiver'.[57] Others were more sceptical. If the Chinese really were such an ancient people, why were they not mentioned either in the Bible or by the Greeks? A drastic revision of the conventional

Jesuit dating made by Father Foucquet from a table compiled for him in Canton in 1724 was generally welcomed, when a version of it was published by the Royal Society. It doubted whether Chinese chronology could be traced with any confidence further back than 400 BC.[58] George Costard, an astronomer who specialized in casting doubts on observations said to have been made in remote periods by eastern peoples, had no confidence in the eclipse of 2155 BC. He considered that the Chinese were incapable of such calculations until they had received instruction from the Jesuits.[59] His comments were sent to Peking, where the Fathers tried to refute them.[60] The fact that Voltaire also believed in Jesuit dating was not for most Englishmen an argument in its favour.[61] In the second half of the eighteenth century few English authors were willing to support ambitious claims for Chinese antiquity. William Jones suggested that they might even be a colony settled by Indians.[62]

When Du Halde moved from assessing the age of Chinese religion to describing the beliefs of Confucianism, he moved onto even more dangerous ground. What exactly was the nature of that 'sovereign Lord of the Universe' whom he said the Chinese had worshipped since their origins? He was, Du Halde wrote, called 'Chang ti', 'Supreme Emperor', or 'Tien', which could be literally translated as 'heaven'. That term was ambiguous. Du Halde admitted that it could be interpreted as 'an intelligent being, Lord and Creator of heaven, earth and all things' or merely as 'the visible material heaven'. He was cautious in committing himself, but left his readers in little doubt that he accepted the first interpretation.[63] Although he found serious deficiencies in their teaching about the creation, the nature of the soul and of a future state, Du Halde was still in no real doubt that the ancient Chinese had been theists. In later ages there had been many deviations into idolatry on the one hand and atheism on the other. But reform had been brought about by Confucius, a greater man even than Socrates. Confucius had reasserted the worship of 'the Lord of Heaven' and had taught an excellent morality. Consequently he was treated in China at the present time with 'the highest degree of dignity'.[64] He was not, however, deified, as the Jesuits' opponents alleged. Idolatry and atheism had reared their heads again, and some modern Confucianists were contaminated, but a pure strain of theism had survived and was still kept alive. Some of the learned remained faithful. This version was to be restated in the later Jesuit compilation, the two-volume *General Description of China* translated in 1788.[65]

Such propositions were fiercely debated within the Catholic Church. Critics of the Jesuits argued that the main strain of Confucianism was essentially atheistic; 'Tien' could only be interpreted in a materialist sense. Far from being monotheists, even 'learned' Chinese worshipped their ancestors and made a god out of Confucius. In as far as British readers were aware of these debates, it would seem reasonable to expect that they would have been unsympathetic to the Jesuit point of view. For Protestants religious conversion was a matter of inner conviction and faith; accommodation on fundamentals was alien to them. Nevertheless, some of the most influential compilations summarized Du Halde without criticism.[66] Doubts about the Jesuit version do, however, appear in the notes to Thomas Percy's edition of the Chinese play, *Hau Kiou Choaan*, of 1761.[67] Percy was a notable scholar who cited an impressive list of sources about China in western languages. He believed that 'most of the modern literati understand the word *Tien*, etc in their ancient books in a low material sense and are downright atheists'. 'Filial piety' was carried to 'idolatrous excess'. Confucius was regarded with 'a degree of reverence, which it is difficult to distinguish from idolatry'.[68] At least one other cleric, Francis Lockier, Dean of Peterborough, agreed with him that 'the great men and celebrated philosophers among the Chinese are all atheists – a sort of Spinozists'.[69]

What if anything those Englishmen who went year after year to Canton made of Chinese religion is not recorded. Some of those who travelled to Peking and elsewhere with Lord Macartney's embassy of 1793 wrote down their impressions. They seem in general to have been puzzled by what appeared to be the diversity and eclecticism of cults. Buddhist temples seem to have caught their attention most. Educated Chinese struck Lord Macartney as 'free thinkers'; Confucianism had deteriorated into 'a corrupt superstition'.[70] Barrow believed that the Confucianists had not 'the least idea of a *personal being* to the deity'. Confucius's teaching was 'too sublime and too metaphysical' for the Chinese. Religion in China was little more than fortune telling.[71]

Unusually for a European of his time, Barrow had a kind word for the Buddhist priests, or 'Bonzes', as they were usually called. They had 'a sort of pride and dignity in their deportment'.[72] He thought that they had been unfairly slandered in missionary accounts. Buddhism was certainly an object of detestation to missionaries working in China, with which they attempted no accommodation whatsoever.[73] They were happy to direct against the Buddhists many of the accusations which they tried to deflect from the Confucianists. The followers of 'Fo' were both idolaters and atheists. As one of the Jesuit letters from Canton translated into English put it, their priests and their pagodas seemed to be a hellish parody of the Christian church.[74] 'There is not so great an impediment to the progress of christianity as is this ridiculous and impious doctrine', wrote another.[75] Du Halde simply called them 'ministers of Satan'.[76] Such verdicts appeared in British summaries.

Readers of the Jesuits would have become aware that the worship of Fo was not confined to the Chinese. Fo was thought to have been an historical figure who had brought his doctrines to China from India at a date variously estimated. His influence could be found in other parts of Asia, too. A number of the French Jesuits who were to serve in China had passed through Siam at the end of the seventeenth century. There they found veneration for 'Sommona Codom',[77] who appeared to be Fo by another name, and 'Talapoins', who were the equivalent of Bonzes. In Japan Fo was usually called 'Saka'. The cults of the Lamas in Chinese Tartary seemed to be essentially similar. The English account of Ceylon by Robert Knox had identified 'another great God, whom they call Buddou . . . Him they believe once to have come on earth'.[78] Readers of books like Engelbert Kaempfer's *History of Japan* or La Loubère's *A New Historical Relation of the Kingdom of Siam* were given some indication of the spread of Buddhism throughout Asia. Kaempfer added the further complication that Buddha was also an incarnation of Vishnu in the Hindu pantheon.[79]

Buddhism puzzled those eighteenth-century scholars who were aware of it. Accounts suggested that it was an extremely diverse phenomenon, varying from Lamaism in Tibet to the Theravada Buddhism of south-east Asia. If there was a body of scriptures, no European had access to it. Many accounts referred to Buddha as a god, but it was generally assumed that Buddha under his various names was a man. There was, however, doubt as to how many Buddhas there had been and when they had lived. The general opinion was that Buddhists really were atheists, whatever they might say in public to comfort and mislead the mass of their followers. Bayle, for instance, wrote that the 'inner doctrine' of Buddhism is 'nothingness'; the aim of man is to revert to nothing, to 'inaction and inner rest'.[80] La Loubère thought that the Siamese Talapoins 'admit not any intelligent being, which judges of the goodness or badness of humane actions'. They have no idea of 'a God creator' or 'of any God'. 'Supream felicity' is 'an eternal unactivity, and a real impassability. *Nireupan*, say they . . .'. It meant annihilation.[81]

English additions to such European knowledge as existed about Buddhism were very slight. Michael Symes spent some time in Burma in 1795 giving an account of temples and rituals in his book on the kingdom of Ava.[82] William Jones tried to fix the Buddha as an historical figure living in India at a specific point in time. Checking his own researches in Sanskrit sources with French reconstructions of Chinese chronology, he tentatively dated him at 1000 BC.[83] Warren Hastings's two missions to Tibet[84] added relatively little to what was known of Lamaism from the descriptions already published by Jesuits. Hastings asked Bogle, his first envoy, to inquire fully into the Dalai Lama, the 'incarnation of this legislator, prophet or God, Budda or Fo'.[85] Little of what he may have found out appeared in print. Pallas, on the other hand, on his journeys into central Asia at roughly the same time,[86] discovered a great deal about Lamaism. The publication of his journals probably gave Europeans the fullest account yet available, if not a very sympathetic one. Pallas had gained his knowledge mostly from Christian Kalmyks whom he encountered. 'Like other superstitions', he thought that Lamaism was 'the fabrick of priests, and illusions by which they contrive to awe the ignorant multitude'. He doubted whether they had any real concept of a 'higher supreme being'.[87]

Translations of Pallas and of other material from Russian sources about Siberia provided information about what was called 'Shamanism' as well as about Buddhism. Shamanism was said to be the ancient indigenous belief of the peoples of Siberia. On the surface it was no more than 'a mass of absurdities and the grossest superstitions'; but even the Shamans showed some slight awareness of 'the general notions of natural religion, as well as various ceremonies of the Mosaic law'.[88] The Mongols at the time of Cingis Khan had been 'strict deists'.[89]

That traces of natural religion, deism and Moses could be found even in such apparently improbable places as Siberia and Mongolia reveals much about eighteenth-century European approaches to religion. Travel accounts had depicted what appeared to be immense diversity throughout Asia: Muslims, Zoroastrians, Hindus, Sikhs, Buddhists of various sorts, Shamanists, Shintoists, varieties of Christians and Jews, to mention only those on whose identification there was some agreement. Such a multiplicity of religions suggested at first sight a chaotic and disordered world. One of the participants in Berkeley's dialogues between Christians and free thinkers drew this conclusion:

> Lastly extending my view to all the various nations which inhabit this globe, and finding they agreed on no one point of faith, but differed one from another, as well as from the forementioned sects, even in the notion of a god, in which there is as great diversity as in the methods of worship, I thereupon became an *atheist*.

The reply was that his reasoning was superficial. If he searched hard enough he would find beneath the surface diversity the same 'sublime truths, which are the fruit of mature thought and have been rationally deduced by men of the best and most improved understandings' throughout history.[90] Diversity was a challenge to find patterns and similarities, to classify and to explain in religion as in other disciplines of eighteenth-century scholarship.[91] The appearance of Moses in

Siberia strongly suggests that scholars had succeeded in bringing a degree of order out of apparent disorder.

Success in classifying religions and relating them to one another owed a great deal to the consensus among eighteenth-century Europeans about the nature of religion. As was stressed at the beginning of this chapter, few dissented from the view that religions were uniform structures of belief, instituted at some specific point in history by God's agency, outside the Jewish-Christian revelation, by men. These creations of divine or human intelligence all had much the same concerns. The traveller or scholar aware of these therefore knew what questions to ask, questions of course framed by his own Christian background. What did the scriptures teach about the nature of the deity, about the soul, about salvation? What were the forms of worship and the establishments of priests? Was there an inner doctrine for the élite and an outer doctrine for the masses? These questions provided a framework for classifying religions. Answers to them tended to reveal variations on certain themes and even marked similarities between the Asian religions themselves and between them and Christianity, which was never regarded as an Asian religion.

To modern readers, patterns and similarities among the answers would seem to a very large extent to have arisen from the form of the questions, which had assumptions of similarity built into them. Some contemporaries were certainly aware of this. The young Nathaniel Halhed in Bengal protested against 'the vanity of reconciling every other mode of worship to some kind of conformity with our own' and of foisting 'allegorical constructions, and forced allusions to a mystic morality . . . upon the plain and literal context of every pagan mythology'.[92] Such iconoclasm was, however, rare. More elaborate explanations were usually sought. Those that were offered seem to have fallen into two categories, to some degree related to the different approaches to knowledge about Asia discussed in the previous chapter. One way of explaining patterns and similarities in Asian religions was essentially historical. Religions had developed from a common point of origin and their relationships with one another could be traced historically. The other approach was based on the study of human nature and of man. The similarities in religion could be attributed to the underlying unity of human nature throughout the world. Differences in religions reflected differences in men's circumstances.

The Christian view of the history of the world, resting on the authority of the Bible, remained the dominant historical explanation of the world's religions. The Bible's first books had been dictated by God to Moses. They described the creation of the earth at a date which could be calculated with reasonable accuracy. With the sons of Noah, men had begun to separate themselves into distinct peoples. The scattering of the peoples followed, when God decided to frustrate men's presumption in trying to build the tower at Babel. In the age of the Patriarchs before Babel, God had instructed men directly. The religion of the Patriarchs was therefore the worship of God in the way that God required. Unfortunately, with the passing of time, the peoples who had migrated away from Babel began to deviate from this simple, pure worship taught by God. Hopes, fears and stupidity led men to worship idols, natural objects or other men and to invent rituals and mysteries. God continued to maintain direct contact with only one of the world's peoples, with Abraham and his descendants. To them in the fullness of time came the Christian revelation.

Increasing knowledge of Asian religion did, however, suggest that although the lapses of ancient peoples had been grievous, they had not fallen into total darkness. None seemed to have forgotten everything that their ancestors had once learnt. Natural atheism, as opposed to the deliberately cultivated atheism of Europeans and some Asians like the Buddhists, was usually discounted, except by determined sceptics like Hume.[93] Even the Siberians had some remote intimations of Moses. Michael Symes was pleased to find that the 'half-humanized' Andaman Islanders, 'the most ignorant and barbarous of mankind', still acknowledged a God.[94] The more sophisticated Asian peoples appeared to have preserved quite definite traces of the original religion of the world. Berkeley thought that the 'gentiles' in general, and especially the Parsis and Brahmins, had a tradition which showed 'manifest traces' of the world's history as written by Moses.[95] The Jesuits of course believed that the secluded Chinese had deviated very little until quite late in their history.

Orthodox Christians in the eighteenth century also accepted that folk memories of patriarchal religion could be reinforced by nature. Through the study of a divinely ordered world men could come to understand something of the purposes of its creator. As a sermon preached at the anniversary of the Society for the Propagation of the Gospel put it in 1759: 'For all men are endowed by nature, or grace, with such rational powers, that they can discover their relation to God as their creator and sovereign, with the principal branches of their duty to him, to themselves and to other men.'[96] The proper study of nature had produced good pagans, Aristotle and Plato, to whom it now seemed that Confucius, Zoroaster and perhaps some Brahmins could be added, men who had acknowledged a supreme being and the immortality of the soul and who had taught a refined morality.

A few Christians were even prepared to go beyond the memory of the Patriarchs and the teaching of nature and to argue that there were some elements of Asian religions that could only be explained by direct divine revelation. God had perhaps spoken to others apart from the people of Israel. In the later Middle Ages it had sometimes been argued that the ancient Egyptians had enjoyed his confidence. They had stored up these divine truths in their indecypherable hieroglyphs, while passing some of them on to Pythagoras. Eighteenth-century writers often assumed that mysterious learning was locked away in the hieroglyphs, but speculation that this might be wisdom directly imparted by God seems to have ceased.[97] Other candidates existed, however. Some Jesuit authors detected symbolic references to Christ's incarnation and crucifixion in Chinese classics, implying that, whether they were aware of it or not, their authors been divinely inspired.[98] Hyde had suggested that God had chosen Zoroaster as a vehicle for revelation.[99]

Hyde was also interested in another possibility that might help to explain some of the features of Asian religions that Christians found similar to their own: might not Christianity have been more widespread in Asia in its early ages than it was now? Hyde was asked by James II at Oxford, ' "whether the Chinese had any divinity?" to which Dr Hyde answer'd "Yes, but 'twas idolatry, they being all heathens, but yet they have in their idol-temples statues representing the Trinity, and other pictures which shew that antient Christianity had been amongst them".'[100] This was not an interpretation of the Chinese much pressed by the Jesuits, although they did in some cases apply it to Hinduism and to Buddhist Lamaism. Hindus were thought by some to have a 'confused idea' of the Trinity and of other Christian doctrines, which they had probably learnt from the Apostle Thomas.[101] The Dutch Protestant Baldaeus also detected signs of Christianity among Hindus.[102] Medieval traditions of Christian communities in central Asia seemed to be confirmed by what the Jesuits took to be traces of Christianity still visible in Lamaism. The Dalai Lama seemed to them a parody of the Christian incarnation.[103]

By the end of the eighteenth century more elaborate explanations of apparent similarities between Asian religions and Christianity had been abandoned, at least in Britain. Revelations not mentioned in the Bible were treated with scepticism, while there appeared to be no firm evidence that St Thomas, the Nestorians or any other early Christian group had been able to make a significant impact on the major religions of Asia. Nevertheless, the proposition that there were common elements in Christianity and non-Christian religions was rarely questioned; to attribute these to a common past before Babel or to God's ability to speak to all men through nature remained strict orthodoxy. For instance, Thomas Maurice, an Anglican clergyman who prided himself on resisting free thinking at the time of the French Revolution, believed that:

> ... in the pure and primitive theology derived from the venerable patriarchs, there were certain grand and mysterious truths, the object of their fixed belief, which all the depravations, brought into it by succeeding superstition were never able entirely to efface from the human mind. These truths, together with many of the symbols of that pure theology were propagated and diffused by them in their various peregrinations through the Higher Asia, where they have immemorially flourished; affording a most sublime and honourable testimony of such a refined and patriarchal religion having *actually existed* in the earliest ages of the world.[104]

Some of the implications of orthodox arguments could be exploited by the unorthodox, who had historical explanations for the similarities of religions which were highly controversial. To the orthodox Christian the existence of apparent similarities between the Jewish–Christian tradition and other religious traditions merely meant that the other traditions had drawn some things from it. They were partially corrupted offshoots and imitations. To the critics of orthodoxy similarities suggested that the Jewish–Christian revelation was not the unique vehicle for God's providence that it was claimed to be. They saw it either as one of a number of roughly similar religions which had developed in different parts of Asia or as one of a number of manifestations of the religious urge in man responding in much the same way to the teaching of God through nature. This was the position of the deists. God did not instruct men through special dispensations and revelations; he spoke openly to man's reason. The fact that travellers and scholars found essential agreement about the existence of a supreme being or a future state with rewards and punishments in so many religions showed that human reason would reach much the same conclusions everywhere.

Although there was a considerable output of deist writing in late seventeenth-century and early eighteenth-century England, English deists do not seem to have made much use of findings about Asian religion. In the late seventeenth century Henry Stubbe had circulated a manuscript which appears to have portrayed Islam as a simple statement of natural religion, unencumbered by dogma like the doctrine of the Trinity.[105] Such points were not, however, to be fully developed in print until the publication of *La Vie de Mahomed* in 1730 by the French freethinker, Boulainvilliers. He argued that the doctrine of the unity of God and the moral teaching of Islam were the work of a man who had clearly been deeply versed in true natural divinity.[106] The great exponent of Asian religions against Christianity was of course Voltaire. He, too, saw the Koran as a statement of universal natural religion.[107] So, too, was Confucianism. Turning the Jesuit versions against their authors, he argued that the admirable doctrines which the Jesuits had described were not some intimations of a remote patriarchal religion, but simple moral truths for which Confucius had claimed no divine inspiration.[108] Matthew Tindal, an English deist, had implied something similar in his *Christianity as Old as Creation* of 1731.[109] Voltaire also believed that the doctrines of the Brahmins and the ancient Persians, as described by Hyde, embodied the principles of natural religion.[110] So to Voltaire there was nothing unique about Christianity. It was one of a number of attempts to encapsulate in a religious code certain fundamental truths understood by reason. Christianity as it had evolved by the eighteenth century was not even the most creditable of such attempts. Asian religions, with the possible exception of Islam, were generally less dogmatic and irrational in their beliefs and much less bloodthirsty and intolerant in their practice.

Voltaire had few English imitators, but his works were quickly translated and drew much comment, most of it hostile. English deism was in retreat in the second half of the eighteenth century, and orthodoxy was very much in the ascendant. The conventional reply to Voltaire was to admit that there might be merits in non-Christian religions, especially where a people supposed to be at a relatively high level of civilization had been open to the benign teaching of God through nature. But by comparison with the splendour of Christianity, these good points did not amount to much. Natural religion had never been adopted; it never was 'either in profession or practice, the religion of any country upon earth since the world began'.[111] Even if the teaching of nature could be applied strictly, it would still be inadequate. Nature could only be fulfilled by revelation. The more the claims of other religions were pressed, the more orthodox Christians pointed out their practical deficiencies, whatever their precepts might be. Utilitarian notes were increasingly sounded at the end of the century. Christianity, especially Protestant Christianity, produced improvements in the human condition; Asian religions did not. Islam had long been identified as one of the causes of the supposed decline of the lands of the Near East from their ancient prosperity. In a much admired set of sermons in Oxford in 1784, Joseph White, or rather the 'ghost' writers whom he employed, restated the case: Islam was 'naturally destructive of the great principles of human welfare', whereas Christianity was 'naturally conducive to them'.[112] Priestley thought that Hindu devotional practices, like Catholic ones, did not lead to 'the due government of the passions, and consequently a proper conduct in life'.[113]

An important part of the deists' and freethinkers' attack on the claims of Christianity was to question the Jewish–Christian view of history. To Christians evidence that accounts of the creation and early history of the world approximating to the Mosaic version could be found in other religions, indicated that these religions preserved some recollections of a common past. On the other hand, if it could be shown that these religions were very much older than Moses stated the world to be, then the early books of the Old Testament were by no means the unique word of God; they were probably an imitation of some much more ancient tradition from some other part of Asia. Most Asian religions claimed an antiquity that was incompatible with Biblical dating. As more knowledge became available about them, the disaffected took them up and pressed their claims, while the orthodox felt obliged to refute them or to try to reconcile them with the Bible. This was not a new problem. Since the sixteenth century scholars had been producing fragments of texts purporting to make great claims for the antiquity of the Egyptians or the Chaldeans. This induced other scholars to undertake elaborate labours reducing such chronologies to the point where they could be reconciled with the Bible. Such works of reconciliation continued to appear in the eighteenth century, but it became increasingly common to regard the texts as supposititious; Berkeley could not see why any 'learned man, should imagine those things deserve any regard'.[114] In the later seventeenth century Chinese chronological traditions were being published in Europe, together with Jesuit attempts to reconcile them to the Bible. As has been shown, English scholars were interested but increasingly sceptical spectators of such matters. Voltaire, however, was far from sceptical, seizing on the Jesuit findings and proclaiming that the Chinese empire was 4000 years old. While other peoples' history was mere allegory and fable, the Chinese had unimpeachable written records to prove theirs.[115] In the second half of the eighteenth century English scholars became Europe's interpreters of Hindu chronology with its immense claims to antiquity. The by now aged Voltaire had no hesitation in accepting these, too. He decided that the Indians were even older than the Chinese.[116] But English opinion was not prepared to accept Hindu chronology, even if British authors had publicized it. To general satisfaction William Jones was able to play the role of a latter-day Jesuit in an essay which showed how Hindu history could be reduced to Biblical proportions.[117]

The willingness of critics of Christian orthodoxy to engage their opponents in disputes over chronology is clear evidence of the continuing vitality, even late in the eighteenth century, of an historical approach to the study of religions. In such disputes both sides started from the assumption that religious concepts were borrowed by one people from another and then set textual authorities against one another to establish the succession of lenders and borrowers. There were, however, some who doubted the value of these exercises, as indeed Voltaire was inclined to do when he was not trying to beat the Christians at their own historical game. Bolingbroke expressed these doubts most trenchantly. The textual authorities which were cited to prove that one religion was older than another were in fact so defective that they proved nothing at all. He thought that the Bible was entirely unreliable as an historical source: it was full of 'additions, interpolations and transpositions, made we neither know when nor by whom'. But he was not interested in replacing the Bible with the sacred books of another people. 'Profane chronology' was so modern, so broken, so precarious 'as to be equally unreliable'. In short, 'antient history never will gain any credit with any reasonable man'.[118]

If attempts to compare and classify religions by relating them to one another historically were to be abandoned because of lack of historical evidence of sufficient quality, what alternatives were available to reduce the diversity of religions into some pattern of order? The most promising one seemed to be to relate religions to a combination of human nature and the state of the society where particular religions were practised. This approach assumed that religions were not inherited from one central source; they were devised by men independent of one another. But they were not devised at random. Some pattern could be found in them. At bottom all religions reflected what Hume called 'the essential and universal properties of human nature'[119] and were the product of 'that *Proteus* the mind of man', as the English translator of the *Ceremonies and Religious Customs of the Nations of the Known World* put it.[120] Hume thought that human nature devised religions in response to 'the events of life'[121] and its inability to explain those events. In a primitive society fear and uncertainty would dominate, to produce a multitude of often malignant deities. A more advanced society with greater control over its environment or knowledge of natural forces would move closer to monotheism and the idea of a beneficent creator.

In the hands of Hume, this kind of 'natural history' of religion was of course very hostile to Christian assumptions. It left no role for divine providence. It was, however, also very hostile to conventional deist assumptions as well. It left no role for universal human reason. In spite of the extreme conclusions implied by Hume, some Christians could adopt the natural historians' way of studying religion. It seems to be very marked in William Robertson's treatment of Hinduism. He, too, saw religions developing from primitive responses to ignorance and fear towards the recognition of a supreme being with the spread of 'science and philosophy'.[122]

Present-day students of religion are likely to be sceptical of both approaches, and to suggest that to provide them with historical pedigrees or to relate them to very generalized propositions about human nature and social development are not necessarily helpful ways of trying to understand religions. What believers believe may well elude categories and generalizations. But to expect eighteenth-century scholars not to categorize or to generalize is to expect a great deal.

The diversity of Asian religions provided theologians and scholars with much to debate. How far this diversity impressed itself on a wider public and what conclusions were drawn from it are less clear. The picture presented in nearly all travel accounts and books about Asia which were commonly read would have implied that, while there was little in any Asian religion worthy of imitation or adoption by Europeans, they were not objects of total detestation either. It was unusual for Asian religions to be described as devil worship or unalloyed idolatry whose adherents were inevitably bound for hellfire. If even intelligent, well-read men could show a great deal of prejudice against Islam for its supposed bigotry and fanaticism, it is likely that the unsophisticated still felt deep hostility to 'Turks'. Nevertheless, if the public at large retained anything of what appeared in travel literature, it would incline them to see some elements of ancient truths and natural reason in Asian religions. They would also have learnt that many Asians showed evidence of personal piety and attempted to regulate their lives by high ethical standards. This would have commended them to eighteenth-century opinion. To an extent that would have been much less marked either in the seventeenth or in the nineteenth centuries, religions were judged by their social effects and the quality of life of their adherents. For many, how one lived could be as important as what one believed. Much store was set by sincerity both in Christians and non-Christians. Hypocrisy, failure to live up to one's principles, was a great fault. Mandarins who appeared to profess a high moral code, but who extorted wealth were bitterly condemned. Papists, Muslims or Hindus who worshipped with apparent sincerity and lived blameless lives were commended, however erroneous their belief might be.

If it was indeed the case that such parts of the eighteenth-century public as had any awareness of Asian religions were not unrelentingly hostile to them, there were obvious limits to this tolerance. Articulate British opinion remained solidly Christian. Christians might feel some indulgence towards non-Christian religions, but they could never put them on any sort of equality with Christianity. Deists and freethinkers who might have been willing to do so were losing influence in the second half of the eighteenth century. The number of Englishmen who voluntarily adopted an Asian religion seems to have been microscopic. One or two who had studied Hinduism were tempted to assimilate some of what they took to be its beliefs to Christianity.[123] Such attempts were not to gather any sort of momentum until changes in the religious climate of Britain brought some interest in mysticism and devotional cults as well as in rationalism and good works. Such changes were, however, peripheral by comparison with the reassertion of Christian fundamentalism, usually known as Evangelicalism, which became so potent by the end of the eighteenth century. Insistence on the funda-mentals of Christian belief inevitably brought with it a rather harsher attitude to non-Christian religions. It also provided the stimulus for a new and much more vigorous phase in Protestant missions from Britain to Asia.

Few Christians in Britain had ever denied that attempts to spread Christianity in Asia were at least theoretically desirable. For most of the eighteenth century, however, there was not much inclination to launch missions. The difficulties seemed to be overwhelming. Although Chardin had talked about religion to thousands of Asians, he had never known a genuine case of conversion by a Muslim or a 'gentile'. He concluded that such people would only change their religion as the result of direct divine intervention.[124] The translator of the *Ceremonies and Religious Customs of the Known World* agreed that the conversion of the Muslims 'must be the work of Heaven itself', and felt that the 'great and haughty kingdoms of the pagans in Asia' offered an equally unpromis-ing field: 'they have but very slender ideas of our power and learning; they are obstinately wedded to the institutions of their forefathers and wise men, under whom they have enjoyed great worldly happiness and grandeur; they are superlatively conceited of the brightness of their lights and understandings'. He considered that the example of Catholic missions operating in Asia was a discouraging one. He did not believe that the 'few ignorant though well meaning zealots, and crafty agents, which the Church of Rome sends among them' had made any impact on Asia.[125] Prejudice against Catholic missions seems to have been a real deterrent to imitating them. Catholics were thought either to accept nominal conversions or to impose conversion by force, when they had the chance, as with the Mexican and Peruvian Indians. Defoe dismissed 'the conversion as they call it, of the Chinese to Christianity' as 'so far from the true conversion required to bring heathen people to the faith of Christ, that it seems to amount to little more than letting them know the name of Christ, and to say prayers to the Virgin Mary and her son in a tongue which they understand not, and to cross themselves and the like'.[126] The Society for the Propagation of the Gospel were warned against attempting 'to regain the ground Christianity has lost' to Islam by resorting to 'the most wicked arts of worldly policy, and by wars'.[127]

Nevertheless, a few English Protestants had been giving serious thought to missions to Asia since late in the seventeenth century. Humphrey Prideaux reported that Robert Boyle had tried to interest the East India Company in missions. He himself believed that 'since God hath by his providence' put the Indians in the Company's settlements 'under our government, he will require of us an account of their souls'. Schools and churches should be set up. 'I confess we have work enough at home, God Almighty help us; but this is no sufficient reason, when an opportunity is offered to serve Him elsewhere for us to neglect it'.[128] A beginning was made in 1710. The Society for Promoting Christian Knowledge began to pay subsidies to the German Lutheran missions operating under Danish auspices in southern India. A sum averaging £360 a year, including income from an estate left 'many years ago, to propagate the Gospel in the East-Indies' was paid to them.[129] This sum had risen to about £1000 a year by the 1770s. A running total of converts was reported to the Society; in 1774 over 2,000 were claimed at Madras.[130]

The military victories won overseas in the mid-eighteenth-century wars stimulated calls for a more active missionary policy. 'A new field is now open to our labour. By the blessing of God and his Majesty's arms, it stretches itself to the utmost parts of the globe. Our armies have gone before us; they have made the most distant countries accessible to our missionaries.'[131] If the British continued to leave 'the miserable inhabitants to perish in their idolatry, without pity and without remorse', God might 'take from you all these extensive conquests'.[132] Missions to India were specifically enjoined.[133] But the first British missionary was not sent to join the Germans until 1788, and he only remained at his post for a short time. Whatever might be said in sermons, the official policy of the East India Company remained deeply suspicious of missions. It was thought that they would antagonize the Indian population and pose an unnecessary hazard to the Company's still fragile hold on its new provinces. Clauses to a bill in 1793, which would have compelled the Company to see to the 'religious and moral improvement' of India and to appoint suitable men as 'school masters, missionaries or otherwise' were defeated. The arguments used against them were traditional ones. Charles Fox described 'all systems of proselytism as wrong in themselves, and as productive in most cases of political mischief'.[134] In the same year when Lord Macartney arrived in Peking, he told his Chinese hosts that the English were not like other Europeans, 'being persuaded that the Supreme Governor of the Universe was equally pleased with the homage of all His creatures when proceeding from sincere devotion . . . One of the principal differences between us and them was our not having the same zeal for making proselytes which they had'.[135]

By 1793, however, new forces were gaining ground in British Protestantism, which did not consider that Asian peoples could be saved by 'sincere devotion' alone and which were prepared to use more formidable weapons of political persuasion than annual sermons. The 1790s were a crucial decade in British missionary history. The old-established Anglican Society for Promoting Christian Knowledge and its offshoot, the Society for the Propagation of the Gospel, were being joined by dynamic new societies drawn from Evangelical Anglicanism, Methodism and Dissent. The new societies inevitably looked to Asia, where their aid was being sought by Evangelically minded Company servants in Bengal.[136] A group of Baptists were the first to take up the task. Drawing support from comparatively humble sections of British society, such as the Northamptonshire artisan, William Carey, who was one of the first missionaries, the Baptists began operations on a very small scale in Bengal in 1793.

The growth of Christian missions introduced an important new dimension into British awareness of Asia. Missionaries developed contacts with Asian people that were in many respects different from those of administrators and businessmen. They were obliged to study Asian institutions and languages to a depth often beyond that attained by others. They also became important channels through whom knowledge about Asia was publicized at home. Whatever may be thought of the quality of material in them, missionary letters, magazines and tracts were aimed at a mass audience. Many nineteenth-century men, women and children came to see the world through missionary eyes.

NOTES

1 F. E. Manuel, *The Eighteenth Century Confronts the Gods* (Cambridge, Mass., 1959), pp. 6–7.
2 F. Caron, *A True Description of the Mighty Kingdoms of Japan and Siam*, ed. C. R. Boxer (1935), p. 42.

3 Cited in R. W. Frantz, *The English Traveller and the Movement of Ideas* (reprint New York, 1968), p. 144.
4 See above, p. 14.
5 Reprinted in *Four Treatises Concerning the Doctrine, Discipline and Worship of the Mahometans* (1712), p. 181.
6 *Ibid.*, p. 79.
7 *De Vita et Rebus Gestis Mohammedis* (Oxford, 1723); *La Vie de Mahomet*, 2 vols (Amsterdam, 1732).
8 *Vie de Mahomet*, i, pp. cvi, xlii.
9 *The Koran, commonly called the Alcoran of Mohammed* (1734), Dedication.
10 3rd edn. (1744–6), i. 397.
11 *Of the Mahometan Religion, Two Books . . . from the Latin of Adrian Reeland* (1712), p. 13.
12 *Four Treatises Concerning the Mahometans*, p. 181.
13 *The Koran*, Discourse, p. 61.
14 'Letter of Rusticus' in vol. xxiii (1753), 271.
15 'Of the Standard of Taste', *Philosophical Works*, ed. T. H. Green and T. H. Grose (1882), iii. 267–8.
16 *Essai sur les moeurs*, ed. R. Pomeau (Paris, 1963), i. 257.
17 *Decline and Fall of the Roman Empire*, ed. J. B. Bury (1896–1900), v. 337.
18 *Works of Sir William Jones* (1806), v. 523.
19 *Travels through Arabia and other countries in the East* (Edinburgh, 1792), ii. 184.
20 *A Faithful Account of the Religion and Manners of the Mahommetans*, 2nd edn. (Exeter, 1734), Preface.
21 R. M. Wiles, *Serial Publication in England before 1750* (Cambridge, 1957), p. 44.
22 *The Complete Letters of Lady Mary Wortley Montagu*, ed. R. Halsband (Oxford, 1965–7), i. 318.
23 *A Journey from Bengal to England* (1798), ii. 48–9.
24 *Sermon Preached before the Incorporated Society for the Propagation of the Gospel . . . by the Bishop of Lichfield* (1788), pp. xii–xiii; J. White, *Sermon on the Duty of Attempting to Propagate the Gospel . . . in India* (1785), p. 32.
25 See above, p. 12.
26 This point is made in V. Pinot, *La Chine et la formation de l'esprit philosophique en France 1640–1740* (Paris, 1932), p. 309.
27 On him see R. Schwab, *La Renaissance orientale* (Paris, 1950); J. Chaybany, *Les Voyages en Perse et la pensée française au xviiie siècle* (Paris, 1971).
28 Jones, *Works*, iv. 588–9.
29 *Sermon Preached before the Incorporated Society for the Propagation of the Gospel . . . by the Bishop of Norwich* (1790), p. 7.
30 For translations of collections of Jesuit letters, see above, p. 83. For the Lutherans, see *Several Letters relating to the Protestant Danish Missions at Tranquebar in the East Indies* (1720); *An Account of the Religion, Manners and Learning of the People of Malabar*, trans. J. T. Philipps (1717).
31 'A Description of the Country of Tranquebar', *Gentleman's Magazine*, xv (1745), 144–5.
32 Reprinted in P. J. Marshall, *The British Discovery of Hinduism in the Eighteenth Century* (Cambridge, 1970).
33 *Ibid.*, p. 194.
34 *Ibid.*, p. 215.
35 *An Historical Disquisition concerning the Knowledge which the Ancients had of India*, 2nd edn. (1794), p. 322.
36 *A Comparison of the Institutions of Moses with those of the Hindoos* (Northumberland, 1799), pp. 156–7.
37 Marshall, *Discovery of Hinduism*, p. 238.
38 L. Scrafton, *Reflections on the Government of Indostan*, 2nd edn. (1770), p. 16.

39 Niebuhr, *Travels*, ii. 420.
40 G. Forster, *Sketches of the Mythology and Customs of the Hindoos* (1785), p. 59.
41 *Speeches of the Managers and Counsel in the Trial of Warren Hastings*, ed. E. A. Bond (1859–61), i. 37.
42 *A Comparison*, pp. 130–4.
43 *Modern Geography* (1802), ii. 255, 258.
44 Marshall, *Discovery of Hinduism*, pp. 105, 158.
45 *Travels of Several Learned Missionaries of the Society of Jesus* (1714), p. 12.
46 Scrafton, *Reflections*, pp. 3–5.
47 The essay is reprinted in Marshall, *Discovery of Hinduism*, pp. 262–90.
48 Discussed in P. J. Marshall, 'Warren Hastings as Scholar and Patron', in *Statesmen, Scholars and Merchants*, ed. A. Whiteman, J. S. Bromley and P. Dickson (Oxford, 1973), pp. 246–8.
49 Scrafton, *Reflections*, p. 18.
50 Evidence to Select Committee of House of Commons, 1781, *Reports from Committees of the House of Commons* (1806–8), v. 37.
51 H. B. Morse, *Chronicles of the East India Company trading to China* (1926–9), v. 117–18.
52 T. Pennant, *Outlines of the Globe* (1798–1800), iii. 92. For confusions about these books, see R. Etiemble, 'De la pensée chinoise aux "Philosophes" français', *Revue de Littérature Comparée*, xxx (1956), 467–8.
53 It was originally entitled *Memoirs and Observations . . . made in a late journey through the Empire of China*.
54 See above, p. 83.
55 *General History of China* (1736 edn.), ii. 1–2, iii. 15–16.
56 Vol. i. 29.
57 Vol. iii (1759), 655 ff.
58 *Philosophical Transactions of the Royal Society*, xxxvi (1729–30), 403.
59 *Ibid.*, xliv (1746–7), 478–9.
60 *Ibid.*, xlviii (1753), 309–13.
61 Eg. S. Watson, 'Observations on Voltaire's Account of China', *Gentleman's Magazine*, xxviii (1758), 59–60.
62 *Works*, i. 98–108.
63 *General History*, iii. 15–17.
64 *Ibid.*, iii. 293–8.
65 *Ibid.*, ii. 162 ff.
66 Eg. Salmon, *Modern History*, i. 26–7; *Modern Part of the Universal History*, iii (1759), 499–500.
67 See above, p. 81.
68 Vols i. 156 *n*, 163 *n*, ii. 51 *n*.
69 J. Spence, *Anecdotes of Books and Men*, ed. J. M. Osborn (Oxford, 1966), i. 299.
70 *An Embassy to China*, ed. J. L. Cranmer-Byng (1962), pp. 233–4.
71 *Travels in China*, 2nd edn. (1806), pp. 457, 460, 486.
72 *Ibid.*, p. 422.
73 On early western views of Buddhism, see H. de Lubac, *La Rencontre du Bouddhisme et de l'occident* (Paris, 1952), pp. 49–104.
74 J. Lockman, *Travels of the Jesuits into Various Parts of the World*, 2nd edn. (1762), i. 58.
75 L. Le Comte, *A Complete History of the Empire of China* (1739 edn.), p. 326.
76 *General History*, iii. 50.
77 *Sramana Gautama*, 'the ascetic Gautama', H. Yule and A. C. Burnell, *Hobson-Jobson* (1968 reprint), p. 366.
78 *An Historical Relation of the Island of Ceylon* (1681), p. 72.
79 *History of Japan* (1728), i. 36.
80 *A General Dictionary, Historical and Critical* (1734–41), ix. 350 *n*.
81 *Relation of Siam*, pp. 125–9.

82 *An Account of an Embassy to the Kingdom of Ava* (1800).

83 Marshall, *Discovery of Hinduism*, pp. 272–3.

84 See above, p. 88.

85 C. R. Markham, *Narratives of the Missions of George Bogle to Tibet and of Thomas Manning to Lhasa* (1876), p. 10.

86 See above, p. 89.

87 J. Trusler, ed., *The Habitable World Described* (1788–97), ii. 246, 259.

88 J. S. Georgi, *Russia: or a Compleat historical account of all the Nations which compose that Empire*, trans. W. Tooke (1780–3), iii. 295–6.

89 *Modern Part of the Universal History*, ii (1759), 259.

90 'Alciphron, or the Minute Philosopher', *Works of George Berkeley* (Oxford, 1871), ii. 36, 51.

91 M. Foucault, *The Order of Things* (1970).

92 Cited in Marshall, *Discovery of Hinduism*, p. 145.

93 'Natural History of Religion', *Philosophical Works*, iv. 309.

94 *Embassy to Ava*, p. 133.

95 'Alciphron', Berkeley, *Works*, ii. 267.

96 *Sermon Preached before the Incorporated Society for the Propagation of the Gospel* . . . by the Bishop of St David's (1759), p. 11.

97 E. Iversen, *The Myth of Egypt and its Hieroglyphs in European Tradition* (Copenhagen, 1961), p. 60.

98 Pinot, *La Chine et l'esprit philosophique*, pp. 350–66.

99 See above, pp. 102–3.

100 *The Life and Times of Anthony Wood*, ed. A. Clark (Oxford, 1891–1900), iii. 236.

101 Lockman, *Travels of the Jesuits*, ii. 272.

102 'A True and Exact Description of the Most Celebrated East India Coasts', *A Collection of Voyages and Travels*, ed. A. and J. Churchill (1745 edn.), iii. 745.

103 C. Wessels, *Early Jesuit Travellers in Central Asia 1603–1721* (The Hague, 1924); Du Halde, *General History*, iv. 188.

104 *Memoirs of the Author of Indian Antiquities* (1819–20), pt. iii. 98–9.

105 P. M. Holt, *A Seventeenth-century Defender of Islam: Henry Stubbe and his Book* (1972).

106 *Vie de Mahomed*, pp. 242–5.

107 *Essai sur les moeurs*, i. 272.

108 *Ibid.*, i. 220.

109 Cited in W. W. Appleton, *A Cycle of Cathay* (New York, 1951), p. 50.

110 *Essai sur les moeurs*, i. 61, ii. 915–16.

111 *Sermon Preached before the Incorporated Society for the Propagation of the Gospel* . . . by the Bishop of Norwich (1790), p. 9.

112 *Sermons Preached before the University of Oxford*, 2nd edn. (1785), p. 404.

113 *A Comparison*, p. 157.

114 'Alciphron', Berkeley, *Works*, ii. 265.

115 *Essai sur les moeurs*, i. 66–7.

116 Marshall, *Discovery of Hinduism*, pp. 32–3.

117 *Ibid.*, pp. 35–7.

118 *Letters on the Study and Use of History* (1752), pt. i. 95–6, 104, 118.

119 *Philosophical Works*, iv. 361.

120 In 7 vols (1733–9), iv, p. iii.

121 *Philosophical Works*, iv. 315.

122 *Historical Disquisitions*, pp. 305–19.

123 A case is examined in R. Rocher, 'Alien and emphatic: the Indian poems of N. B. Halhed', in *The Age of Partnership: Europeans in Asia before Dominion*, ed. B. B. Kling and M. N. Pearson (Honolulu, 1979), pp. 215–35.

124 *Voyages en Perse* (Amsterdam, 1735), iii. 434.

125 Vol. iv, pp. vi–vii.

126 *The Farther Adventures of Robinson Crusoe*, ed. G. A. Aitken (1905), p. 246.
127 *Sermon Preached before the Incorporated Society for the Propagation of the Gospel . . . by* John Denne (1730), p. 64.
128 *The Life of the Reverend Humphrey Prideaux* (1748), pp. 152–71.
129 *An Account of the Origins and Designs of the Society for Promoting Christian Knowledge* (1737), pp. 5–6.
130 *Ibid.* (1774), pp. 72, 105.
131 *Sermon Preached before the Incorporated Society for the Propagation of the Gospel . . .* by the Bishop of Oxford (1762), p. 16.
132 Letter in *Gentleman's Magazine*, xxxvii (1767), 152.
133 White, *Sermon on the Duty of Attempting the Propagation of the Gospel*; *Sermon Preached before the Incorporated Society for the Propagation of the Gospel . . .* by the Bishop of Lincoln (1786), p. 22.
134 *Sketch of the Debate in the House of Commons on . . . May 25, 1793* (1793), p. 42.
135 *Embassy to China*, ed. Cranmer-Byng, p. 167.
136 A. T. Embree, *Charles Grant and British Rule in India* (1962), pp. 118–20.

5

Asia and the Progress of Civil Society

By the seventeenth century a tradition of dividing the world into continents to which separate identities were attributed was deeply rooted in European thought about geography. Improbable as it might seem that a huge diversity of peoples over an immense area had significant features in common, this did not deter searches for what were regarded as the characteristics of 'eastern', 'oriental', or Asian peoples. Nearly all European commentators agreed that the distinguishing feature that they had in common above all others was imperviousness to change. Asians were intensely conservative. They never adopted new ideas or new practices. Thus descriptions of Asian peoples in the Bible or by the Greeks were virtually identical with those given by contemporary travellers.

What came to be regarded as the most authoritative statement about Asian changelessness in the late seventeenth century occurred in the Preface to the *Travels* of the revered Chardin.

> It is not in Asia as in our Europe, where there are frequent changes more or less, in the forms of things, as the habits, buildings, gardenings and the like. In the East they are constant in all things; the habits are at this day in the same manner, as in the precedent ages; so that one may reasonably believe, that in that part of the world, the exteriour forms of things (as in their manners and customs) are the same now, as they were two thousand years since, except in such changes as may have been introduced by religion, which are nevertheless very inconsiderable.[1]

Chardin's opinion that Islam had introduced only 'inconsiderable' changes in the peoples of the Middle East was that of most seventeenth-century writers. The Arabs of the deserts in particular were thought to be embalmed specimens of a remote past still living in the present. 'The customs, manners and genius of the Arabs, except in matters of religion, are in effect the same at this day that they were betwixt three and four thousand years ago.'[2] Arabic was often cited as an example of the way in which Asian languages remained static. Whereas European languages changed and developed so that the usage of one age ceased to be that of another, Chardin said that the Arabic of the Koran was still the model for correct speaking in contemporary Arab countries.[3] The Turks were accepted to be a relatively new people to the Middle East, but they, too, were thought scrupulously to pre-serve the ancient characteristics which they had brought with them from their original homeland. They were Scythians from the wastes of central Asia and so 'severity, violence and cruelty' remained their dominant characteristics.[4] Belief in the intense conservatism of the Jews reinforced beliefs that the peoples of the Middle East did not change.

All seventeenth-century accounts of the Hindus stressed that they clung to the past with the utmost tenacity. They 'are desirous to do, and to believe as their ancestors have before them; to fare as they have fared, and as they have sped to speed'.[5] They were thought not 'to have advanced one footstep from the false rudiments either of religion or customs of the old world'.[6] 'Their difference in washings, meates, drinkes, and such like arise rather from the tradition of their fathers enjoyned to their posteritie.'[7] Bernier added his imprimatur to conven-tional wisdom when he stated that neither the language nor the beliefs of the Hindus had changed since ancient times.[8]

The Chinese were believed to be another intensely conservative people. Du Halde summed up the verdicts of all Jesuit writers when he stressed that the Chinese strictly observed 'order, and the ancient customs' and firmly repressed any 'troubles and commotions which are commonly caused by the love of novelty, to which the vulgar are but too much inclin'd'.[9] The whole Chinese social and political system was said to be based on reverence for age and attempts to adhere to the past. Children obeyed their parents; all revered their ancestors. The duty of the government was to prevent deviation. Thus China 'continues still, like a great river that never ceases rolling along the streams that fall from its first fountain'.[10]

Those late seventeenth-century writers who tried to explain why Asian peoples did not change usually suggested environmental factors, especially climatic ones. The effect of terrain and climate on the behaviour of men had greatly interested Aristotle and many other classical writers. Such speculations were to be revived in the sixteenth century, notably by Jean Bodin.[11] Bodin specifically considered the differences between those who lived in 'northern', 'southern' or 'temp-erate' climates. The heat of the south tended to make men slothful and conservative. This was applied to Asia by the English geographers of the seventeenth century, Nathanael Carpenter and Peter Heylyn. Car-penter described southerners as 'obstinate and perverse in standing to their own propositions'. He gave as examples the refusal of the Indians and 'the Chinois' to change 'a platforme of religious discipline', 'once settled'.[12] Heylyn, who had elaborate theories about the influence of 'heavenly bodies' on particular parts of the world, argued that when vigorous northern peoples such as the Turks, the Tartars or the Greeks invaded southern Asia they, too, became 'effeminate'.[13] Chardin's explanations were similar. 'The climate of each people is always as I believe, the principal effect of the inclinations and customs of the men, which are no more different among them than that the temper of the air is different from one place to another.'[14] In Asia 'the hot climates enervate the mind as well as the body' and so Asians were incapable of intellectual exertion; they were content with knowledge that is 'so restrained that it consists only in learning and repeating what is contain'd in the books of the ancients . . . 'Tis in the north only that we must look for the highest improvement and the greatest perfection in the arts and sciences'.[15] La Loubère, another admired French authority, generalized from his experiences in Siam that the climate also rendered Asians unfit for exertion in war. 'The over-quick imagination of the excessive hot countries, is not more proper for courage . . . I say moreover, that every one born in the Indies is without courage; although he is born of European parents . . . The best constituted men are those of the temperate zones.'[16]

Important as it was considered to be, environment alone was usually not thought a sufficient explanation of Asian constancy in old ways by writers of the later seventeenth century. The effect of governments must also be taken into account. If the Jesuits were to be believed, the stability of all things Chinese was in large measure due to a carefully contrived policy enforced by the imperial authorities from age to age. Elsewhere in Asia, the despotic nature of Asian government, regarded as almost universal, appeared to be a powerful force against change. To men like Chardin and Bernier despotism stifled change, because it killed all incentive to improvement in the cultivation of land, in manufacturing, in art or in thought. They believed that the individual's quest for his own advantage was the engine of improvement throughout the world. But individuals would only seek their own advantage in conditions of security. Despotism destroyed security. No man could protect the fruits of his labour from a rapacious state. There was no point in taking risks to improve farming, manufacturing or trade; the rewards would simply fall into the maw of the government. Rich men would be rare and those that were rich could not afford to appear so by encouraging the arts of graceful living. Without patronage craftsmen would not work. There was not even any incentive for individuals to acquire learning. The learned went unrewarded; all preferment was given at the whim of the ruler to sycophants. In a society ruled by a despot no one ventured to put his head over the parapet. All remained sunk in fearful sloth and apathy. Islam was thought to reinforce the deadening effects of despotism. Everywhere that it became established it created 'sloth and idleness, and the neglect of every art and science . . . They discourage every attempt towards the advancement of learning, which might shew the absurdity of the maxims they are governed by'.[17]

Europeans were well aware that at a certain level the history of Asia was one of rapid and violent change. By the end of the seventeenth century all the great empires had been shaken by the struggles for the throne, while China had been convulsed in mid-century by the Manchu conquest. But it was believed that this instability was merely superficial. Whatever happened to rulers, the framework of society, institutions and ideas were unshakeable. This vast tableau of peoples supposedly set in an unchanging mould was, second only to the diversity of religions, the Asian phenomenon which attracted most attention.

The contrast with Europe seemed to be glaring. Educated Englishmen in the late seventeenth century did not believe that they lived in a society immune from fundamental change. They, too, had experienced dynastic upheaval and internal conflict between 1640 and 1660 and again in 1688; but changes seemed to go much deeper. The social hierarchy, institutions and beliefs all seemed to be in flux. There was a new awareness of economic forces and they were discussed in a new way.[18] To many the economic basis of society seemed to be shifting rapidly. Those who had been assured of a dominant position in the past now seemed to be threatened. There was much discussion of this at the time of the Civil War and again in the 1690s and the early decades of the eighteenth century, when old landed families and even well-established mercantile interests were thought to be going down before the rise of the financial manipulators, the war-mongering generals and company promoters. To some the constitution, defended so successfully in 1688, seemed to be in danger from an increasingly powerful executive able to spread corruption. The willingness of men to be corrupted was symptomatic of increasing love of luxury and the decline of old civic virtues. The Church of England had beaten off the attacks of Popery, but it was now besieged by Dissent and by freethinkers. The 'ancients' were trying to defend traditional sound learning against the experimental methods of the 'moderns'.

Many faced the prospect of change with equanimity, believing in improvement: greater knowledge of the universe and of the ways of man, more political and religious liberty, economic growth and opportunities for individual advancement. Others were far from optimistic. Expectations of progress in human affairs or even in nature were still

alien to some men with a classical upbringing. Deterioration or cycles
of relative improvement followed by deterioration were what they
expected. To some who thought like this Britain at the end of the
seventeenth and beginning of the eighteenth century was showing
unmistakable signs of decline. The debate between this disaffected
minority of pessimists and the increasingly dominant largely Whig
orthodoxy of optimists after 1688 gave a particular slant to interpretations of Asia in Britain.[19] In France admiration for Asia was usually a
polemical weapon used by reformers and radicals, whose praise for
supposedly rational Asian systems of belief and well ordered societies
was well understood to imply criticism of obscurantism and misgovernment in Europe. In Britain deists and other critics of religious
orthodoxy used Asia in the same way, if usually with very much less of
the stridency that marked attacks on the Church in France.[20] But on
social and political issues the most vocal critics in early eighteenth-
century Britain were not reformers; they were outraged conservatives.
In as far as it was used at all, Asia was the weapon of the traditionalists
not of the radicals. Thus it was the supposed Asian constancy in ancient
ways rather than Asia as a model for a more rational ordering of life that
featured in polemics. So long as the debate between tradition and
change continued, Asian imperviousness to change would find at least
a few British admirers. But as modernity and optimism triumphed
almost completely by the middle of the eighteenth century, peoples who
were thought to be unchanging stood more and more condemned.

At the end of the seventeenth century Sir William Temple was the
most obvious example of a self-confessed 'ancient', deeply sceptical
about the achievements of his own age and the prospects of progress,
who admired the ancient civilizations of Asia. In his 'Essay of Ancient
and Modern Learning' Temple argued that not only were contemporary 'moderns' in no way obviously superior to the ancients of Europe,
but that behind the European ancients were even more venerable and
splendid civilizations, those of India and China. 'For whoever observed
the account already given of the ancient Indian and Chinese learning
and opinions will easily find among them the seeds of all those Grecian
productions and institutions.'[21] Not only was it the source of learning
on which modern Europe had yet to improve, but in his essay 'Of
Heroic Virtue' Temple argued that China had kept its pristine excellence to a remarkable extent in a world prone to deterioration. China
was 'the greatest, richest and most populous kingdom now known in
the world'. Chinese practice excelled 'the very speculations of other
men, and all those imaginary schemes of the European wits . . . the
Utopias, or Oceanas of our modern writers'.[22]

To a modern scholar of imperial China, Temple's great disciple,

Swift, with his reverence for the ancients against the moderns, his 'vast preference for the humanities over the natural sciences' and his 'patrician uneasiness with material utility as the touchstone of value', seemed to have very close affinities with Confucian culture.[23] Although overt references to China or any other Asian society are relatively few in Swift's writings, a persuasive case has recently been made for suggesting that the more admirable characteristics of the Houyhnhnms and some of those of Lilliput in *Gulliver's Travels* are in fact thinly disguised references to China as it had been depicted by Temple.[24] In a short piece published in 1738 and attributed in part at least to the young Samuel Johnson, another critic of Whig orthodoxy, the reader is told that he will 'find a calm, peaceful satisfaction when he reads the moral precepts and wise instructions of the Chinese sages' and unflattering comparisons are made with the England of Walpole.[25]

On the other hand, English readers of Chardin and of Bernier, who did so much to popularize ideas of Asian changelessness, were left in no doubt that change was the natural expectation of man. Failure to change in Asia was not an admirable constancy but was stagnation. Defoe, who has been seen as the embodiment of 'the restless desire to tinker with and change society and nature',[26] agreed with them. He could not share Temple's or Swift's admiration for the Chinese. They were 'a contemptible herd or crowd of ignorant, sordid slaves, subjected to a government qualified only to rule such a people'.[27] Much more of this was to be heard in the years ahead.

New knowledge about Asia gathered during the second half of the eighteenth century generally seemed to reinforce belief in the conservatism of Asians. It became a received truth from which it was safe to begin much speculating and theorizing. 'That their customs in general remain unaltered . . . is a fact that admits of no doubt', wrote one scholar; he had read a '*multitude* of writers' who had told him that.[28] 'The modern description of India is a repetition of the ancient and the present state of China is derived from a distant antiquity to which there is no parallel in the history of mankind', Adam Ferguson wrote in his *Essay on the History of Civil Society*, one of the pioneering social studies of the Scottish Enlightenment.[29] To John Richardson, the orientalist who moved from Scotland to Oxford, author of *Dissertation on the Languages, Literature and Manners of Eastern Nations*, 'the least attention to oriental manners will clearly show, that the characteristic habits of these people, even at this hour, are in every respect, similar to the most remote accounts.'[30]

By the second half of the eighteenth century the contrast between an apparently stagnant Asia and modern Europe seemed to be even more marked than it would have been fifty years or so earlier. That Britain was a society undergoing rapid change was now universally accepted, but anxieties about the consequences of change seemed to be much less pronounced than they had once been. This did not necessarily mean that Englishmen of the reign of George III were facile optimists about human conditions or the life of the individual; but relatively few men seem to have believed that British society and institutions were deteriorating or that the ancients or even previous generations had been wiser than contemporaries were. The future was not without danger: men might become effete and corrupt and the constitution might be subverted. But such eventualities were by no means inevitable. That an era of decay should follow an era of improvement was not thought to be in the nature of things; it would be the consequence of human weakness and error. If men conducted their affairs properly, further increases in human knowledge and material well-being could confidently be expected. In the past, when some at least feared the future, societies, like those of Asia, which were supposed to cling obstinately to the ways and wisdom of their forebears might seem to have some merit; now they seemed merely to be deliberately forgoing the normal human expectation of progress.

In the second half of the eighteenth century there was a marked tendency to categorize societies on a scale according to the amount of progress they had in fact realized. This was particularly the interest of the social philosophy of the Scottish Enlightenment as studied at Edinburgh or Glasgow, by David Hume, Adam Smith, John Millar, William Robertson, Adam Ferguson and the lawyer, Lord Kames. Serious-minded writers of travel books also played the game of putting societies into categories. John Barrow, for instance, began his book on China with the statement that he hoped to 'enable the reader to settle, in his own mind, *the point of rank China may be considered to hold in the scale of civilized nations*'.[31] William Marsden included in his *History of Sumatra* a division of peoples into five 'classes', from 'the refined nations of Europe' down to the Caribs, the inhabitants of New Holland, the Laplanders and Hottentots, 'who exhibit a picture of mankind in its rudest and most humiliating aspect'.[32] Few writers, if any, would have disagreed with those he placed at the top and the bottom. Asian societies would come somewhere in between. Some, like the Tartars or the Arabs of the desert, would be put low down on the scale. They were thought to be nomads who had made little attempt to subjugate nature and to organize political life beyond a rudimentary level. The peoples of the Near East, the Persians, Indians and Chinese were much more difficult to place. Interestingly, Marsden thought that the Chinese should perhaps be put on the same level as the 'highest' European states. Other writers put them lower. By most contemporary standards the great Asian states were undoubtedly 'civilized'. It was recognized that in the past some of them had actually been more 'polished' than any European society. But their lack of development told against them. The Chinese were a particularly puzzling case. China to Adam Smith had 'been long one of the richest, that is, one of the most fertile, best cultivated, most industrious and most populous countries in the world. It seems, however, to have been long stationary'.[33] Hume felt that the Chinese had 'a pretty considerable stock of politeness and science', which might have been 'expected to ripen into something more perfect and finished than has yet arisen from them'.[34] 'From the middle to the end of the sixteenth century, compared with Europe in general', wrote Barrow, China 'had greatly the superiority, if not in science, then at least in arts and manufactures, in the conveniencies and luxuries of life. The Chinese were, at that period, pretty much in the same state in which they still are; and in which they are likely to continue.' He went on to make a comparison between China and Russia. At first sight their conditions seemed to be very similar, but while the one, Russia, 'is in a state of youthful vigour, advancing daily in strength and knowledge; the other is worn out with old age and disease'.[35] Lord Macartney concluded that, 'whilst we have been every day rising in arts and sciences, they are actually become a semi-barbarous people in comparison with the present nations of Europe'.[36] Whatever point on the scale of nations Asian peoples had reached, there they had stuck, if anything slipping back rather than progressing further.

Stagnant societies must be made up of stagnant individuals. W. G. Browne, who travelled in the Levant in the 1790s, wrote that 'impatience, activity and sanguine hope are the habits of an European. . . . The habits of the Oriental on the contrary, are indolence, gravity, patience. His ideas are few in number and his sentiments in course equally rare.'[37] 'Continually seated, they pass whole days musing, with their legs crossed, their pipes in their mouths, and almost without changing their attitude. It should seem as if motion were a punishment to them', added Browne's French contemporary, Volney.[38] 'Almost their whole life is spent in idleness; to eat rice, drink water, smoke tobacco, sip coffee, is the life of a Mussulman', an earlier French authority had written.[39] Hindus were thought to be 'strangers to that vigor of mind, and all the virtues grafted on to those passions which animate our more active spirits'.[40] In Bengal a female traveller found that 'indolence . . . prevails, to such a degree as seems to absorb every faculty'.[41]

The difference between a vigorous, progressive Europe and a torpid, apathetic Asia presented an obvious challenge to the natural historians of man. Very few eighteenth-century writers were prepared to offer a racial explanation in the physiological sense for the different performances of Asian and European man. They were not assumed to be separate species with inherently different capacities. Any such assumption would encounter very serious obstacles. In the first place, separate species of men postulated separate acts of creation for which there was absolutely no authority in the Bible. On the contrary, the Bible made it clear that all men originated from a single source until the dispersal of the peoples after Babel. Even the Scottish philosopher, Lord Kames, who did believe that there were 'different species of men as well as of dogs',[42] was deterred by the force of Scripture from taking his arguments very far. It was even unusual for differences between Europeans and Africans to be attributed to separate racial origins.[43] To attempt to do so for differences between Asians and Europeans would encounter the additional difficulty that it was widely believed that secular as well as sacred history indicated that European man had originally come from Asia and was therefore closely related to Asian man. The Goths, the supposed ancestors of most northern European peoples, including those of the British Isles, were thought by many to have come from Tartary.[44] An Irishman, Colonel Vallancey, offered a variation of this theory in which he described the original inhabitants of Britain as what he called 'Persians or Indoscythae'.[45] William Jones seemed to be able to trace the earliest Europeans back to Asia with the firmest grounds of all in his studies of language. By 1786 he was able to point to the similarities in the structure of Sanskrit, Greek, Latin and even the 'Gothick' and 'Celtick' languages, which could not 'possibly have been produced by accident'. They must have had 'a common source'.[46] In a Discourse 'on the Origin and Family of Nations' of 1792 he stated that the Romans, the Greeks and the Goths could all be traced back to Asian roots not only through their languages but also through their religious beliefs. Three Asian peoples, the Indians, the Arabs and the Tartars, were the original peoples of the whole earth.[47]

Thus Genesis was powerfully reinforced. The peoples of the world had a common origin. Asians and Europeans were not separate species of men. Those who wished to explain their differences must look elsewhere. Environmental explanations, the effect of terrain and climate, already widely used in the later seventeenth century, gained in popularity. They were extensively used by Montesquieu in *The Spirit of the Laws*, a book which enjoyed immense prestige in England after it appeared in 1748.

To produce a vigorous progressive people, Montesquieu and those who thought like him argued that the environment should not be either bountifully favourable to human existence nor too bleakly hostile to it. If life was too easy, men would not struggle for improvement; if it was too difficult, they could make no progress whatever efforts they made. The deserts of Arabia or the tundra of Siberia were in themselves sufficient reason why their inhabitants had not climbed more than a few steps up the ladder of human progress. The Tartars had perhaps reached a step or two further. Montesquieu[48] and Ferguson[49] called them 'barbarians' rather than 'savages'. 'Barbarians' were defined as peoples capable of uniting under some kind of political rule, at least for a period, whereas 'savage' peoples always remained fragmented into small groups. But the political systems of the barbarians were temporary and rudimentary, incapable of maintaining a framework within which men could progress towards civilization. In the case of the Tartars' environment, an abundance of poor quality land was seen as the explanation of their lack of progress. Because of its high altitude, 'Tartary' was said to be too cold for effective corn-growing.[50] The people therefore remained pastoralists; 'chained to the shepherd-state', they could 'never advance to be husbandmen'.[51] The vast plains of central Asia meant that they had no need to form lasting settlements. John Bell recorded that in Mongolia 'there is not so much as a single house to be seen. All the people, even the prince and high priest, live constantly in tents; and remove with their cattle, from place to place, as conveniency requires.' So peripatetic a people could not be expected to progress. Bell believed that, 'Satisfied with necessaries, without aiming at superfluities, they pursue the most ancient and simple manner of life'.[52] Ferguson agreed: 'The unbounded plain is traversed at large by hordes, who are in perpetual motion, and who are displaced and harassed by mutual hostilities.' Proper human development required that men should live in settled communities in clearly demarcated areas.[53]

Montesquieu believed that the Asian environment tended to extremes. Men either lived in cold, barren conditions, as the Tartars did, or in hot, lush countries from the Middle East to China. There was no 'temperate' zone, as in Europe,[54] where men unhampered by extremes of hot and cold strove to improve lands of moderate fertility. For the great mass of Asians who lived in the torrid 'south', life was superficially easy. The land was fertile, producing crops with little effort. This was just as well, since the climate sapped men's vitality and made all effort a burden. Physical inertia was irresistible. Men became 'effeminate', a term repeatedly applied to Asians. Great heat produced mental inertia, too. There could be no curiosity, no enterprise, no generous sentiments, and therefore no intellectual progress. The mental powers of Asians were deeply influenced by the heat of the climate. They lacked the energy for sustained reasoning, but they had quick and fertile imaginations. Hence their poetry was without balance and proportion, although it was full of fanciful and luxurious images. This combination of imaginative sensitivity without intellectual rigour further inhibited change. Once they had formed an impression, Asians could not exert themselves to change it. So, Montesquieu concluded, everything about them is today as it was a thousand years ago.[55]

Environmental explanations for the supposed lack of progress in 'southern' Asian societies were widely accepted in late eighteenth-century England. The twelfth edition of Thomas Salmon's very popular *New Geographical and Historical Grammar*, revised by William Robertson in 1772, was characteristic.

> The warmth of these Eastern climates has doubtless ever contributed to the indolence and effeminacy of its inhabitants; it may be doubted whether they ever had the industry and active spirits of the inhabitants of Europe, who found the necessity of labour for their support, which the Asiatics had less occasion for, through the luxuriancy of their soil.[56]

Ferguson believed that the heat made men 'feverish in their passions, weak in their judgements, and addicted by temperament to animal pleasures'.[57] William Marsden considered that 'the limited progress of arts and sciences' in Asia could be attributed to the relative ease with which life could be sustained, which had eliminated 'the spring of importunate necessity'.[58] Those parts of India with which the British were becoming increasingly acquainted, especially Bengal, seemed to be a text-book illustration of the debilitating effect of a 'southern' Asian environment. Its heat and its fertility had reduced its people to an 'effeminacy and resignation of spirit, not to be paralleled in the world'.[59] The geographer, James Rennell, described the 'softness and effeminacy induced by the climate, and the yielding nature of the soil, which produces almost spontaneously'.[60] 'Breathing in the softest of climates', Robert Orme wrote, 'having so few wants and receiving even the luxuries of other nations with little labour from their own soil, the Indian must become the most effeminate inhabitant of the globe'.[61] In the case of India much was also made of one of the incidental consequences of environment, diet. Some diets, meat-eating and beer-drinking, for example, promoted energy; others, consuming rice and drinking water, sapped it.

For all their popularity, environmental explanations were obviously a very blunt instrument for explaining the characteristics of peoples as diverse as those of Asia. Montesquieu postulated two types of climate, 'northern' and 'southern'. Yet most travel books gave some indication of the immense variations within his northern and southern belts. For instance, John Richardson pointed out that people called Tartars lived in the legendary cities of Samarkhand and Bukhara and the fertile country surrounding them as well as on the northern steppes of Mongolia.[62] Even the most casual reader of Jesuit accounts could hardly fail to notice the great difference between the climate and terrain of northern and southern China. Environmental factors also seemed to give little help to those who wished to understand why Asia had lost its early lead in the arts and sciences. There was no evidence that the climate had changed. Baghdad had not enjoyed a temperate climate when it had been a great centre of learning under the Abbasid Caliphs. Some scholars were inclined to suggest that where improvement had taken place in Asia in the past it had been the work of vigorous northern invaders not as yet reduced to torpor by the climate. Jean Bailly produced an elaborate theory based on this supposition,[63] but it did not carry much conviction with contemporaries.

Most writers, including Montesquieu himself,[64] accepted that there were limits on too strict an interpretation of human development solely in environmental terms. William Falconer, in a book called *Remarks on the Influence of Climate* (and on a whole series of other environmental factors, too), warned that they could only be used to explain 'general', not 'particular' human characteristics.[65] David Hume in an essay 'Of National Characters' was one of many who challenged environmental determinism. He argued that what he called 'moral' factors seemed to assert themselves regardless of environment. By 'moral' factors he meant 'circumstances which are fitted to work on the mind', such as forms of government, religion, and what was commonly called 'education'. He used China as one of his examples. In climate and terrain China was very varied, yet he thought it had 'the greatest uniformity of character imaginable'.[66] Debate between those who stressed environmental influences and those who stressed moral ones was usually a matter of degree. There were few who were wholly committed to one or the other and there was little rigour about the arguments. Most writers chose to leave the issue open. Carsten Niebuhr's statement that 'Climate, government and education, are, undoubtedly, the great agents which form and modify the characters of nations'[67] was characteristically nebulous. So, too, was the *Universal History*'s attempt to explain the effeminacy of Asian peoples as 'chiefly owing to the warmth of the climate, though perhaps heightened by custom and education'.[68] Gibbon who thought that environment determined the character of 'barbarians', while 'moral causes' were more important for 'civilized nations'[69] was unusually precise over a matter on which contemporaries more and more came to believe that ultimate precision was hardly possible.

For nearly all writers the moral factor above all others which produced stagnation throughout Asia was a form of government, inevitably despotism. But whereas an earlier generation had accepted the existence of despotism everywhere in Asia as axiomatic, by the second half of the eighteenth century there was a minority prepared to contest this. Voltaire was the international patron of this minority. He insisted that despotism was much rarer in the world than was commonly supposed.[70] The usual definition of Asian despotism was that rulers were under no restraints, either from the need to obtain their subjects' consent to any of their actions or to adhere to any fixed law in their dealings with their subjects. The individual was without rights or security. Government was a matter of the ruler's whim. This, Voltaire insisted, was not even true of the Turks.[71] One of the leading British authorities agreed with him. Sir James Porter, who had been ambassador at Constantinople, believed that Turkish government was in fact 'much less despotic than the government of some Christian states'. Turkey was rather 'a species of limited monarchy'. The Koran established a 'code of law between prince and people', which was interpreted by the *Ulama*, not by the Sultan. In practice, no doubt, the Turkish government was riddled with abuses, but it was still intended to be a government according to law.[72] Any idea that Muslim states were governed without fixed laws was hardly compatible with the British experience of administering their new Indian provinces. The criminal law and part of the civil law in Bengal when the British conquered it was the law of Islam. To help inexperienced Englishmen supervise the courts legal texts were translated into English. In his Preface to one of these translations William Jones pointed out that subjects' rights to property were clearly guaranteed.[73]

Early British rule in India also made it clear that Hindus were a people with an ancient legal system. The first English version of Hindu law, a translation of a Code provided by Bengal pundits, appeared in 1776. It revealed elaborate provisions for the protection and inheritance of property. Translations from genuine legal texts, including the 'Laws of Manu', followed. How far rights to property, especially to property in land, had in fact been observed in India became matter for bitter controversy. Some of the East India Company's servants came to share the views which Bernier had done so much to publicize: Indian rulers, Hindu and Muslim, had overridden all private rights to land whenever they had seen fit, the implication being that the British might do likewise. Others denied this. Property rights had always been recognized. Edmund Burke was one of a number of those who had never been to India who joined in the fray. He feared that men like Warren Hastings were trying to construct a British oriental despotism in Bengal and denied that they had any historic right to do so. In Reports of parliamentary committees, speeches in the House of Commons and ultimately in charges against Hastings before the House of Lords, he insisted that Indian government had always been government according to law. Arbitrary power and seizure of the subject's property had no more sanction in the Indian tradition than they had in the British. From time immemorial Indians had possessed 'property moveable and immoveable, descendable property as well as occasional property, and property held for life'.[74]

The European verdict on Chinese government delivered in the seventeenth century was that it was a kind of regulated absolutism. The Emperor did not need to obtain the consent of his subjects to his decisions, but he did govern by fixed laws and through properly-constituted channels, even if his will was ultimately sovereign. Eighteenth-century Jesuit accounts made the same points. In the last edition of their reports to be translated into English, the Abbé Grosier's *General Description of China*, appearing in 1788, the Emperor was said to govern his people like a father. 'He is the undisputed master of the lives of his subjects; yet he seldom employs this prerogative but to provide for their safety and promote their happiness.'[75] This version remained acceptable to some English commentators. The geographer Pinkerton believed that, 'The Emperor is indeed absolute; but the examples of tyranny are rare, as he is taught to regard the people as his children and not his slaves.'[76]

An alternative version was, however, coming into fashion. Montesquieu believed that the missionaries were wrong and that China 'is a despotic state, whose principle is fear'.[77] Englishmen who went to China in 1793 agreed with him. Barrow thought that 'this fatherly care and affection in the governors, and filial duty and reverence in the governed, would with much more propriety, be expressed by the terms of tyranny, oppression and injustice in the one, and by fear, deceit and disobedience in the other'.[78] The laws were easily manipulated by those who administered them, giving the subject very little security. Lord Macartney recognized the existence of an 'ancient constitution', but considered that the government 'as it now stands is properly the tyranny of a handful of Tartars over three hundred millions of Chinese'.[79]

Whatever might be the case about China, information about Asian government in the second half of the eighteenth century was beginning to suggest a diverse pattern, so that generalization about oriental despotism should perhaps be treated with caution. British scholars, however, showed little caution. Voltaire's questioning of received wisdom won few adherents. A book by Anquetil Duperron, intended to refute theories with Asiatic despotism, was never translated into English.[80] Montesquieu was much more influential. He became the great exponent of the idea of Asiatic despotism to his contemporaries. 'Power in Asia ought then to be always despotic', he wrote. There was nothing in the history of Asia which suggested freedom; slavery would always flourish there.[81] Adam Ferguson wrote very much in the manner of Montesquieu. The 'calamity' of despotism had fallen on Asia, and 'the chains of perpetual slavery' were 'rivetted on the East'.[82] Lectures on Asian history were given in Edinburgh University in 1780. Such a topic was a bold innovation, but the theme of the lectures by John Logan was very stereotyped indeed. 'One form of government hath prevailed in Asia from the earliest records of history to the present time. A despot, under the name of Great King, or King of Kings, possesses supreme or unlimited power. . . . Sovereign and slave compose the only distinction of ranks in the East'.[83]

The connection between despotism and lack of development or progress in human societies was reaffirmed throughout the eighteenth century. The argument that despotism also stifled progress by destroying all those groups between the ruler and the mass of the people from whom exertion could be expected was given further emphasis. According to the great Scottish historian, William Robertson, 'It is the distinguishing and odious characteristic of the Eastern despotism, that it annihilates all other ranks of men, in order to exalt the monarch . . . Under the Turkish government, the political condition of every subject is equal.'[84] What seems to have been new in eighteenth-century discussions of the effects of despotism is a stress on the psychological damage wrought by it. Under despotism men were not fully men. The springs of creativity dried up. Montesquieu wrote that education under despotism was hardly necessary. The subject need only know enough to fear the ruler and adhere to the state religion.[85] The author of a section of the *Universal History* pointed out that: 'The indifference of the Asiatick nations under the Turkish empire with respect to virtue, their ignorance, and abject state of mind, are the necessary consequences of their form of government . . . The tyrant, to make use of arbitrary power with impunity, is forced to enervate the minds and the courage of his subjects . . . The property of despotic power is to silence the passions . . . Passions are necessary in a nation, and are its life and soul: the people who have the strongest are in the end triumphant.'[86] William Jones used a similar argument. Despotism invariably had the effect of 'benumbing and debasing all those faculties, which distinguish men from the herd, that grazes: and to that cause he would impute the decided inferiority of most Asiatick nations, ancient and modern, to those in Europe, who are blest with happier governments.'[87]

Nearly all writers linked religion with forms of government as the most important 'moral' influences on the character of nations. That

Islam inhibited change because it killed all desire to acquire new knowledge was still fervently believed throughout the eighteenth century. It was a point on which Oxford professors in Anglican orders, like Joseph White,[88] and French freethinkers, such as Volney, could agree. Volney thought that Islam was the greatest single reason for the 'ignorance of the people' in the Near East.[89] Among its other vices, Islam was thought to make the faithful believe in predestination. They therefore became fatalistic and would not exert themselves to master the forces of nature and improve human conditions. 'A bigotted predestinarian', the Turk 'resolves sickness or health, pleasure or pain, with all, even the most trifling incidents of life, into the mighty power and uncontrollable will of the Supreme Being.'[90] He was committed to 'fatality, and the absolute denial of the freedom of the human will'.[91]

Increased knowledge of India seemed to confirm earlier beliefs that Hindus were an intensely conservative people and that Hinduism itself was in large measure responsible for their aversion to change and progress. Many of the clichés of twentieth-century journalism about Hinduism as an obstacle to 'development' started their life in the eighteenth century. Hinduism was believed to enforce a rigid social system, which denied the possibility of personal advancement through individual effort. William Robertson regretted that caste divisions seemed 'to be adverse to improvement either in science or in arts' and to 'circumscribe the operations of the human mind within a narrower sphere than nature has allotted to them'.[92] On the other hand, on the evidence of the *Gita*, Robertson pointed out that Hinduism actually taught that 'man was formed, not for speculation or indolence, but for action'.[93] Conventional views were, however, against him on this point. Hindu values were thought to be other-worldly, teaching men the virtues of passivity and renunciation rather than energy and achievement. The pursuit of 'Abstraction from all sensible objects and the union of the soul with God', Priestley believed, 'ends in nothing but a stupid apathy and insensibility'.[94] 'Hindoo philosophy' was 'more fit for the visionary cell of the recluse, than to promote universal spirit and industry'.[95] Similar comments were made about Buddhism when it was identified.

The 'moral' causes for Chinese stagnation were less easy to define. The government was increasingly believed to be despotic and therefore to deny to individuals the security for persons and property that was necessary for improvement. On the other hand, there was no established religion and no persecution of opinion. Barrow was even surprised to find what he called a free press.[96] The values of the Chinese were not thought to be other-worldly, at least in practice; Thomas Percy considered that: 'A love of gain is so strongly impressed on the minds of the Chinese, and every thing in their situation and country contributes so much to inspire and feed it, that we must expect to find it predominant over all other considerations.'[97]

If China seemed at first sight to show some of the conditions thought necessary for human progress as Europeans understood it, its actual record of immobility suggested that there were serious obstacles, too. Conformity might not be enforced by religious establishments, censorship or government tyranny, but it was still enforced. Jesuits continued to write of that 'progressive submission, which rises gradually from the bosom of the family, even to the throne'.[98] Barrow believed that the 'moral sentiments and actions' of the Chinese were 'swayed by the opinions and almost under the entire dominion of the government'.[99] To the seventeenth-century Jesuits and indeed to seventeenth-century Englishmen, such voluntary submission of heart and mind to authority seemed admirable. It was the embodiment of patriarchy, that is of authority accorded to age and of political subordination on the model of the family.[100] To later eighteenth-century writers, however, the price to be paid for such social stability was much too high. Barrow's analysis is an interesting illustration of this. He may or may not have observed China with any perception, but he does reflect changing European views of the human personality. Barrow believed that outward submission and rigid conformity to established codes of behaviour were enforced in China at the expense of all natural human feelings, between husband and wife, parent and child, and in social life generally. The Chinese were therefore strangers to 'the happiest, the most interesting and sometimes also the most distressing moments of life'. Their children never behaved like children: 'A Chinese youth of the higher class is inanimate, formal, and inactive, constantly endeavouring to assume the gravity of years.'[101] A people in whom feeling and passion were repressed became sterile and uncreative. Other writers made similar points. Percy called Chinese 'customs, manners and notions . . . the most artificial in the world'.[102] Johann Reinhold Forster thought that 'the Chinese, in all their performances, show a very inferior and servile genius, without any spirit'.[103] Lord Kames considered that the Chinese were not likely to produce literature of distinction because they had 'little opportunity for exerting manly talents in their lives'.[104] The implication of all these comments was clear: only a society which allowed full play to the human spirit would progress. China was not such a society.

Concern for human passion and spontaneity in late eighteenth-century writing about Asia reflects a preoccupation that was apparently spreading through British upper-class society. This preoccupation has been called the cult of 'affective individualism'.[105] Individual happiness and self-fulfilment were in the first instance considered to be more important than subordination to larger groups. Happiness came through cultivating 'natural' feelings towards others rather than through imposed discipline and repression. But in the properly-developed individual, feelings would be kept under self-imposed restraint. A society composed of such individuals would in fact have greater strength and cohesion than would be the case in an authoritarian society. Secure in what was due to him, the fulfilled individual would voluntarily accept obligations to his family and to his fellow-citizens. Society thus rested on the solid basis of interlocking self-interests.

Asian societies were presumed to rest on a very different and much less secure basis. Proper individual development and therefore proper social development were virtually impossible in them. Despotic government, the tyranny of custom and religious bigotry all repressed natural feeling. Instead of the balance which the Englishman was to achieve between passion and voluntary restraint, the Asiatic alternated between lifeless conformity and unbridled indulgence. The contrast between Europe and Asia seemed to be most marked in sexual matters. To many Englishmen 'domestic affection' between husband and wife was becoming 'the prime legitimate goal in life'.[106] Sexual relations in Asia seemed utterly bleak by comparison. The point was repeatedly made. It is 'an invariable maxim', Barrow wrote, 'that the condition of the female part of society in any nation will furnish a tolerably just criterion of the degree of civilization to which that nation has arrived.' Where women are degraded, 'as is the case in all the despotic governments of the Asiatic nations, tyranny, oppression and slavery are sure to prevail'.[107] William Eton in his book on the Turkish empire wrote that, 'Much of the civilization of modern Europe has been with justice attributed to the influence of female society: to this are owing the high and noble passions which excite mankind to deeds of active patriotism and benevolence and the softer pleasures which ornament and endear the social circle.' The Turks, he thought, were 'barbarians; whose love is sensuality without friendship or esteem'.[108] John Malcolm wrote in the same vein about Iran. On 'the laws and customs which regulate the relative situation and intercourse of the sexes . . . perhaps, beyond all other causes, depends the moral state of a country, and its progress in general improvement.' Polygamy 'and the degrading usage of secluding the female sex, which Mahomed practised, have no doubt, had an influence scarcely secondary to any other cause, in retarding the progress of civilization among those races which have adopted his faith.'[109] In short, it was generally assumed that in Asia there was no middle ground between total repression and unrestrained indulgence, between the eunuch and the harem. Genuine feelings of love and affection were unknown.

Human relations in general seemed to follow a similar pattern throughout Asia. In their dealings with others Asians either showed meaningless formality or were openly domineering. Men either cringed as inferiors seeking to ingratiate themselves or lorded it as superiors harshly oppressing. Disinterested social intercourse among equals who took pleasure in one another's company was very rare indeed. To eighteenth-century Englishmen sociability and the interchange of unforced good feelings were a very important part of life. When they encountered it among Asians they commented on it with enthusiasm. Lord Macartney recorded with delight that some of the Chinese officials appointed to accompany his embassy eventually came 'to love us as individuals; . . . though in public ceremonious, in private they were frank and familiar. Tired of official formalities, they seemed often to fly to our society as a relief and to leave it with regret.'[110] There are indications that the desire for expression of what were taken to be natural feelings, for people who would be 'frank and familiar', was already inclining eighteenth-century Englishmen to value the apparently unsophisticated, the Tibetans, the hill tribes of eastern India or the Bedouins of the desert, and above all the Pacific islanders, rather than the élites of the Asian cities. There was natural virtue in simplicity, but behind the polished façade of the apparently inscrutable Hindu, Muslim or Chinese lurked cruelty, lust and avarice.

Sweeping conclusions were drawn from the personality deficiencies diagnosed in so many Asians. Both their art and their politics were the worse for them. Asian art had none of the balance which reflected a balanced personality. It gave way too easily to unrestrained voluptuousness and to over-imaginative imagery. On the other hand, a society in which natural sociability and mutual regard among individuals had not been allowed to develop was a society of mutually antagonistic atoms, only kept from injuring one another by fear of authority. Patriotism or public spirit could not exist. Asians were said to be 'men' but not 'citizens'. Minds 'depressed by despotism' could not 'embrace the idea of a common interest'.[111]

Cornelius de Pauw insisted that those who hoped to understand the 'character of nations' should examine 'modes of living' and 'rural economy' before they considered the traditional 'moral' factors, 'religion and government'.[112] There was in fact a strong school of British or, to be more exact, Scottish thinkers who agreed with him. By the middle of the eighteenth century they had devised what was essentially an economic scale by which to measure and compare the progress of nations. A number of writers began to argue along these lines in the

1750s, but the most coherent statements were made by Adam Smith.[113] In his lectures at Glasgow in 1762–3 Smith is recorded as having said: 'There are four distinct states which mankind pass thro: – 1st, the age of hunters, 2dly, the age of shepherds, 3dly, the age of agriculture; and 4thly, the age of commerce.'[114] Lord Kames had made a similar statement in 1758: 'Hunting and fishing in order for sustenance, were the original occupations of men. The shepherd life succeeded; and the next stage was that of agriculture. These progressive changes in the order now mentioned, may be traced in all nations, so far as we have any remains of their original history . . . it was agriculture which first produced a regular system of government.'[115] It became a common assumption that all societies passed through these stages or roughly similar ones. There could be no doubt that most European countries were by the eighteenth century well into Smith's 'age of commerce'. Equally, as later chapters will show, it seemed clear that the Indians of North America, most African peoples and those of the Pacific were at best in the second stage. This was also true of some Asians. Adam Smith thought that the Tartars and the Arabs remained pastoralists. What stage the Indians, the Chinese or the Turks had reached was much more problematic. Smith seems to have regarded them as commercial societies which had atrophied. 'In manufacturing art and industry', he wrote, 'China and Indostan, though inferior, seem not to be much inferior to any part of Europe'.[116] But he considered that China had become a 'stationary' economy in which the amount of labour available and 'the funds destined for maintaining it' seemed to remain perpetually at the same level, enabling the mass of the population to maintain a very low standard of subsistence. He implied that the reasons for this state of stasis were 'moral' ones. Many centuries ago China had probably 'acquired that full complement of riches which the nature of its laws and institutions permits it to acquire'.[117]

Some writers tried to place certain eighteenth-century Asian countries on the rung of the ladder of progress reached by Europe in the early middle ages. Feudal analogies became fashionable for a time. In his *Observations concerning the Distinction of Ranks in Society* John Millar, Professor of Civil Law at Glasgow, suggested that 'great lords' who had been 'reduced into a sort of feudal dependence upon a single person' could be found in India, Burma, Laos, Siam, Malaya and in the Ottoman Empire.[118] John Richardson wrote that in 'Persia, Tartary and India, and other Eastern countries, the whole detail of government, from the most ancient account down to the present hour, can hardly be defined by any other description' than feudal. By this he meant the rule of 'one great king to whom a number of subordinate princes pay homage and tribute'.[119] According to Michael Symes,

Burmese government 'exhibits almost a faithful picture of Europe in the darker ages, when, in the decline of the Roman empire, the principles of feudal dependence were established by barbarians from the north'.[120] 'The Malais', Pierre Poivre wrote, 'are governed by feudal laws.'[121]

Statements such as these do not suggest that much precision was being used in defining feudalism. But their general drift is clear. For certain parts of Asia at least the concept of an all-powerful despotism was being questioned. The power of rulers might to some extent be curbed by the power of aristocracies. Nevertheless, the alternative was not an attractive one. The feudal past in Europe was not a period for which eighteenth-century historians had much sympathy. In Robertson's view feudalism was based on principles of 'disorder and corruption' and produced 'the most fatal effects'.[122] Asian societies whose institutions could be described as feudal were likely to be unstable and backward. In Burma, Symes wrote, 'the feudal system which cherished ignorance and renders man the property of man, still operates as a check to civilization and improvement'.[123] Poivre described the feudalism of the Malays as a 'capricious system, conceived for the defence of the liberty of a few against the tyranny of one, whilst the multitude is subjected to slavery and oppression'.[124]

With the British conquest of Bengal questions of Asian social and economic development ceased to be matters merely of idle curiosity. Nearly all observers believed that the British were ruling over a province suffering from periodic famine, declining trade and widespread poverty. As early as 1772 an academic political economist, Sir James Steuart, was asked to give his advice on what should be done. Adam Smith also took a keen interest in Bengal, while many of the young men who went to India in the East India Company's service had at least a smattering of the new learning. As historians have done since, all concerned found it much easier to point out what was wrong with early British rule than to provide any very cogent analysis of the indigenous economy.[125] There seems, however, to have been general agreement that even without the malign effects of recent British policies, Bengal was in a state of arrested development. However feudalism was defined, feudal analogies were not usually thought to be very helpful. But systems of land tenure were considered to be unsatisfactory; property rights were insufficiently defined and inadequately protected. Ultimately the British administration tried to remedy what they saw as defects and to provide definition and security.[126] The analysis was essentially the same as that of Bernier and Chardin: despotism had stunted the growth of the East and the curbing of despotism would enable growth to begin again. Indeed 'old François Bernier' retained his authority into the 1850s, when Marx and Engels quoted him to one another on despotism, 'the *absence of private property* in land' and other elements of their theory of the 'Asiatic' mode of production, yet another assertion that Asia left to itself never changed.[127]

If for Adam Smith and his contemporaries, despotism, feudalism or some other political order incapable of maintaining security were the enemies of economic progress, the reverse was also true. A society incapable of economic progress beyond a certain point would have many other defects. 'Commerce and manufacture gradually intro-duced order and good government, and with them, the liberty and security of individuals, among inhabitants of the country', Smith wrote.[128] Ferguson, who believed that 'the commercial and political arts have advanced together', specifically applied this to the case of China. The few substantial merchants in China were a ray of hope in a backward society. 'While his countrymen act on the plans and under the restrictions of a police adjusted to knaves, he acts under the reasons of trade and the maxims of mankind.'[129] Sir James Steuart agreed that 'commerce and industry' were 'bulwarks against passions, vice and weakness'.[130] Societies which had carried commerce to a high level would even be more effective militarily than despotisms where the armed forces seemed to dominate. By the 1760s Ferguson was aware that the commercial nations of Europe were now capable of spreading their empires 'from the sea of Corea to the Atlantic Ocean'.[131]

In their attempts to explain why they thought that Asians had been unable to change significantly over long periods of time, the natural historians of man made it abundantly clear that they were recording human failure. Some writers of an earlier generation might have seen constancy as admirable; by the end of eighteenth century it is hard to find any who did. Even a man as dubious about progress as Samuel Johnson, made Imlac tell the young prince in *Rasselas* that: The 'north-ern and western nations of Europe . . . are now in possession of all power and all knowledge. . . . When I compared these men with the natives of our own kingdoms and those that surround us, they appeared another order of beings. In their country it is difficult to wish for any thing that may not be obtained: a thousand arts of which we have never heard are continually labouring for their convenience and pleasure; and whatever their own climate has denied them is supplied by their commerce.'[132] This power and knowledge had been won by men who had exerted themselves; peoples who could not or would not exert themselves stagnated.

Eighteenth-century Europeans found little need to question assumptions that Asia did not change. By the end of the previous century trends in both religious and secular thought were creating expectations of progress at least among more and more intellectuals.[133] The contrast with Asia seemed to be real enough. Travellers determined to find the world of the Bible or of Alexander still surviving in contemporary Asia could do so without too much difficulty. Things which caught the eye of the traveller – dress, building, technology – did indeed give the impression of having changed very little. Acquaintance with hitherto unknown cultures, such as Hindu India or Confucian China, with their insistence on strict conformity to precepts said to be of immense antiquity and their claims to very remote historical origins, can only have reinforced such appearances. As Europeans' belief in their own capacity for progress and their enthusiasm for it gathered momentum during the eighteenth century, to suggest that Asians shared this capacity would not merely fly in the face of accepted evidence; it would endanger a much-cherished facet of Europe's self-esteem.

If depictions of a stagnant Asia flattered Europe as a whole, they were especially flattering to Britain. Oppressive despotisms and obscurantist religions, the normal 'moral' elements in Asian immobility, were but the 'Popery' and 'slavery' of authoritarian Catholic Europe writ large. Britain was presumed to be a country governed under known laws and with the consent of at least some sections of its population; British Protestantism rested on reason and placed no obstacles in the way of scientific inquiry and the pursuit of individual advantage.

There were a few, however, even in the generally optimistic climate of the late eighteenth century, who found warnings as well as matter for self-congratulation in contemplating the atrophy of Asia. China in particular was taken to be a 'polished', 'commercial' nation that had become corrupted. Scottish writers were sometimes willing to use it as a parable of what Britain should avoid. For them a healthy society depended on individuals maintaining their 'virtue', that is their public spirit and sense of community. In rich, complex societies each man inevitably tended to pursue his own selfish advantage and to specialize narrowly in his own particular job. Thus he was in danger of losing his versatility and becoming a self-interested cog in a machine rather than a full citizen.[134] Ferguson thought this had happened in China. The government of China might seem at first sight to be an admirable machine for efficient routine administration, especially 'in raising, and in consuming the fruits of the earth'. It was staffed by carefully chosen graduates, highly skilled 'in detail and the observance of forms'. But the system was fundamentally weak: it allowed no scope for 'the exertions of a great or liberal mind'. There was no public spirit. In a crisis no one would 'stand forth in the dangers of their country'.[135] Lord Kames chose India for his example of the dangers of over-specialization. There it made men 'ignorant and unsociable'; 'men by inaction degenerate into oysters'.[136] India and China had become effete societies, inert victims for invaders. Britain should take note.

Such anxieties do not, however, seem to have been widely shared. The free, enterprising individual, active both for his own and his country's good, was generally seen as the agent of Britain's progress. The climate, government, religion and manners of Asia had all made it impossible for such individuals to flourish there.

NOTES

1 *Travels of Sir John Chardin into Persia and the East Indies* (1686).
2 *The Universal History*, vii, pt. i (1744), 244.
3 *Voyages en Perse* (Amsterdam, 1735), iii. 143.
4 P. Rycaut, *Present State of the Ottoman Empire* (1668 edn.), p. 3.
5 E. Terry, *A Voyage to East-India* (1655), p. 362.
6 J. Fryer, *A New Account of East India and Persia*, ed. W. Cooke (1909–15), i. 118.
7 *Relations of Golconda in the early seventeenth century*, ed. W. H. Moreland (1931), p. 14.
8 *Travels in the Mogul Empire*, ed. A. Constable and V. Smith (1914), p. 340.
9 *General History of China* (1736 edn.), i. 5.
10 G. Magaillans, *A New History of China* (1688), p. 61.
11 The history of thought on the effects of environment on men is examined in C. Glacken, *Traces on the Rhodian Shore* (Berkeley, 1967).
12 N. Carpenter, *Geography Delineated* (Oxford, 1625), pt. ii. 241–2.
13 *Cosmography in Four Books* (1674 edn.), pt. i. 15.
14 *A New and Accurate Description of Persia* (1724), ii. 139.
15 *Ibid.*, ii. 157.
16 *A New Historical Relation of the Kingdom of Siam* (1693), p. 90.
17 T. Salmon, *Modern History; or, the Present State of all Nations* (1744–6), i. 390.
18 J. Appleby, *Economic Thought and Ideology in Seventeenth-century England* (Princeton, 1978).
19 For recent studies of this debate, see J. G. A. Pocock, *The Machiavellian Moment* (Princeton, 1975) and I. Kramnick, *Bolingbroke and his Circle* (Cambridge, Mass., 1968).
20 See above, p. 117.
21 *Works of Sir William Temple* (1814), iii. 457.
22 *Ibid.*, iii. 328, 342.
23 J. Levenson, *Confucian China and its Modern Fate* (1965 edn.), i. 15.
24 G. J. Pierre, 'Gulliver's Voyages to China and Moor Park', *Texas Studies in Language and Literature*, xvii (1975), 427–38.
25 'Eubulius on Chinese and English Manners', *Yale Edition of Samuel Johnson*, x, *Political Writings*, ed. D. J. Greene (New Haven, 1977), 15–16.
26 Kramnick, *Bolingbroke*, p. 193.

27 *Farther Adventures of Robinson Crusoe*, ed. G. A. Aitken (1905), p. 255.
28 T. Harmer, *Observations on Divers Passages of Scripture*, 2nd edn. (1776), i. p. iv..
29 1st published 1767, see edition by D. Forbes (Edinburgh, 1966), p. 111.
30 2nd edn. (Oxford, 1778), p. 153.
31 *Travels in China*, 2nd edn. (1806), p. 4.
32 *The History of Sumatra* (1783), pp. 169–70.
33 *Wealth of Nations*, ed. R. Campbell, A. Skinner and W. Todd (Oxford, 1976), i. 89.
34 Essay 'On the Rise and Progress of the Arts and Sciences', *Philosophical Works*, ed.
    T. H. Green and T. H. Grose (1882), iii. 183.
35 *Travels*, pp. 29, 384.
36 *An Embassy to China*, ed. J. L. Cranmer-Byng (1962), p. 222.
37 *Travels in Africa, Egypt and Syria* (1799), p. 426. Cf. pp. 192, 220 below.
38 *Travels in Syria and Egypt* (1787), ii. 461.
39 M. Tournefort, *A Voyage to the Levant* (1718), i. 15.
40 L. Scrafton, *Reflections on the Government of Indostan*, 2nd edn. (1770), p. 16.
41 Mrs Kindersley, cited K. K. Dyson, *A Various Universe* (Delhi, 1978), p. 62.
42 *Sketches of the History of Man* (1788 edn. Edinburgh), i. 20.
43 See below, pp. 241–5.
44 See above, p. 88.
45 *Essay on the Primitive Inhabitants of Great Britain and Ireland* (1807).
46 P. J. Marshall, *The British Discovery of Hinduism in the Eighteenth Century* (Cambridge,
    1970), p. 252.
47 *The Works of Sir William Jones* (1806), i. 129–33.
48 *Spirit of the Laws*, trans. T. Nugent (New York, 1949 edn.), pt. i. 276.
49 *Civil Society*, pp. 98–9.
50 *Modern Part of the Universal History*, ii (1759), 251.
51 Kames, *Sketches of the History of Man*, i. 102.
52 *Travels from St. Petersburg in Russia to diverse parts of Asia* (Glasgow, 1763), i. 275.
53 *Civil Society*, p. 120.
54 *Spirit of the Laws*, pt. i. 266.
55 *Ibid*, pt. i. 225.
56 P. 430.
57 *Civil Society*, p. 112.
58 *History of Sumatra*, pp. 48–9.
59 R. Orme, *Historical Fragments of the Mogul Empire* (1805 edn.), p. 421.
60 *Memoir of a Map of Hindoostan* (1788 edn.), p. xxi.
61 Orme, *Historical Fragments*, p. 472.
62 Richardson, *Dissertation on Eastern Nations*, p. 148.
63 *Lettres sur l'origine des sciences* (London and Paris, 1777).
64 This is stressed in R. Shackleton, *Montesquieu: a Critical Biography* (Oxford, 1961),
    pp. 312–14.
65 (1781), p. iv.
66 *Philosophical Works*, iii. 249.
67 *Travels through Arabia and other Countries in the East* (Edinburgh, 1792), ii. 194.
68 *Modern Part of the Universal History*, xvi (1765), 12.
69 *Decline and Fall of the Roman Empire*, ed. J. B. Bury (1896–1900), iii. 71.
70 *Essai sur les moeurs*, ed. R. Pomeau (Paris, 1963), i. 836, ii. 322.
71 *Ibid.*, i. 832.
72 *Observations on the Religion, Laws, Government and Manners of the Turks*, 2nd edn. (1771),
    pp. xiv, xx.
73 Jones, *Works*, iii. 511–12. See also S. N. Mukherjee, *Sir William Jones: A Study in
    Eighteenth-century British Attitudes to India* (Cambridge, 1968), p. 132.
74 Cited in P. J. Marshall, *The Impeachment of Warren Hastings* (Oxford, 1965), p. 183.
75 Vol. ii. 2–5.

76 *Modern Geography* (1802), ii. 90.
77 *Spirit of the Laws*, pt. i. 125.
78 *Travels*, p. 360.
79 *Embassy to China*, ed. Cranmer-Byng, p. 236.
80 *Législation orientale* (Amsterdam, 1778).
81 *Spirit of the Laws*, pt. i. 269.
82 *Civil Society*, pp. 103, 254.
83 *A Dissertation on the Governments, Manners and Spirit of Asia* (1787), pp. 10–12.
84 *The Progress of Society in Europe*, ed. F. Gilbert (Chicago, 1972), p. 145.
85 *Spirit of the Laws*, pt. i. 32–3.
86 *Modern Part of the Universal History*, xvi (1765), 65–6.
87 Jones, *Works*, i. 149.
88 *Sermons Preached before the University of Oxford*, 2nd edn. (1785), pp. 389–90.
89 *Travels through Syria and Egypt*, ii. 397.
90 R. Chandler, *Travels in Asia Minor* (Oxford, 1775), pp. 280–1.
91 R. Clayton, *A Vindication of the Histories of the Old and New Testament* (1759 edn.), p. 387.
92 *An Historical Disquisition concerning the Knowledge which the Ancients had of India*, 2nd edn. (1794), p. 233.
93 *Ibid.*, p. 285.
94 *A Comparison of the Institutions of Moses with those of the Hindoos* (Northumberland, 1799), pp. 156–7.
95 Pinkerton, *Modern Geography*, ii. 254.
96 *Travels*, p. 392.
97 *Hau Kiou Choaan; or The Pleasing History* (1761), ii. 166 *n*.
98 Grosier, *General Description of China*, ii. 373.
99 *Travels*, p. 359.
100 L. Stone, *The Family, Sex and Marriage in England 1500–1800* (1977); K. V. Thomas, 'Age and Authority in Early Modern England', *Proceedings of the British Academy*, lxii (1976), 205–48.
101 *Travels*, p. 142.
102 *Hau Kiou Choaan*, iv. 201.
103 'Observations on some Tartarian Antiquities', *Archaeologia*, ii (1773), 231.
104 *Sketches of the History of Man*, i. 201.
105 Professor Stone's phrase in *Family, Sex and Marriage in England*.
106 *Ibid.*, p. 268.
107 *Travels in China*, pp. 138–9. See below, p. 220.
108 *A Survey of the Turkish Empire* (1798), p. 242.
109 *History of Persia* (1815), ii. 587, 622.
110 *Embassy to China*, ed. Cranmer-Byng, p. 214.
111 H. Verelst, *A View of the Rise, Progress and Present State of the English Government in Bengal* (1772), p. 139.
112 *Philosophical Dissertations on the Egyptians and the Chinese* (1795), i, p. xi.
113 See the discussion in R. L. Meek, *Social Science and the Ignoble Savage* (Cambridge, 1976), pp. 99 ff.
114 Cited, *ibid.*, p. 117.
115 Cited, W. C. Lehmann, *Henry Home, Lord Kames, and the Scottish Enlightenment* (The Hague, 1971), p. 184.
116 *Wealth of Nations*, i. 224.
117 *Ibid.*, i. 89.
118 4th edn. (1806), pp. 214–18.
119 *Dissertation on Eastern Nations*, p. 151.
120 *An Account of an Embassy to the Kingdom of Ava* (1800), p. 316.
121 *Travels of a Philosopher* (1769), p. 69.

122 *Progress of Society in Europe*, p. 17.
123 *Embassy to Ava*, p. 123.
124 *Travels*, p. 69.
125 For recent surveys of contemporary debates, see R. Guha, *A Rule of Property for Bengal* (Paris and The Hague, 1963); W. J. Barber, *British Economic Thought and India* (Oxford, 1975); S. Ambirajan, *Classical Political Economy and British Policy in India* (Cambridge, 1978).
126 See below, pp. 162–3.
127 Cited in S. Avineri, *Karl Marx on Colonialism and Modernization* (New York, 1969 edn.), pp. 450–3.
128 *Wealth of Nations*, i. 412.
129 *Civil Society*, pp. 143, 261.
130 Cited A. O. Hirschman, *The Passions and the Interests* (Princeton, 1977), p. 85.
131 *Civil Society*, p. 153.
132 *The History of Rasselas, Prince of Abissinia* (1759), Ch. 11.
133 For a recent discussion, see R. Nisbet, *History of the Idea of Progress* (1980), pp. 118–67.
134 Pocock, *Machiavellian Moment*, pp. 497 ff; D. Winch, *Adam Smith's Politics* (Cambridge, 1978).
135 *Civil Society*, pp. 226–7.
136 *Sketches of the History of Man*, i. 194–5.

6

Asia: Images of a Continent in 1800

Viewed from Asia itself the impact of Europe on the continent as a whole was still very small by 1800. Viewed from London the prospect looked rather different: the outlines of two kinds of conquest of Asia by Britain were becoming apparent. The first conquest was in the mind; the second was more substantial – the spread of British military power and commercial predominance.

Intellectual conquest of Asia had come about by 1800 by the mapping and measuring of the continent, the classifying of its people, and the analysis of their religious, social and political institutions. The natural historians of man had assessed Asia and had assimilated it into their theories about the nature of man. The sense of wonder that had lingered into the late seventeenth century, appearing for instance in references to India in geographies as 'the best and goodliest land in the world', 'an earthly paradise',[1] had been dispelled. In its place was a confidence that most of what needed to be known about Asia was now becoming known and that it could be related to what was known about mankind everywhere.

The strength of Britain's military presence in Asia was demonstrated in a most spectacular way in 1799 with the overthrow of Tipu Sultan of Mysore, who had frequently been likened in the English press to Hannibal, vainly opposing the new Rome. A year later the Governor General, Lord Wellesley, wrote that: 'The glorious termination of the late war in Mysore . . . [has] established the ascendancy of the British power over all the states of India.' Henceforward it would be necessary 'to consider the extensive and valuable possessions' of the British in India 'as a great empire'.[2] British power outside India was also increasing. At the end of the 1790s Britain effectively replaced France as the European state with the greatest influence in the Ottoman empire. Britain's nineteenth-century role as protector of the empire against dismemberment was beginning. In 1801 British armies sent through the Mediterranean and the Red Sea expelled the French from Egypt. The Royal Navy was active in the Red Sea and the Persian Gulf. An embassy was sent from India to Tehran to draw Iran into the British defensive system. The Dutch were driven out of Ceylon. With the settlement of Penang and the conquest of Malacca British power was being asserted on the coasts of Malaya. An expeditionary force to capture Batavia, capital of the Dutch empire in Asia, was in contemplation. Britain had a very large stake in China's foreign trade and was prepared to occupy Macao by force if need be. Interest in the possibility of trade with Japan was growing.

The two conquests, intellectual and military, were not necessarily connected. The impulses behind them could be very different. For instance, the intellectual mapping of Asia was to some extent an international enterprise. Knowledge was shared even if political and commercial privileges were not. Nevertheless, connections between the gathering of knowledge and the assertion of power clearly do exist, although they are complex and vary from area to area. Commercial contact, military operations and the experience of administering territory in Asia all obviously provided new opportunities for gathering knowledge. But trading and ruling helped to determine what would be regarded as acceptable knowledge. It is not necessary to believe that western oriental scholarship became the handmaid of imperialism[3] to accept that much of what was gathered was related to the needs of merchants or administrators and that scholars often came to share their points of view. More difficult to resolve is the question of the degree to which knowledge already acquired about Asian peoples and assumptions based on that knowledge helped to pave the way for deeper British involvement in Asia. To assume that British power spread over Asia in fulfilment of some programme of conquest devised by the natural historians of man would be totally to distort the historical record. No such programme existed; the use of power was opportunistic, and generally with very little thought for the ultimate consequences. Nevertheless, it would be hard to deny that increasing willingness to intervene in Asian politics and in the last resort to contemplate undertaking the responsibility for ruling Asian peoples had at least some relation to supposed knowledge about Asia available to Europeans by the end of the eighteenth century. Those who took decisions, either in the British government or in the East India Company, increasingly believed that they understood the workings of Asian societies, knew how to exploit their weaknesses, and could even attempt to remedy such weaknesses under European rule.

Even late in the eighteenth century the prospect of an empire in Asia was a repugnant one for many Englishmen. Eastern conquests were associated with many evils in the conventional view of Roman history: the growth of a great professional army likely to intervene in affairs of state, the corruption of political life by an unbounded flow of wealth and luxury, and the emergence of authoritarian proconsuls who oppressed their Asian subjects and were a threat to liberty at home. In his first chapter Gibbon condemned Trajan's 'dangerous emulation' of Alexander in seeking to carry conquest beyond the Danube 'against the nations of the east'. In parliamentary debates about India parallels between imperial Rome and the dangers in Britain's new imperial role were repeatedly drawn. By contrast, the most cherished image of Britain was that of a small, 'virtuous' 'republic', living within its bounds, preserving its ancient freedom, but becoming rich through a world-wide trade driven with fairness and frugality.[4] According to the editor of one of the great collections of 'voyages', conquest might make 'a nation rich and powerful by the spoil of others; but then it carries the seeds of its destruction in the very principles of its greatness; for where military power is the source of grandeur there must be perpetual hazards, not only as to the issue of foreign contests, but from the frequent convulsions of intestine troubles. . . . But an application to commerce cannot be charged, at least not justly, with any of these inconveniences. We may trade with people without subduing them, and we may become potent, rich and happy without injuring.'[5] By the 1760s Adam Ferguson was well aware that European armies could now carry all before them in Asia, and he greatly feared for the consequences, 'if that ruinous maxim should prevail, that the grandeur of a nation is to be estimated from the extent of its territory; or, that the interest of any particular people consists in reducing their neighbours to servitude.'[6]

By 1800 most of these fears had vanished and Englishmen generally took a pride in an empire in Asia won by conquest. The British believed that they had remained 'a free though conquering people'.[7] Complacency of this sort was no doubt largely an unreflecting response to events. A record of almost uninterrupted military successes stilled doubts and aroused patriotism. But writers of all kinds also contributed to reconciling the public to Asian conquests. As they portrayed Asia, it was ceasing to appear as the rich seductress, infecting its conquerors with its vices of luxury and despotism; it was poor, weak and backward. Conquest was more likely to carry progress and enlightenment to Asia than to sap the virtue of Europe.

In short, the proposition that growing British power in Asia generated knowledge about Asians seems to be incontrovertible; the obverse – that knowledge of Asia generated British conquest – is unlikely to be true in any direct sense, although assumptions generally held about Asians at the end of the eighteenth century increased European confidence in the exercise of power in Asia.

*   *   *

By 1800 the acquisition of knowledge about Asians and of dominion over them had gone much further in India than anywhere else. As a previous chapter has indicated,[8] the record of British scholarship in India by the end of the eighteenth century was becoming a distinguished one. The study and teaching of languages were on a firm basis. Large collections of texts, both Hindu and Islamic, were accumulating in India and in Britain, and authoritative translations were being made from them. Men like William Jones, Charles Wilkins and later Henry Thomas Colebrooke are recognized to be the founders of Indology as an academic discipline in the west. The rest of Europe learnt from Britain. At first sight there appears to be a wide gap between the work of such men and the crude necessities of the East India Company in its rise to dominance. Warren Hastings, the patron of the scholars, insisted that learning should be sought for its own sake.[9] The scholars largely concerned themselves with a remote Indian past, which they often portrayed in glowing terms. Jones proclaimed that the Hindus had once been 'splendid in arts and arms, happy in government, wise in legislation, and eminent in various knowledge'.[10] The relevance of such noble sentiments to a harassed young Company servant supervising the extraction of taxes from an impoverished peasantry in the marshes of deltaic Bengal can at best have seemed to be marginal.

Yet even so refined a spirit as Sir William Jones was much concerned with the practical problems of administering justice and applied himself to the preparation of legal texts for the use of the Company's courts. Scholarship had many other practical applications. But ultimately perhaps of greater significance than obvious instances in which knowledge was directed to the particular needs of ruling are the general assumptions on which the Company constructed its administrative system. Historians have often debated the balance between what might be regarded as ideological commitment and practical necessity in the shaping of various phases of British policy in India. The practical necessities confronting what was still in 1800 a weak and ill-informed administration need little emphasis. On the other hand, there is much evidence to show that the late eighteenth-century Company servants were often men with strongly held *a priori* beliefs, expressed freely in the voluminous minutes and despatches that they were required to send home,[11] in which policy is frequently justified by sweeping assertions about Indian society. Such assertions were rooted in the great body of writing about India, from scholars and travellers alike, which had been accumulating throughout the eighteenth century, as much as in actual observation of Indian conditions.

After much experiment the Company's government in India had acquired certain clearly defined features by 1800. At its higher levels it had become a government by Europeans. Ultimate authority was exercised by Governors and Councils with Collectors and Judges responsible for local administration. The scope of these officials' activities and the extent to which they involved themselves in regulating the lives of their subjects was, however, relatively restricted. Above all else the East India Company's government was concerned with finance, with the assessment and collection of taxation on land supplemented by customs revenue and the profits of state monopolies. It was also concerned with the maintenance of law and order and the administration of justice. Beyond these functions it attempted little.

Practical necessity will certainly go a long way towards explaining why a predominantly white government, autocratic in its powers but limited in its functions, should have come into existence in the first Indian provinces administered by the British. The East India Company, as was no doubt inevitable for a trading body with limited resources and no political ambitions, had largely reproduced the pattern of indigenous Mughal government with changed personnel at the top. But the Company's servants appear to have been much influenced in what they did by assumptions about Indian society which had become commonplace long before the British conquest.

On strictly practical grounds there were in fact formidable objections to excessive reliance on Europeans for the higher posts of the administration. Apart from their obvious lack of any of the expertise required for ruling an alien people, the Company servants had blatantly used power for their own interest. Displacement of Indians began, however, in the 1760s and was virtually complete by the mid-1780s. It is commonly supposed that Indians were demoted because of the particular prejudices of Lord Cornwallis, the first Governor General to be appointed without previous Indian service. In fact they lost their offices because of prejudices which were both much older and much more widely held.[12] Mughal officials in Bengal and southern India were usually, though often erroneously, supposed to be separated both by their ethnic origins and by their Muslim beliefs from the mass of the population over whom they ruled. They were, for instance, described as 'adventurers from Persia . . . strangers to the customs and indifferent to the welfare' of the people of Bengal.[13] They were presumed to be the characteristic agents of the despotic Islamic governments which extended from Turkey to India, the kind of men whom Bernier over a hundred years earlier had dismissed as 'slaves, ignorant and brutal'.[14] At the mercy of an unpredictable and rapacious monarch, they were cruel and extortionate in their turn. To remove such men would be to liberate the Hindu masses from their oppressors. As early as 1758 Robert Clive made this point in a famous letter to Pitt:

'. . . as under the present government they have no security for their lives and properties, they would rejoice in so happy an exchange as that of a mild for a despotic government'.[15] The last of the great Muslim officials in Bengal was removed in 1772. In retrospect the author of a pamphlet published in 1790 believed that, since 1772, 'British mildness and forbearance' have 'at last happily exploded Mahommedan severity'.[16]

For some years after 1772, however, Indian officials continued to exercise important functions under the East India Company. These were the Hindu *muttaseddis* and *diwans*, revenue administrators who had been the workhorses of Mughal government. Warren Hastings recognized their value for the British as well, but they, too, became objects of suspicion and dislike. Extortion by cruelty was attributed to Muslim officials; extortion by guile and fraud was thought to be the vice of the milder Hindu. The government and the mass of the people suffered from both. In 1786 one of the Company's self-confessed revenue experts wrote that: 'The depravity, ignorance and misconduct of native Hindoostanny agents in every branch of government has often been the theme of general declamation as being notorious, lamentable, irremediable.'[17] They must give way to Europeans, who, it was supposed, could learn the minutiae of Indian government with little difficulty. 'The collection of the revenue, is in itself simple . . .', wrote another expert of the 1780s. 'Common sense, a competent knowledge of the language, application, and rectitude of intention are all the qualities required either for this, or in the distribution of justice.'[18] 'Rectitude of intention' was by far the most important of these attributes. Black as the record of the early Company servants had been, with the aid of proper rewards and punishments a sense of honour and public service could be aroused in young Europeans. Subjection to despotic government in a debilitating climate ensured that Indians could see no further than their own interests in the narrowest sense. They would never change.

A change in the personnel at the top was not intended to produce a revolution in the way in which the new British provinces were governed. Again there were obvious practical reasons why a weak and uncertain alien administration should choose to disturb its new subjects as little as possible, but again long-standing British assumptions about the nature of Indian society also suggested inaction. Bengal and the Company's possessions in southern India had long been held by Europeans to be highly fertile and to be inhabited by a hard-working, extremely productive Hindu population, diligent tillers of the soil and weavers of cloth. The early Company servants fully endorsed such opinions. For instance, Lord Cornwallis wrote: 'We have by a train of the most fortunate events obtained the dominion of one of the most fertile countries on the face of the globe, with a population of mild and industrious inhabitants.'[19] Such people required no prompting from the new government to generate wealth. They needed only to be left alone in peace and security. Any attempted change could be positively damaging to the Company's interests. The intense conservatism of Hindus was a truism of the travel writers which was rarely questioned by the administrators. Hindus were an 'effeminate' people who would accept new masters without resistance so long as their way of life was not threatened; but if innovations were imposed on them, even these abject worms might turn and rebel. On this point the degree to which the men of letters and the men of action shared the same assumptions was demonstrated in an unusually explicit way in 1781. A group of ex-Company servants gave evidence to a Select Committee of the House of Commons on the disruption allegedly being caused in Bengal by attempts to extend English law to sections of the Indian population. Dire warnings about the possibility of armed rebellion were uttered. The committee which heard this evidence found that it agreed with what they already believed. Edmund Burke, who took the lead on the committee, urged Parliament to restore 'peace' to Bengal by giving the Indians laws that were in accordance with 'the genius, the temper, and the manners of the people'. With the aid among others of William Jones, a scholar and poet who had yet to set foot in Asia, Burke felt able to draft a bill to protect Indians 'in the enjoyment of all their ancient laws, usages, rights, and privileges'.[20]

For all their caution about disturbing Hindu conservatism or arousing Muslim 'fanaticism', by 1800 the East India Company had in fact embarked on policies which, contemporaries clearly recognized, implied major changes in areas likely to be of critical importance for many Indians, that is, law and land tenure. Those who supported such policies might speak of practical need, but their approach to the problems of ruling the new provinces was often highly abstract and theoretical. Recent studies have shown how much such approaches drew from European models and controversies rather than from direct Indian experience.[21] When the advocates of what were essentially European solutions to supposed Indian problems tried to show their relevance to local conditions they often did so by repeating old-established clichés about the nature of Asian society in general.

That stagnation and poverty had been produced in many parts of Asia by 'moral' causes, that is by the abuses of government, as well as by climate and physical environment was by far the most influential of the stereotypes inherited by British administrators in India. The pursuit of individual advantage was believed to be the engine of improvement in all human societies. In Asia human enterprise was generally blighted by government oppression. Thus even the naturally industrious population of the Company's supposedly highly fertile provinces produced much less than could reasonably be expected. The replacement of predatory Indian officials by disinterested and benevolent Europeans would do something to encourage the tender plant of personal ambition in the Company's subjects; but more was needed. As early as 1769 the Directors had been urging their servants in Bengal to do all they could to ensure 'security for the property and persons of the natives.'[22] Positive security came ultimately from clearly defined rights to property enforced by known laws impartially administered by properly constituted courts. To introduce such concepts into a society whose fabric had been rotted by centuries of despotism would inevitably involve a considerable degree of innovation. Two, deeply-revered, received truths about India thus seemed to conflict: the evils of despotism could only be remedied at the risk of affronting Indian conservatism. But in retrospect at least it seemed as if a successful compromise had been achieved by 1800. John Bruce, the East India Company's official historiographer, summed up what he saw as the nature of the compromise between the need to change and the need to ensure continuity: the outward forms of indigenous 'institutions and laws' had been preserved, while being tempered, in his words, with 'the mild spirit of the British government'.[23]

Land tenure and the administration of justice were regarded as the essential underpinning for security for the individual and were therefore the crucial areas in which the compromise between Indian form and British spirit were worked out. Only if a man had land in his own personal possession and held it by a title that could not be questioned would he exert himself to improve it. So British rule must be concerned with defining rights to land on an individual basis with a precision and certainty that were quite alien to previous régimes. On the other hand, it would be extremely dangerous to attempt to subvert the existing structure of rural society. Established claims to land should be given the new form of recognition. Elaborate historical inquiries were undertaken to reveal which of the various competing layers of Indian society had the better claim to the new rights. Put crudely, the famous 'settlements' of the revenue, concluded on one set of assumptions in Bengal in 1793 and evolving on another set in Madras later on, can be described as attempts to fit new systems of rights onto what were taken to be existing structures of society, that is as compromises between innovation and preservation.

Compromise on the same principles was also sought in the administration of justice. Security for the individual could only be ensured if the law was fixed in a form that could be known by all and was administered in an impartial and predictable way. This would no doubt require some innovation, since even if crude assumptions about the absence of formal law in Asian societies had been disposed of, it was still presumed that justice in India was done in a haphazard way, heavily influenced by corruption and the needs of the state. But the substance of the law must on no account be changed. Hindu and Muslim law had a religious sanction; to displace them would be to provoke certain resistance. Even the Muslim criminal law, regarded as being contrary to 'reason and natural justice',[24] must be preserved. The terms of the compromise were that Indian law, given definite and predictable form by the publication of what were imagined to be authoritative translations, should be administered by British courts employing such British concepts as equality before the law. As a further refinement, the British doctrine of the separation of the powers, by the exclusion of executive influence from judicial proceedings, must be upheld even against the British themselves. 'In this country, as in every other', wrote the Bengal Council, 'security of property must be established by a system upheld by its inherent principles, and not by the men who are to have the occasional conduct of it. The body of the people must feel and be satisfied of this security before industry will exert itself.'[25] To modern scholarship the aim of tempering the substance of Indian law with the spirit of British administration seems entirely unrealistic. The new legal system broke almost completely with the past. The law applied by its courts has been called a 'hybrid monstrosity'.[26] Nevertheless, the achievements of the compromise were celebrated in 1800 by the Bengal Council. While they had been granted 'the confirmation of their ancient laws in all matters connected with their religious prejudices, or their domestic relations', the inhabitants of the British provinces also enjoyed the benefits of living under a government modelled on 'principles drawn from the British constitution'.[27]

Nothing in Britain's imperial experience had prepared Englishmen for the tasks, suddenly thrust upon them in the second half of the eighteenth century, of trying to govern millions of Indians. In such circumstances there was little alternative to proceeding with extreme caution and trying to deviate as little as possible from indigenous institutions in as far as these could be comprehended. Caution was indeed the dominant note in the Company's administration throughout the eighteenth century. Yet other notes, often surprisingly self-confident and strident ones, can also be heard, and policies which within limits were innovatory in intention, and often even more so in effect, were introduced. That it took some Englishmen only a relatively short space of time before they felt able to pronounce on what was needed to improve their new Indian provinces was due as much to the achievements of the natural historians of man as it was to their own capacity to deduce conclusions from closely observing an alien society. Even before they went to India, young Englishmen learnt that Asian societies were not necessarily opaque and mysterious. Criteria that applied to other societies also applied to them. Comparisons could be made with other peoples and the place of the various Asian nations on the scale of mankind as a whole could be ascertained. Empirical observation was not needed to convince Englishmen that the mass of Indians were docile and hardworking, if invincibly conservative, that their Muslim overlords were cruel and extortionate, that property of all kinds was insecure, or that the administration of justice was at best corrupt and uncertain. Observation might confuse the issue; these were the maxims of many books. Such maxims were commonly regarded as being the clearest signs guiding the faltering footsteps of the early administration of India.

There has been considerable speculation about possible links between the flowering of French scholarship on the Middle East and the expedition to conquer Egypt in 1798. By contrast British scholarly interest in the area was much less vigorous and British political ambitions were less grandiose. Even so, what was taken to be the accumulated wisdom of travellers and writers certainly influenced the calculations of ministers as they deployed British power and diplomacy on an ever-increasing scale throughout the Levant at the end of the eighteenth century.

At the end of the seventeenth century British accounts of the Ottoman Empire had made much of its apparent defects and had even prophesied its eventual downfall, but in spite of recent reverses, they clearly regarded it as a power to be reckoned with.[28] A hundred years later the same defects were still being diagnosed in remarkably similar terms, but there was now no doubt that the Turkish decline was very far advanced. The empire appeared to be in an abject state, prey to the powers of Europe. British interests could only be protected by vigorous intervention.

Loss of people seemed to provide the most striking evidence of decline. William Eton believed that the total population of the empire had sunk to only one fifth of what it had been in the sixteenth century.[29] The cities were shrunken and much of the countryside was totally deserted. Numerous comparisons were drawn between areas that had flourished in antiquity but were now an impoverished wilderness. Technology remained rudimentary and agriculture was very backward indeed. The mass of the population were impenetrably ignorant, but the élite were little better. When the 'Grand Vizier' was told by the commander of the British military mission that the earth was round, 'this information caused no small degree of surprise to the Turkish minister . . . "If", he observed, "the earth is round, how can the people, and other detached objects on the half beneath be prevented from falling off?" '[30] Defeat by the Russians and the Austrians suggested that the Turkish military system was on its last legs.

By the end of the eighteenth century explanations of this disastrous decline were very stereotyped indeed; despotism and the malign effects of Islam were held to be responsible. Although there had been some debate about the nature of the Turkish government, the general view that it was despotic was restated with great force at the end of the eighteenth century. 'The Turkish government properly speaking is a system of slavery', wrote Habesci in 1784.[31] To Eton, Turkish despotism was 'a power calculated to crush the growing energies of mind, and annihilating the faculties of man'.[32] As earlier generations had done,[33] other commentators believed that the 'spirit' which had sustained the Turks had been fierce discipline and religious fervour. This was now totally sapped. The Turks had become soft and effete. Close observers of the empire in the last decade of the eighteenth century could hardly fail to notice that if parts of the old order were giving way, 'modernization' was being attempted in a patchy way. European technicians and experts were being employed to improve the armed forces and introduce new systems of education.[34] British writers who commented on these changes varied in their assessments from deep pessimism[35] to very reserved caution[36] about the prospects of effective reform.

The dismemberment of the Ottoman Empire in the near future was viewed with enthusiasm by some sections of British opinion. Burke told the House of Commons that the Turks were 'worse than savages . . . Any Christian power was to be preferred to these destructive savages.'[37] Eton thought that: 'Humanity itself is disgraced by the prolongation of Turkish despotism.'[38] For those who directed British foreign policy the matter was rather more complex. During the 1790s Britain's objections to Russian gains at Turkey's expense began to harden. The consequences for the European power balance were the first consideration, but in 1792 Henry Dundas, effectively minister responsible for India, expressed 'fear for our possessions in India' if the Aegean Islands, Egypt or the Red Sea were to pass under Russian control.[39] In 1798 Britain had to react to an entirely new threat to Turkey, this time from the French invasion of Egypt. To Dundas and to those of his colleagues who accepted his diagnosis, the French presence in Egypt constituted a very serious danger to India. It immediately threw Britain and Turkey together to an unprecedented degree. The Turks were given a sweeping guarantee of all their territories in a treaty of alliance of 1799. A military mission of 76 officers and men was dispatched to train the Turkish army for operations against the French. The first ambassador directly appointed by the King rather than by the Levant Company, Lord Elgin, arrived in Constantinople, accompanied by an entourage of painters and scholars. French trade in the Levant was virtually extinguished and, once British naval control of the Mediterranean had been restored, Britain gained an overwhelmingly powerful position in Turkish markets.

Much deeper involvement in the affairs of the Ottoman Empire did little to dispel gloom about its future prospects. British officers who served with the Turkish army admired the courage of the soldiers but believed that they were little more than 'an armed rabble'.[40] 'Under a Turkish government everything becomes debased', wrote Sir John Moore.[41] 'Superstition' and 'the radical vices of their government' were said to make effective military reform impossible.[42] Direct British involvement had been needed to blunt the French offensive at Acre and only large British forces had driven them out of Egypt. Disengagement from Turkish affairs in the future would not be easy.

Developments at the end of the eighteenth century showed that the Ottoman system was at its most vulnerable in the outlying provinces and brought an intensification of British commitments in two of them, Egypt and Iraq. Egypt was regarded by Europeans as a province which was potentially very rich but which suffered even more than other parts of the empire from misgovernment as the Mamluke Beys struggled to reduce the power of the Ottoman representatives. Foreign travellers, such as Niebuhr and Volney, joined with British ones in painting a melancholy picture of oppression and poverty. W. G. Browne believed that taxes were 'now multiplied to a point beyond which, consistently with the being of the peasantry, they cannot well be extended'.[43] Formal British interests in Egypt developed somewhat fitfully in the later eighteenth century. An agent appointed in 1775 had been very active in countering French diplomacy in the 1780s but his appointment was later allowed to lapse.[44] The French invasion in 1798 transformed the situation. The French must of course be evicted, but Dundas began to speculate on whether a permanent British presence there should not replace them. 'If any great European power shall ever get possession of that country, the keeping it will cost them nothing, and that country so getting possession of Egypt will in my opinion be possessed of the master key to all the commerce of the world.'[45] Before launching the campaign which ended in the surrender of the French Egyptian army in 1801, the British Cabinet apparently discussed the future of Egypt. Annexation was ruled out, but it was hoped that a restored Turkish régime could be induced to reform its ways by the presence of a limited British military contingent.[46] Nothing came of such plans and the British army finally evacuated Egypt in 1803.

Statements of regret for opportunities missed in the view of some men who had served in Egypt are striking evidence of increasing British confidence in their capacity to rule eastern peoples, not only in India. George Baldwin, formerly consul, thought that under British rule 'the peasant could enjoy the fruit of his labour', while a thousand ships a year would carry goods between Britain and Egypt.[47] Sir Robert Wilson reflected on how much 'happier' and 'more advantageous' it would have been for the Egyptians had Egypt 'been constituted an Indian colony' under Britain.[48] Moore looked to the regeneration of Alexandria and considered that 'it was in the power of the English to do more in Egypt than it would ever be in that of any other nation'.[49]

British involvement with Iraq was much less significant. In 1798 a British agent was sent on the orders of the government to Baghdad, where among other duties he was to stiffen the resistance of the Turkish Governor to any French penetration. Harford Jones, the first Baghdad agent, quickly began to speculate on the deployment of British forces in Iraq should the Ottoman Empire break up.[50]

The outer rim of Arabia was also being drawn into the British orbit. Trade from India to the Red Sea ports languished and Muscat also seemed to be in decline, while Niebuhr reported that his great journeys revealed 'a country interesting in many respects; but . . . in general neither rich nor fertile'.[51] Nevertheless, precautions were taken against the French even here. Ships of the Royal Navy patrolled the Red Sea. For a time an expeditionary force from Bombay was sent to the islands at its Indian Ocean end. Agreements to exclude the French were signed with Muscat in 1798 and 1800.

Declining commercial contacts but increasing attempts to exert diplomatic influence also marked British relations with Iran at the end of the eighteenth century. Travellers were very discouraging about Iran's prospects. Stable government was thought to have broken down completely. George Forster reported that Persia has 'suffered severe devastations and has been grievously depopulated'. 'At this day, Persia may be said to exhibit a vast tomb, piled up with the victims of ambition, avarice and revenge.'[52] John Malcolm, the envoy sent by the Governor General of India to Iran in 1800, was less melodramatic but still found a 'Government not two stages removed from a state of barbarism'.[53] In his case the attempted exertion of influence and the advancement of scholarship went together. On this visit and two subsequent ones he collected material for his *History of Persia* of 1815. Although the reputation of this huge book is now somewhat equivocal, it was widely admired by contemporaries and was regarded with some justification as the most significant contribution to European under-standing of modern Iran since the publication of Chardin's account.

The dispatch of British troops and envoys all over the Levant and south-west Asia in the years 1798 to 1800 assumed a deeply pessimistic assessment of the state of society throughout the region. There was poverty and deterioration everywhere. Nowhere could vigour and sta-bility be expected. Alarmists like Dundas supposed that a French army could fight their way from the Mediterranean to India. All British policy-makers assumed that rulers could be manipulated and cajoled into some kind of British system. Even though there were no plans to extend British territorial control and the burst of activity at the very end of the eighteenth century is not the prelude to Middle Eastern empire, individuals increasingly expressed the opinion that British rule over parts of the region was feasible and might be desirable from the point of view of the inhabitants, if not from Britain's.

The pessimism underlying British judgements of the Middle East around 1800 was not new in essentials. It embodied beliefs about the effects of Islam and despotism which had been current throughout the eighteenth century, even if they were sharpened by the self-consciously hardheaded assessment of the new 'scientific' travellers. To statesmen who shared these beliefs, the countries of the Middle East seemed to be incapable of offering effective resistance to France or Russia of them-selves; British intervention in the region would be both necessary and relatively easy to put into effect. As has frequently been pointed out, the 'Great Game' of the defence of India began in the 1790s; by then it was already being assumed that the apparently weak and unstable states of the Middle East would be no more than pawns in the game.

Britain's stake in south-east Asia was growing in importance by 1800. British trade through shipping based in India was increasing rapidly throughout the region, while the domination of the Netherlands by France exposed Dutch settlements to British conquest whenever adequate forces were available. The occupation of Java late in the Napoleonic War was to involve the British for the first time in the problems of ruling a large population in south-east Asia, but two imperial enclaves already existed by the end of the eighteenth century. One of these, Benkulen in Sumatra, was of long standing; the other, Penang, off the coast of Malaya was acquired in 1786. Benkulen stimulated one major study of the people over whom the East India Company ruled, William Marsden's *History of Sumatra*, published in 1783. Marsden was clearly proud of Englishmen's capacity to rule Asians.

> By the Company's power, the districts over which it extends are preserved in uninterupted peace. . . . The natives themselves allow it . . . ; and those dismal catastrophes, which, in all the Malay Islands

are wont to attend on private feuds, but very rarely happen. . . . The Resident is also considered the protector of the people, from the injustice and oppression of the chiefs.[54]

Penang had not yet produced a major literary work. But impressions of the supposed characteristics of Malays, Chinese and other inhabitants were being noted in the East India Company's records together with advice on how they should be managed.[55]

So far this chapter has been exploring possible connections at the end of the eighteenth century between changing British assessments of Asian peoples and changing relationships between these people and Britain. For China there is no obvious change of relations. Trade grew greatly in volume but it remained clamped into a set of regulations which continued in force from the mid-eighteenth century until 1842. Yet, perhaps paradoxically, assessments of the Chinese generally changed in Britain more drastically than did assessment of any other Asian people.

Late eighteenth-century accounts of the Ottoman Empire, Iran, India or south-east Asia all stressed weakness by comparison with Europe, but the weaknesses that they chose to expose were generally those which had appeared in late seventeenth-century books. Verdicts may have grown harsher over a hundred years, but they were essentially the same verdicts. On China verdicts were radically different. Although the late seventeenth-century portrayal of China had not been one of universal admiration, there was fairly general agreement that an efficient bureaucracy under the emperor's direct control maintained a rigorous but benevolent sway over a vast population, reinforcing the sound practical morality by which the people lived and encouraging them to raise abundant crops and apply their much famed skill to various manufacturing crafts. The Chinese system was not only benevolent and efficient, but, above all other things, it was presumed to be stable. It had lasted for centuries with only superficial change. It would continue for centuries.[56]

By the end of the eighteenth century many writers were coming to doubt even Chinese stability. Lord Macartney was the most elegant of the sceptics.

The empire of China [he wrote] is an old, crazy, first rate man-of-war, which a fortunate succession of able and vigilant officers has contrived to keep afloat . . . but whenever an insufficient man happens to have the command upon deck, adieu to the discipline and safety of the ship. She may perhaps not sink outright: she may drift some time as a wreck, and will then be dashed to pieces on the shore; but she can never be rebuilt on the old bottom.

Macartney considered that Britain would now have very little difficulty in extracting whatever concessions she wished from China by force, but any plan for territorial acquisitions was, he thought, 'too wild to be seriously mentioned'.[57] Habesci, who had been to Peking in 1784, agreed that the Chinese imperial system was 'in those circumstances which enable one to foretell its decay'. Government and 'manners' had both become corrupt. 'Anarchy resides there . . .'. He, too, recognized Britain's potential power, but unlike Macartney he hoped that it would be used. From Canton the British should seize Kwang-tung province. The example of those who became their 'free and happy subjects' would stimulate a revival throughout China.[58] John Barrow, who accompanied Macartney, was another who thought that China would not be exempt in 'this age of revolutions'. He had heard reports of secret societies opposing the Manchus.[59] Such doubts about China's future were repeated by those who wrote in Britain at second hand. For instance, William Falconer described China as having become a 'weak and insignificant' power, although he supposed that its size and distance from Europe would preserve it from conquest.[60]

Late eighteenth-century writers took issue with seventeenth-century versions of China on a number of specific grounds. At least since the middle of the century, the nature of the imperial Chinese government had been undergoing a reassessment. Rather than depicting a kind of tempered absolutism in which the emperor's great powers were restrained by scrupulous observance of traditional rights and duties and by taking the disinterested advice of highly qualified officials, it became fashionable to dismiss China as yet another oriental despotism.[61] The government was not patriarchal and benevolent in its actual dealings with the people; it was harsh and tyrannical. Whatever might be the theory, in practice the emperor's control over his officials was thought to be limited. On closer inspection these officials turned out not to be philosopher rulers but to be grasping extortioners. A very great deal was written about corruption. In a report on the prospects for its trade with China, issued in 1791, the East India Company felt it necessary to refute 'voyage writers, among other superficial observers' and assert categorically that the Chinese government was 'the most corrupt in the universe'.[62] John Barrow thought that 'men in power' rarely let the affluent Chinese escape their 'rapacious grasp'.[63] Bribery was said in Pinkerton's *Modern Geography* to be a 'universal vice'.[64]

Earlier accounts had suggested that the Chinese were guided in their lives by an ancient code of ethics which was admirable by European standards. To a later generation it seemed that these precepts had little effect either on those in authority or on the mass of the people. Macartney concluded that 'morality is a mere pretence in their practice'.[65] 'The general character of the people', according to Barrow, was 'strongly marked with pride, meanness and ignorance'.[66] What Falconer had learnt led him to conclude that: 'It is an established rule in that country, that every one should, at any rate, be attentive to his own interest, and promote it by any means in his power, violence excepted. Fraud therefore is not regarded as a crime.'[67]

Falconer had, however, also learnt that to pass moral strictures on the mass of the Chinese population in the abstract left much unexplained. Devotion to 'interest' and 'deceit' were, he believed, forced upon them by poverty. Many of the earlier Jesuit writers had recognized the existence of poverty for all the intensely productive use of land and other resources which they so much admired. By the end of the eighteenth century virtually all British writers accepted that poverty was very widespread indeed among the Chinese. Little attention was paid to the French physiocrats who still praised Chinese agriculture. The British debate was not about the existence of poverty but about its causes. Members of the Macartney mission produced an estimate of the population of the empire, said to be derived from official Chinese records, of 333,000,000 people. To Macartney himself this figure was a sufficient explanation for poverty. The 'multitudes' of people were 'so great as to exceed the means of subsistence by labour'. So 'vast numbers perish of hunger and cold' every year. 'Partial famine' frequently occurred in particular provinces, while the very poor were driven to infanticide or to selling their children.[68] Malthus made a study of the evidence on China, which led him to conclude that it was 'more populous, in proportion to the means of subsistence, than perhaps any other country in the world'. The 'reward of labour' was 'as low as possible', the mass of population being ground down 'to the most abject state of poverty'.[69] Others who had been to China doubted whether the pressure of people on resources was as acute as the figures suggested. The acerbic Barrow, ever ready with an interpretation which showed Chinese civilization in a poor light, was inclined to attribute poverty to the low productivity of Chinese labour. 'Industrious they certainly are', he wrote, 'but their labour does not always appear to be bestowed with judgment.' Minute holdings, poor implements, especially ploughs, lack of livestock, and techniques of husbandry, which were 'not to be mentioned with many European nations' all produced a low yield from the land. He thought that the Netherlands could easily support a population as dense as China's.[70] Habesci agreed with him. 'In China, the cultivation of which is so renowned, much land lies uncultivated', yet multitudes begged for their living.[71]

Seventeenth-century writers believed that Chinese science and learning had stagnated and would not stand comparison with those of

Europe. Late eighteenth-century comments were even more scathing. Macartney took a scientist, a Dr Hugh Gillan, with him to report on Chinese attainments. Gillan produced a catalogue of ignorance. Physic 'can hardly be said to exist among them'. They knew next to nothing about anatomy and physiology. 'Natural history, natural philosophy and chemistry, as sciences, are equally unknown to them'.[72] In a separate report on technology he was equally dismissive.[73] Even the skill and the beauty of line and colour in the applied arts which had so excited earlier generations of connoisseurs now seemed tawdry. From the middle of the eighteenth century, the Chinese taste, which had enjoyed something of a boom in the 1740s, began to lose ground in Britain. The vogue for attempting buildings in a supposed Chinese manner was for the most part over by the 1750s.[74] Chinoiserie in furniture and interior decoration remained fashionable rather longer. But mostly used as a medium for rococo styles, Chinese motifs declined in popularity with the rise of neo-classicism. Efforts were made to combine China and Antiquity, but after 1800 the Brighton Pavilion was to be the only significant attempt to create a Chinese interior to an English building. Only in porcelain and earthenware was Chinoiserie to have a long life, 'willow pattern' making its appearance about 1780.[75]

The success of English porcelain with or without 'Chinese' decoration was a clear sign of another shift in taste away from China in the second half of the eighteenth century. The demand for Chinese porcelain, purchased through Canton by the East India Company or by individuals licensed to carry goods on its ships, tailed off sharply at the end of the century. In 1791 the Company decided to end porcelain purchases and by 1800 private imports had greatly diminished.[76] In part this reflects steep increases in duties on the Chinese items which made them uncompetitive, but for some time connoisseurs had come to prefer English goods, whatever the price. Wedgwood won his markets not by cheapness but by convincing the fashionable world that he could recapture 'the elegance and simplicity of the ancients'.[77] A volume of the *Universal History* published in 1759 stated that Meissen ware 'so much exceeds the Chinese especially in the beauty of the colours and fineness of the painting', and looked forward to the time when British porcelain would also be superior to Chinese.[78] When Barrow wrote at the end of the century, he was sure that this had happened. The Chinese, he thought, could not 'boast of giving to the materials much elegance of form. With those inimitable models from the Greek and Roman vases, brought into modern use by the ingenious Mr. Wedgwood, they will not bear a comparison. And nothing can be more rude and ill designed than the grotesque figures and other objects painted, or rather daubed, on their porcelain.'[79] Such opinions were endorsed at the highest level. Matthew Boulton was summoned to Queen Charlotte's 'boudoir', where she 'shewed me her chimney piece and asked me how many vases it would take to furnish it. "For," said she, "all that China shall be taken away . . .".'[80]

At the end of the seventeenth century a number of English writers had been willing to see in China models for imitation by Europe. By the end of the eighteenth century virtually no one did. At best China remained an obstinately stagnant society when progress was coming to be regarded as the normal expectation of humanity. For many writers, however, the case seemed to be worse than that. China was in decline, its system of government was deteriorating, its people were getting poorer, and its future was likely to be bleak.

Pessimism about China at the end of the eighteenth century may have been supported by what contemporaries regarded as new evidence, from the Macartney mission especially, but disparagement of China was not of itself new in English writing by 1800. The decline in the taste for things Chinese or pseudo-Chinese in mid-century was matched by a decline in esteem for China. Publications censorious of the Chinese steadily increased in the second half of the century. Thomas Salmon's *Modern History* in its revised form of 1744 concluded that 'the Chinese seem to be a nature of exquisite hypocrites . . . , guilty of all manner of fraud, vice and extortion.'[81] The very harsh account of the Chinese in Anson's *Voyage Round the World* appeared in 1748.[82] *The Modern Part of the Universal History* of 1759 wrote of the 'avarice, bribery, and corruption' which 'reign through the whole empire, from the highest tribunals down to the lowest office'.[83] Thomas Percy in the notes which he attached to his *Hau Kiou Choaan, or, the Pleasing History* of 1761[84] was often extremely scathing. He described the Chinese in general as 'to the highest degree greedy of gain, libidinous and vindictive'.[85]

Assuming, as seems certainly to be the case, that mounting scepticism about China was not based on any systematically observed deterioration from the China of K'ang-hsi to the China of late Ch'ienlung, that is that the object observed was thought to have remained more or less constant, the explanation for the reassessment of China would seem to lie either in the kind of observers that went there or in the values of British society in general.

A persuasive case can certainly be made for important changes in those who observed China and in their point of observation. By the end of the eighteenth century Europeans were hearing relatively less from missionaries at Peking and much more from those connected with the China trade at Canton. At Peking the missionaries had some access to the court and government of the empire at its highest level where Confucian culture was at its most refined. Writing from the imperial capital, they were naturally inclined to stress centralized power and the benevolence of the régime. Moreover, the Jesuits in particular, who were trying to present Christianity in an acceptable form to Chinese intellectuals by reconciling it to some aspects of the Chinese tradition, had an obvious interest in presenting the Chinese tradition in an acceptable light to Christians at home. Jesuit accounts were inevitably influenced by their point of view in the Rites controversy.[86] On the other hand, the European merchants at Canton were dealing at a distance with a local administration which despised them in principle but which was also keenly interested in soaking them for money. Allegations of official corruption at Canton seem to be well founded. Merchants also had no incentive to palliate what they saw. They tended to paint their sufferings in the most lurid light, hoping to stimulate their governments to intervene with the Chinese authorities.

But the shift of emphasis from Peking to Canton, from missionary to merchant, ultimately leaves much about British reactions to China unexplained. At any time in the eighteenth century British readers were never wholly dependent on one set of sources rather than another. There were sceptics about China among Jesuit and non-Jesuit writers early in the century; towards the end of it favourable accounts of China written by missionaries or by secular authors were still being published in English.[87] Thus the English public always enjoyed some freedom to choose what published version of China it would or would not believe. That it should in general have been inclined early in the eighteenth century to believe the missionaries (for all its normal inhibitions about the Society of Jesus) and, judging from the evidence of compilations of all sorts or from the known opinions of men like Thomas Percy, Oliver Goldsmith or Samuel Johnson,[88] have increasingly ceased to believe in them from mid-century, seems to require a deeper explanation than a shift in the angle of vision. It seems to be related to changes in British culture as a whole.

The most ambitious recent attempt to draw a connection between attitudes to China and cultural change in the widest sense was made by Professor Louis Dermigny as a small part of his massively authoritative *La Chine et l'Occident: Le Commerce à Canton au xviiie Siècle*.[89] Dermigny argued that there was in fact continuity between the Sinophiles of the early eighteenth century and the later Sinophobes. In his view both admiration for supposed Chinese excellences and denigration of supposed vices can be related to what he called 'la montée bourgeoise' in Europe as a whole.[90] Jesuit portrayal of a rationally ordered meritocracy found favour with a wider public because it was a parable of 'bourgeois' aspirations. As these aspirations came to be attained throughout Europe, the triumphant bourgeoisie had no more need of parables. They began to ridicule their own creation. Bourgeois assertiveness was most marked in England; hence the decline of respect for China began there first, but it spread to France by the 1770s.

Such an interpretation encounters difficulties when applied to Britain. In France the Jesuit version of China was certainly taken up by critics of religious, social or political orthodoxy and presented as a rational alternative to the existing order of royal autocracy, aristocratic privilege and clerical intolerance. Admiration for China can therefore be identified, at least by some definitions, with bourgeois values. In Britain the situation was rather different. The leading exponents of China seem not to have been radicals in an obvious sense, but self-confessed 'ancients', like Temple, or disaffected Tories, like Swift or Johnson when young, who appealed to the past against the present with its commercialism and mania for change. Defoe, the supreme apostle of bourgeois values for so many critics, despised the unprogressive Chinese.[91] On the other hand, Professor Dermigny is surely correct in relating the growing scepticism about China from the middle of the eighteenth century to major cultural changes in Britain. It is no doubt possible to describe these changes as the assertion of bourgeois values, but it is not particularly instructive to do so. It is hard to relate them to any obvious shift in the economic base of society, and the new values seem to have been embraced by English upper-class society as a whole.

Even late in the seventeenth century the Jesuit version of China reflected aspirations that were still widely held in England. A tightly disciplined, highly stable society based on unquestioning obedience to authority of parents or emperor seemed admirable to many. Patriarchy, which China was said to embody, was still an ideal.[92] A society preserving its ancient traditions back to a remote antiquity was the best recipe against inevitable decay. To later generations patriarchy involved the suppression of all that was most valuable in human relations, that is spontaneous and genuine feelings. The remote past was little guide to the present. Stagnation not decay was the main danger. China was judged not by how well it adhered to its ancient traditions but by how it performed at the present time in terms of military power, effective government, scientific knowledge, technological skill and the living standards of the mass of the population. The growth of the China trade certainly played some part in this shift of interest. It brought to Canton large numbers of men who regarded themselves as practical observers of present conditions rather than scholars studying Confucian classics and speculating with Mandarins on the nature of *T'ien*. But the change in the kind of observer was still relatively trivial in its effects. British society as a whole now wanted assessments of the present state of China rather than theories about its past. The observers shared the values of the society from which they came. Even if there had been no alternative to the Jesuits' version, for a British reading public from the middle of the eighteenth century to go on admiring an ordered, unchanging China would have been for them to deny many of the values which they now accepted.

The example of how the British perceived China in the eighteenth century seems to illustrate in a particularly striking way the relationship between knowledge and interpretation for Asia as a whole during the period. To suppose that interpretations only changed as the result of new knowledge would no doubt be unduly naive. In fact, for the case of China almost the reverse seems to be true. As far as Britain was concerned, new knowledge was relatively limited during the eighteenth century, but interpretations changed radically. The conclusion which this suggests is that, whatever may be true for the sixteenth century with which his great books are concerned,[93] Professor Lach's concept of Asia 'making' Europe would be much less tenable for the eighteenth century. It would be an exaggeration, but one closer to reality, to argue that Europe 'made' and remade Asia in the eighteenth century to fit its own changing preoccupations rather than to suggest that European preconceptions were fundamentally altered by new knowledge of Asia.

The case of China also suggests some very tentative conclusions about possible connections between British assessments of Asian peoples and British dominance over them. A change for the worse in British esteem for the Chinese took place without the experience of exercising power over them. On the other hand, a decline of regard was in no way of itself a sufficient cause for efforts to extend British dominion. There was general recognition that the Chinese could now do little to resist forceful British intervention, but calculations of many kinds seemed to argue against such intervention. Only when these calculations were no longer seen to apply would the British resort to force. Nevertheless, the reassessment of China meant that force had now become a theoretical option, as it was in so many other parts of Asia.

The natural historians of man prided themselves that they were willing to study all men without preconceptions and prejudices. They deferred neither to Scripture nor to the wisdom of antiquity. For instance, in his *Letters on the Study and Use of History* Bolingbroke dismissed the 'ridiculous and hurtful vanity' of those who 'make their own customs and manners and opinions the standard of right and wrong, of true and

false'. The best antidote to such vanity was 'to accustom ourselves early
to contemplate the different nations of the earth in that vast map which
history spreads before us'. Yet in the very same sentence Bolingbroke
reveals what modern critics regard as his cloven hoof, an anatomical
deformity which they consider that he shared with many of his like-
minded contemporaries,[94] when he adds that history will display different nations 'in their rise and their fall, in their barbarian and
civilised states'.[95] He had no standard other than the 'customs and
manners' of his own society by which he could judge whether a people
had or had not 'risen' to a 'civilized' state. Civilization and barbarism
were European not universal terms. As European 'customs and manners' changed, so did the criteria by which Europeans judged Asia.
Those used by the natural historians of man might differ from earlier
ones but they were not necessarily any less free of what Bolingbroke
called 'those national partialities and prejudices which we are apt to
contract in our education'.[96]

By the criteria of Christian orthodoxy non-Christian Asians were
likely to fall short of full civility, although the Jesuits were very generous in their assessment of the Chinese. The natural historians of man
appeared to offer rather easier terms. Their criteria for civility were
secular and this-worldly: peace, stability, a reasonable degree of prosperity, concern for the arts and learning. By such tests the Chinese
certainly and perhaps other Asian peoples as well seemed to be
qualified for civility. Early in the eighteenth century the Chinese were
generally given a place among the 'polished' peoples of the world. In
the second half of the eighteenth century, however, the rules began to
change. Civility required a commitment to progress through individual
achievement. To the English in particular it also involved new patterns
of personal behaviour and personal relations in which genuine feelings
were balanced by self-imposed restraint. Such tests were too hard for
the Chinese and even harder for other Asians.

Much new information was collected about Asia in the eighteenth
century, but for the most part it was poured into moulds already
prepared in Europe. Relativism was rare. Asians might or – much more
commonly – might not achieve levels of civility defined in Europe; it
was very unusual for them to be seen as offering alternative models of
civility. Both those who observed Asia at first hand and those who
commented on others' observations agreed on this. Their points of view
were usually very similar. Few men who went to Asia could judge and
assess except in the terms then current in Europe. The travellers were
often themselves philosophers or practitioners of the new discipline of
the study of man. Even when they were not themselves learned, traditions were established, as with the questions prepared by the Royal

Society at the end of the seventeenth century,[97] of what travellers were expected to see and report upon.

British intellectual, military or commercial 'conquest' was spreading over Asia at some speed by 1800, although the incidence of all three was still very uneven. Japan and the vast areas of central Asia and Siberia were still completely outside the orbit of British trade or British political influence. What was known of them was gleaned almost entirely at second hand from other European sources. China was thought to be increasingly well known, even if trade was only permitted at a single port and the reception of the Macartney embassy showed that the Chinese would accept no political connection with Britain. The British were still ignorant about much of south-east Asia, but the appearance of Symes's and Marsden's books suggested an increasing degree of expertise. With the waning of the Dutch East India Company Britain's commercial and military supremacy over other European powers in the region clearly emerged. In India Britain's pre-eminence in every sense seemed to be unassailable, although from the brief wartime captivity of the Scottish Sanskrit scholar, Alexander Hamilton, in Paris a great development of Indology in France and Germany was to follow.[98] The British had as much influence in Iran, negligible as it was, as any European power apart from Russia. British scholars may have fallen well behind French ones in the study of the Middle East, and above all of Egypt, but very important collections of Egyptian objects were being brought to London as a consequence of the defeat of the French in 1801, and French diplomatic, military and commercial influence throughout the Levant had all been curbed for the time being.

As British interests spread throughout Asia by 1800 much wider sections of British society must have had some awareness of Asia than would have been the case earlier in the eighteenth century. What this awareness amounted to presumably varied very greatly. To politicians of the age of Pitt and Dundas, Asia had become a great chess board on which pieces were moved to protect British India. British commercial dealings with Asia were still transacted within the framework of the Levant and East India Companies, although the East India Company especially was coming under pressure to modify its privileges. More and more British manufacturers were taking an interest in Asia as a larger outlet for British exports. For the members of the new Protestant missionary societies Asia, if as yet only India, was a new field for endeavour in the making of converts.

In trying to analyse the interest taken by eighteenth-century scholars in Asia a distinction has been made between the traditionalists seeking new light on man's early history as partially revealed through the Bible and the classics of Greece and Rome and the natural historians of man studying man as a phenomenon in nature. The older tradition was increasingly assailed, but its vitality remained largely intact and the carrying-off of the Rosetta stone signalled that at last major discoveries about the ancient world were to be made from Asian sources. The chapters on Asia in Thomas Malthus's *Essay on Population* of 1798 are a striking example of the way in which material on Asia was being incorporated into the early landmarks of modern social science, the culmination of the new approaches.

More specialized studies of Asia were also developing by 1800. Arabic, Hebrew and more rarely Persian had long been studied at British universities. Indian languages began to be taught at the East India Company's new College, soon to be at Haileybury, from 1806. In 1801 the East India Company opened a Library and Museum. The British Museum had acquired a number of varied Asian objects over the years, but it only became a serious centre of study with the arrival of the great haul of Egyptian material taken from the French. The Society of Antiquaries undertook study of the Rosetta stone.

For some eighteenth-century poets, essayists and designers pastiches of Asian originals had provided a medium for experiment. For the most part the experiments had been with form rather than with content. A supposed Asian manner had been used as a vehicle for very western moral sentiments or as an alternative to more conventional rococo designs to express lightness and grace. By 1800 Chinoiserie and the oriental tale had generally run their course. Indian motifs had a short vogue in architecture, culminating in the Royal Pavilion at Brighton, while Egyptian themes were still featuring prominently in neo-classical design. Most oriental adaptations in literature or the visual arts had been more or less ephemeral, but in poetry oriental influences, mediated through Beckford and William Jones for the most part, were continuing to produce creative responses well into the nineteenth century.[99]

Asia can hardly, if at all, have impinged on the lives of the great mass of the British population by 1800 in any of the ways so far described. They can have had little awareness of high politics or of strategies for commercial expansion or for mass conversions. They are not likely to have been connoisseurs or to have been well read in either the old or the new approaches to the study of man. But if they read at all, they probably had an acquaintance with some part of the travel literature, which kept its popularity so well to the end of the century, or with random references to Asia in the press, magazines, books for children or similar material. The growth of imports from Asia meant that many more people handled Asian commodities and that for the most part these were no longer of a very exotic kind: plain Indian cottons and the increasingly ubiquitous tea, rather than wrought silks or porcelain. First-hand knowledge of Asia also grew greatly as military and naval expeditions went to the Middle East and India and as the East India Company's civil and military services expanded. For some families in England and Scotland service in India became a regular expectation. Such expectations encouraged interest in Asia. Study of the printed catalogue issued in 1786 for a commercial library in Edinburgh, an important source of candidates for the East India Company, has revealed 'a profusion of oriental titles of all kinds . . . We must conclude such prodigal acquisition is a particularly impressive example of the expanding and accelerating concern with the orient which marked the last quarter of the century'.[100]

What unsophisticated readers or those who did not read at all made of Asia is hardly easier to fathom for 1800 than it is for 1700. The demand for chap books was evidently still vigorous at the beginning of the nineteenth century and their form and content appear to have changed little over a hundred years. Tales of chivalry remained popular.[101] Some of them were given Asian settings, but still ones appropriate to the Crusades rather than to the East India Company. For instance, in *The Surprising Adventures of the Seven Champions of Christendom*, evidently published around 1800, St George had dealings with the King of Egypt (whom he converted to Christianity) and the Sultan of Persia, while St David went off to 'the court of Tartary'.[102] Sir John Mandeville lasted right through the eighteenth century as a standby for the chap-book sellers. An edition of *The Foreign Travels and Dangerous Voyages of that Renowned English Knight*, thought to be dated 1785, has him setting out from St Albans in 'Michaelmas 1732', and its illustrations show him, wearing eighteenth-century dress, sailing in an eighteenth-century ship; the Asian countries through which he travels, however, are still those of medieval legend.[103] Early in the eighteenth century new material about Asia began to be filtered into the chap books by those who plundered the *Arabian Nights*; a chap-book version was advertised in 1708, very soon after the first English translation of Galland.[104] By 1800 Sinbad and Aladdin had become standard chap-book heroes. They had also begun their careers on the stage. In 1788 'Aladdin and his Wonderful Lamp' appeared for the first time as a London Christmas pantomime.[105] From the 1790s it became increasingly common to give pantomimes an 'eastern', supposedly Indian, Persian or Arabian, setting. Early in the nineteenth century Chinese pantomimes came into vogue. Charles Dibdin's 'Whang Fong; or, the Clown of China' of 1812 is said to have marked the point at which 'orientalism' in pantomime became firmly established.[106]

Plates from William Alexander, the 'draughtsman' who had accompanied Lord Macartney, were the models for the more ambitious Chinese pantomimes' costumes and scenery. Even so, impressions of Asia conveyed by chap book or pantomime can at best have been hoary legend or more recent fantasy. Other publications were, however, beginning to compete with chap books for a mass readership, especially religious and moral tracts and educational material aimed at Sunday schools in particular. By 1800 geography was said to be 'part of the most common education; the elements of it are taught in our parish schools; and accordingly, there are scarcely any, except in the lowest ranks of society . . . to whom, those parts of the other quarters of the globe, where their own nation has settlements or trade are totally unknown.'[107] William Carey, the future Baptist missionary, taught geography in a Northamptonshire village school. From reading travel books and from his own teaching, Carey 'was led to contemplate the moral and spiritual degradation of the heathen, and to form the noble design of communicating the Gospel to them'.[108] What the children in his or any other school retained of Asia from such lessons is another matter altogether.

Conclusions about so wide a range of perceptions of Asia must be very tentative. One common feature does, however, suggest itself. Belief in the unfathomable and mysterious East was by 1800 largely confined to poets or those who read chap books. For others Asia had been reduced to ordinary human dimensions, and by what were taken to be universal standards, not very impressive human dimensions at that. Huge and powerful empires had turned on closer acquaintance into weak, vulnerable states; rare luxuries were replaced by everyday items of consumption or raw materials for manufacturers; belief in the ancient wisdom of Egypt or the refined natural morality of the Confucianists had given way to conviction that Asians were ignorant and confirmed in their ignorance by religious bigotry.

An Asia diminished in scale to the prosaic and humdrum was also by 1800 an Asia to be put to use for an increasing number of Englishmen. New commodities and markets were to be found in it. Its states were to be drawn into alliances. Honourable and well-rewarded careers could be made in it, especially in India. It could provide the life's work for scholars. The metaphor was even adopted by painters, who saw themselves by 'guiltless spoliation' carrying back 'picturesque beauties of those favoured regions'.[109] Territorial empire had come to be accepted by most sections of British opinion by 1800, although there is no evidence that extensive additions to it were widely desired. Nevertheless, if imperialism is defined as the exercise of power in various ways by one people over another, something like an imperial state of mind was coming into existence in Britain with regard to Asia by the beginning of the nineteenth century.

NOTES

1 R. Fage, *A Description of the Whole World* (1657), pp. 49–50.

2 *The Despatches, Minutes and Correspondence of the Marquess Wellesley*, ed. M. Martin (1836–7), ii. 312, 320.

3 In outline such a case has recently been put forward by E. Said in his *Orientalism* (1978). A collection of articles discussing the issues raised by Professor Said appeared in the *Journal of Asian Studies*, xxxix (1980).

4 On these concepts, see especially J. G. A. Pocock, *The Machiavellian Moment* (Princeton, 1975).

5 *Navigantium atque Itinerantium Bibliotheca* (1764 edn.), ii. 1055. This edition was revised by John Campbell, see above, p. 49.

6 *An Essay on the History of Civil Society*, ed. D. Forbes (Edinburgh, 1966), p. 154.

7 J. Bruce, *Historical View of the Plans for the Government of British India* (1793), p. 39.

8 See above, p. 76.

9 See above, p. 76.

10 P. J. Marshall, *The British Discovery of Hinduism in the Eighteenth Century* (Cambridge, 1970), p. 251.

11 On this point see especially R. Guha, *A Rule of Property for Bengal* (Paris and The Hague, 1963) and A. T. Embree, 'Landholding in India and British Institutions', *Land Control and Social Structure in Indian History*, ed. R. E. Frykenberg (Madison, 1969), pp. 35–52.

12 This point is elaborated in P. J. Marshall, 'Indian Officials in Eighteenth-century Bengal', *Bengal Past and Present*, lxxxiv (1965), 95–120.

13 H. Verelst, *A View of the Rise, Progress and Present State of the English Government in Bengal* (1772), appendix, p. 234.

14 *Travels in the Mugal Empire*, ed. A. Constable, revised V. Smith (1914), p. 230.

15 G. Forrest, *Life of Lord Clive* (1918), ii. 176.

16 *A Short Review of the British Government in India* (1790), p. 67.

17 James Grant, quoted in Marshall, 'Indian Officials', *Bengal Past and Present*, lxxxiv. 105.

18 John Shore, *ibid.*, 106.

19 *Selections from the State Papers of the Governors-General of India: Lord Cornwallis*, ed. G. W. Forrest (Oxford, 1926), ii. 113–14.

20 21 Geo. III, c. 70, sec. 1. For the background of the bill, see *The Writings and Speeches of Edmund Burke*, v, ed. P. J. Marshall (Oxford, 1981), 140–2.

21 See especially Guha, *Rule of Property*.

22 *Fort William–India House Correspondence* (New Delhi, 1949–), v, ed. N. K. Sinha, 242.

23 *Historical View of the Plans for the Government of British India*, p. 29.

24 Bengal to Directors, 10 Aug. 1791, India Office Records, E/4/50, p. 303.

25 *Selections from State Papers: Cornwallis*, ii. 123.

26 J. D. M. Derrett, *Religion, Law and the State in India* (1968), p. 298.

27 *Wellesley Despatches*, ed. Martin, ii. 312–13.
28 See above, pp. 16–17.
29 *A Survey of the Turkish Empire* (1798), pp. 282–3.
30 W. Wittman, *Travels in Turkey, Asia Minor, and across the Desert into Egypt* (1803), p. 133.
31 *The Real State of the Ottoman Empire* (1784), p. 258.
32 *Survey*, p. 17.
33 See above, p. 16.
34 S. J. Shaw, *Between Old and New: The Ottoman Empire under Selim III* (Cambridge, Mass., 1971).
35 Eton, *Survey*, p. 101.
36 J. Dallaway, *Constantinople Ancient and Modern* (1797), pp. 42–3.
37 Speech on 29 March 1791, *Parliamentary History of England*, xxix. 77.
38 *Survey*, p. 439.
39 Speech of 29 Feb. 1792, *Parliamentary History*, xxix. 949.
40 J. P. Morier, *Memoir of a Campaign with the Ottoman Army in Egypt* (1801), p. 19.
41 *Diary of Sir John Moore*, ed. J. F. Maurice (1904), i. 396.
42 Wittman, *Travels in Turkey*, p. 244.
43 *Travels in Africa, Egypt and Syria* (1799), p. 56.
44 H. L. Hoskins, *British Routes to India* (New York, 1928), pp. 43–8; R. J. Said, 'George Baldwin and British Interests in Egypt', London Ph.D thesis, 1968.
45 *Private Papers of George, Second Earl Spencer*, ii, ed. J. S. Corbett (1914), 318.
46 S. Ghorbal, *The Beginnings of the Egyptian Question and the Rise of Mehemet Ali* (1928), p. 64.
47 *Political Recollections Relative to Egypt* (1801), pp. 224–5.
48 *History of the British Expedition to Egypt* (1802), p. 232.
49 *Diary*, ii. 51.
50 M. E. Yapp, 'The Establishment of the East India Company's Residency at Baghdad', *Bulletin of School of Oriental and African Studies*, xxx (1967), 329.
51 *Travels through Arabia and other Countries in the East* (Edinburgh), 1792, ii. 322–3.
52 *A Journey from Bengal to England* (1798), ii. 178, 234.
53 J. W. Kaye, *Life and Correspondence of Major-General Sir John Malcolm* (1856), i. 133.
54 P. 180.
55 Eg. despatch of 25 Jan. 1794 in H. P. Clodd, *Malaya's First British Pioneer: the life of Francis Light* (1948), pp. 97–101.
56 See above, p. 129.
57 *An Embassy to China*, ed. J. L. Cranmer-Byng (1962), pp. 212–13.
58 *Objects Interesting to the English Nation* (Calcutta, 1793), i, pp. ii–iii, 234.
59 *Travels in China*, 2nd edn. (1806), pp. 380, 395–6.
60 *Remarks on the Influence of Climate* (1781), p. 207.
61 See above, p. 141.
62 *House of Commons Sessional Papers of the Eighteenth Century* (Delaware, 1975), xci. 3–4.
63 *Travels in China*, pp. 379–80.
64 (1802), ii. 91.
65 *Embassy to China*, p. 223.
66 *Travels in China*, p. 419.
67 *Remarks on Climate*, pp. 206–7.
68 *Embassy to China*, pp. 244–6.
69 *An Essay on Population*, 'Everyman' edn. (1914), i. 128–30.
70 *Travels in China*, pp. 566–86.
71 *Objects Interesting to the English Nation*, p. 223.
72 *Embassy to China*, p. 279.
73 *Ibid.*, pp. 291 ff.
74 E. Harris in J. Harris, *Sir William Chambers* (1970), p. 176.

75 H. Honour, *Chinoiserie* (1961).
76 G. Godden, *Oriental Export Porcelain and its Influence on European Wares* (1979), pp. 48–9, 80.
77 N. McKendrick, 'Josiah Wedgwood: an Eighteenth-century Entrepreneur', *Economic History Review*, 2nd ser., xii (1959–60), 425.
78 *Modern Part of the Universal History*, iii. 620.
79 *Travels in China*, p. 305.
80 R. J. Charleston, 'Porcelain as Room Decoration in Eighteenth-century England', *Chinese Export Porcelain*, ed. E. Gordon (New York, 1977), p. 100.
81 Vol. i. 22.
82 See above, pp. 81–2.
83 Vol. iii. 578.
84 See above, p. 81.
85 Vol. ii. 147 *n*.
86 See above, pp. 107–8.
87 See above pp. 85–6.
88 On him see T. C. Fan, 'Dr Johnson and Chinese Culture', *Occasional Papers of the China Society*, vi (1945).
89 3 vols (Paris, 1964).
90 Vol. i. 36.
91 See above, p. 133.
92 L. Stone, *The Family, Sex and Marriage in England, 1500–1800* (1977), p. 152.
93 *Europe in the Making of Asia* (Chicago, 1965–).
94 For a very trenchant expression of such criticisms, see M. Hodgen, *Early Anthropology in the Sixteenth and Seventeenth Centuries* (Philadelphia, 1964), Ch. 12.
95 (1752), i. 29–30.
96 *Ibid.*, i. 31.
97 See above, p. 45.
98 R. Rocher, *Alexander Hamilton* (New Haven, 1968).
99 E. S. Shaffer, *Kubla Khan and the Fall of Jerusalem* (Cambridge, 1978).
100 P. Kaufman, *Libraries and their Users* (1969), pp. 139–40.
101 See above, p. 54.
102 British Library press-mark Ch. 820/28.
103 *Ibid.*, 1076.1.3.
104 F. J. Harvey Darton, *Children's Books in England* (Cambridge, 1958), p. 71.
105 L. Hughes, *The Drama's Patrons* (Austin, 1971), pp. 159–60.
106 D. Mayer, *Harlequin in his Element. The English Pantomime 1808–36* (1969), pp. 140–63.
107 *Edinburgh Review*, iii (1803–4), 67.
108 J. C. Marshman, *The Life and Times of Carey, Marshman and Ward* (1859), i. 9.
109 Thomas and William Daniell, cited P. Mitter, *Much Maligned Monsters* (Oxford, 1977), p. 127.

PART III

7

Savages Noble and Ignoble:
Concepts of the North American Indian

The editor of a popular reference work of the late eighteenth century, reflecting on the implications of Europe's discovery of America, reminded his readers that it had 'not only opened a new source of wealth to the busy and commercial part of Europe, but an extensive field of speculation to the philosopher, who would trace the character of man under various degrees of refinement, and observe the movements of the human heart, or the operations of the human understanding, when untutored by science or untainted with corruption.'[1] In these words William Guthrie summed up one of the dominant themes in almost 300 years of contact between Europe and the Americas. The concept of an innocent primitive had been present in western culture almost from its literate beginnings, but the age of discoveries had brought him from a remote past to the present, distant in space but no longer in time, available for scrutiny, dissection, perhaps emulation. For a moment it seemed as if the African would take pride of place when the fifteenth-century Portuguese obsession with Prester John gave rise to the image of the *bon éthiopien*[2]; then the Atlantic voyages at the end of the century produced a beguiling rival in the person of the American 'Indian'. Columbus's account of his landfall in October 1492 among the Arawaks of the Bahamas described a people physically handsome, quick-witted, gentle and welcoming. Later revelations of the Aztec empire showed a darker, more horrific side to American societies; but over and above individual variations lay the fundamental question of the origin of the inhabitants of the New World. Most scholars argued ingeniously in favour of the traditional, and Biblical, monogenetic explanation, but even so awkward questions arose. How had the Americans reached their present home? Who were their ancestors? Had their present characteristics developed before or after the migration, if indeed there had been a migration? Finally, and the same question was to be asked of the Negro, could the American Indian be classed as human at all, in the sense that a Spaniard or a Turk or a Scotsman – for all their obvious differences in custom, religion and language – clearly were?[3]

The debate was coloured by prejudice and instinct, for if the idea of a carefree innocent living according to the laws of nature was a persistent one, the concept if not the terminology of the 'ignoble savage' was also rooted deep in the European consciousness. Outside the battlements of medieval Christendom had swirled misty and monstrous shapes: giants, troglodytes, men with six arms, unipeds, hermaphrodites – aberrant, sub-human figures moving on the edge of the known world.[4]

A fearful expectation is reflected in the accounts of the early transatlantic voyages: Columbus had written almost apologetically after his first voyage, 'I have so far found no human monstrosities, as many expected . . .'.[5] Vespucci, describing his explorations a few years later along the Atlantic coast of South America, wrote of the inhabitants in generally favourable terms, but then added lurid details of polygamy, human sacrifice and cannibalism. So alien, so diverse, did the peoples of the New World appear that no simple category could embrace them all. The differing interpretations shared one assumption, however; for the ethnocentric nature of medieval Christian thought was repeated in later centuries. It was Europeans who had ventured forth and 'discovered' America and its inhabitants, not the reverse. Europe was the centre, America the periphery; Europe the superior, America the inferior.[6]

The contrasting concepts of primitivism were well illustrated in the English experience in America during the late seventeenth century when developments strengthened many of the earlier prejudices discussed in chapter 1. Once more, New England was racked by Indian warfare, this time the bloody 'King Philip's War' of the 1670s. In Massachusetts, which bore the brunt of the fighting, perhaps two-thirds of the inhabited places were affected, and one-tenth of the adult males captured as the Wampanoag and Narragansett Indians swept down on the settlements. The war produced a crop of passionate diatribes against the Indians, and the first of the captivity narratives which were to become so fashionable a literary form. John Josselyn's *Account of Two Voyages to New-England*, published in London in 1674, is probably representative of the settler view of the Indians in the period just before the war. The Indians were given grudging good marks for their physical characteristics – 'tall and handsome timber'd people, out-wristed, pale and lean Tartarian visag'd, black-eyed which is accounted the strongest for sight . . .'. Their 'disposition', however, was a different matter: 'Very inconstant, crafty, timorous, quick of apprehension, and very ingenious, soon angry, and so malicious that they seldom forget an injury, and barbarously cruel. . .'.[7] Within two years the first of the war narratives appeared, slim volumes usually published both in Boston and London, which recounted Indian bad faith, murders, pillage and torture. The language erred on the side of extravagance: the Indians were 'like wolves, continually yelling and gaping for their prey'; they were 'bloody and deceitful monsters'; 'perfect children of the Devil'.[8] These denunciations were not totally anti-Indian in a generic or racial sense, for the writers admitted the importance of the role played by the loyal Indians who remained faithful to their alliance with the white settlers. Their numbers fell not far short of those fighting for Philip (who was finally killed by an Indian), but they suffered indiscriminately from both the insurgent Indians and the settler forces. The number of Indian converts living in the 'praying towns' which had been a symbol of devotion among some sections of the Puritans to missionary work, declined drastically; and after the war their movements were limited. The war hardened attitudes and, as one scholar puts it, 'rather than bringing the demise of the white man in New England, signalled instead the beginning of the end for the Indian tribes.'[9] A more acerbic critic refers to these wars, indeed, not as 'Indian wars', 'Pequot wars', or 'King Phillip's War' – settler terms which have been used by historians – but as wars of Puritan conquest.[10]

Most appalling to the readers of the war accounts were the killing and mutilation of women and children, though they would not have to look far for similar accounts in contemporary Europe – certainly no farther than Grimmelhausen's *Simplicimus*, with its relation of atrocities committed against the rural population of central Europe during the Thirty Years War. One of the earliest of the narratives described in doleful terms the fate of a white woman: 'They took her, first defiled her, then skinned her Head, as also the Son, and demist them both, who immediately died.'[11] Even this incident paled before the lurid tales of Indian captivities – prolonged martyrdoms, from which some of the sufferers, having endured much, made miraculous escapes. The perspective was usually a religious one; Puritan in tone, the narratives were designed not to inform the reader about the Indians but to enlighten him about God's providence. At best, the captivity narratives were simple, moving tales of fortitude and suffering. They became bestsellers, but their commercial success led to their imitation in the eighteenth century by dozens of inferior (sometimes fictitious) accounts rattled off by hack writers which were mere tirades of anti-Indian feeling.[12] Although there was some continuation of missionary work among the Indians it was on a reduced scale, and had to contend with the attitude expressed by Cotton Mather in his *Magnalia Christi Americana* early in the eighteenth century: 'Though we know not *when* or *how* these Indians first became inhabitants of this mighty continent, yet we may guess that probably the devil decoyed those miserable salvages hither in hopes that the gospel of the Lord Jesus Christ would never come here to destroy or disturb his *absolute empire* over them.'[13]

At the same time as the dramatic war narratives were issuing from Boston, farther south a different view of the Indian was being encouraged among the early settlers of Pennsylvania. The contrast reflects in part differences between the Indians of the two areas, but more than that a determination by the organizers of the new colony that the indigenous inhabitants should be fairly treated, their rights recognized, and war avoided. William Penn reached America for the first time in 1682, and the next year produced a sympathetic account of the Indians which was translated into Dutch, German and French. Their way of life was marred only by their taste for alcohol (introduced by Europeans, as Penn lamented) and by their revengefulness. Although untutored in religious matters, where they lived 'in a dark Night', they had a firm belief in a God or Creator, and in the immortality of the soul. Their government was through a chief advised by a council of elders, and their deliberations were marked by a 'natural Sagacity'. Penn then went on to describe their daily life in terms which were to become as familiar to English readers as the harrowing tales of Indian torture:

> In Liberality they excel, nothing is too good for their friend; give them a fine gun, coat, or other thing, it may pass twenty hands, before it sticks; light of heart, strong affections, but soon spent; the most merry creatures that live, feast and dance perpetually; they never have much, nor want much: wealth circulateth like the blood, all parts partake . . . they care for little, and the reason is, a little contents them: in this they are sufficiently revenged on us; if they are ignorant of our pleasures, they are also free from our pains. They are not disquieted with bills of lading and exchange nor perplexed with chancery-suits and exchequer-reckonings: we sweat and toil to live, their pleasure feeds them, I mean, their hunting, fishing and fowling. . . .[14]

A versified description of Pennsylvania printed in Philadelphia a few years later put the matter into rhyme:

> Without much care they eat, they drink, they sleep,
> Their care for worldly riches is but light,
> By day they hunt, and down they lie at night.
> Those infidels that dwelleth in the wood,
> I shall conclude of them so far so good.[15]

Much the same image of the Indian was presented by the learned German immigrant to Pennsylvania, F. D. Pastorius, whose geography of the colony was published at Frankfurt in 1700. He described a life of simplicity and honesty, and commented, 'these savages have never in their lives heard the teaching of Jesus concerning temperance and contentment, yet they far excel the Christians in carrying it out . . . [and] put to shame many thousands of false nominal and canting Christians.'[16] In a later passage he contrasted the peaceful behaviour of these 'unsavage savages' with the bloodshed of a contemporary Europe torn by incessant warfare. The point had been made earlier by that sensitive and melancholy writer, Thomas Traherne, who compared the travel narratives with his own experience of Restoration England: 'By this you may see who are the rude and barbarous Indians: for verily there is no savage nation under the cope of Heaven, that is more absurdly barbarous than the Christian World. They that go naked and drink water and live upon roots are like Adam, or Angels in comparison of us.'[17]

By the end of the seventeenth century, then, two distinct streams of English writing on the North American Indian were evident. They are best represented by the New England war narratives of the 1670s on the one hand, and by the slightly later Pennsylvania accounts on the other. To reconcile the two was difficult, and by and large compilers and commentators at home selected the materials which supported their own attitudes and prejudices. Some simply included everything, as did Richard Blome in his *America* of 1687. In Blome's pages, alongside Penn's enthusiastic praise, lies a menacing description of the Virginian Indians of Powhatan's time, 'a Giant-like people, very monstrous in proportion, behaviour and attire'. The New York Indians were 'very serviceable and courteous to the English'; those of New England on the other hand were, inexplicably, given to massacre, torture or even cannibalism.[18] The failure of the English accounts to agree on a general image of the Indian was a microcosmic illustration of the difficulties faced by the scholars of Europe who struggled to form some kind of synthesis of the peoples of the New World from the avalanche of descriptive materials which descended on their desks. A favoured solution, which helped to explain much, was that they were men in an early stage of development, primitive Europeans in a sense. The assumption survived the period we are concerned with. It is in Peter Heylyn's *Microcosmos* of 1636, rather precisely dated: 'He that travelleth in any part of America not inhabited by the Europeans shall find a world very like to that we lived in, in or near the time of Abraham the Patriarch about three hundred years after the flood.' It is expressed in Adam Ferguson's *Essay on the History of Civil Society* in 1767: 'It is in their [the Indians'] present condition that we are to behold, as in a mirror, the features of our own progenitors.'[19]

Some of the implications of this were developed by John Locke, who seems to have been widely read in the French as well as English accounts. To Locke, America, or most of it, was a wilderness – a land in its natural state, uncultivated, where a thousand acres were needed to yield the same sustenance to 'the needy and wretched inhabitants' as ten acres in England. Though surrounded by land for the taking, many of the inhabitants of America lived in a state of miserable poverty; a king there was worse fed, housed and clothed than a labourer in England. 'Thus', concluded Locke in a striking phrase, 'in the beginning all the World was America' – in the sense that the world once was, as America remained, untilled and undeveloped. Likewise, society in America outside Mexico and Peru, was primitive and unformed. There were chiefs, but their powers were more respected in time of war than in peace, and the succession was determined in the last resort by martial valour. This, Locke again claimed, was 'a pattern of the first ages in Asia and Europe'.[20] If America did not represent a state of nature in Hobbesian, anarchic terms, neither did it hold out a model for Europe to imitate. In his *Essay concerning Human Understanding*, although Locke stressed that throughout the world customs cherished in one part were denounced or ignored elsewhere, he could find little in American behaviour which Europeans might usefully observe and follow. Rooted in their early stage of economic and social development, the Indians were classed by Locke with children, idiots and illiterates in their inability to reason in abstract, speculative and comparative terms. It was not a question of permanent, immutable inferiority. A Virginian Indian brought up and educated in England, argued Locke, might become as good a scholar as any Englishman. But the existing state of the Indian Locke summed up in terms as bleak as those used by Buffon, de Pauw and Robertson in the next century. 'Their notions are few and narrow, borrowed only from those objects they have most to do with, and which have made upon their senses the frequentest and strongest impressions. Such kind of general propositions are seldom mentioned in the huts of Indians . . .'.[21]

One characteristic of the English accounts of the Indians published in the seventeenth century was their brevity, their thinness, their reliance very often on hearsay information. There was no equivalent of the detailed, first-hand knowledge of the *Jesuit Relations*. Penn's comments on the good Indian were based on scanty personal experience. The New Englanders who wrote so dogmatically about the bestiality of the Indians along their frontiers had rarely, if ever, seen the inside of an Indian village, still less experienced daily life among an Indian people. George Alsop, in his description of the Indians of Maryland, after asserting that they were mostly seven feet tall, retreated in despair from the task of explaining their institutions. 'Their Government is wrapt up in so various and intricate a Laborynth, that the speculatv'st Artist in the whole World, with his artificial and natural Opticks, cannot see into the rule or sway of these Indians.'[22] If the apparent lack of political structure among the Indians puzzled most Europeans, they found still more baffling the religious ceremonies and beliefs of the Indians. Having allowed that the existence of some sort of religion, however idolatrous it might be, was evidence of the civility of the Indians, European observers turned a critical eye on its practitioners. The shamans, guides in supernatural matters, were referred to in a variety of terms, which had in common only their tone of contempt – jugglers, quacks, impostors, wizards. Alsop again owned himself at a loss – the rites and ceremonies of the Indians were 'so absurd and ridiculous, that its almost a sin to name them'.[23] Even better-informed observers fell into a tendency to describe Indian institutions and customs in terms of European parallels, a practice criticized by William Robertson when he wrote (but not until 1777) that 'There is not a more frequent or a more fertile source of deception in describing the manners and arts of savage nations . . . than that of applying to them the names and phrases appropriate to the institutions and refinements of polished life.'[24]

The early eighteenth century saw some improvement in this respect, with the publication by Robert Beverly and John Lawson of accounts which were based on contact with the southern Indians, and were influenced by a determination to show the Indian as he was, to abstain from passing more judgments. 'Close to Indian culture, but not pitted against the natives in a fight for land or survival, they developed clearer perspectives on aboriginal life.'[25] Beverly's *History and Present State of Virginia*, first published in London in 1705, was the earliest attempt to write a history of Virginia throughout the seventeenth century, and it included in Book III as full a description of the Indians as Beverly could muster from personal observation and from earlier authors. In Beverly's *History*, its modern editor has written, 'the Indians are neither noble savages nor sons of the devil, but human beings possessing some of the virtues and vices common to mankind'.[26] This was not an easy balance to strike, for 1676 had seen fighting in Virginia as well as in New England, this time in the form of Bacon's rebellion. Central to the uprising was the Indian and his land, threatened by Bacon's insistence that they were 'wholly unqualifyed for the benefitt and protection of the law'.[27] Beverly's account of Indian customs, government, daily life and the rest followed conventional form. He described the system of hereditary chieftaincy, and noted how important decisions were entrusted to a Grand Council. The Indians possessed neither individual property nor land, and before the coming of the English managed without a currency. Physically, 'they are straight and well proportion'd, having the cleanest and most exact limbs in the world: They are so perfect in their outward frame, that I never heard of one single Indian, that was either dwarfish, crooked, bandy-legg'd, or otherwise mis-shapen.'[28]

The most original part of Book III was the section on religion. Beverly was one of the few Englishmen who had ventured inside an Indian ceremonial place of worship – an exploit which he considered might have cost him his life. He was particularly interested in the current debate among French writers as to whether the Indians had any formal notion of a deity. Beverly insisted that the Indians believed both in a God who was beneficent and a Devil who was malign; but the longest and most critical emphasis of his account was on the position and practices of the Indian priests or 'conjurers', with their divinations, enchantments, and burnt sacrifices. Detachment went by the board as Beverly saw the Indians veering towards the servility which he instinctively associated with Popery. 'In this state of nature, one would think they should be as pure from superstition, and overdoing matters in religion, as they are in other things: but I find it is quite the contrary; for this simplicity gives the cunning priest a greater advantage over them.'[29]

Four years later John Lawson's *New Voyage to Carolina* was published in London. Lawson admitted the inadequacy of the English accounts, compared with the French, and this he put down to the fact that the most experienced English travellers in America were 'Persons of the meaner sort, and generally of a very slender education'.[30] Lawson, whose surveys on the frontier had led to his appointment as surveyor general of North Carolina in 1708, was determined to redress the balance. His detailed descriptions of Indian habitations, dress, food, ceremonies and child-birth formed one of the most perceptive accounts yet given by an Englishman of the customs and habits of an Indian people. Life in the wilderness was not without its blemishes – despite the fact that Englishmen who had experienced the Indian way of life were usually reluctant to leave it. In a not very convincing attempt to explain the Indian torture of captives Lawson noted that the Indian's existence was so hard that death alone was no punishment. Ironically, Lawson himself was to be put to death by the Indians in 1711. One of the worst Indian faults was greed; for wampum, wrote Lawson, an Indian would do anything, from selling his wife to murder. On the other hand, envy and jealousy were unknown to them, and a man was valued, not for his property or riches, but for his personal qualities. Lawson concluded his book with a sweeping indictment of European behaviour towards the Indians. Many of the 'Indian wars', he believed, were the fault of the Europeans, who had cheated the Indians, and in general introduced them to the vices rather than the virtues of European civilization. In a passage in which he pleaded for the fair treatment of Indians, the apprenticeship of their children to settlers, perhaps even intermarriage, Lawson wrote:

> They are really better to us, than we are to them; they always give us victuals at their quarters, and take care we are arm'd against hunger and thirst: We do not so by them (generally speaking) but let them walk by our doors hungry, and do not often relieve them. We look upon them with scorn and disdain, and think them little better than beasts in humane shape, though if well examined, we shall find that, for all our religion and education, we possess more moral deformities, and evils than those savages do, or are acquainted withal. We reckon them slaves in comparison to us, and intruders, as oft they enter our houses, or hunt near our dwellings. But if we will admit reason to be our guide, she will inform us, that these Indians are the freest people in the world, and so far from being intruders upon us, that we have abandoned our own native soil, to drive them out, and possess theirs.[31]

One reason for the more sympathetic attitude to the Indians was the changing situation in North America. There the French, albeit with Indian allies, were the main threat by the end of the seventeenth century. On the inland frontiers the hovering Indians might still be a frightening menace, but in the metropolitan centres of the eastern seaboard they seemed a remote danger. Their numbers had declined drastically during a century of contact with the English and their diseases, alcohol and weapons. In 1697 Lieutenant-Governor Andros of Virginia put the total number of Indian fighting men in the colony at only 362,[32] a figure slightly increased by Beverly in his *History*. For his part, Lawson thought that 'there is not the sixth savage living within two hundred miles of all our settlements, as there were fifty years ago.' As the struggle between England and France in North America intensified, both local and imperial efforts turned to winning Indian support. In the north the Iroquois confederacy was the main target of these efforts, in the south the Cherokees, Creeks and Choctaws. Of these an imperial official pointed out, 'while they are our friends, they are the cheapest and strongest barrier for the protection of our settlements'.[33]

It was as part of this general endeavour that in 1710 four Iroquois sachems from the Mohawk valley made a well-publicized visit to London. They were wined and dined, entertained and fêted, theatrical performances were given in their honour. Throughout all this they seem to have conducted themselves with dignity. In the words of the chronicler Abel Boyer they were 'Men of good presence, and those who have convers'd with them, say, that they have an exquisite sense, and a quick apprehension.'[34] The portraits of the 'Four Kings' by John Verelst confirm the impression of authority and poise which struck their London hosts. Other cruder pictorial representations were also issued, and several pamphlets and ballad-sheets, one of which coolly lifted Lawson's description of the Indians of North Carolina, and applied it to the Iroquois several hundred miles distant.

Not all onlookers were impressed by the visit or the visitors. In 1712 Defoe was at pains to point out why the street gangs of Queen Anne's London were called 'Mohocks'. With a reference to the region 'from whence our four pretended Indian Kings came lately of their own Fools Errand', Defoe claimed that the Mohawks 'were always esteemed as the most desperate, and most cruel of the natives of North-America'.[35] Nor did an effort to build a missionary enterprise with the goodwill of the Mohawk sachems meet with any more success than an earlier attempt of 1704. A missionary, an interpreter and a school master were sent out in 1712, and set up quarters among the Mohawks about forty miles from Albany. Although the mission had some initial success among the children, it made little impression upon the adult Iroquois, who cheerfully continued their roving, hunting life, their polygamy, and their addiction to rum. The four sachems proved broken reeds in missionary terms, for 'they sunk themselves into their old brutal life, and tho' they had seen this great city [London], when they came to their own woods, they were all savages again'.[36]

In England satirists took the opportunity of using London's colourful visitors as weapons with which to attack some aspects of existing society, a device already used by Lahontan in France and rapidly becoming commonplace. The appearance of the Iroquois sachems in an article by Steele in the *Tatler* of May 1710, and in a longer one by Addison in the *Spectator* of April 1711, was no evidence of interest in the Indians as such. But implicit in the feigned wonderment at churches where people gossipped but did not worship, at clothes whose only purpose seemed to be to stifle the wearer, and at those strange, rampaging beasts, Whigs and Tories, who were 'born with a secret antipathy to one another, and engage when they meet as naturally as the elephant and the rhinoceros',[37] was the assumption that somewhere existed simpler, healthier societies where freedom rather than artificiality ruled, and nature replaced convention. Since the earliest urban civilizations, since the first written records, doubts seem to have existed about the benefits brought by technical and economic progress. Inherent in man, it seemed, was a wistful looking-back to a less sophisticated existence, to a golden age of simplicity and virtue. Eighteenth-century literature is crowded with examples of nostalgic escapism, some of it not too seriously intended, as when Boswell wrote to a friend in February 1767: 'You are tempted to join Rousseau in preferring the savage state. I am so at times. When jaded with business, or when tormented with the passions of civilized life, I could fly to the woods.'[38] Sometimes the vision centred on a mythical resting-place where man had once been, or which he might still find: Elysium, the Isles of the Blest, the Garden of Eden. The golden age was one of happy innocence revealed in Ovid's *Metamorphoses* (here in a translation of 1621):

> The Golden Age was first; which uncompelled
> And without rule, its faith and truth excelled.
> As then, there was no punishment, nor fear;
> Nor threatening laws in brass prescribed were;
> Nor suppliant crouching pris'ners shook to see
> Their angry judge: but all was safe and free.
> To visit other worlds, no wounded pine
> Did yet from hills to fruitless seas decline.
> Then, unambitious mortals knew no more,
> But their own country's nature-bounded shore . . .[39]

Sometimes the vision took shape around an actual people. Pompeius Trogus, writing in the 1st century BC, described the Scythians in terms which make familiar reading to anyone acquainted with the 'noble savage' literature of the seventeenth and eighteenth centuries: 'The people of that country recognize no boundaries, for they do not work the land . . . Justice is served by the tribe's inherent respect for it, not by laws . . . They shun gold and silver just as the rest of mortals seek it . . . they desire nothing they do not possess.'[40]

But the distance between thesis and antithesis was never great. For every writer yearning for a half-forgotten pastoral existence, there was another complacently boastful of the technical wonders of his own age. Between them stood the sceptics and doubters, critical of much in contemporary European society, yet sharply aware of the difficulty of transferring the conventions of a distant, simpler age to the more complex problems of the present. It was an extension of the discussion on the overseas discoveries initiated by the writings of Las Casas on the Indians, which in turn were part of 'the continuing debate between two conflicting European traditions. Over against the acquisitive instinct, which had been sharply stimulated among Europeans by the sudden availability of silver and gold, this great medieval mendicant is setting the simple virtues of a society free from gold.'[41] By the eighteenth century the developing wealth and strength of Europe had made the contrast at once more poignant and more difficult to resolve. As Mandeville explained in the preface to his *Fable of the Bee* (1714), 'the main design of the Fable . . . is to shew the impossibility of enjoying all the most elegant comforts of life that are to be met with in an industrious, wealthy and powerful nation, and at the same time be bless'd with all the virtues and innocence that can be wish'd for in a golden age.'

*   *   *

Across the Channel, the French, by the turn of the century, had proceeded further than the English in producing serious and detailed studies of the North American Indians, notably in the writings of the Jesuits. The *Relations* of the years 1632 to 1673 were complemented by the great series of *Lettres édifiantes et curieuses* of the eighteenth century, but except for some isolated fragments and summaries little American material from either series was translated into English.[42] By failing to make use of these collections, English scholars lost the opportunity to benefit from a remarkable series of observations. Despite their preconceptions and instinctive attitudes, the Jesuits, living among the Indians and observing them at close quarters, produced an incomparable picture of the tribes of the northeast at the moment of their calamitous contact with the European and his material culture, deadly diseases and alcohol, and aggressive religion. The Jesuit writings brought the Indian to a life far removed from the crude stereotype which appeared in the accounts of those explorers, traders and soldiers whose encounters with the Indians tended to be brief and sometimes bloody.

The early *Relations* tended to follow common practice with their careful listing of Indian characteristics into good and bad, virtuous and vicious. This process presupposed a whole set of moral values and behaviour patterns, inevitably European and Christian, which were then applied to the Indians under scrutiny. It judged the American Indian not in relation to his own environment and traditions, but with reference to criteria which had developed in a distant setting. In the American context both the praise and condemnation of European observers had little meaning. A gulf existed in comprehension between the Europeans, long since committed to a social system based on private possessions and property, and the Indians with their deep-rooted communal instincts. After the first shock of seeing Indian life and behaviour at close quarters faded, the Jesuits' training turned them towards a more dispassionate evaluation of the Indian and his situation as a 'natural man'. Initial optimism that, given time and patience, the Indians could be converted was replaced by a more realistic grasp of the Indians' reluctance to abandon old ways and traditional beliefs. Assumptions that the Indians had no religion were replaced by a slow and perplexed awareness of the intricacies of Indian beliefs, relating as they did to every form of activity, from hunting to healing. Jérôme Lalemant, the Jesuit superior at Quebec, advocated tolerance and understanding: 'One must be very careful before condemning a thousand things among their customs, which greatly offend minds brought up and nourished in another world. It is easy to call irreligion what is merely stupidity, and to take for diabolical working something that is nothing more than human.'[43] Morality and Christianity were not inseparable; heathenism, humanity and virtue were not necessarily incompatible. The Jesuits, like many other travellers, came to appreciate that there was no uniformity of taste and custom in the world, that 'If one were mounted on a tower high enough to survey at his ease all the nations of the earth, he would find it very hard, amid such strange varieties and such a medly, to say who are wrong and who are right, who are fools and who are wise.'[44] There was to be an echo of this in a popular English compilation of the early eighteenth century, though its source was William Penn rather than the Jesuits: 'Is it not vanity in any one people to call another barbarous, because their customs differ?'[45]

Ironically, English readers, ignorant for the most part of the *Relations*, had ready access to the publications of those categorized by Gilbert Chinard as 'les Adversaires des Jesuites', and particularly of two writers with first-hand experience of New France, the Recollet monk, Louis Hennepin, and the soldier and adventurer, Lom d'Arce de Lahontan.[46] Their books were very different in form, content and purpose from the meticulous accounts of the Jesuit fathers. They were written for profit and self-glorification, and they followed a wavering line between truth and fiction, reality and imagination. They also achieved a European circulation and popularity in a way which the scholarly *Relations* never did. Hennepin's *Description de la Louisiane* appeared in 1683; it went through three French editions in five years, and was quickly translated into Italian, Dutch and German. His *Nouvelle Découverte* of 1697 and *Nouveau Voyage* of 1698, for all the problems of authenticity which they present, gave the earliest account in print of the upper Mississippi valley. They painted a beguiling picture of Louisiana; a fertile land, temperate, well-wooded, with pleasant lakes and rivers, and an abundance of animal life – 'the most delightful portion and the earthly paradise of America'. Only the region's aboriginal inhabitants flawed the scene. Much of Hennepin's comment on the Indians was general in character; when he was more specific, then he referred to the Illinois and Sioux (both little known to European readers at this time) as well as the more familiar Iroquois. In his book which had widest circulation in England, *A New Discovery of a Vast Country in America* (1698), Hennepin stressed the contrast between the physical prowess of the Indians and their crude, brutish life. He could see glimpses among them of a 'brotherly love' which would shame many Christians, but there was no hope of genuine conversion until they were civilized. 'These miserable dark creatures listen to all we say concerning our mysteries, just as if 'twere a song; they are naturally very vitious, and addicted to some superstitions that signifie nothing; there customs are savage, brutal and barbarous; they will suffer themselves to be baptised ten times a day for a glass of brandy, or a pipe of tobacco.'[47] The summary of Hennepin's writings contained in Harris's collection of voyages of 1705 reflected the monk's sour view of the Indians. The section began with, 'the Iroquese are an insolent and barbarous nation, and have shed the blood of more than two millions of people', and ended with Hennepin's assertion, 'I do not deny but that the missionaries have faithfully discharg'd their ministry: but the seed has fallen upon an ungrateful soil'.[48]

Popular though they were, Hennepin's books were overshadowed by the *New Voyages to North-America* of Lahontan, printed and reprinted in French, English, German and Dutch. In simple, vivid prose Lahontan told of his adventures among the Indians. Resentful at his treatment in France, eager to write a bestseller and a defence of his actions, Lahontan fused his personal experiences and commercial instincts into a book which was at once a panegyric to the simple life of the Indian, and a bitter attack on the vices and follies of European society. His Indian, living without laws, kings, property or priests, was a truly happy man. Lahontan declared his intent in the preface: 'Nations which are not debauch'd by the neighbourhood of the Europeans, are strangers to the measures of meum and tuum, and to all laws, judges, and priests'.[49] The frontispiece showed an Indian contemptuously trampling over the regalia of European government and religion. It is the polemical aspect of Lahontan's writings which mainly attracted the attention of later commentators; often overlooked is that his book was a compendium of information on the Indians in readable, illustrated form. Even in France, for each reader who had studied the *Jesuit Relations*, many more were familiar with Lahontan's descriptions (based largely on the Iroquois) of Indian courtship and marriage, medicine men, sweathouses, herbal remedies, funerals, hunting, war, treatment of prisoners and the like. In England, Lahontan became the most accessible and quotable of all the French writers on North America. Superficial and generalized, with a sprinkling of tall stories to enliven the narrative, the *New Voyages* of 1703 gave a manageable account for English readers of Indian life in the forests of North America. Nor could they overlook the wider implications of Lahontan's observations:

> The savages are utter strangers to distinctions of property, for what belongs to one is equally anothers . . . Money is in use with none of them but those that are Christians, who live in the suburbs of our towns. The others will not touch or so much as look upon silver, but give it the odious name of the *French Serpent* . . . They think it unaccountable that one man should have more than another, and that the rich should have more respect than the poor. In short, they say, the name of savages which we bestow among them would fit our selves

better, since there is nothing in our actions that bears the appearance of wisdom . . . among them the true qualifications of a man are, to run well, to hunt, to bend the bow and manage the fuzee, to work a cannoo, to understand war, to know forrests, to subsist upon a little, to build cottages, to fell trees, and to be able to travel an hundred leagues in a wood without any guide, or other provision than his bow and arrows.[50]

The most acerbic part of Lahontan's book came in the *Supplement*, the celebrated dialogue between Lahontan and the Indian Adario (based loosely and anagrammatically on the real-life Huron, Kondiaronk), who according to the author had lived in Quebec, New York and France before returning thankfully to his wilderness habitat. Adario was an early and influential literary example of an exotic visitor reacting in appalled fashion to his first sight of Europe. Through him Lahontan attacked established religion, and the French legal system with its vindictive judges, harsh laws and use of false witnesses. In contrast, remarked the Huron, 'We live quietly under the laws of instinct and innocent conduct, which wise nature has imprinted upon our minds from our cradles.' In passages of persuasive and caustic satire Lahontan's Indian asked how anyone could live as a Frenchman did, dressed in the clothes of a fool, behaving as a hypocrite in an unjust society. In reply to the author's protests about the hardships of savage life, Adario proffered an enticing invitation: 'At that rate you prefer slavery to liberty . . . Why would you not choose to live upon the broth of all sorts of good and substantial meat? Our partridges, turkeys, hares, ducks, and roe-bucks; do not they eat well when they're roasted or boil'd? What signifies your pepper, your salt, and a thousand other spices, unless it be to murder your health? Try our way of living but one fortnight, and then you'll long for no such doings.'[51] Adario's offer was one which more Europeans accepted than could be conventionally explained; and once accustomed to life among the Indians few wished to return to settled life among their own kind.[52]

Lahontan's writings confirmed that the American Indian, whose image had owed much to the evangelizing Catholicism of the sixteenth and seventeenth centuries, was fast becoming the property of the sceptic, the rationalist, even the atheist. In Europe generally, the emergence of the Indian as an accusing critic owed little to observation in America, and much to disillusionment with existing political, social and religious forms. This disillusionment, sharper in France than in England, was reflected in the utopian literature which described imaginary voyages to imaginary lands.[53] However bizarre these countries and their inhabitants, certain common elements predominated. They usually had a deistic form of religion, held property in common, and lacked the formalized laws, institutions and political structures of the western world. Occasionally, as in Defoe's *Robinson Crusoe*, they showed a solitary man able to live a virtuous existence, close to nature, and bereft of all the mechanical aids and sophistications of civilization. Some included outright condemnation of that civilization, memorably expressed by Swift's king of Brobdingnag as 'a heap of conspiracies, rebellions, murders, massacres, revolutions, banishments, the very worst effects that avarice, faction, hypocrisy, perfidiousness, cruelty, rage, madness, hatred, envy, lust, malice and ambition could produce'. Apart from *Crusoe* and *Gulliver*, probably the most widely read of these books was Fénelon's *Aventures de Télémaque*, published in Paris in 1699, and quickly translated into the main European languages. In England it went through dozens of editions, and became almost required reading for generations of young people. The ideal commonwealth described to Telemachus clearly owed something to accounts of the North American Indians, though the land was situated somewhere off the coast of Africa. Its inhabitants lived simply in skin tents or bark houses; they were healthy and long-lived; they abhorred riches and all material possessions, which 'soften, intoxicate and torment the possessors of them, and tempt those that are depriv'd of them to acquire them by injustice and violence: and how can that be called a good, which serves only to make men wicked?' There were no laws, institutions, private property or judges; instead the people followed 'the true dictates of nature'.[54] Four years later Lahontan seemed to give credibility to just such a people with his account of the Huron and Iroquois Indians.

Another sort of credibility was provided by the visual arts, for the Indian appeared before European eyes in countless paintings, engravings and statues.[55] To generalize from this vast range is difficult, but certainly the best-known depictions tended to idealize the Indian, and as late as Lafitau (1724) traces linger of|De Bry's sentimental figures of the late sixteenth century. Charles le Brun's cartoon of the peoples of America – all that is left of his great painting which decorated Louis XIV's court at Versailles – has a magnificent, statuesque Indian towering over his creole neighbours. It is perhaps the finest delineation of the *bon sauvage*. Indian visitors to Europe were invariably portrayed in dignified poses, whether they appeared in European-style clothing as did Verelst's Mohawks of 1710 and Isaac Basire's seven Cherokee chiefs of 1730, or half-naked as did the Creek chieftain, Tomo Chachi, in an engraving of 1734. Later in the century Joshua Reynolds's portrait of Joseph Brant was only one of several which showed the Indian leader as a striking example of savage nobility. The farther removed from the American wilderness the artist, the more sympathetic was his image of its aboriginal inhabitants. Drawings made on the spot tended to be less flattering, but these remained largely unpublished. The 'Codex Canadensis', a manuscript book of sketches dating from about 1700, has dozens of lively if unsophisticated depictions of Indians in full decorative paint with something of the bizarre and horrific about them. Even more chilling was the drawing by Alexandre de Batz in 1732 of a grim-faced Tomica warrior displaying the scalps of three Natchez enemies. Equally unprepossessing were the Indian warriors sketched or caricatured by Brigadier George Townshend during the campaigns of the Seven Years War in Canada. Farther north the Cree Indians were shown in homelier activities by the English fur trader, James Isham, whose drawings had them dressed in a rather unbecoming mixture of European and Indian clothes hunting beaver rather than striking the formalized poses characteristic of many of the published illustrations.

Fictional representation of the American Indian in this period is nondescript, and his sporadic appearance in plays, novels and poetry is of limited significance.[56] His delineation is casual, and usually he is a background figure in a setting which is vaguely American. He is only one of a whole gallery of exotic types; he rubs shoulders with Mexicans and Peruvians, Africans and Turks, Chinamen and Persians. He varies in type from noble innocent or faithful companion to war-painted villain, skulking behind a tree, tomahawk in hand and scalping-knife at belt. His character and behaviour depend less on careful observation than on the exigencies of the plot, and he is often of uncertain ethnic type. Even when he features more prominently he is overlaid with a heavy sentimentality or encumbered with classical allusions. So the Indian hero of John Shebbeare's novel *Lydia* wears 'the air, attitude, and expression of the beauteous statue of Apollo', while 'the perfection of his form and the expression of his visage were such that the Grecian sculptors of the famed statue of Laocoon, or the fighting gladiator, might have studied him with instruction and delight'.[57] Not until the novels of Henry Mackenzie in the 1770s did the North American Indian appear in fiction as a believable human being, an individual rather than a stock type. Even his prominence in satirical literature reflected his availability rather than deep intrinsic interest in him and his ways. For the philosopher who wished to bring a sophisticated visitor to Europe there was a wide range of alternatives, but for a writer who needed a guest from a more primitive culture to be confronted with the irrationalities of English or French behaviour the choice was limited. The African Negro was occasionally used, but was part of another controversy in which his colour and identity as a slave domi-nated. The Pacific islander did not emerge into the limelight until the era of Cook and Bougainville. Little was known about the peoples of south and central America outside the areas of immediate Spanish control. So the North American Indian was an obvious claimant, and the travel narratives provided ample material for writers to use him for illustrative or polemic ends.

The amount of this material continued to increase during the eighteenth century, and although much of it was inaccurate and repetitious, there were also investigations of the Indian which were of a more scholarly and comparative nature. Among a series of early eighteenth-century books which scrutinized peoples in distant parts of the world alongside those known from antiquity[58] was Joseph-François Lafitau's *Moeurs des Sauvages Ameriquains* (1724). To his wide reading on the subject, Lafitau added the valuable ingredient of personal experience, for he was a member of the Jesuit mission at Saint-Louis du Sault near Montreal from 1712 to 1717. Lafitau expressed his aim thus: 'I have not limited myself to learning the characteristics of the Indians and informing myself about their customs and practices, I have sought in these practices and customs, vestiges of the most remote antiquity.'[59] This search plunged Lafitau and his readers into a series of detailed parallels between the American Indians and the peoples of the world of classical antiquity. Lafitau's prime purpose was a religious one. As a Jesuit, he was repelled by the attitude of the freethinkers and sceptics, and their attacks on the Church. Even some missionaries had described primitive peoples as being without any religion, a fundamental error which could only encourage the atheists. Accordingly, by far the longest chapter in Lafitau concerned the religion of the Indians. It began with the forthright utterance, 'men need a religion', and ended almost 200 pages later with the comment, 'I have said enough on this matter to show that religion had the same origin for all the peoples'.[60] Apart from its information on the religious beliefs and customs of the Indians, Lafitau's work contained a meticulous reconstruction of life among the Iroquois and Huron. There is the detail of the earlier *Jesuit Relations*, but fitted now into a general framework of social and political organization. It is noteworthy, for example, that Lafitau's chapter on the women's occupations in the village was longer than the one on the men's, evidence of his appreciation of the women's role in Iroquois society, where the woman was head of the household, and exerted influence and power within the village community and the tribe at large. The sweeping generalizations of previous writers about the 'liberty' and 'freedom' of the Indians were severely modified in Lafitau, who understood that Indian society had constraints and traditions just as binding as the laws and conventions of European states. Lafitau was a realist who made no special claims for the lifestyle of the Indians, and rarely hinted that Europeans could benefit from direct imitation, although he considered that 'they think justly about their affairs, better than the mass of people do among us'.[61]

In his insistence on the close similarities between the Indians and the peoples of Europe's Graeco-Roman past, Lafitau might have been expected to give, if not a new respectability to the Indian, at least a new direction to observations. That his work was not more immediately influential stemmed partly from its awkward style, partly from the fact that its author was a Jesuit. Even so, much of Lafitau's material, if not all his conclusions, should have been of interest to his contemporaries. The same year, 1724, saw the belated publication of Fontenelle's *Discours sur l'origine des fables* whose methodology bore a resemblance to Lafitau's but with a different end in view. Fontenelle used contemporary travel literature on the American Indians and Homer's detail on the ancient Greeks to postulate a primitive mentality common to all peoples at an early stage of their existence. To Fontenelle, myth and fable provided the keys to unlock this mentality, otherwise impossible for the modern mind to discern or comprehend. It was a mentality narrow and undeveloped, for Fontenelle concluded that the myths represented, as the paraphrase of a modern commentator puts it, 'the unintentional errors, the faulty perceptions of infantile reason, of ignorant barbarians akin to peasant dolls and fibbing children'.[62] Lafitau's researches gave a quite different dimension to the subject, but there is no evidence that Rousseau and Diderot – for all their avowed interest in primitivism – had studied his work, and Voltaire had read it only to mock it. 'He would derive the Americans from the ancient Greeks and these are his reasons: the Greeks have myths; some Americans have them too. The first Greeks went hunting; the Americans go too. The first Greeks had oracles; the Americans have sorcerers. In the festivals of Greece there was dancing; there is dancing in America.'[63] In Britain, by contrast, there was serious use and appreciation of Lafitau's work later in the century. In 1757 the author of *An Account of the European Settlements in America* wrote that Lafitau's was 'a work which deserves to be read amongst us much more than I find it is',[64] and certainly in the years that followed the leading scholars of the 'Scottish Enlightenment' made good use of it.

Though of lesser weight and quality, in some ways a companion set to Lafitau's volumes was another Jesuit work, Father Charlevoix's *Histoire et Description Générale de la Nouvelle France* (1744). A straightforward compilation, it contained a great deal of reliable factual information, and towards the end Charlevoix's *Journal historique*, a series of letters containing the author's personal impressions of his travels through New France in 1720–22 which became one of the most popular sources on the American Indian, and was translated into English. After an early confession that he could discover nothing 'but a chaos and confusion' in the government of the Indians, Charlevoix produced a reasonable summary of the way in which the Hurons and Iroquois regulated their affairs. He described the role of the elders, the system of hereditary chieftainship through the female succession, the absence of private property; and then went on to reflect on the disputed question of authority in more sensible fashion than those writers who, because the Indians lacked a formal structure of government in European terms, could see nothing but either uninhibited freedom or complete anarchy. Restrained by the council of elders, who were without personal political ambition, the chiefs 'generally have no great marks of outward respect paid them, and if they are never disobeyed, it is because they know how to set bounds to their authority . . . obedience is founded in liberty . . . free from any apprehension of its degenerating into tyranny'.[65]

Charlevoix's volumes were the last of the great French compilations on Canada, which by 1760 was in the hands of the British. The work of publication, condensing and serialization continued for a little while in the *Lettres édifiantes et curieuses*, but little material from this long series, which began in 1702, seems to have reached England either in translation or in its original printed form. More was known in England in the first half of the century of the new areas of French endeavour to the south, in the lush, fertile lands of Hennepin's 'Louisiane'. There, the Indians bore little resemblance to the familiar forest-dwellers of the north. They were Natchez, sun-worshippers, living along the east bank of the Mississippi in 'one of the most beautiful and fertile countries in the world'. Their chieftain, with the title Brother of the Sun, ruled despotically, and the French accounts described a society more akin to that of pre-conquest Mexico than to the Algonkian peoples of the northeast with their atomistic social and political way of life. The most prominent building in a Natchez town was the temple, crammed with idols and with the bones of previous chiefs and their strangled followers. There a perpetual fire burned, guardians maintained an unceasing vigil, and outside the people lived in superstitious submission.[66] It was from one of these unfriendly Jesuit descriptions that Montesquieu obtained his example of despotic power which forms the celebrated two-sentence Chapter XIII, Book V, of *L'Esprit des lois*. 'When the savages of Louisiana want fruit they cut down the tree to take it. This is despotic government.'[67] There was nothing here of the liberty-loving Indian of Lahontan or the *Jesuit Relations*. Moreover, Louisiana was settler country – or intended to be so in the ambitious schemes of French officials and promoters – and although the sparse reality never approached the grandeur of the visions of John Law and others there were enough colonists to lead to tension with the Natchez, and to a massacre in 1729 which was described in gruesome and well-publicized detail in Europe.

Some observers realized that the French were at least partly to blame, and one of these, Le Page du Pratz, later wrote a long and discerning account of the Natchez, based on eight years' living among them. In 1751–3 Le Page wrote a series of articles in French, extracts of which were translated and published in the *Gentleman's Magazine* for 1753. These were expanded into a book, his *Histoire de la Louisiane*, published in Paris in 1758, reviewed at length in the *Monthly Review* of the same year, and issued in a poor English translation in 1763.[68] As against earlier French interpretations of the Natchez wars, where the Indians were referred to in familiar settler terms as 'perfidious savages', Le Page insisted that 'one does grave injustice to call "Savages" men who know how to make good use of their reason, who think justly, who are prudent, faithful, generous, much more than certain civilized nations'. But his main emphasis was on the compatibility of the Natchez with their environment, and on the inappropriateness of applying conventional European criteria to their lifestyle. 'Let no one be surprised then if I call a city that which is a pile of straw huts which form the dwellings of Americans naked of arts and of the tools necessary to building. Having only wood, earth and straw with which to build, they deserve praise more than scorn, having constructed from such materials dwellings, both comfortable and secure, capable of resisting all the violence of wind and the other visitations of nature.'[69]

By the time Le Page's book was published France was losing its North American empire in the midst of the fiercest wars the continent had known. To the normal casualties expected from the clash of European troops were added the horrors of Indian fighting, deplored by observers on both sides. It was to this involvement of the Indians in European hostilities that Voltaire was referring when he wrote to Rousseau in August 1755 bewailing the fact that the outbreak of fighting in North America and the European example had made 'les sauvages presque aussi méchants que nous'.[70] Henry Timberlake, a Virginian who fought with and against Indians in the war, pointed out how the attitude of the Cherokees changed as they became caught in the spreading hostilities: 'They were pretty hospitable to all white strangers, till the Europeans encouraged them to scalp; but the great reward offered has led them often since to commit as great barbarities on us, as they formerly only treated their most inveterate enemies with.'[71] The image of the Indian as victim rather than villain appeared in books and periodicals in both England and France during the war years. The speeches made by the Indian chiefs at the Albany Conference in 1754 were widely reported, sometimes as examples of Indian oratory, but also to remind readers of the help given by the Indians to the first English settlers:

> At this time which we have now spoken of, the white people were small, but we were numerous and strong; we defended them in that low state: But now the case is altered; you are numerous and strong, but we are few and weak; therefore we expect that you will act by us in those circumstances as we did by you in those we have just now related. We view you now as a very large tree, which has taken deep root in the ground, whose branches are spread very wide.[72]

A similar botanical image was used by a writer at the same time describing the Iroquois as proud warriors but not bloodthirsty barbarians: 'whenever their country and liberty are out of danger, their passionate desire of peace as far exceeds vulgar bounds as their ardour in war . . . peace they always express by the emblem of a fair tree, whose top reaches to the sun, and whose roots are extended through all the nations that are leagued in the same chain with them.'[73] In the enlarged edition published in London in 1747 of his *History of the Five Indian Nations*, Cadwallader Colden pursued the same theme. An Iroquois chief reminded him of 'the bust of Cicero', while of the Iroquois in general he wrote: 'A poor, generally called barbarous people, bred under the darkest ignorance; and yet a bright and noble genius shines through those black clouds. None of the greatest Roman heroes have discovered a greater love of their country, or a greater contempt of death, than these people called barbarians have done, when liberty came in competition.'[74] Yet another writer insisted that 'Liberty in it's fullest extent is the darling passion of the Americans. To this they satisfy everything. This is what makes a life of uncertainty and want supportable to them.'[75] In other publications British treatment of the Indians was compared unfavourably with the French – the *Monthly Review* asserted, 'we make use of them only as tools to serve a present purpose: court them when we have need of them, and when the business is over, neglect and despise them, cheat and leave them in the lurch'. But as if to show the danger of seeking consistency of interpretation, the same periodical a few months later reviewed a book first published in Boston which pictured the Indians in familiar settler terms: 'no honesty, no honour; dread labour, more than poverty; spend all their time in eating or sleeping, except what is employed in travelling, hunting, and dancing; are much addicted to deceit and lying . . . eat the very flesh of their enemies'.[76] There were other accounts reminiscent of the most hostile Puritan war narratives of the previous century, John Maylem's *Gallic Perfidy* of 1758, for example, with its extravagant depiction of the colonists' Indian foes:

With visage foul, and horrid awful grin;
Red, black and green besmear'd their mighty fronts,
With snaky braids, and dreadful ornament,
And pitchy feathers platted on their hair;
Obscene and naked, daub'd with various paints.[77]

Although the *Universal History* was as dependent on its sources as the other collaborative works of the period, in the sections on America there are clear indications of editorial sympathies with the Indian cause in the wars with European settlers. In one volume the official French interpretation of the Natchez rising of 1729 was queried, in another the conduct of the Massachusetts settlers during the Indian wars of the seventeenth century was criticized.[78] The triumphs of the Seven Years War were applauded, of course, but a few thoughtful voices expressed sympathy with the plight of the Indians. One observer put into verse the supposed thoughts of an Indian auxiliary as he surveyed the French and British armies confronting each other at Quebec in 1759.

For see! these sons of rapine have now drawn
Their swords upon each other, and referr'd
Their idle and imaginary claims
To the decision of a war; let us
Look on with pleasure, still remembering
That when an European falls, there falls
A tyrant and a robber; for what claim
Has either hostile nation, but the claim
Of the rapacious vulture to the hare
Or of the tyger to the helpless fawn?[79]

Even the rising of 1763 of the Ottawa chief Pontiac, supported by the Senecas and other tribes, brought understanding of the Indian cause as well as the inevitable condemnation of the scenes of massacre and desolation. Peter Collinson, a London merchant who was a Fellow of the Royal Society and a correspondent of Benjamin Franklin, had already warned that 'our ill usage of the Indians, by cheating and breach of promise, deceiving, and incroaching on their lands with impunity, brings on Indian wars'.[80] The title of Franklin's own *Narrative of the Late Massacres*, published in Philadelphia in 1764, was a reference, not to Indian atrocities, but to the slaughter of Moravian Indians by the Paxton Boys in Pennsylvania. It was recognition by the imperial government of the dangers of uncontrolled westward expansion which had led it to a series of measures aimed at bringing responsibility for the frontier Indians under its control rather than that of colonial governments susceptible to local pressures. Superintendents of Indian Affairs were appointed, and in 1763 the Proclamation issued which sought to restrict westward movement into 'Indian country' by settlers, traders and land speculators. These steps were taken for practical rather than humanitarian reasons; they were not enough to prevent Pontiac's rising, and their effectiveness disappeared as revolutionary sentiments grew in the colonies over this and other issues. But they were a sign of a new attitude in British governing circles which a later generation would call trusteeship. These are hints of this attitude, too, in one of the more sober accounts of the fighting which followed Pontiac's rising, William Smith's narrative of Henry Bouquet's expedition against the western tribes in 1764. One of Bouquet's achievements was to negotiate the handover by the Shawnees of their British prisoners – men, women and children – but he was taken aback to find some captives unwilling to return, and others parting from their Indian captors only with reluctance. Even after the transfer had taken place, some prisoners remained in touch with the Indians, a spectacle which caused Smith to write: 'Those qualities in savages challenge our just esteem. They should make us charitably consider their barbarities as the effects of wrong education, and false notions of bravery and heroism; while we should look on their virtues as sure marks that nature has made them fit subjects of cultivation as well as us.'[81]

In the excitement and drama of the American campaigns of the period it was easy to lose sight of the fact that, out of the public eye, European explorers were still making important discoveries – across the prairies and the great plains; along the Missouri, Arkansas and Red Rivers; in Texas, Arizona and Dakota. They were meeting unfamiliar Indian peoples, the horse-riding Blackfeet, Apache and Comanche among them, but although detailed accounts were often written of the encounters few found their way into print at the time. Much of the information was 'classified', either for reasons of state or because of commercial rivalry; other narratives remained unknown and unread, not necessarily because of official obscurantism but often through the inertia of government departments. Some of the shrewdest comments on the Indians were recorded by the fur traders, British and French, but again little was published. The traders were influenced neither by settler fears nor by literary images; their references to the Indians, usually set in the context of commercial considerations, were brief and to the point, but knowledgeable. Unlike traders on the west coast of Africa in the same period the fur traders travelled and often lived with their suppliers. One of the few accounts to reach print by a trader of the Hudson's Bay Company, and that almost twenty years after the event, was Samuel Hearne's journal of his wanderings in 1769–72 across the Barrens to the shores of the Polar Sea. In his description of the 'Northern' or Chipewyan Indians who were his companions and guides there is no hint of the noble primitive; instead, there is a vivid depiction of the harshness and brutality of wilderness life in the sub-Arctic North. The softness, adornments and sophistication of European society had no relevance to the Chipewyan lifestyle, as Hearne realized when in the midst of describing the sturdy appearance of the Indian women, he mused on relative concepts of feminine beauty.

> Ask a Northern Indian, what is beauty? he will answer, a broad flat face, small eyes, high cheek-bones, three or four broad black lines a-cross each cheek, a low forehead, a large broad chin, a clumsy hook-nose, a tawny hide, and breasts hanging down to the belt. Those beauties are greatly heightened, or at least rendered more valuable, when the possessor is capable of dressing all kinds of skins, converting them into the different parts of their clothing, and able to carry eight or ten stone in summer, or haul a much greater weight in winter.[82]

Another, and in a way more surprising, publication came from Madrid with the issuing in 1757 of one of the last Jesuit accounts from America, the *Noticia de la California*. Translated into English, French and Dutch, the work allowed a rare glimpse of Spanish activity in the remotest province of Spanish America, Lower (*Baja*) California. The description of the Indians was harsh by any standards, even allowing for the difficulties the Jesuits had encountered in establishing their missions there, and stands in marked contrast to the assessment of the Indians of the region in George Shelvocke's journal of his voyage round the world in 1719–22. Based on a stay of five days, it pontificated in no uncertain manner on the virtues of the Indians. Their behaviour, Shelvocke wrote, was 'endowed with all the humanity imaginable, and they make some nations (who would give these poor people the epithet of savages or barbarians) blush to think that they deserve that appellation more than they'. They held everything in common, knew nothing of luxury, pride and covetousness. 'In a word they seem to pass their lives in the purest simplicity of the earliest ages of the world, before discord and contention were heard amongst men . . . In short, in every respect, they seem to enjoy a perfect tranquillity.'[83]

The Venegas account represented a bitter and disillusioned epitaph on one and a half centuries of devoted missionary effort in North America. It was more than an indictment of the particular Indians of southern California; it was a revelation of the fading of Jesuit hopes in the face of the corruptibility and degradation which the missionaries saw in the American Indian. It was as remote from the realities of indigenous existence as Shelvocke's shallow praise.

> The characteristicks of the Californians, as well as of all the other Indians, are stupidity and insensibility; want of knowledge and reflection; inconstancy, impetuosity, and blindness of appetite; and excessive sloth and abhorrence of all labour and fatigue; and incessant

love of pleasure and amusement of every kind, however trifling and brutal; pusillanimity and relaxity: and in fine, a most wretched want of every thing which constitutes the real man, and renders him rational, inventive, tractable, and useful to himself and society. It is not easy for Europeans, who were never out of their own country, to conceive an adequate idea of these people . . . Their understanding comprehends little more than what they see: abstract ideas, and much less a chain of reason, being far beyond their power; so that they scarce ever improve their first ideas; and these are in general false, or at least inadequate.[84]

The effect of these varied writings on the American Indian can be seen in the outpouring of philosophical treatises which brought to the middle decades of the eighteenth century a ferment of intellectual discussion and excitement. These writings reflect, within certain limits, an acquaintanceship with the accounts of overseas areas and peoples, and a readiness to draw on them for corroborative evidence. No reputable *philosophe* would theorize on the nature of man without producing some well-chosen references to the American Indian, the Chinese, the African Negro or the Hottentot. Michèle Duchet has pointed out that the travel literature of the period could be juggled to construct a model or an antithesis. One might see a people without a history, without writing, without religion – in short, a people living in a void, 'opposé au monde plein du civilisé'. Or one could use the example of the same savage people – without masters, priests, laws, property – to show 'le désenchantement de l'homme social et l'infini bonheur de l'homme naturel'. Those convinced of the superior happiness of the savage will overlook the harshness and uncertainty of his life; those convinced of the benefits of civilization will ignore the issue as to whether the inhabitants of modern states are not the 'vrais anthropophages'.[85] In this context the increasing volume of descriptive literature on the Indian had a dual effect. It provided ammunition for both defenders and critics of existing European societies; it also widened the intellectual horizons of some at least of the thinkers of the period. Studies of the American Indian, in the view of one scholar, 'may well have played a rather special role, perhaps going beyond that of a catalyst and approaching that of an independent primary source'.[86]

This is not immediately evident in either of the two most influential French thinkers of the period, Montesquieu and Rousseau. *L'Esprit des lois* (1748), while stressing the importance of man's physical environment, had little to say on the North American Indians. It accepted the conventional notion that the end of savage government was 'natural liberty', and related this to the economic base of savage society. Montesquieu wrote that people who did not farm 'enjoy great liberty; for as they do not cultivate the earth, they are not fixed: they are wanderers and vagabonds; and if a chief should deprive them of their liberty, they would immediately go and seek it under another, or retire into the woods'.[87] No North American examples were produced of this situation, and the reference to the Indians of Louisiana, with their sun-worship and authoritarian rulers, was rather used as evidence for Montesquieu's supposition that the warmer the climate the more despotic the form of government was likely to be. In accounts of the spartan, simple life Roman authors such as Tacitus were more likely to be called on, and Montesquieu's threefold classification of government into republican, monarchical and despotic allowed little room for the less formal institutions of the North American Indian. In Rousseau, by contrast, savage forms of government played an altogether more important role, though his perspective and his examples were global rather than exclusively American. In the *Discours sur l'inégalité* (1755) Rousseau sketched man in a state of nature, a fine physical specimen but living alone, inarticulate, with basic animal needs – little different from the African gorilla or the East Indian orang-outang of the travellers' narratives. From this first pre-political and pre-social stage, which for want of historical evidence Rousseau admitted was conjectural, man slowly evolved, developing powers of speech, the use of simple tools, family connections. During this stage we can see man in a domestic environment, perhaps a communal or tribal one, living under a loose patriarchal government. To Rousseau this was the golden age of individual liberty and happiness, not the pre-social stage of animal existence which was the setting of natural man. Man was as yet unfettered by formal laws and government; there was no private property, no division of land or wealth. It was the existence described in the accounts of travellers in Africa, America and the East which Rousseau cited in his lengthy footnotes to the *Discours*. In *Du Contrat Social* of 1762 Rousseau produced a specific example of how the first societies were governed: 'The heads of families deliberated together on specific business, the young readily yielded to the authority of experience . . . Even today the savages of North America are still governed in this way, and very well governed.'[88] Man's evolution from this stage into one with private property, inequality of wealth and power, overbearing government and constant warfare, represented to Rousseau a steady deterioration which had led to that enslavement and debasement of man which he saw all around him.

At the same time a very different thesis was being propounded in France by Turgot, but his writings were not published until later, and more significant was the similar work finding its way into print from a group of scholars at the universities of Edinburgh and Glasgow who were to achieve a European reputation as the founders of the 'Scottish

Enlightenment' of the second half of the century. Selecting the mode of subsistence as the essential element by which a society could be identified, they established four categories – hunting, pastoral, agricultural and commercial. Implicit in the theory was the assumption that each successive stage was an advance on the previous, that societies might be expected in time to progress from the rudimentary first stage to the sophisticated fourth stage.[89] It was a view which stood in direct opposition to Rousseau's claim that economic specialization and intellectual development were root causes of human misery, and it was out of sympathy with the primitivist appeal to the virtues of the simple life, with equality, lack of property and freedom from formal laws. David Hume, in many ways the intellectual precursor of this group, had made the fundamental point clear in his *Treatise of Human Nature* (1739): ' 'Tis by society alone [man] is able to supply his defects . . . By society all his infirmities are compensated: and tho' in that situation his wants multiply every moment upon him, yet his abilities are still more augmented, and leave him in every respect more satisfied and happy, than 'tis possible for him, in his savage and solitary condition ever to become.'[90] The publication of Rousseau's *Discours* led to an immediate response from Adam Smith. In his 'Letter to the Authors of the Edinburgh Review' of 1755 he described it as 'a work which consists almost entirely of rhetoric and description', and argued that Rousseau, 'intending to paint the savage life as the happiest of any, presents only the indolent side of it to view'.[91] In his first book, *The Theory of Moral Sentiments* (1759), Smith related the differing behaviour of the 'civilized' and 'savage' worlds to physical circumstances, so that 'Hardiness is the character most suitable to the circumstances of a savage; sensibility to those of one who lives in a very civilized society.' The progressivist implications of Smith's writing were made clear when he noted that man's insistence on improving his material conditions led him 'to cultivate the ground, to build houses, to found cities and commonwealths, and to invent and improve all the sciences and arts which ennoble and embellish human life, which have entirely changed the whole face of the globe, have turned the rude forests of nature into agreeable and fertile plains.'[92]

Adam Ferguson challenged another aspect of primitivist thought when in his *Essay on the History of Civil Society* (1767) he wrote that 'property is a matter of progress . . . the industry by which it is gained, or improved, requires such a habit of acting with a view to distant objects, as may overcome the present disposition either to sloth or enjoyment'.[93] Or, as Kames expressed it a few years later, 'Without private property there would be no industry, and without industry, men would remain savages forever'.[94] Elsewhere in his *Essay* Ferguson seemed to be pointing directly at the American Indian as he discussed man in his pre-political state: 'The savage, whose fortune is comprised in his cabin, his fur, and his arms, is satisfied with that provision, and with that degree of security, he himself can procure. He perceives, in treating with his equal, no subject of discussion that should be referred to the decision of a judge.'[95] To Lahontan or Rousseau, this lack of legal machinery might appear an advantage; to the Scottish writers it was part of a general deprivation which marked and condemned the savage state and from which mankind must progress, 'from ignorance to knowledge, and from rude, to civilized manners'.[96] Early in his book, Ferguson had stressed a point of crucial importance to this school of thought: 'If we admit that man is susceptible of improvement, and has in himself a principle of progression, and a desire of perfection, it appears improper to say, that he has quitted the state of his nature, when he has begun to proceed . . .' Although he conceded that commercial nations could suffer from 'internal decay' and 'ruinous corruptions', he was adamant that the potential virtues of a savage state could be realized only in an advanced one, and that 'men in being civilized had gained more than they had lost.'[97]

In the writings of the 'four stages' theorists the American Indians were used to provide well-documented examples of the early stages of mankind's existence, but their conclusions applied to the savage world at large. Scientists were also pondering the implications of the travellers' accounts, and their considerations were likewise influenced by the contemporary emphasis on environmental factors. The problem of the basic humanity or otherwise of the primitive peoples revealed in the accounts had been largely resolved, though some queries remained. The fashionable concept of the 'Great Chain of Being' in which all living matter was arranged in hierarchical order, with scholars prowling along the chain in an obsessive search for 'links' and 'gaps', encouraged the subdivision of mankind into civilized and savage, 'polished' and 'monstrous', to use Shaftesbury's terms. The article on Cosmology in the *Encyclopédie* put it firmly and concisely: 'Everything in nature is linked together . . . beings are connected with one another by a chain of which we perceive some parts as continuous, though in the greater number of points the continuity escapes us.'[98] Inevitably, the search for the most celebrated 'missing link' of all, that joining men and the higher apes, focused on the dim shapes of distant beings half-glimpsed by explorers and travellers. When stories of men with tails or shaggy skins had been discounted, then it was the Hottentot who came under the closest and most suspicious scrutiny. Generally, the American Indian escaped this particular scrutiny. His humanity was accepted, and discussion was limited to the causes and nature of his savagery. By the mid-eighteenth century, environment (with particular emphasis on climate), and long isolation from the civilizations of both East and West, were the favoured explanations. They were couched in general and global terms; but the publication in 1749 of the first volume of Buffon's *Histoire naturelle* brought the American Indian into the centre of the debate.

Louis Leclerc, Comte de Buffon, was one of the most renowned European scientists of the century. He was no obscurantist theologian, no apologist for the activities of Europeans overseas; yet, almost unwittingly (if his later reactions are any guide) he provided a full-blown scientific theory which seemed to prove that American Indians were inferior to Europeans. It sprang from Buffon's attempts to explain the differences between the animal world of Europe and America. He started from the assumption that America was a new land in which nature itself was harsher and more overbearing than in Europe. The continent's physical environment was bleak and forbidding, its mammals were feeble and undersized – and so was man. In a chilling passage Buffon described the American Indian in terms which were all the more devastating because of their appearance of scientific authority. In America, he wrote:

> man, scarce in number, was thinly spread, a wanderer, where far from making himself master of this territory, as his own domain, he ruled over nothing; where never having subjugated either animals or the elements, nor farmed the waters, nor governed the rivers, nor worked the earth, he was himself no more than an animal of the first order, existing within nature as a creature without significance, a sort of helpless automaton, powerless to change nature or assist her . . . the savage is feeble and small . . . the activity of his body is less an exercise or voluntary movement than an automatic reaction to his needs; take from him hunger and thirst, and you will destroy at the same time the active cause of all his movements; he will remain either standing there stupidly or recumbent for days on end.[99]

To Buffon, the American was immature, not degraded. News of Bering's discoveries which reached Europe in the 1740s convinced him that there had been a double migration, one from Asia into northwest America, the other from Greenland into northeast America. In this way Buffon reconciled religion and science which the discovery of America had originally seemed to set at odds. To Buffon the crucial fact was that the Americans were recent arrivals, and the continent's lack of civilization, he explained, 'is owing to the paucity of its inhabitants'. This was followed immediately by a resounding indictment of those inhabitants, 'for though each nation had peculiar customs and manners, though some were more savage, cruel, and dastardly than others; yet they were all equally stupid, ignorant, and destitute of arts and of industry'.[100] Elsewhere Buffon allowed himself to look forward several centuries to a time when America, settled and exploited, would 'become the most fruitful, healthy, and rich of all', and in more general terms pointed out that 'Man, white in Europe, black in Africa, yellow in Asia and red in America, is only the same man tinted with the color of the climate.'[101] These qualifications were lost to sight in the controversy caused by the publication in 1768 of Cornelius de Pauw's *Recherches philosophiques sur les Américains*. Building on the foundations laid by Buffon, whose later protests, retractions and modifications were ignored, de Pauw stressed the hopeless and permanent inferiority of the American Indian. Replete with fashionable diatribes against clerics and colonialists, its pages tinged with Voltairean scepticism and scientific methodology, de Pauw's book quickly achieved a European reputation. In place of the sickly romanticism which had, for many, turned the Indian into an unbelievable creature of the imagination, de Pauw seemed to bring a stringent sense of inquiry to the subject, and as a controversialist proved more than a match for his main detractor, Dom Pernety. In reality, de Pauw used and misquoted sources without scruple, but his influence was undeniably powerful. Together with the geographer, Samuel Engel, he wrote the article on America for the *Supplément à l'Encyclopédie* of 1776, and there he described once more 'immensité des horizons, dispersion des Indiens, multiplicité des langues, difficulté des communications entre les différentes tribus, faiblesse de l'homme américain et âpreté de la nature, ancienneté du peuplement et retard historique.'[102] In Germany, Kant in 1764 had compared the American Indians to the ancient Spartans, but after digesting de Pauw he described them as degraded and incomplete beings.[103] And although Buffon disowned some of de Pauw's more extreme statements, when he returned to the subject of the American savage in his *Epoques de la Nature* in 1778 he depicted a passive, terror-stricken figure, at the mercy of the elements and of beasts of prey – victim rather than master of his environment.[104]

In France, the Abbé Raynal, in the various editions of his influential *Histoire philosophique et politique des deux Indes*, also showed the impact of the theories of Buffon and de Pauw. A collaborative work, the *Histoire* owed much to the distinctive pen of Diderot who had little doubt of the theoretical supremacy of the savage state over the civilized. The savage suffered only the ills of nature, the civilized man the miseries of an unjust social order and of degrading and brutalizing work.[105] But if this was much in evidence in the *Histoire*, so was the concept of the infancy of America and its inhabitants. In the English edition of 1777, Raynal regretted that in America 'the image of rude unpolished nature is already disfigured' by the activities of 'rapacious and cruel christians' (the Spaniards), but pointed out that in those regions the warm climate had made the native inhabitants debauched and indolent. Farther north the climatic factor seemed to work the other way round: the arduous life of the Indians in a cold climate resulted in impotence – 'all their strength is employed for their own preservation'. Then, in terms which owed much to Buffon, Raynal sketched the outlines of a fearsome physical environment where the inhabitants were dwarfed by an intimidating display of natural forces: 'Their perpetual contest of one element with another; of the earth engulphing the waters in her internal cavities; and of the sea encroaching upon, and swallowing up large tracts of land . . . exposes the inhabitants of the globe to evident dangers, and fills them with apprehensions concerning their fate . . . This terror . . . is observed to operate most strongly in countries such as America . . . Man, once possessed with fear, considers a single calamity as the parent of a thousand others. Earth and heaven seem equally to conspire his ruin.'[106]

It was at this time that the first battles of the War of American Independence were taking place, a war in which Indians were once more involved as auxiliaries. To the scholars' condemnation of the Indian as a man was added the familiar denunciation of the Indian as a cruel and inhuman adversary. In a debate in the House of Commons on 6 February 1778 bloodstained images of the Indian were conjured up by opponents of the government's policies. Edmund Burke 'stated the mode of an Indian war, which was so horrible, he said, as to exceed the ferocity of all barbarians mentioned in history. The only emoluments they receive: who signalize themselves in battle, are human scalps, human flesh, and the gratification arising from torturing, and some-times eating, their captives in war.' Governor Thomas Pownal sup-ported Burke's contentions in equally lurid language: 'The mutual feelings of humanity, which have set bounds to ravage, desolation, and bloodshed, among civilized peoples, are totally absorbed by an unre-strained effusion of the passions of revenge, bloodthirstyness, and carnage, even to extermination among the American savages.'[107] In the general reference works there was some clumsy stitching together of the views of Buffon and Raynal with the denigration of Indian conduct during the war. The net result was unappealing: the Indians emerged as malignant, insidious, dastardly, faithless and dangerous.[108]

Some counterbalance to these unfavourable interpretations was provided by the last spurt of published accounts in Britain before the success of the revolutionary movement in the colonies took responsibil-ity for the fate of most American Indians elsewhere. The books of Robert Rogers, James Adair and Jonathan Carver, with their generally sympathetic accounts of the southern and western tribes, sold well, and Carver's in particular was long to remain in print.[109] But none could compare in circulation and scholarly esteem with William Robertson's *History of America* in 1777, which became the main channel through which the views of Buffon and de Pauw reached the British literary public. Principal of Edinburgh University, author of the *History of Scotland* and the *History of Charles V*, Robertson was an author of European fame and, in Britain, enormous popularity. In his *History of America*, though he held aloof from the more vitriolic criticisms of de Pauw, he saw the North American Indian in terms which were distinctly unflattering. His portrayal of the New World, a vast inhospitable region where the few European colonies made small inlets of civilization, is immediately recognizable as stemming from Buffon and de Pauw. More scrupulous in his use of sources than the latter, Robertson was still influenced by his work. To Robertson, whose footnotes are evidence of the great range of published sources he had examined,[110] America with its variety of peoples extending from the relatively advanced Incas to the more primitive tribes of both South and North America, was a laboratory wherein the scholar could 'complete our knowledge of the human species'. Attempts by Lafitau and others to trace connections and common origins between the Americans and the peoples of the classical world were treated with derision. Instead, environmental factors dominated: 'The character and occupations of the hunter in America must be little different from those of an Asiatic, who depends for subsistence in the chase. A tribe of savages on the banks of the Danube must nearly resemble one upon the plains washed by the Mississippi. Instead then of presuming from this similarity, that there is any affinity between them, we should only conclude, that the disposition and manners of men are formed by their situation.'[111]

Robertson agreed with de Pauw that the smooth skins and beardless faces of the Americans indicated a lack of strength, even of manhood. Feebleness of body, he insisted, was universal among the American Indians, who were 'not only averse to toil, but incapable of it; and when roused by force from their native indolence, and compelled to work, they sink under tasks which the people of the other continents would have performed with ease.' Application, inventiveness, industry, were all lacking. The wretched savages, Robertson solemnly observed, 'will spend so many years in forming a canoe, that it often begins to rot with age before they finish it'. The physical perfection of the Indian, on which so many writers had commented, Robertson explained by a mortality rate among infants so high (and sometimes deliberate) that only the very fittest survived to manhood. To see the rules of reason prevailing among these savages was nonsense: the Indians had no terms to express abstract ideas, most could not even count. 'A naked savage, cowering over the fire in his miserable cabin, or stretched under a few branches which afford him a temporary shelter, has as little inclination as capacity for useless speculation. His thoughts extend not beyond what relates to animal life; and when they are not directed towards some of its concerns, his mind is totally inactive.'[112]

Two years after Robertson's book there appeared the revised and enlarged third edition of John Millar's *Origin of the Distinction of Ranks*. More clearly than any other product of the Scottish Enlightenment it revealed the mixture of classical writings with contemporary travel narratives as source material: within two or three paragraphs Herodotus, Caesar, Kolben, Hawkesworth, Homer and the Bible might follow each other in quick succession. Lafitau, Buffon, and de Pauw, more talked about than read by some of Millar's academic contemporaries, one suspects, had also been thoroughly scrutinized. Despite the medley of sources, Millar's arguments were clear and persuasive. The direct environmental factor was discounted as the dominant element in the shaping of societies; instead, Millar explained, the uneven progress of different societies depended on a complex interaction of historical and geographical forces. Though orthodox in his emphasis on the method of subsistence Millar struck out from there in bold and original fashion. His long opening dealt with 'the rank and condition of women in different ages', for to Millar the treatment of women was one of the identifying marks by which the progress of a society could be judged. The hard, wandering life of the savage left him neither time, energy nor inclination for 'contrivance and correspondence with the other sex'. Such attentions might not only distract him, perhaps fatally, from the business of survival, but would be inconsistent with other aspects of his behaviour, summed up by Millar as an indulgence in theft, rapine, torture and cannibalism. This is an elaboration of Buffon and de Pauw, but there are also echoes of the criticisms being made of sexual and family relations in Asia by British writers in this same period. The precarious life of a savage, though it gives him robustness and hardihood, teaches him none of the restraints on his appetite present in civil society. Although even the most brutish existence 'contains the seeds of improvement, which . . . are capable of being brought to maturity', the process is long and difficult because without writing 'the experience and observations of each individual are almost the only means of procuring knowledge'. Finally, there was a thinly-veiled attack on Rousseau:

> Many writers appear to take pleasure in remarking that, as the love of
> liberty is natural to man, it is to be found in the greatest perfection
> among barbarians, and is apt to be impaired according as people make

progress in civilization and the arts of life. That mankind, in the shape of mere savages, are in great measure unacquainted with government, and unaccustomed to any sort of constraint, is sufficiently evident. But their independence, in that case, is owing to the wretchedness of their circumstances, which afford nothing that can tempt any one man to become subject to another.[113]

The books of Robertson and Millar marked a new stage in the popularization of the four-stages theory – 'In every inquiry concerning the operations of men when united together in society, the first object of attention should be their mode of subsistence. Accordingly as that varies, their laws and policy must be different' – and linked it to Buffon's scientific categorization. The resultant amalgam not only explained the difference between one people and another, and the way mankind had advanced from a savage to a civilized state, but it provided a model into which the flow of information about overseas societies could be incorporated. Theological inferences, even the much-cited peoples of antiquity, began to fade a little as the stress on a cultural evolution linked to physical environment and forms of subsistence became dominant. As far as the American Indian was concerned, the demands of white settlement and enterprise, and the speculations of philosophers and scientists, seemed to join in denigration of his very existence. It is true that the *bon sauvage* retained his place in the European imagination: to read Chateaubriand is to look back to Adario and forward to Hiawatha. But there was always an element of unreality about the noble primitive, a gap between the vision and the actuality. Since the first days of colonization the settlers had shown little patience with the concept. It was essentially a stylized literary and philosophical product. As Bernard Sheehan put it, 'Confronted by a particular reality, it tended to dissolve.'[114]

The endeavour of the Jesuits and the pro-Indian writers was earnest enough. Often there was a genuine effort to understand and to learn, but cultural arrogance and condescension were powerful if sometimes subconscious forces. And in Europe a whole school of primitivist writers took the Indian from his natural habitat, the wilderness where he had come to terms with his environment, and experimented with him in a mock and alien setting as a man of reason. In the end the image proved powerless to protect the Indian. During the War of American Independence pictorial representations of an Indian holding aloft a cap of liberty became an accepted symbol of the aspirations of the thirteen colonies, but to the triumphant new nation which emerged from the war the Indian was an irritating, sometimes dangerous nuisance. Even when the government in Washington was sympathetic to the plight of the trans-Mississippi tribes, it had little control over the thousands of settlers, speculators and adventurers heading west. In British Canada the settler-Indian conflict was later in coming, and less abrasive when it did, but considerations of space and numbers were responsible for this rather than any adherence to a favourable definition of the Indian. Lahontan's freedom-loving dweller of the forests had long been replaced by the adventurous figure of the wilderness fur-trader as the antithesis of urban man. Whether the Indian resisted the white intruder or co-operated with him, his ultimate fate was determined by others. The European cult of the noble savage was overborne by a rougher, American belief – 'The only good Indian is a dead Indian'. This was a belief supported by interest, not merely by sentiment. As the representation of the Indian as a man of nature lingered still in the literature and visual arts of the nineteenth century – in the novels of Fenimore Cooper, the poetry of Longfellow, the paintings of George Catlin – on the western frontiers the sword was proving mightier than the pen.

NOTES

1 William Guthrie, *A New Geographical, Historical and Commercial Grammar* (9th edn., 1785), p. 763.

2 See Henri Baudet, *Paradise on Earth: Some Thoughts on European Images of non-European Man*, transl. Elizabeth Wentholt (New Haven, 1965), p. 20.

3 See L. E. Huddleston, *Origin of the American Indian: European Concepts 1492–1729* (Austin, 1967).

4 See Richard Bernheimer, *Wild Men in the Middle Ages: A Study in Art, Sentiment, and Demonology* (Cambridge, Mass., 1952).

5 *The Voyages of Christopher Columbus. . . .* , ed. Cecil Jane (1930), p. 263.

6 See W. E. Washburn, 'The Meaning of "Discovery" in the Fifteenth and Sixteenth Centuries', *American Historical Review*, LXVIII (1962), 1–21.

7 John Josselyn, *An Account of Two Voyages to New-England* (London, 1674), pp. 124, 125.

8 W. Hubard, *The Present State of New-England. . . .* (1677), pp. 33, 41, 42; Increase Mather, *A Brief History of the War with the Indians in New-England* (1676), pp. 19, 27.

9 Alden T. Vaughan, *New England Frontier: Puritans and Indians 1620–1675* (Boston, 1965), p. 320.

10 Francis Jennings, *The Invasion of America: Indians, Colonialism, and the Cant of Conquest* (Norton Library edition, New York, 1976), pp. 178–9. A useful summary of the contrasting interpretations of recent historians on the subject is contained in

    So Dreadfull a Judgment: Puritan Responses to King Phillip's War, 1676–1677, eds. Richard Slotkin and James K. Folsom (Middletown, Conn., 1978), pp. 3–45.

11 *Narratives of the Indian Wars 1675–1699*, ed. C. H. Lincoln (New York, 1913), p. 28.

12 See R. H. Pearce, 'The Significance of the Captivity Narrative', *American Literature*, XIX (1947–48), 1–20.

13 Vaughan, *New England Frontier*, p. 20.

14 Printed in Richard Blome, *The Present State of His Majesties Isles and Territories in America* (1687), pp. 99–100.

15 *Narratives of Early Pennsylvania, West New Jersey and Delaware, 1630–1707* (New York, 1912), p. 303.

16 *Ibid.*, pp. 384, 385, 420.

17 Thomas Traherne, *Centuries* (1969 edn.), p. 116.

18 Blome, *Present State*, especially pp. 193, 204, 233.

19 Robert F. Berkhofer, Jnr., *The White Man's Indian: Images of the American Indian from Columbus to the Present* (New York, 1978), pp. 47, 131.

20 John Locke, *Two Treatises of Government*, ed. Peter Laslett (Cambridge, 1967), pp. 312, 314–15, 319, 357.

21 John Locke, *An Essay Concerning Human Understanding* (Everyman edn., 1948), pp. 13, 14.

22 George Alsop, *A Character of the Province of Maryland* (1666), p. 60.

23 *Ibid.*, p. 66.

24 William Robertson, *The History of America* (1812 edn.), II, 204.

25 Gary B. Nash, 'The Image of the Indian in the Southern Colonial Mind', *William and Mary Quarterly*, XXIX (1972), 222.

26 *The History and Present State of Virginia by Robert Beverly*, ed. L. B. Wright (Chapel Hill, 1947), p. xxvi.

27 On this see W. E. Washburn, *The Governor and the Rebel: A History of Bacon's Rebellion in Virginia* (Chapel Hill, 1957).

28 *History of Virginia*, p. 159.

29 *Ibid.*, p. 211.

30 *A New Voyage to Carolina by John Lawson* ed. H. T. Lefler (Chapel Hill, 1967), p. 5. Further editions appeared in 1712 and 1722; long passages from Lawson were plagiarized in John Brickell, *The Natural History of North Carolina* (Dublin, 1737).

31 *Ibid.*, pp. 243–4.

32 For this, and the ruthless treatment generally of the remaining Indians in Virginia in this period, see Gwenda Morgan, 'The Hegemony of the Law: Richmond County 1692–1776', unpublished Ph.D thesis (John Hopkins, 1980), especially Ch. 1, 'The Extinction of the Savages'.

33 Georgina C. Nammack, *Fraud, Politics and the Dispossession of the Indians: the Iroquois Land Frontiers in the Colonial Period* (Norman, Okla., 1969), p. 16.

34 R. P. Bond, *Queen Anne's American Kings* (Oxford, 1952), pp. 16, 105.

35 *Ibid.*, p. 77.

36 David Humphreys, *An Historical Account of the Incorporated Society for the Propagation of the Gospel in Foreign Parts* (1730), pp. 309–10.

37 Bond prints the Addison article in full in *American Kings*, pp. 81–5.

38 Quoted in A. O. Lovejoy, 'Monboddo and Rousseau', in *Essays in the History of Ideas* (Baltimore, 1948), p. 38.

39 Printed in H. C. Porter, *The Inconstant Savage: England and the North American Indian 1500–1660* (1979), p. 45.

40 Printed in A. O. Lovejoy *et al.*, *A Documentary History of Primitivism and Related Ideas* (Baltimore, 1935), p. 328.

41 J. H. Elliott, 'Renaissance Europe and America: A Blunted Impact?', in *First Images of America: the Impact of the New World on the Old*, ed. Fredi Chiapelli (Berkeley, 1976), I, 12.

42 The two-volume selection compiled by John Lockman, *Travels of the Jesuits* (1743), contained only one letter from North America (II, 474–507).

43 *The Jesuit Relations and Allied Documents*, ed. R. G. Thwaites (Cleveland, 1896–1901), XXXIII, 145.

44 *Ibid.*, XLIV, 297.

45 John Oldmixon, *The British Empire in America* (1708), I, 161.

46 See Gilbert Chinard, *L'Amérique et le Rêve Exotique dans la Littérature Française au XVIIᵉet au XVIIIᵉ Siècles* (Paris, 1934), pp. 151–87.

47 *A New Discovery of a Vast Country in America by Father Louis Hennepin*, reprinted from the second London issue of 1698, ed. R. G. Thwaites (Chicago, 1903), p. 460.

48 *Navigantium atque Itinerantium Bibliotheca*, ed. John Harris (1705), II, 906, 915.

49 *New Voyages to North-America by the Baron de Lahontan*, reprinted from the English edition of 1705, ed. R. G. Thwaites (Chicago, 1905), p. 7.

50 *Ibid.*, pp. 420–1. See also the summary of Lahontan in Harris, *Bibliotheca*, II, 915–28, and especially pp. 924–5.

51 Lahontan, *New Voyages*, pp. 582–3.

52 See James Axtell, 'The White Indians of Colonial America', *William and Mary Quarterly*, XXXII (1975), 55–88.

53 See Geoffroy Atkinson's two studies: *The Extraordinary Voyage in French Literature before 1700* (New York, 1920), and *The Extraordinary Voyage in French Literature from 1700 to 1720* (Paris, 1927).

54 The passages quoted here are from the sixth English edition of *The Adventures of Telemachus* (1707), Bk II, 107–21.

55 For reproductions of those mentioned here see Hugh Honour, *The New Golden Land: European Images of America* (New York, 1975), and W. P. Cumming *et al.*, *The Exploration of North America 1630–1776* (1974).

56 See Benjamin Bissell, *The American Indian in English Literature of the 18th Century* (New Haven, 1925).

57 Quoted Honour, *New Golden Land*, p. 125.

58 See for example J. F. Bernard, *Cérémonies et coutumes religieuses des peuples idolâtres* (Paris, 1723–43).

59 *Customs of the American Indians compared with the Customs of Primitive Times by Father Lafitau* ed. W. N. Fenton, E. L. Moore (Toronto, 1974), I, 27.

60 *Ibid.*, 92, 281.

61 *Ibid.*, 90.

62 Frank E. Manuel, *The Eighteenth Century Confronts the Gods* (Cambridge, Mass., 1959), p. 44.

63 See Lafitau, *Customs*, I, p. xcviii.

64 [William Burke?], *An Account of the European Settlements in America* (1757), I, 161.

65 P. F. X. de Charlevoix, *Journal of a Voyage to North-America. . . .* (London, 1761), I, 301; II, 24.

66 Thwaites, *Jesuit Relations*, LXV, 135 ff.; LXVIII, 120 ff.

67 Quoted Robert Shackleton, *Montesquieu: A Critical Biography* (Oxford, 1961), p. 235.

68 See Joseph G. Tregle, Jnr., 'Le Page du Pratz: Memoir of the Natchez Indians', in *The Colonial Legacy*: Vol III, *Historians of Nature and Man's Nature* (New York, 1973), pp. 59–90.

69 *Ibid.*, pp. 77, 80.

70 *Rousseau: Oeuvres Complètes*, II, ed. Michel Launay (Paris, 1971), 268.

71 Henry Timberlake, *Memoirs. . . .* (1765), pp. 52–3.

72 *Gentleman's Magazine*, XXV (1755), 256.

73 [William Smith], *Some Account of the North-American Indians* (1754); these remarks were paraphrased in a long review in *Monthly Review*, X (1754), 285–93.

74 See Wilbur R. Jacobs, 'Cadwallader Colden's Noble Iroquois Savages', in Leder, *Colonial Legacy*, III, 47, 55.
75 [Burke?], *Account*, I, 169.
76 Reviews in *Monthly Review*, XII (1755), 483; XIII (1755), 275.
77 Quoted Richard Slotkin, *Regeneration through Violence: the Mythology of the American Frontier* (Middletown, Conn., 1973), p. 249.
78 *An Universal History*, XL (1763), 371 ff.; XXXIX (1763), 287, 302 ff.
79 *Gentleman's Magazine*, XXXV (1765), 526.
80 *Ibid.*, XXXIII (1763), 419.
81 William Smith, *An Historical Account of the Expedition against the Ohio Indians* (Philadelphia and London, 1766), p. 28.
82 *A Journey from Prince of Wales's Fort in Hudson's Bay to the Northern Ocean . . . by Samuel Hearne*, ed. Richard Glover (Toronto, 1958), pp. 56–7.
83 *A Voyage Round the World by George Shelvocke*, ed. W. G. Perrin (1928), p. 224.
84 Miguel Venegas, *A Natural and Civil History of California* (1759), I, 64–5.
85 Michèle Duchet, *Anthropologie et histoire au siècle des lumières* (Paris, 1971).
86 Ronald L. Meek, *Social Science and the Ignoble Savage* (Cambridge, 1976), p. 3.
87 *Spirit of the Laws*, trans. T. Nugent (New York, 1949 edn.), pt. i. 277.
88 Bk. III, Ch. 5.
89 See above, pp. 146–7.
90 Cited in A. C. Chitnis, *The Scottish Enlightenment: A Social History* (1976), p. 94.
91 Meek, *Ignoble Savage*, p. 116.
92 Chitnis, *Scottish Enlightenment*, p. 94.
93 June Rendall, *The Origins of the Scottish Enlightenment* (1978), p. 144.
94 Chitnis, *Scottish Enlightenment*, p. 102.
95 Rendall, *Origins*, p. 156.
96 *Ibid.*, p. 144.
97 W. C. Lehmann, *Adam Ferguson and the Beginnings of Modern Sociology* (New York, 1930), p. 78.
98 See A. O. Lovejoy, *The Great Chain of Being, a Study of the History of an Idea* (Cambridge, 1950).
99 Buffon, *Oeuvres complètes*, XV, 443–6; translated and quoted in Antonello Gerbi, *The Dispute of the New World: the History of a Polemic, 1750–1900* (Pittsburgh, 1973), pp. 5–6.
100 *Natural History, General and Particular, by the Count de Buffon*, trans. William Smellie (2nd edn., 1785), III, 110, 169.
101 Gerbi, *Dispute*, pp. 14, 15n.
102 Duchet, *Anthropologie et histoire*, p. 205.
103 Gerbi, *Dispute*, pp. 329–30.
104 Duchet, *Anthropologie et histoire*, p. 247.
105 For Diderot's contributions see Hans Wolpe, *Raynal et sa Machine de Guerre* (Stanford, 1957), pp. 186–252.
106 *A Philosophical and Political History of the Settlements and Trade of the Europeans in the East and West Indies translated from the French of the Abbé Raynal by J. Justamond* (1777), II, 333, 358, 457; IV, 447.
107 *Gentleman's Magazine*, XLVIII (1778), p. 611.
108 To borrow some key words from John Payne, *Universal Geography* (1791), II, 663.
109 See Henry Savage, *Discovering America 1700–1875* (New York, 1979), p. 48.
110 In his Bk IV on America and its inhabitants Robertson used almost one hundred different sources. On North America his favourite authority was Charlevoix, cited about seventy times, with Lafitau running second with a score or so of references.
111 Robertson, *History of America*, II, 30.
112 *Ibid.*, 62–3, 72–3, 94.

113 References here are to the 1779 edition printed in W. C. Lehmann, *John Millar of Glasgow 1735–1801* (Cambridge, 1960), pp. 190–1, 197–8, 230, 244, 294.
114 Bernard W. Sheehan, *Seeds of Extinction: Jeffersonian Philanthropy and the American Indian* (Chapel Hill, 1973), p. 112.

8

'One Rude Chaos': Accounts of West Africa in the Slave Trade Era

Europe's interest in the American Indian, however much it derived from the burgeoning of intellectual and theological curiosity about the New World, grew as the empires of trade and settlement developed in size and importance across the Atlantic. The Indian, depending on time and place, might be guide, supplier, ally, enemy. He could never be ignored, and rarely did Europeans feel unchallenged superiority over him. At the least, he was a lurking, hovering presence, the original inhabitant of the land now coveted by the newcomer, and a subject of perennial, sometimes guilty, fascination. Whatever perceptions Europeans possessed of his lifestyle, it needed no great leap of the imagination to see the Indian as a forerunner, for better or worse a primitive version of a modern Frenchman or Englishman. Physical differences were slight, and colour was not an issue – many Indians were no darker in hue than southern Europeans, and exposure to the elements and the application of animal grease were generally held accountable for their 'tawny' complexions.

By contrast, Europe's attitude towards the Negroes of Africa was influenced from an early stage by suspicion and uneasiness. The West African littoral, unapproachable in many places by sea-going vessels, hot, steamy and fever-ridden when reached, held few temptations for European settlers. Penetration inland was difficult and dangerous, and although the Portuguese trade in gold and ivory whetted European commercial instincts, the exploitable resources of the region compared unfavourably with those of America with its seemingly inexhaustible supplies of silver, plantation products, fish, furs and timber. By the time that French and English settlements were taking root in America, West Africa was firmly placed in the European mercantile world as a dependency of America, for its most important role was to supply slave labour for the European plantations there. In both economic and imaginative terms, Africa was for long simply 'une annexe des Antilles'.[1] The slaves, shipped out from a number of points along 3000 miles of coastline stretching from Senegal to Angola, were 'black', regardless of variations in their actual skin colour. In the West African Negro the light-skinned European was confronted with the twin issues of colour and slavery, both missing from his contact with the American Indian, and both redounding with thunderous implications – theological, commercial and cultural.

Europe's reaction to the blackness of the Negro has been exhaustively examined by recent scholars. Their findings show that many of the attitudes traditionally associated with the era of the slave-trade were already present in the European consciousness. D. B. Davis insists, 'to see slavery as the only source of racial prejudice is to oversimplify one of the most complex and troublesome questions in modern history . . . it is possible that there was something in the culture of Western Europe that inclined white men to look with contempt on the physical and cultural traits of the African'.[2] As indicated earlier, examples of this condescension and distrust among Englishmen in the sixteenth and seventeenth centuries are plentiful;[3] and assumptions of superiority sharpened as England's role in the slave trade increased. The first permanent English posts on the West African coasts were established in the 1630s; the Royal African Company received its charter in 1672; by the early eighteenth century Britain was the dominant power in the African trade. This growth in activity was matched by an increase in the number of accounts of West Africa published in England, mostly written by slave traders or by naval officers involved in protecting the trade. Their writings tended to harden the existing association of Africa, Negro, blackness and slavery, as did the accounts of the New World plantations with their black slaves and white masters.

The various publications of Richard Blome in the 1670s and 1680s illustrate knowledge and attitudes at the beginning of our period. Editor of several travel collections and 'cosmographies', Blome began his section on 'Guiny' in his *Geographical Description* of 1670 with the claim that 'the Inhabitants, especially before the crossing of the Portugals, were rude and barbarous, living without the knowledge of a God, Law, Religion or Government, very dis-ingenious, not caring for Arts or Letters'. Even after the coming of the Europeans, the Africans remained 'much addicted to Theft . . . perfidious, Lyers . . . great Idolaters . . . of late they have tried many forms of religion, as Judaism, Mahometism, and Christianity; but care not much for any'.[4] In later works Blome produced brief sketches of English plantation slavery, though neither his work nor that of any other English compiler of the period approached in detail and comprehension that of the French writers on the Caribbean islands, notably Jean-Baptiste du Tertre and Jean-Baptiste Labat. Writing in 1672 on the hard lot of African slaves in Barbados, Blome noted that they had a meagre diet, were worked hard, and ill treated – 'yet are they well contented with their conditions'. Contentment had disappeared from the scene when Blome returned to it in 1687, for whereas 'the masters live in all affluence of pleasure and delight . . . the lodging of these poor wretches is worst of all; for having laboured all the day in so hot a country, without any nourishing diet, at night they must be content to lie hard, on nothing but a board, without any coverlet, in their huts or rather hog-sties'.[5] Hans Sloane added some gory details a little later when in his *Voyage to Jamaica*, published in 1707, but relating to a visit he made twenty years earlier, he included a horrific list of slave punishments – castration, burning, dismemberment – which was still being cited at the end of the eighteenth century.

More impressive than the rather thin English descriptions of plantation slavery in the Americas was the mounting pile of accounts of West Africa published in the first half of the eighteenth century. Tapped by most writers on the subject, they have recently been analysed in thorough fashion by Dr A. J. Barker, who effectively argues against the notion that in the period before the great abolition debates of the late eighteenth century the African Negro was widely regarded as sub-human. 'A wild, untutored cousin', possibly, but unmistakably human in his final conclusion, and he insists that 'the Negro image was little different from that of the rest of the uncivilized world'.[6] There are problems about this, for if this material is compared, not with the pro-slavery writings of Long and his successors but with contemporaneous accounts of other non-European peoples, then what emerges is the sharper, more denigratory tone of the language used. This may be because the accounts are fewer in number and narrower in approach than those relating to North America, for example, which attracted a rich variety of narratives written from different viewpoints – by settlers, missionaries, traders and explorers. In the books on West Africa the slave trade dominates both the observations and the observers. The latter operated on the edges of African society, their knowledge of African languages was rudimentary or non-existent, and their accounts often selected those features of African life which the reading public would find at once shocking and titillating. The accounts were also constricted by geographical limitations in a way unknown on the expansive American frontier. Although the West African coast was fairly well mapped between Arguin and Calabar, only the Senegal and Gambia rivers had been followed any distance inland by Europeans. Farther east, there was no realization of the significance of the Niger delta, and no first-hand knowledge of either the geography or the peoples of the interior. The accounts of Leo Africanus were still studied in an effort to identify the shadowy inland states whose names the coastal traders often heard but were quite unable to place.

The first, and one of the most important, of the accounts to appear in the eighteenth century was William Bosman's, published in Dutch, French, English, German and Italian editions from 1704 onwards.[7] Bosman, who had been on the Gold Coast as a senior Dutch factor between 1688 and 1702, looked at the area and its inhabitants with the jaundiced eyes of a veteran trader. 'To begin. The Negroes are all without exception, crafty, villanous and fraudulent, and very seldom to be trusted; being sure to slip no opportunity of cheating an European, nor indeed one another. A Man of Integrity is as rare among them as a white falcon . . . they indeed seem to be born and bred villains.' Bosman's imprecations were not simply or even mainly racial in character; they rather represent the age-old complaint of the merchant confronted with difficult customers or unreliable suppliers. Bosman himself made the point that his remarks agreed 'with what authors tell us of the Muscovites', and he wrote in even more caustic terms of his English trading rivals – sottish drunkards who died like flies. Elsewhere, the Negro appeared in a different but equally unflattering light, as indolent and apathetic: 'nothing but the utmost necessity can force them to labour . . . are so little concerned at their misfortunes that 'tis hardly to be observed by any change in them whether they have met with any good or ill success . . . they are no sooner at their resting-place, but, like the beasts, they sleep perfectly undisturbed by any melancholy reflections'.

Bosman stressed the difficulty of learning the local languages and dialects among an illiterate people, and reckoned it a ten-year task. He could usually understand what was said to him, but was defeated in his attempts at pronunciation and constructing a vocabulary. 'I think 'tis folly to attempt farther', he concluded. Despite this drawback, Bosman ventured into the realm of religious beliefs, pointing out that, although contact with Europeans had induced some of the coastal peoples to declare themselves believers in a single deity who had created the world, in time of trouble they reverted to fetish-worship. Others clung to their belief that 'Man was made by Anansie, that is, a great spider'. These observations by Bosman on West African religious beliefs were to be used to good effect by Pierre Bayle in his *Réponse aux questions d'un provincial* of 1731, when in his efforts to discredit the Renaissance reverence for paganism he claimed to see detailed conformities between fetish-worship and the religions of Greece and Rome. To Bayle the one was as irrational and absurd as the other – 'a vulgar, stupid adoration of mere things, an affront'.[8]

On government among the Africans Bosman tried at first to correlate it with familiar European forms such as monarchies and republics, but generally found it 'very licentious and irregular, which only pro-

ceeds from the small authority of their chief men or cabocero's'. Nor
was he much taken with the Africans' military skills – 'their ridiculous
gestures, stooping, creeping and crying, make their fight look more like
monkeys playing together than a battle'. But as Bosman moved along
the coast to Whydah and Benin, government became more formal and
impressive. At Whydah he described the court of an absolute king.
Treated as a demi-God he ate off special utensils, while his great men
lay prostrate on the ground. His rule was supported by a financial
system which employed a thousand tax collectors to bring in revenue.
Even more striking was Bosman's account of the court at Great Benin,
with its splendid bronzes, and the Oba in his audience chamber,
'sitting on an Ivory Couch under a Canopy of India Silk'.

Bosman's work with its careful observation had a value which was
seldom to be equalled during the next half-century. Its worth is evident
if we compare it with the African sections in Harris's collection of
voyages, published in the same year, 1705, as the English edition of
Bosman. Although Harris included much detail on North Africa, he
could put together only a few pages on 'Negroland', and those were
taken mainly from Leo Africanus. Characteristic were the comments
on the inhabitants of Bornu, a state as yet known to Europeans only
through the Muslim geographer. 'Have garments and beds of skins in
winter, but in summer they only cover their privities with a piece of
leather. They are not distinguish'd from one another by proper names,
but by nick names taken from their stature, fatness, or some other
quality; for they have no possession of religion: their wives and children
are common, and in a word, the whole scene of their lives is brutish.'[9]
There was much in the full version of Leo Africanus to balance this, but
other observers reaching print at this time did scant justice to the range
and complexity of societies which confronted them. James Houston, a
surgeon in the employ of the Royal African Company who reached
Sierra Leone in 1722 confined his remarks on the indigenous inhabitants to one dismissive paragraph: 'I shall only say in one word, that
their natural temper is barbarously cruel, selfish and deceitful, and
their government equally barbarous and uncivil . . . As for their Customs, they exactly resemble their fellow creatures and natives, the
Monkeys.'[10]

The 1730s saw a minor spate of books on West Africa, beginning
with the belated publication in 1732, in the fifth volume of the Churchill
collection, of the late-seventeenth century account by Jean Barbot,
Agent-General of the French West India Company. Containing almost
600 pages of observations, some first-hand, others hearsay, with considerable repetition and plagiarism, it remains a difficult source to use
and assess. As in Bosman's work there is no doubt that the areas

described were peopled not by some sub-human species but by Africans living in societies with their own rules, customs and institutions. The lengthy explanation at the beginning on the range of observations gave some indication of this: 'the inhabitants in general; their employments, professions, natural genius and temper; their habit, houses, cottages, hamlets, villages, and towns, with all things appertaining to them; their languages, manners, customs, religion, government, and distribution of justice civil or criminal; the several kingdoms, principalities, or states; their power, courts, laws, wars, armies, weapons, and taxes paid by the subjects.'[11] Some of the stereotypes of Bosman's book are also in Barbot, of treacherous, cruel blacks, but also some extenuating circumstances. If the blacks behaved in an unreasonable fashion, then this might well be the effect of European abuses – 'many of the European nations, trading amongst these people, have very unjustly and inhumanely, without any provocation, stolen away, from time to time, abundance of the people'. Then, too, the standard accusation that the blacks 'were naturally inclinable to seek their ease, and averse to labour', did not always withstand scrutiny. Along the Gold Coast, Barbot noted 'very many who industriously apply themselves to some particular profession, or handicraft, as merchants, factors or brokers, gold and black-smiths, fishermen, canoe, or house carpenters, salt-boilers, potters, mat-makers, husbandmen, porters, watermen or padlers, and soldiers' – though he attributed much of this industry to European influences.

The accompanying volume in the Churchill collection contained Thomas Phillips' journal, again printed many years after the event – a disastrous slaving voyage for the Royal African Company in 1693–4. Early on came the stress on the sensuality of 'negroe women, who talk'd to us many smutty English words, making lascivious undecent gestures with their bodies, which were all naked, excepting a little clout about their waste, hanging down to the middle of the thigh, which they would often take up to shew us their merchandize.'[12] This set the tone for a sensationalized account whose vivid, readable detail helped to shape English images of West Africa in the eighteenth century: cannibalism, baboons which ravished and killed women, the stench of the slave pens, the terrors of the middle passage on which half the slaves and many of the crew died. In the midst of this horrific narrative came some homespun philosophizing about the lot of the 'poor creatures . . . nor can I imagine why they should be despised for their colour, being what they cannot help, and the effect of the climate it has pleas'd God to appoint them. I can't think there is any intrinsick value in one colour more than another, nor that white is better than black, only we think it so because we are so'.

The weighty Churchill volumes containing the Barbot and Phillips accounts were followed in the next few years by cheaper and more accessible accounts by Snelgrave, Atkins and Moore. Apart from its revelation of Muslim traders now reaching the coastal areas from the north, the most valuable and certainly the most quoted part of Snelgrave's book concerned the conquest of Whydah by Dahomey in 1727. The story was full of details of human sacrifice, slaughter of captives, and cannibalism, which were to be repeated many times during the course of the century. These events persuaded Snelgrave to produce a justification of the slave trade which became standard: that slavery, of a sort, was known and accepted within Africa, and that in the existing anarchic situation many survived through being transported overseas who would have been killed if they had remained. Once on the American plantations, they enjoyed a standard of living better than in their homeland. When one added to these considerations the advantages which accrued to England then, 'in a word, from this trade proceed benefits, far outweighing all, either real or pretended mischiefs and inconveniences'.[13]

This defence of the slave trade was repudiated by John Atkins, a surgeon on board a naval vessel protecting the Royal African Company's trade in the early 1720s. Snelgrave's contention that Africans were taken across the ocean 'to preserve them from sacrifice and cannibals, to convey them to a land flowing with more milk and honey, to a better living, better manners, virtue, and religion', he condemned as a hypocritical pretence.[14] Nor did he accept hearsay evidence of cannibalism. He thought it unlikely that Africans – abstemious meat-eaters compared with the English – were likely to gorge themselves on human flesh. 'The true Anthropophagi', he commented, 'are only the diverse insects infesting us.' But Atkins' opposition to the slave trade did not extend to any favourable estimation of the Negro as such. Like many Europeans before him, he was struck by the physical and alien distinctiveness of the West African: 'the black colour, and woolly tegument of these Guineans, is what first obtrudes itself on our observation, and distinguishes them from the rest of mankind'. He rejected the conventional explanations for this, and was bold enough to suggest that 'the black and white race have, *ab origine*, sprung from different-coloured first parents'. This, together with the influence of diet and way of life, led to a series of distinctive racial characteristics – summed up elsewhere by Atkins in unflattering terms as a weak brain, ignorance, indolence and a lack of natural passions and affections.[15]

For African authority Atkins had little respect, and added to the now-familiar abuse of black peoples, 'cautious of planting too much, and wasting their labour ... unplagued with to-morrow, or the politicks of Europe', an array of unprepossessing African rulers. 'King Pedro' at Sesthos was produced as 'A sample of Negro majesty . . . the King's dress was very antick: he had a dirty, red bays gown on, chequer'd with patch-work of other colours, like a jack pudding . . . he had an old black full-bottom'd wig, uncombed; an old hat not half big enough and so set considerably behind the fore-top, that made his meagre face like a scare-crow.' The King of Wydah was just as prepos-terous: 'His palace is a dirty, large bamboo building, of a mile or two round, wherein he keeps near a thousand women, and divides his time in an indolent manner, between eating and lust; he is fatned to a monstrous bulk; never has been out since he became King (nigh twelve years).'

Along with sweeping, catastrophic generalizations – 'the further we depart from Morocco on this west side, or Egypt on the east, there is always found less industry and more ignorance' – came a sense of change within African society, of the impact of outside influences. In an unusually lengthy examination of African religions Atkins pointed out that there was nothing extraordinary in a primitive people worshipping the elements, or prominent physical objects, but that overlying this in some areas was an intimation of the Christian deity and of the concept of good and evil. Atkins could see European influence at work in other respects, too, for example in those parts of the Gold Coast where the Africans seemed to him more honest – though this might be caused by fear. Some of these observations would have carried more conviction if Atkins had been on the coast for longer than the fifteen months he had spent there twelve years earlier. Throughout his writings there is a clear insistence on Negro inferiority, and his comment on the wretched, servile existence of the English garrison at one of the coastal factories is not without significance in terms of wording: '. . . are all of them together a company of white Negroes, who are entirely resigned to the Governour's commands, according to the strictest rules of discipline and subjection'.[16]

Francis Moore, a Royal African Company factor whose account of the Gambia was published in 1738, supported Atkins' condemnation of the slave trade. Since its coming, he noticed, 'all punishments are chang'd into slavery', including those for the most petty misde-meanours. Moore's description of the tyrannical behaviour of African rulers was reprinted almost immediately in the *Gentleman's Magazine*, but only, it seems, to make a domestic political point: 'the African monarch imitates his royal brethren of Europe, in most particulars; for he gets as much as he can by fair means, and then as much more as he is able by force or fraud'.[17] Among the supplementary matter in Moore's book were lengthy extracts from the Arab geographies of El-idrisi and

Leo Africanus, and an account of an expedition by Bartholomew Stibbs up the Gambia in 1723. This took him only sixty miles above the Barracunda 'Falls' which, 200 miles from the sea, marked the end of navigation for boats of any size. There was no further attempt to reach the interior of the region for another seventy years, and although Moore spent five years on the Gambia he remained convinced that it was part of the Niger. Unlike some of his contemporaries, Moore had a sense of the relationship between a people, their natural environment, and their technical skills. He described in lengthy detail the rebuilding of a Company factory by African labour 'without any iron-work, trowels, squares, or carpenters rules'. All this had some reference to the preface of the book, which included a sketch of black Africa in the past, before the coming of Islam:

> The Negroes were entirely ignorant of arts and letters, and of the use of iron: they lived in common, having no property in lands nor goods, no tyrants, nor superior lords; but supported themselves in an equal state upon the natural produce of the country . . . ambition or avarice never drove them into foreign countries, to subdue or cheat their neighbours. Thus they lived without toil or superfluities. And this the Greeks and Romans believed to be the first state of mankind, which they describe in the golden age . . .[18]

Much the same point was made by William Smith, who had been on the coast in 1726 and 1727 carrying out surveys for the Royal African Company. His explanation for the 'laziness' of the Gambians was that a bountiful nature supplied all their wants and enabled them to live a simple life 'without any great art or industry of their own; the ground in this part of the earth, seems, in some measure, to be exempt from the general curse. As for clothing they want, the beau and the belle, the fop and the coquet, the pests of all society, assemblies and conversations in Christendom, have no being here.'[19] African nakedness had been transmuted into a virtue, indolence into an ideal; we are in the world of Fénelon and Lahontan. In a section devoted to an account supposedly given to Smith by his shipboard companion, the experienced Royal African Company factor, Charles Wheeler, there is more of this: a defence of African polygamy as being similar to Old Testament patriarchal behaviour, and in any case preferable to the European practice of one wife and several mistresses. In an improbable sentence suspiciously reminiscent of the satirists, Wheeler was made to say, 'Nature is the best school, her lessons are true, and her dictates are universal.' Elsewhere this was spelt out in more detail: 'A Guinean by treading in the paths prescrib'd him by his ancestors, paths natural, pleasant and diverting, is in the plain road to be a good and happy man; but the European has sought so many inventions and has endeavour'd to put so many restrictions upon nature, that it would be next to a miracle if he were either happy or good.' Further on there is an anticipation of the anti-colonial sentiments of later in the century: 'The discerning natives account it their greatest unhappiness, that they were ever visited by the Europeans . . . say they, it is observable, that wherever Christianity comes, there come with it a sword, a gun, powder and ball.'

The main body of Smith's narrative contained striking descriptions of Whydah and Benin, of wars and massacres. It printed an eye-witness account by an English factor of an attack by Dahomean forces on Allada in 1724: 'When we went out there was scarce any stirring for bodies without heads, and had it rained blood, it could not have lain thicker on the ground.' Smith himself described Whydah in 1727 just before its sacking by the Dahomean army. The language was not unlike that used by Bougainville of Tahiti some years later:

> All who have ever been here, allow this to be one of the most delightful countries in the world. The great number and variety of tall, beautiful and shady trees which seem as if planted in fine groves for ornament, being without any underwood, or weeds, as in other parts of Guinea; also the verdant fields are every-where cultivated, and not otherwise divided, than by those groves, and in some places a small foot-path; together with a great number of pretty little villages, encompassed by a low mud-wall, and regularly plac'd over the face of the whole country. All these contribute to afford the most delightful prospect that imagination can form.

Idyllic though Whydah was, Benin seemed to Smith nearest in kind to a European monarchy as he set out the grandeur of the king's court, the length of the streets, its well-stocked markets and handsome houses. Like Snelgrave, Smith was struck by the appearance in the coastal areas of Muslim merchants. There was much of interest in Smith's book, and much to be wary about. A stay of nine months, eighteen years before the book's publication, had provided a surprising amount of detailed information, some of it used to support a polemic argument, and some of it contradicted by other contemporary accounts. Generally, the book approached nearer the Amerindian type of primitivism familiar to English readers than did Michel Adanson's later and more celebrated account, *A Voyage to Senegal*, published in English translation in 1759. Although this French botanist, detached from the necessities of the slave trade, painted a beguiling picture of parts of Senegal and some of its inhabitants – 'There are some of them perfect beauties. They have a great share of vivacity, and a vast deal of freedom and ease, which renders them extremely agreeable' – most of what was impressive about the area he traced to European influence. His experiences in Senegal, where he learned enough Wolof to make him exceptional among the European writers on the region, did not change his unfavourable opinions about West Africans in general – 'the most artful beggars, and the most dextrous thieves in the universe . . . negligent and idle to excess.'[20]

The stately collections of voyages and travels which appeared in the middle decades of the century provided more material but no consistency of interpretationn and they printed comparatively few new accounts. Osborne's collection of 1745, for example, included Pigafetta's sixteenth-century account of the Congo with its gory but generally discredited description of cannibalism in the region. There, it was alleged, man-eating was catered for on a commercial scale: 'They keep a shambles of man's flesh, as they do, in these countries, for beef and other victuals . . . if they can have a good market, they sell; or, if they cannot, they deliver them to the butchers to be cut in pieces, and so sold, to be roasted or boiled.' Fullest and most authoritative of the collections as far as Africa was concerned was Astley's of 1745–7. The second volume, 732 pages long, was given over entirely to accounts of West Africa, ranging from some which had been printed in Purchas to more recent works such as Francis Moore's. Particularly valuable were the extracts from French works, including Labat's *Nouvelle Relation de l'Afrique Occidentale* of 1728 based on the papers of André Brue, governor of Senegal up to 1720. Alongside lurid reports of cannibalism and human sacrifice was much information which gave a sense of peaceful and productive communities. Near the Gambia, for example, Brue noted that 'Scarce a spot lay unimproved. The low grounds, divided by small canals, were all sowed with rice . . . through these were raised banks to keep in the water, so that their rice may be fed. The higher grounds were planted with millet, or maiz, and pease of different kinds.'[21] Among the other French accounts put forward by Astley for English readers for the first time was Loyer's of 1714 which included a preface which summed up the views of many writers: 'The reader will, no doubt, be surprized to hear of kingdoms where monarchs are peasants; of towns built with nothing but reeds; of vessels for sailing, each composed out of a single tree; above all he will wonder to be told of a people who live without care, speak without rule, transact business without writing, and go-about without cloaths; people, of whom some live in the water like fish, and others in holes of the earth, like worms, whose nakedness, and almost insensibility they possess.' The same kind of explanatory note, in more restrained language, was given in Thomas Salmon's *Universal Traveller* a few years later: 'In Guinea there are some sovereign princes, whose dominions are very extensive, rich, powerful, and arbitrary; monarchs limited by no laws, or any other restraints: and there are a multitude of others, to whom the Dutch, and other Europeans have given the name of king, whose dominions do not exceed the bounds of an English parish, and whose powers and revenues are proportionably mean.'[22]

If we admit the fragmentary nature of many of the European observations, the delay between writing and publication, the problems of translation, the inexpert character of many of the witnesses, and then add to this the shifting nature of African coastal societies in this period, it is not surprising that no consistent picture emerges. As the editor of a volume of the *Universal Modern History* complained: 'In writing the history of Guiney, we labour under difficulties from the too great abundance of materials, which are thrown together in one rude chaos . . . Materials are jumbled together, without regard to method or diction; the very perusal of which is more laborious, and fatiguing than the whole of the execution besides.'[23] The *History* itself supplied an appropriate example of this confusion. The introductory section on Africa in volume XIV contained editorial passages of runaway virulence. Africans were 'proud, lazy, treacherous, thievish, hot, and addicted to all kinds of lusts, and most ready to promote them in others, as pimps, panders, incestuous, brutish, and savage, cruel and revengeful, devourers of human flesh, and quaffers of human blood, inconstant, base, treacherous, and cowardly; fond of, and addicted to, all sorts of superstition and witchcraft; and, in a word, to every vice that came in their way . . .'. The following pages contained equally critical generalizations. Africa was 'known to have been burning with human impurities; insomuch, that one would rather take it for a volcano of the most impure flames, than for a habitation of human creatures.' All attempts to explain the colour of the Negro were in vain, and the editor could only conclude 'that the true cause of this peculiar blackness of their bodies is still as much unknown to us, as that of the swarthiness of their minds'. Finally, came a triumphant linking of Negrophobia with the hostility towards Islam which (as chapter 4 shows) was common in eighteenth-century England: 'a religion so nicely suited to the depravity of the natives . . . that it did not need the help of the sword to make it spread itself far and near'.

Yet in the long descriptive sections on West Africa which followed, the writings of Bosman, Snelgrave, Barbot, Atkins and the others were used with discretion and intelligence. Due attention was paid to towns, commerce and agriculture, and there was little attempt to sustain the dire accusations of the introductory sections. It is impressive in itself that two of the sixteen volumes of the modern part of the *History* were devoted exclusively to Africa. Another volume, indeed, contained a frank editorial admission of subjective bias – 'it is seldom that a people does not fix the standard of beauty among themselves'. But the overwhelming impression given by the collections is unfavourable. The emphasis was placed on the sexual appetites of the Negro, exemplified by polygamy of the most extravagant proportions and by depravity so shocking as to incur suspicion of sexual relations between black women and apes; on cannibalism and human sacrifice, often associated with Dahomey's conquest of Whydah in 1727; and on despotism of a tyrannical and unpredictable nature. Most accounts of primitive peoples were tinged with ethnocentrism, but nowhere was the assumption of superiority clearer and the critical observations harsher than in the African accounts. 'The reporting', Philip Curtin points out, 'often stressed precisely those aspects of African life that were most repellent to the West and tended to submerge the indications of a common humanity.'[24] As knowledge of the coast increased, so did willingness to differentiate between various African peoples – though often only to the extent of whether they made 'good' or 'bad' slaves. But in the general sections they tended to be categorized as 'Negro', 'Black', or 'African', stereotypes which ignored or lessened individual characteristics, and which were applied regardless of variation in language, custom and appearance. Scholars have shown recently how much useful information about the reality of African societies can be prised out of the eighteenth-century accounts, but as D. B. Davis puts it, 'the most memorable images that emerged from the travel literature were not of industrious farmers or weavers, but of a people who mutilated their bodies and drank human blood, and of kings who lived in palaces decorated by thousands of human skulls'.[25] The impact of these accounts on an educated Englishman was summed up by the 4th Earl of Chesterfield who explained, in one of his exhortatory letters to his son, that 'the Africans are the most ignorant and unpolished peoples in the world, little better than the lions, tigers and leopards and other wild beasts, which that country produces in great numbers'.[26]

The most important counter to the synthesis of subordination and inferiority which marked the African accounts came from imaginative writers in England who set up their own stereotype. Moved by the piteous lot of the enchained black, they produced in poetry, novels and plays a pathetic, sentimental image of a noble primitive, a suffering prince, of which Aphra Behn's *Oroonoko* was the most celebrated. Adapted by the dramatist Thomas Southerne, Mrs Behn's novel was turned into a play which was performed at Drury Lane in 1695 and during the eighteenth century formed a standard item in the repertory of London and provincial theatres. The leading part, with its depiction of a black prince enduring much for love and honour before stoically meeting a grisly death at the stake, was played by David Garrick among others. But Oroonoko, as Mrs Behn's description shows, approximated in behaviour and in all physical characteristics except colour to the most correct type of Englishman. 'His nose was rising and Roman, instead of African and flat: His mouth the finest shaped that could be seen: far from those great turn'd lips, which are so natural to the rest of the Negroes. The whole proportion and air of his face was so nobly and exactly form'd, that bating his colour there could be nothing in nature more beautiful, agreeable and handsome.'[27] Likewise, Defoe was at pains to stress in *Robinson Crusoe* that the sympathetic Man Friday was not a Negro: 'He had all the sweetness and softness of an European in his countenance, too, especially when he smiled. His hair was long and black, not curled like wool; his forehead very high and large; and a great vivacity and sparkling sharpness in his eyes. The colour of his skin was not quite black, but very tawny, as the Brazilians and Virginians . . . his nose small, but not flat like the negroes; a very good mouth, thin lips, and his teeth well set, and white as ivory.'[28] Sometimes another appeal was sounded, though without much conviction as far as the Negro was concerned, that appreciation of physical differences between races was an entirely subjective matter. An article in the *Gentleman's Magazine* for 1735 denied that there was any 'difference of genius' between white and black men, and set the 'sickly whiteness' of the one against the 'majestic glossiness' of the other. The writer, in the guise of a free Negro, then went on – 'Let a white man expose his feeble face to the winds; or heat at high-noon, as we do. Will he bear it too, as we do? No: he will be sick; pale and red, by turns, be haggard and sun-burnt.'[29]

In the sentimental literature of the period generally European preconceptions shaped the image of the black slave. The more his thought-processes seemed akin to those of a sensitive Englishman, the more acceptable he became as a human being, and the more deplorable was his lot as a slave. So the slumbering, dreaming slave of James Scott's verses of 1761 could be exchanged, with the alteration of an adjective or two, with the entrapped hero of many romantic ballads as he

> Recalls the joys he felt of old,
> When wandring with his sable maid,
> Thro' groves of vegetable gold,
> He clasp'd her yielding to his raptur'd breast,
> And free from guile his honest soul exprest.[30]

This identification of common characteristics and feelings between white and black reached its height in the publicity given to the handful of Negroes who, against all the odds, attained some sort of celebrity in English society. There was Job Ben Solomon from the Senegambia who translated Arabic manuscripts for Hans Sloane and could write out the

Koran from memory; Francis Williams from Jamaica, who composed Latin verse; Philip Quaque from Cape Coast, educated in England, ordained priest by the Bishop of London, and returning home as 'Missionary, Catechist and Schoolmaster' to his fellow Africans; Ignatius Sancho, born on a slave ship, and brought to England where he became a familiar figure in the literary and political world of Johnson's London; Olaudah Equiano, kidnapped into slavery, then gaining freedom in England where in the late 1780s he played a leading role in the abolitionist campaign.[31] But the varied achievements of this small group did little to alter the generally servile image of the Negro in Britain. It was easy to argue, as Hume did, that their accomplishments were those of a parrot – simply an ability to imitate. There were few attempts to draw connections between the 10,000 or more blacks who lived in Britain, and the nature and potential of their African homeland. Many had come at one remove, of course, from a Caribbean plantation rather than direct from West Africa. Even so, there seems to be a problem both of comprehension and imagination here. The gap between the black page-boy, street beggar or quiet porter, and the fetish-worshipping, barbaric environment which the travel accounts described as the home of the black race seemed too wide to bridge or explain.

Since the late fifteenth century the explorations and observations of Europeans overseas had provided growing evidence of human diversity. As Jean Bodin expressed it in his *Six bookes of a commonweale* in 1586, 'even as we see a varietie in all sorts of beasts . . . in a like way we may say, there is in a manner as great difference in the nature and disposition of man'.[32] Cultural differences were not necessarily associated with racial differences, although as we have seen some Spanish writers of the sixteenth century had postulated the biological inferiority of the American Indians in an attempt to justify their subordination and servitude. Assumptions of the unity of the human race came under pressure as doubts grew about the Biblical teaching on monogenesis at the same time as European dominance was established over wide areas of the world and their inhabitants. Robert Burton had expressed the puzzle in his *Anatomy of Melancholy* in 1621 when he enquired: 'Whence proceed that variety of manners, and a distinct character (as it were) to several nations? . . . some are wise, subtile, witty; others dull, sad, heavy . . . some soft, some hardy, barbarous, civil, black, dun, white.'[33] Although some writers strained to find cultural similarities, a process which led to some far-fetched and tenuous parallels, the Negro was hard both to trace and place. Once observers (or at least English and Dutch ones) had pointed out that African fetish-worship reminded them of the superstitious idolatry of Papists they usually abandoned their quest to find 'likenesses'. To most, fetish-worship was not religion as such. William Smith, having dealt with Muslims and Christians on the coast of Gambia, then turned to those 'who trouble themselves about no religion at all', the fetishists. 'Some have a lion's tail; some a bird's feather, some a pebble, a bit of rag, a dog's leg; or, in short, any thing they fancy.'[34] Labat produced a different list – 'some a horn, some a crab's claw, some a nail, a flint, a snail's shell, a bird's head, or a root' – but no more enlightenment.[35] In a work of considerable scholarship Charles de Brosses pursued the matter further, but his *Culte des Dieux Fetishes* of 1760 placed fetishist societies firmly at the bottom of the scale of human development. To worship objects, plants and animals had nothing in common with true religion, he insisted. It was a further example of the 'ferocious stupidity' of such societies, whose inhabitants lived in ignorance and fear. 'They know nothing, and they have no desire to know anything. They pass their lives without thinking, and they grow old without emerging from childhood, all of whose faults they retain.'[36]

On the deeper question of whether the Negro was part of the human race at all the debate was hesitant and inconclusive. Doubts about the origins of the American Indians had been resolved within a monogenetic framework by emphasizing the process of diffusion which followed the original act of creation. Details were given, even of precise routes supposedly followed, and as late as 1775 James Adair in his *History of the American Indians* was happily proving that they were descendants of the lost tribes of Israel. But the blackness of the Negro proved a more intractable obstacle. Inevitably, stark physical differences led some to postulate more fundamental divisions within mankind. By some, the Negro was regarded as an aberrant, degenerate departure from the original model – to use the language of the *Universal Modern History*, 'black skins, swarthy minds' – though quite how this had happened was not easy to explain. When Sir William Petty in the 1670s set out a proposed plan which was to include all living creatures, he clearly believed that there were more than physical differences between Europeans and Africans. 'Europeans do not only differ from the aforementioned Africans in collour, which is as much as white differs from black, but also in their haire . . . in the shape of their noses, lipps and cheek bones, as also in the very outline of their faces and the mould of their skulls. They differ also in their naturall manners, and in the internall qualities of their minds.'[37]

This latter assertion was by no means universally accepted. François Bernier in a paper of 1684 in the *Journal des Sçavans* relied on physical attributes, and particularly colour differences, in distinguishing the various species of man, but did not read distinctions of mental or spiritual qualities into his classification. Even so, he expressed a common but potentially ominous belief when he allowed the American Indians to be the same species as Europeans, but not the African Negroes. 'What induces me to make a different species of the Africans, are, 1. their thick lips and swab noses, there being few among them who have aquiline noses or lips of moderate thickness. 2. The blackness which is peculiar to them, and which is not caused by the sun, as many think.'[38] The attempt to link skin colour to latitude became increasingly difficult as generations of black slaves grew up far removed from their African homeland, at the same time as white planters living in the tropics kept their racial characteristics. As a late seventeenth-century essayist put it, 'A negroe will always be a negroe, carry him to Greenland, give him chalk, feed and manage him never so many ways.' He went on to argue that the Negro's colour was 'innate or seminal', owing nothing to climate or Biblical curses, and queried whether it was of any importance anyway, or 'only accidental to beauty which consists wholly in proportion and symetry?'[39] Others propounded a more sophisticated version of the climatic explanation. John Harris in the editorial introduction to his collection of voyages of 1705 added psychological influences:

> Suppose for instance, in the case of the Cafres or Negroes of Africa, New Guinea, Madagascar, &c. might not the naked bodies of the first inhabitants of those parts, by the vast heat and drought of the climate, become very swarthy, burnt and black; especially of those who went much abroad, and exposed themselves to hunting and fishing, toil and labour in the sun? And is it not natural enough to conceive that these persons, who were bold and active men at hunting, fishing, or feats of war, would come by degrees to value themselves on the colour their bodies had gain'd by such brave and heroic exploits? And would not they despise the effeminate whiteness and softness of those that staid at home?[40]

From this, Harris envisaged the use of cosmetics to make the skin blacker, and a desire among women for prestigious, dark-skinned offspring which would have a colouring effect on the foetus. Few writers of the early eighteenth century seem to have supported any causal relationship between physical and mental characteristics. Richard Bradley, writing in 1721, explained the concept of the Chain of Being, but did not accept that this implied any hierarchical arrangement among races. Although he identified five categories of men, ranging from 'the white men, which are Europeans, that have beards', to 'the blacks of Guiney, whose hair is curl'd, like the wool of a sheep', he considered that the distinction was an external one only – 'for, as to their knowledge, I suppose there would not be any great difference, if it was possible they could all be born of the same parents, and have the same education, they would vary no more in understanding than children in the same house.'[41]

By the middle decades of the eighteenth century this general acceptance of the equality of races was changing form before the vigorous efforts of natural scientists to classify and explain the world of living matter, including mankind. These efforts were constrained by their unwillingness to abandon conventional monogenetic doctrine, for few were willing to follow John Atkins when he wrote in 1734 that 'White and Black must have descended from different protoplasts; and that there is no other way of accounting for it.'[42] Thus John Mitchell, whose paper was published in the *Philosophical Transactions* in 1744–5, went through complicated convolutions with references back to Newtonian optics in his attempt to explain that the colours of all human races were in fact only differing shades of the same colour, thus showing 'that there is not so great, unnatural, and unaccountable a difference between Negroes and white people, on account of their colours, as to make it impossible for both ever to have been descended from the same stock'.[43] Maupertuis, the celebrated natural philosopher who was President of the Berlin Academy of Sciences, advanced in his *Vénus Physique* (1745) and *Système de la Nature* (1751) the theory of mutation to explain differences of species in nature generally and of racial differences in men particularly. But added to this fortuitous assembling of living particles was the influence of climate and diet. 'The heat of the torrid zone is more likely to foment the particles which render the skin black, than those which render it white', so that 'in travelling away from the equator, the colour of the people grows lighter by shades. It is still very brown just outside the tropics; and one does not find complete whiteness until one has reached the temperate zone. It is at the limits of this zone that one finds the whitest peoples'. Once again, there was an effort to reconcile a scientific explanation, this time mutation, with monogenesis. 'Could not one explain by that means how from two individuals alone the multiplication of the most dissimilar species could have followed? They could have owed their first origination only to certain fortuitous productions, in which the elementary particles failed to retain the order they possessed in the father and mother animals; each degree of error would have produced a new species; and by reason of repeated deviations would have arrived at the infinite diversity of animals that we see today.'[44]

Buffon followed the same line: 'Mankind are not composed of species essentially different from each other; that, on the contrary, there was originally but one species, who, after multiplying and spreading over the whole surface of the earth, have undergone various changes by the influence of climate, food, mode of living, epidemic diseases, and the mixture of dissimilar individuals.'[45] This essential unity of mankind might seem to postulate an equality of mankind; but this would be to ignore both the subjective elements of preference, distaste and prejudice which influenced the natural scientists, and the fact that the process of classification which they pursued led them insidiously towards arrangements of order, rank and precedence. So in 1735 the great pioneer among eighteenth-century botanists, Carl Linnaeus, in the first edition of his *Systema Naturae*, brusquely divided mankind into two species, *Homo sapiens* and the unalluring *Homo monstrosus*, with most primitive men falling into the second category.[46] By the tenth edition of 1758 Linnaeus had reached a more elaborate classification in which the American Indian, but still more the African Negro, fared badly in comparison with the European.

> American – red, choleric, erect; thick, straight, black hair; distended nostrils; freckled face; beardless chin; obstinate, gay, free. He paints himself with variegated, red lines. He is ruled by custom.

> European – white, sanguine, muscular; long, blond hair; blue eyes; gentle, most intelligent; a discoverer. He covers himself with clothing suitable to the northern climate. He is ruled by religious custom.

> African – black, phlegmatic, lax; black, curly hair; silky skin, apelike nose, swollen lips; the bosoms of the women are distended; their breasts give milk copiously; crafty, slothful, careless, he smears himself with fat. He is ruled by authority.[47]

There was a counter-argument, based on the ideas of cultural relativism which some observers had expressed in their remarks on the American Indians. It was put forward by Adam Smith in 1759 when he asked, 'What different ideas are formed in different nations concerning the beauty of the human shape and countenance? A fair complexion is a shocking deformity upon the coast of Guinea. Thick lips and a flat nose are a beauty.'[48] More commonly, the stress on environmental differences – which Smith used elsewhere for his evaluation of 'civilized' and 'savage' societies – tended to point towards a hierarchical arrangement. When this was done, the white European (and his overseas progeny) appeared, instinctively and invariably, at the top, and his black antithesis at the bottom. In between were ranged, in less certain order, the other hues and colours of mankind. Buffon produced an unusually precise version of climatic determinism to account for this. 'The most temperate climate lies between the 40th and 50th degree of latitude, and it produces the most handsome and beautiful men. It is from this climate that the ideas of the genuine colour of mankind, and of the various degrees of beauty, ought to be derived. The two extremes are equally remote from truth and from beauty.' More than skin colour was included, for 'it is probable, that both the bile and blood of Negroes are blacker than those of white people, as their skin is likewise blacker' – though quite how this had come about was difficult to explain. As far as other features of the physiognomy were concerned, then custom might be responsible – for nose-flattening, for example – or variations in diet in other cases. Not simply physical differences were at issue; aesthetic, spiritual and intellectual attributes were involved. There was in nature, Buffon argued, a prototype of each species, and for humanity that prototype, the ideal, was the European – to put it more exactly, if we are to take Buffon's boundaries at their face value, those Europeans fortunate enough to dwell between the latitudes of Rome and Paris. The general physical environment was important to Buffon, as we have seen in his discussion of the American Indian, so it was significant that he saw the Negro race as living in 'miserable and precarious' circumstances, like the peoples of the far north and the far south – Eskimos and Aborigines for example – who eked out a marginal existence in harsh, inhospitable regions of the world. The blacks of Africa, in Buffon's words, were 'gross, superstitious and stupid'.[49]

The implications of this line of thought were put in their most pointed form by David Hume, in a long afterthought of a note appended in 1754 to his essay, 'Of National Characters', published six years earlier. Here race and culture, colour and achievement, were aggressively linked. 'I am apt to suspect the Negroes, and in general all the other species of men (for there are four or five different kinds) to be naturally inferior to the whites. There never was a civilized nation of any other complexion than white, nor even any individual eminent in action or speculation. No ingenious manufactures amongst them, no arts, no sciences.'[50] Dr Barker has cogently argued that too much attention has been paid to this celebrated footnote by Hume,[51] but the fact is that it was more than a casual reference. The language is dogmatic, and the sentiments are commonplace. They are to be found in Maupertuis, 'Le blanc est le couleur des premiers hommes'.[52] Even J. R. Forster, whose observations on the peoples of the Pacific were to show much understanding, was unable to shake off the inbred conviction of the superiority of his own kind: 'The native of Senegal is characterised by a timorous disposition, by his jetty black skin, and crisped wooly hair. A majestic size, red hair, a blue languishing eye, a remarkably fair complexion, and a warlike, intrepid, but open and generous temper distinguishes the Teutonic tribes of the north of Europe, from the rest of mankind.'[53] Accusations that the Negro belonged to a sub-human category were rare and half-hearted in this period, but implications that he was an inferior member of the human race were not.

The African accounts of the first half of the eighteenth century had sharpened the problem which Europeans thought they faced in the Negro: his origin, his colour, his place in the human race. The uneasiness felt by many observers was characterized by John Atkins when he wrote that Africa seemed so alien that he felt as though he were on a different planet.[54] The 'barbarity' of Africa continued to be a persistent theme of the publications of the second half of the century. It is found in the standard history in English of France's American and West Indian colonies, Thomas Jefferys' *Natural and Civil History of the French Dominions in North and South America* of 1760. Here the works of Tertre and Labat were used to portray the miserable lot of the slaves on the sugar plantations, but a general 'Comparison of their present and past condition' found in favour of the former. The slaves' European master, harsh disciplinarian though he was, was 'endowed with more humanity and benevolence' than their former ruler in Africa – an 'unlettered savage, who bears despotic sway over a herd of rough brutes, that have scarcely any thing but their walking upon two legs, to give them a title to the name of man, and in whom, if reason shines at all, it is with a faint and glimmering ray'. There was much difference between this scrutiny of the Negro and the largely favourable report on the Canadian Indians in the same book – 'the happiest of all mortals . . . their most admirable quality is that truly philosophical way of thinking'.[55]

The continued prejudice against the African is the more noticeable because by this period the emphasis on the importance of subsistence in a society might be expected to work moderately in his favour. Many of the accounts had information on African agriculture, whose development would seem to put West African societies firmly in the third stage of progression, ahead of those AmerIndian peoples who depended heavily on hunting and fishing for subsistence. A rare example of this adjustment is to be found in Philmore's pamphlet *Two Dialogues of the Man-Trade* (better known through its inclusion in the abolitionist publications of the American Quaker, Anthony Benezet). Philmore argued that the African Negroes were superior in civilization to the 'wild unsettled' Indians of North America, for 'they generally settle together, and employ themselves in agriculture and commerce. Some large nations are represented as industrious and careful in the cultivation of their lands; breeding cattle and carrying on a trade to distant parts.'[56] In contrast, and more typically, Pierre Poivre, the physiocratic French writer who set great store on the state of a region's agriculture as the measure of its advancement, flew in the face of the evidence to produce a very different picture of West Africa: 'The western coasts of Africa . . . are uncultivated, inhabited by miserable savages. These wretched men, who esteem themselves so little as to sell one another, never think on the cultivation of their lands. Content with existing from one day to another under a climate where they have but few wants, they cultivate no more than prevents their dying of hunger.'[57]

Raynal, though he argued strongly against slavery, and produced in the later editions of his *Histoire des deux Indes* a plan for gradual emancipation, saw the climatic environment of Africa as being as unfavourable in its own way towards the progress of human society as the overwhelming physical forces unleashed upon a puny mankind in America. Though he would have no truck either with Biblical legends about the mark of Cain or with theories about the influence of sun upon colour, he was convinced that there was a general correlation between climate and species. In Africa the hot and sultry climate was matched by a people with limited intellectual faculties, 'more indolent, more weak, and unhappily more fit for slavery'. The major religions of the world had no impact on West Africa, where fetish-worship and super-stition reigned. Shelter, clothes, diet, were all of the simplest – 'Arts are unknown amongst them. All their labours are confined to certain rustic employments. Scarce one hundredth part of their country is cultivated, and that in a very wretched manner.'[58]

Further use, or misuse, of the current theories on environmental considerations was made by the former Jamaican judge, Edward Long, first writing in 1772 under the pseudonym of 'A Planter'. He relied heavily on the connection made by James Steuart and other of the Scottish writers between a warm, tropical climate and indolence.[59] This supported Long's belief that without the discipline of slavery the black labourers in the West Indies would 'despise and reject the cultivation of a planter's land' and revert to their African form of existence – 'a banditti of lazy, lawless, Negroes, living in a state of nature'.[60] The argument was taken a decisive stage further by Long in his major work, the three-volume *History of Jamaica*, published in 1774. Some of its most radical ideas were borrowed from the second edition of a pamphlet, *Considerations on the Negro Cause*, published two years earlier by Samuel Estwick, assistant agent in England for the Barbados plan-ters. To conceive of men as being uniformly the same seemed to Estwick to 'unlock that great chain of heaven'. Negroes, he maintained, differed 'from other men, not in kind, but in species'.[61] Prominent in the second volume of Long's *History* was a very individualistic version of the Chain of Being in which the animal world, represented at its highest level by the orang-outang, shaded almost imperceptibly into the Negro race, with a distinct gap intervening before the white race was reached. In contrast to Buffon, who had also looked at the question, Long insisted that the orang-outang was intellectually equal to many Negroes, that sexual intercourse could and did take place, and that in general 'he has a much nearer resemblance to the Negroe race, than the latter bear to white men'. Long's language was crudely abusive, as when he listed the physical differences between Negroes and whites:

> First, in respect to their bodies, viz. the dark membrane which communicates that black colour to their skins, which does not alter by transportation into other climates, which they never lose . . . Secondly, a covering of wool, like the bestial fleece, instead of hair. Thirdly, the roundness of their eyes, the figure of their ears, tumid nostrils, flat noses, invariable thick lips, and general large size of the female nipples, as if adapted by nature to the peculiar conformation of their childrens mouths. Fourthly, the black colour of the lice which infest their bodies . . . Fifthly, their bestial and fetid smell, which they all have in a greater or less degree. . . .[62]

Mentally, the Negro race had not advanced in 2000 years, Long asserted. This was presumably a shaft aimed at James Beattie, who in a rebuttal in his *Essay on Truth* (1770) of Hume's accusations of mid-century, had explained that Africa (and America) lagged behind Europe culturally because they were in the stage Europe had reached 2000 years before. They were younger, not inferior, and he cited the examples of Francis Williams and Philip Quaque as proof 'that Blacks, if properly educated, are capable of the same improvements as Whites'.[63] Now, in an elaboration of Hume, Long insisted that the Negroes were altogether devoid both of genius and morality, and that because of their idleness Africa was 'one continued wilderness'. The slave trade he saw as a healthy culling process in a land where polygamy reigned and one man might have 200 children; it had, he added, the same sordid but beneficial function 'as scavengers in a dirty town'.[64]

Historians have argued about the significance and influence of Long's remarks, and in particular about his suspicion that Negroes were nearer to beasts than to men. This was radical thinking indeed, for the distinction between men, created in God's image and endowed with reason, and all other living creatures, remained a dominant one. In this area Long had little effect, for the polygenetic implications of his writings left him in 'a position of precarious intellectual isolation'.[65] The other work of the period, published in the same year as Long's *History*, which went halfway towards accepting polygenesis, was the first volume of Kames' *Sketches of the History of Man*, and there Long would find no support for his theory of immutable Negro inferiority. Environment and circumstances were the key explanations to Kames. He admitted that there was 'a strong presumption' that white and black were different species, but 'second thoughts' had convinced him that any inferiority in the understanding of Negroes was caused by their condition rather than by any inherent differences. In Africa food, and what clothes and shelter they needed, came easily; as slaves, they were not required or encouraged to think for themselves. But, he concluded, 'Who can say how far they might improve in a state of freedom, were they obliged, like Europeans, to procure bread with the sweat of their brows.'[66]

It is important that Long's comments were made, not in some self-evidently polemic tract, but in what became accepted as a standard work on the largest of Britain's West Indian colonies. Although few would follow the theoretical leap which Long was poised to make, yet the denigrating tone of his references to Africa and its black inhabitants was only an extension of much that was already in print. The point is reinforced by a glance at the compilations of the 1770s and 1780s, where the introductory sections vied with each other in their portrayals of a continent sunk in sloth and barbarity. They do not follow Long ideologically, for where any explanation was offered it was generally limited to environmental factors, but the tone and the language are much the same. William Guthrie complained that 'In Africa the human mind seems degraded below its natural state. To dwell long upon the manners of this country, a country so immersed in rudeness and barbarity, besides that it could afford little instruction, would be disgusting to every lover of mankind.'[67] G. H. Millar considered that the southern parts of the continent were marginally preferable to the equatorial zone, but even these were 'inhabited by such barbarous people, so fierce and savage in their nature, so uncouth and forbidding in their manners and language, and so shy of all intercourse with foreign nations, that our readers need not wonder that we are almost as much in the dark about them as we are about the midland part of the continent'.[68] In another collection, although the slave trade was held partly responsible for Africa's degraded condition, 'the nature of the clime, the brutality of the natives, and the ferocity of the beasts, display the powerful effects of excessive heat both on the vegetable and animal creation; while the successive depredations of different nations have reduced it to the lowest ebb of ignorance and barbarity'.[69]

The abolitionist era brought some degree of challenge to this dire interpretation of the African condition, but familiar ethnocentric assumptions remained common to both sides involved in the debates of the late 1780s and 1790s. Although the single issue of abolition seems to dominate the period, the very fact that Britain's traditional involvement in Africa was possibly drawing to an end led to alternative attitudes and proposals developing in these years. The English botanist, Henry Smeathman, whose recommendations on the Sierra Leone region led in 1787 to the establishment of a settlement there intended to take some of Britain's 'black poor' as well as black loyalists from North America, was heavily critical of the negative impressions which the accounts gave of Africa. He was enthusiastic about what he had seen of Negro agriculture in Sierra Leone, and went on, 'This unhappy race have considerably suffered by misrepresentation. While our moral and philosophical writers have sacrificed them to system, and our travellers to prejudice, our merchants and planters, regarding them as mere beasts of burden, have devoted them to their avarice and custom.'[70] The Sierra Leone experimental settlement never lived up to expectations, and after a fraught and precarious existence of twenty years it finally became in 1807 Britain's first Crown Colony in Africa. It was only one of a dozen or so projects for West African enterprise of one kind or another in the late eighteenth century, and although they accomplished little in the end, they were evidence of a new and different interest in a region long given over to the slave-trade. What is lacking is any fundamental change in attitude towards the indigenous inhabitants. Ruthless exploitation was to cease, but there was no question of equal rights or equal partnership. Rather, the emphasis was that expressed by the Swedish promoter and philanthropist, Carl Berns Wadström, when in a publication of 1789 he pointed out that 'civilized nations have some right to exercise a certain dominion over the uncivilized, provided that this happy dominion be confined to a paternal yoke'.[71]

These sentiments were reflected in the evidence of abolitionist witnesses to the Privy Council in 1789 and the select committee of the House of Commons in 1790 and 1791 as those bodies enquired into the slave-trade. The main thrust of the abolitionists' campaign was directed against conditions on the middle passage and the system of plantation slavery in the West Indies. Africa itself came a poor third, as the abridgement by William Fox of several volumes of evidence given before the select committee showed. In his *Summary* of 1792 Fox was able to compress the evidence relating to Africa into a short opening chapter of only a few paragraphs entitled 'Africans – same as other people'.[72] It summed up the abolitionist case in one important respect: Africans had skills in agriculture and manufacturing; they possessed moral virtues and normal capacities; they were worst where contact with European slave-traders was closest, and 'best, where they have the least intercourse with the latter'. Conditions on the slave coasts were not typical of West Africa in general. Domestic slavery there might be, but it bore no resemblance to the ruthless exploitation of human beings on the Caribbean plantations. For all this, no great claims were made for the level of African development. As Wilberforce told the Commons, 'Their state of civilization [is] in general very imperfect, their notions of morality extremely rude, the power of their governments ill-defined.'[73]

The pro-slavery apologists, by contrast, made much of what they considered to be innate characteristics of the Negro. These varied from indolence to cannibalism, and produced a situation of savage barbarity which made slavery a supportable, even preferable, alternative to life in Africa. This picture of tyranny, bloodshed and misery was based on supposedly eyewitness accounts and still more on the large corpus of published material which now existed on Africa. Recent additions to this came from two books on Dahomey: Robert Norris's *Memoirs of the Reign of Bossa Ahadee, King of Dahomy* (1789), and Archibald Dalzel's *The History of Dahomy, An Inland Kingdom of Africa* (1793). The latter work, in particular, drew on previous accounts of the region from Snelgrave onwards, as well as on Dalzel's own extensive first-hand experience, to produce what his modern editor has termed 'the epitome of African barbarism'.[74] Attention, in particular,\ was focused on the Dahomean capital, Abomey, and its horrific annual festivals where human sacrifice took place on a mass scale. Seventy miles inland, Abomey was far removed from the coasts where the European slavers operated. Dalzel's report of the remarks made by the King of Dahomey to an English factor in 1766 was widely quoted as evidence that African barbarity was inbred, of long-standing, and was not connected with the demands of the European slave-trade. To strike awe and terror were his aims, Kpengla declaimed: 'I, who have not long been master of this country, have, without thinking of the market, killed many thousands, and I shall kill many thousands more . . . neither silk, nor coral, nor brandy, nor cowries, can be accepted as substitutes for the blood that ought to be spilt for example sake.' Elsewhere in the book, Snelgrave's old accusations of cannibalism were resurrected, and a chronological account given of the wars of Dahomey since the early years of the century. For these Dalzel had a single general explanation: 'The insatiable thirst after blood, the barbarous vanity of being considered the scourge of mankind, and the savage pomp of dwelling in a house garnished with skulls, and stained with human gore, seem to be the only motives for the atrocious actions.'[75]

'A mixture of facts, fables and prejudices' is how a modern African historian has described all this.[76] It was in an effort to introduce more fact and less fable into Britain's knowledge of Africa that in 1788 the Association for Promoting the Discovery of the Interior Parts of Africa was founded. Set up by a group of a dozen men of wealth, influence and learning, headed by Sir Joseph Banks, the Association had as its avowed aim 'enlarging the fund of human knowledge'. Knowledge of the world was increasing fast, as its *Plan* of 1788 pointed out, and even in Africa the travels of Bruce in the east, and of Sparrman and others in the south were bringing in new and exciting detail. But 'the map of its interior is still but a wide extended blank, on which the geographer has traced, with a hesitating hand, a few names of unexplored rivers and of uncertain nations'. Though the presence of Muslim traders on the west coast indicated that there were regular routes into the interior, Europe's knowledge of them was slight. 'The source of the Niger, the places of its rise and termination, and even its existence as a separate stream, are still undetermined. Nor has our knowledge of the Senegal and Gambia rivers improved upon that of De La Brue and Moore . . .'.[77]

If the quest for knowledge was an important consideration, it was not the only one. The prospect of opening a new region to British commerce, which at the same time as it replaced the slave-trade as a source of wealth would benefit the Africans and raise their level of civilization, appealed to several groups in Britain. It was expressed in a letter from Olaudah Equiano to Lord Hawkesbury which was printed in the Privy Council report of 1789 on the slave trade: 'A system of commerce once being established in Africa, the demand for manufactories will most rapidly augment, as the native inhabitants will insensibly adopt our fashions, manners, customs, etc. etc. In proportion to the civilization, so will be the consumption of British manufactures . . . Industry, enterprise and mining will have their full scope, proportionately as they civilize. In a word it lays open an endless field of commerce to the British manufacturer and merchant adventurer.'[78] More succinctly, the appeal is also heard in the report for 1790 of the secretary of the African Association, Henry Beaufoy, printed in the Association's *Proceedings*: 'Of all the advantages to which a better acquaintance with the inland regions of Africa may lead, the first in importance is the extension of the commerce and the encouragement of the manufactures of Britain.' The peoples of the African interior, he wrote two years later, 'may soon be united with Europe in that great bond of commercial fellowship'.[79]

With more than one aim before it, then, the African Association built up its knowledge of the interior during the 1790s: explorers were engaged, reports were received from Consuls and other Englishmen with experience of North Africa, interviews were noted down with a whole series of 'Moors'. There were setbacks and disappointments; not all the explorers were competent, some of the more persistent died, and it was difficult to make sense of all the information received. Certain states or cities – it was rarely clear which – took on intriguing if hazy shapes in the western interior. There was Timbuktu, Bornu, Katsina, Hausa. If they were not, Beaufoy concluded in the end, inhabited by descendants of the ancient Egyptians, the Carthaginians, or the ancient Greeks – 'I am much disappointed in finding all those peoples

253

Negroes', one of his informants wrote – still there were compensations. The walled cities were reputed to be populous and wealthy, they traded gold dust, ivory, and fine linens in such quantity 'that in one day you may procure as much as would load fifty large ships'.[80] They were, at the very least, African societies of a different type from those along the 'Guinea' coast.

The most dramatic revelation came from the travels of the greatest of the Association's explorers, Mungo Park. In his journey of 1795–7 he half-solved one of the most perplexing mysteries of African geography when he reached the Niger and discovered that it flowed eastward. With that one observation he reversed traditional concepts of West African geography. And he did more than this, for his account set new standards in dispassionate and perceptive observation, nearer to Cook than to most of his predecessors in Africa. The *Annual Register* for 1799 noted this: 'he seems to have described things as he saw them, \and to have consulted his senses rather than his imagination; he is unwilling to glut credulity by the narration of wonders'.[81] The account of his explorations published in 1799, with its descriptions of the well-established states of the interior, showed (as the *Gentleman's Magazine* put it) that 'the Negroes of these districts are not to be considered an uncivilized race; they have religion, established governments, laws, schools, commerce, manufactures, *wars!*'[82] In Park's own words, he was convinced that 'whatever difference there is between the Negro and European, in the conformation of the nose and the colour of the skin, there is none in the genuine sympathies and characteristic feelings of our common nature'.[83]

It was less Park's reflections on the universality of human sentiments than the implications of his discoveries which seized the imagination of Banks and the African Association. In May 1799 Banks pointed out that Park had 'opened a gate into the interior of Africa' through which Britain must pass, not just with single explorers, but with troops and field guns, to wrest trade out of Muslim hands, establish forts on the banks of the Niger, and generally to control the region. In a letter to Lord Liverpool the next month Banks expanded on the possibilities if Britain would secure 'by conquest or by treaty' if not the whole of the coast from Arguin to Sierra Leone, at least the Senegal River itself. Trade in manufactured goods and gold dust would be established, the slave-trade damaged, and the British company set up to do all this 'would govern the Negroes far more mildly and make them far more happy than they are now under the tyranny of their arbitrary princes, would become popular at home by converting them to the Christian religion by inculcating in their rough minds the mild morality which is engrafted on the tenets of our faith'.[84]

Christianity and commerce, conquest and treaty: with these recommendations to the government at the close of one century, Banks indicated much of what was to follow in Britain's contact with Africa in the next.

NOTES

1 Michèle Duchet, *Anthropologie et histoire au siècle des lumières* (Paris, 1971), p. 36.
2 David Brion Davis, *The Problem of Slavery in Western Culture* (Ithaca, N.Y., 1966), p. 281.
3 See above, pp. 34–7.
4 Richard Blome, *A Geographical Description of the four parts of the World* (1670), Pt. II, 49.
5 Richard Blome, *A Description of the Island of Jamaica; With the other Isles and Territories in America* (1672), p. 85; *The Present State of His Majesties Isles and Territories in America* (1687), p. 39.
6 A. J. Barker, *The African Link: British Attitudes to the Negro in the Era of the Atlantic Slave Trade, 1550–1807* (1978), pp. 120, 200.
7 William Bosman, *A New and Accurate Description of the Coast of Guinea* ... (1967 reprint of the 1705 English edition, with introduction by J. R. Willis and notes by J. D. Fage and R. E. Bradbury). The references which follow are taken (in order of citation) from pp. 177, 49–50, 117–18, 146, 164.
8 See Frank E. Manuel, *The Eighteenth Century Confronts the Gods* (Cambridge, Mass., 1959), p. 28.
9 *Navigantium atque Itinerantium Bibliotheca* ... ed. John Harris (1705), I, 351.
10 James Houston, *Some New and Accurate Observations* ... *of the Coast of Guinea* (1725), p. 33.
11 J. Barbot, 'A Description of the Coasts of North and South-Guinea', in *A Collection of Voyages and Travels*, ed. J. and A. Churchill, V (1732), 12.
12 Thomas Phillips, 'A Journal of a Voyage', in *ibid.*, VI.
13 William Snelgrave, *A New Account of some parts of Guinea, And the Slave-Trade* (1734), p. 161.
14 John Atkins, *A Voyage to Guinea, Brasil, and the West-Indies* ... (1735), pp. 176, xxiv–v, 122–32, 38–9 (in order of citation).
15 John Atkins, *The Navy-Surgeon* (1734), pp. 20–1.
16 Atkins, *Voyage*, pp. 64–5, 110, 90 (in order of citation).
17 *The Gentleman's Magazine*, VIII (1738), 473.
18 Francis Moore, *Travels into the Inland Parts of Africa* ... (1738), pp. 179, iii.
19 William Smith, *A New Voyage to Guinea* (1744), pp. 28, 245, 248–9, 266, 194 (in order of citation).
20 Michel Adanson, *A Voyage to Senegal* (1759), pp. 39, 75, 117.
21 *A New General Collection of Voyages and Travels*, pub. by Thomas Astley (1745–7), II, 86, 417.
22 *The Universal Traveller*, ed. Thomas Salmon (1752), II, 373.
23 *Universal Modern History* (1760), XVI, 355; XIV, 18, 19, 20, 24; XVII, 290 (in order of citation).

24 Philip D. Curtin, *The Image of Africa: British Ideas and Action 1780–1850* (Madison, 1964), p. 23.

25 Davis, *Slavery and Western Culture*, p. 468.

26 Quoted Roger Anstey, *The Atlantic Slave Trade and British Abolition, 1760–1810* (1975), p. 37.

27 Quoted Winthrop D. Jordan, *White over Black: American Attitudes Toward the Negro, 1550–1812* (Norton Library edn., New York, 1977), p. 28.

28 Daniel Defoe, *Robinson Crusoe* (Penguin edn., Harmondsworth, 1965), pp. 208–9.

29 *The Gentleman's Magazine*, V (1735), 21–3.

30 Quoted Roger Anstey, *Atlantic Slave Trade*, p. 149.

31 On these see Folarin Shyllon, *Black People in Britain 1555–1833* (1977), especially Pt. III.

32 Margaret T. Hodgen, *Early Anthropology in the Sixteenth and Seventeenth Centuries* (Philadelphia, 1964), p. 209.

33 Quoted *ibid.*, p. 221.

34 Smith, *New Voyage*, p. 26.

35 Osborne, *Collection*, II, 323.

36 Quoted Manuel, *Eighteenth Century Confronts the Gods*, Ch. 4.

37 Quoted Jordan, *White over Black*, p. 225.

38 Printed in T. Bendyshe, 'The History of Anthropology', Anthropological Society of London, *Memoirs*, I (1863–4), 361.

39 *Ibid.*, p. 371.

40 Harris, *Bibliotheca*, I, viii.

41 Richard Bradley, *A Philosophical Account of the Works of Nature* (1721), p. 169.

42 Atkins, *Navy-Surgeon*, pp. 23–4.

43 Quoted Jordan, *White over Black*, p. 247.

44 Quoted Bentley Glass *et al.*, *Forerunners of Darwin: 1745–1859* (Baltimore, 1959), pp. 76–7.

45 *Natural History, General and Particular, by the Count de Buffon*, trans. William Smellie (2nd edn., 1785), III, 206.

46 See Hodgen, *Early Anthropology*, p. 425.

47 Printed in John G. Burke, 'The Wild Man's Pedigree', in *The Wild Man Within*, ed. E. Dudley and Maximilian E. Novak (Pittsburgh, 1972), pp. 266–7.

48 Adam Smith, *The Theory of Moral Sentiments*, ed. D. D. Raphael and A. L. Macfie (Oxford, 1976), p. 199.

49 On all this see Buffon, *Natural History*, III, 202–5; also Duchet, *Anthropologie et histoire*, pp. 255 ff.

50 David Hume, *Essays: Moral, Political and Literary*, ed. T. H. Green and T. H. Grose (1875), I, 252.

51 Barker, *African Link*, pp. 115 ff.

52 Duchet, *Anthropologie et histoire*, p. 270 n.

53 J. R. Forster, *Observations made during a Voyage round the World* (1778), p. 227.

54 Atkins, *Voyage*, p. 34.

55 *Natural and Civil History of the French Dominions in North and South America*, ed. Thomas Jefferys (1760), pp. 193, 96 respectively.

56 [Anthony Benezet], *A Short Account of that part of Africa inhabited by the Negroes* (Philadelphia, 1762), pp. 37–8, 72.

57 Pierre Poivre, *The Travels of a Philosopher* . . . (1769), p. 6.

58 *A Philosophical and Political History of the Settlements and Trade of the Europeans in the East and West Indies translated from the French of the Abbé Raynal by J. Justamond* (1777), III, 372–85 *passim*; see also E. D. Seeber, *Anti-Slavery Opinion in France during the second half of the eighteenth century* (Baltimore, 1937).

59 See pp. 275–6 below, also pp. 137–8 above.

60 *Candid Reflections* . . . *on* . . . *the Negroe-Cause by 'A Planter'* (1772), p. 66.

61 Quoted Barker, *African Link*, p. 47.

62 Edward Long, *A History of Jamaica* (1774), II, 351–2; see also his remarks on pp. 353, 370–1, 384.

63 See *The Gentleman's Magazine*, XLI (1771), 595.

64 Long, *History*, p. 384.

65 Barker, *African Link*, p. 51.

66 Henry Home (Lord Kames), *Sketches of the History of Man*, I (Edinburgh, 1774), 32.

67 William Guthrie, *A New Geographical, Historical and Commercial Grammar* (9th edn., 1785), p. 9.

68 G. H. Millar, *The New and Universal System of Geography* (1782), p. 220.

69 [Thomas Bankes], *A New Royal Authentic and Complete System of Universal Geography* (*c.* 1787), p. 315.

70 Printed Christopher Fyfe, *Sierra Leone Inheritance* (Oxford, 1964), p. 97.

71 Quoted Curtin, *Image of Africa*, p. 105.

72 William Fox, *An Abridgement of the Evidence delivered before a Select Committee of the House of Commons in the Years 1790 and 1791* (6th edn., 1792), pp. 1–2.

73 Quoted, with much other relevant material, in R. A. Austen and W. D. Smith, 'Images of Africa and British Slave-Trade Abolition: the Transition to an Imperialist Ideology 1787–1807', *African Historical Studies*, II (1969), 78.

74 J. D. Fage in introduction to *The History of Dahomy, An Inland Kingdom of Africa . . . by Archibald Dalzel* (1967 reprint of 1793 edn.), p. 12.

75 *Ibid.*, pp. 218, 166 respectively.

76 I. A. Akinjogbin, *Dahomey and its Neighbours 1708–1818* (Cambridge, 1967), p. 4.

77 *Records of the African Association 1788–1831*, ed. Robin Hallett (1964), pp. 44–5.

78 Printed in Fyfe, *Sierra Leone Inheritance*, p. 111.

79 See *Records of African Association*, pp. 101, 117.

80 *Ibid.*, pp. 118–19.

81 Kenneth Lupton, *Mungo Park the African Traveler* (Oxford, 1979), p. 114.

82 *Ibid.*, p. 112.

83 Quoted Robin Hallett, *The Penetration of Africa . . . Volume 1 to 1815* (1965), p. 233.

84 *Ibid.*, p. 245 and *Records of African Association*, pp. 211–12.

9

'Enlarging the Sphere of Contemplation'
The Exploration of the Pacific 1760–1800

The impact of the overseas discoveries played a positive if sometimes elusive role in the wide-ranging debate of the seventeenth and eighteenth centuries on the origins and nature of society and government. The discovery of the New World, as Locke had said, 'enlarged the sphere of contemplation'; it had stimulated discussion on how 'civilized' man (that is, usually, European man) had developed from 'savage' ancestors. It was a debate affected by the distant explorations, scientific discoveries and intellectual movements of the post-Renaissance era, and was accompanied by wistful queries as to whether the early stages of mankind's existence were not in some ways more acceptable than the current state – whether man, morally at least, might not have degenerated rather than advanced. As the chapters on Asia have suggested, the terms of the debate were changing. Steeped in classical and biblical traditions, educated Englishmen were still inclined to relate new knowledge of the peoples of the world to those traditions. Yet to more and more scholars this approach seemed increasingly inadequate even for the ancient peoples of Asia who had impinged historically on the world of the Bible or of Greece and Rome. The techniques of the student of nature seemed more appropriate than those of the student of texts. For the peoples of a region never mentioned in classical literature, the natural historians of man came even more into their own.

By the mid-eighteenth century such a region was beginning to attract Europe's attention for reasons commercial, strategic and scholarly – the remote and little-known expanses of the Pacific Ocean. Between the ending of the Seven Years War in 1763 and the outbreak of the French revolutionary wars thirty years later, Britain and France in particular experienced a 'Pacific craze', in which a new type of national hero emerged in the shape of naval explorers and itinerant scientists. Expeditions set off into the unknown, to return three years later laden with specimens from the South Seas, eager to publish descriptions, maps and views of the wondrous places visited and the peoples seen. For no other region do we have such detailed and thoughtful accounts of the indigenous inhabitants over a short period of time. To the published versions can be added a great deal of supplementary observation from individual logs and journals to give a more comprehensive view than usual of the varied reactions of the discovery crews. And in the process of observation there is a clear and two-way link between the conclusions of scholars at home on primitive peoples in general and the explorers' assessments of the specific Pacific peoples they encountered.

In the beginning at least, Europe seemed to be presented with a more convincing *bon sauvage* than either America or Africa had managed to muster. For students of primitive peoples the Pacific held advantages over North America and West Africa, ravaged and contaminated as they were by centuries of European exploitation. In the South Seas there had been no such contact, no slave trade, no frontier wars. Here in unspoilt surroundings would surely be found evidence to prove or disprove the presumptions of the 'noble savagery' school of thought, and indicate more reliably the relationship between western and primitive man. Looking back in 1784 at twenty years of exploration in the Pacific, the editor of Cook's third voyage, Canon John Douglas, stressed the importance of the islands of the South Seas to the scientist and philosopher. They were, he wrote

> untrodden ground. The inhabitants, as far as could be observed, were unmixed with any different tribe, by occasional intercourse, subsequent to their original settlement there; left entirely to their own powers for every art of life; and to their own remote traditions for every political or religious custom or institution; uninformed by science; unimpaired by education; in short, a fit soil from whence a careful observer could collect facts for forming a judgment, how far unassisted human nature will be apt to degenerate; and in what respects it can ever be able to excel.[1]

The motives for the Pacific expeditions after 1763 were not simply, nor even primarily, scientific. This second New World promised resources of such potential that its discovery and control might tip the commercial balance of power in Europe – for Britain confirm the overseas superiority brought by the wartime conquests, for France redress the humiliations of an unsuccessful war. In the one country John Campbell, in his revised edition of Harris's *Navigantium atque Itinerantium | Bibliotheca* (1744–48), urged his countrymen to establish a new commercial empire in the south Pacific, ranging from New Guinea and New Holland in the west to Juan Fernandez in the east, and taking in on the way the supposed southern continent, *Terra Australis Incognita*. The official account of Anson's voyage – that halfway mark in more ways than one between Dampier and Cook – helped in and after its publication in 1748 to maintain British interest in the Pacific. One of the most widely-printed of eighteenth-century travel accounts, it was more than a superb narration of heroism and suffering on the high seas, though this no doubt was the prime reason for its popularity. Its description and views of the Pacific islands of Juan Fernandez and Tinian made their own appeal to the imagination, with reminders of Robinson Crusoe at one level and of Rousseau's Nouvelle-Héloise at another.[2] There is an anticipation here of Tahiti, William Hodges, and much else.

In France, Buffon pointed in the first volume of his *Histoire naturelle* (1749) to the existence of lands of unknown size in the southern hemisphere, and three years later Maupertuis suggested in his *Lettre sur le progrès des Sciences* that one of the most important objectives left to western man was the discovery of the continent and islands of the south Pacific. Much of this preliminary thinking was brought together with the publication in Paris in 1756 of the first great collection of voyages devoted exclusively to the Pacific, *Histoire des Navigations aux Terres Australes* by Charles de Brosses. Plundered by John Callender in his three-volume English edition, confidently entitled *Terra Australis Cognita* (1766–68), this work provided Europe with accessible accounts of the main Pacific voyages: Magellan, Mendaña, Quirós, Torres, Tasman, Dampier, Schouten, Le Maire, Roggeveen, Anson. This was at first sight an impressive roll-call of navigators, but their voyages had produced almost as much confusion as enlightenment. Islands had been sighted and resighted, identified and then lost again; distant volcanic peaks had been mistaken for the outlying promontories of continental land-masses; straits had become bays, and bays straits. The map of the Pacific in 1750 is dotted with island groups whose names shift with every whim of cartographical fashion, and is scarred with squiggles of coastline which hint at intriguing but still unproven lands of continental dimensions. The immensity of the ocean, 10,000 miles in each direction, primitive methods of navigation, and the straitjacket of wind and current which pushed the tracks of sailing ships into a narrow belt, posed apparently insuperable problems to any wide-ranging and methodical exploration.

If the geography of the Pacific was uncertain and fanciful, so was knowledge of its inhabitants. Scattered through the volumes of de Brosses and his camp-follower, Callender, are the explorers' references to the island peoples of the Pacific. Their observations were usually hasty and superficial, often the result of only a few days', or sometimes even a few hours', stay. Encounters varied from friendly to violent, but misunderstanding was more common than comprehension, and all too often contact ended with the blast of cannon and musket on one side and a shower of stones and arrows on the other. It was characteristic somehow that the difficult eastern entrance into the Pacific through the Strait of Magellan was supposedly guarded by a race of giants, symbolic of the fact that Europeans were entering an alien world where their conventional standards did not apply. The strait's discoverer, Magellan, wrote in 1519 of its fearsome inhabitants that they were 'of a prodigious stature, fierce, and barbarous, made a horrible roaring noise, more like bulls than human creatures'. Even when the inhabitants of that bleak, inhospitable region dwindled to more normal size, they remained distinctly unprepossessing, in the words of Jacques Le Maire in 1624, 'rather beasts than men; for they tear human bodies to pieces, and eat the flesh, raw and bloody as it is. There is not the least spark of religion or policy to be observed amongst them: On the contrary, they are, in every respect, brutal'.[3]

Once into the Pacific, the explorers found among the island groups a bewildering and unpredictable variety of appearance and behaviour, the one undeviating norm being that from Magellan to Cook the European found the Pacific native incurably, often frivolously thievish – a constant source of conflict which overshadowed attempts at understanding and led to countless deaths. Added to this was a lack of political structure as Europeans understood it. At the Ladrones shortly before his death Magellan noted that 'Amongst these people there is not the least shew of any order or form of government, but every man does what is agreeable to his own humour and inclination.' Most puzzling of all to Europeans influenced by the belief that physical appearance was conditioned by climatic zone, was the startling difference of colour between inhabitants of the same region. Mendaña wrote of the Solomon Islands in 1567 that 'the inhabitants are black, for the most part, but some of them are red, others white, and others fair'. In 1606 Quirós in his wanderings through Polynesia came to 'the Island of Fair People' (Rakahanga) where he found 'women, who were remarkably handsome and agreeable. Nothing surprised us so much, as the great whiteness of their skins, in a climate where the air and sun, to which they are perpetually exposed, might be expected to spoil their colour.' Two thousand miles farther west Quirós reached the New Hebrides where he saw 'many inhabitants which, to our great surprize, were of three different colours. Some of them were altogether black, others very white, with red beards and hair, and a third sort were mulattoes.' An eighteenth-century footnote added, helplessly, 'It appears impossible to account for this diversity of colour, on the common principles assigned for it; for here are three different colours in one and the same climate, and the two (the white and black) totally unmixed.'[4]

The whole area impressed Quirós as a 'terrestrial paradise', but the more pragmatic Dutch gathered different conclusions. In 1616 at 'Cocoa Island' Schouten was beset 'by a vast number of canoes, filled with a mad sort of people, armed with great clubs'. At Papua he was even less taken with the inhabitants, 'whose ridiculous fancies, in their manner of dress, superadded to their own natural deformity, made them appear little short of monsters in human nature'.[5] Tasman likewise was left with some dark impressions of the Pacific, notably of his most important discovery of New Zealand where several of his men were killed in 1642 at a spot he named the Bay of Murderers (Golden Bay today). The incident, he wrote in his journal, 'is a teacher to us, to hold this land's inhabitants as enemies'. It seemed confirmation of the warning set out in his instructions, that 'the Southlands are peopled with very rough wild people'.[6]

Away in the northwesterly stretches of the great ocean the accounts coming from the Spaniards in the Philippines of the inhabitants of the nearby island groups tended to conform more closely to European images of carefree primitives. The Caroline islanders, for example, though they were 'perfectly savage', and lived without material comforts, were 'very cheerful, and contented with their condition'. Even more attractive were the Ladrone islanders described in Father Gobien's history of the islands published at Paris in 1700, and extensively quoted by de Brosses and Callender. Before Magellan reached the island group, wrote Gobien, 'the natives lived in the most perfect freedom and independence, subjected to no laws, but every man lived as it best pleased himself'. Pursuing a simple, vigorous existence, they were a healthy and long-lived people 'exempt from cares and solicitude for the future'. This state of innocence and simplicity was interrupted by the arrival of the Europeans, and a bitter harangue on the effect of that intrusion was put by Gobien into the mouth of a native chief persuading his countrymen to rebel against Spanish rule: 'These Europeans [says this Indian] would have done better, had they continued quiet at home . . . They seem to have arrived here, only to afflict and torment us.'[7] Notwithstanding all this, de Brosses when he reflected on the explorers' accounts had no doubt that further investigation, contact and finally colonization would be in the interest of both Europe and the Pacific lands. The indigenous inhabitants would lose a certain innocence, but they would gain much, and not only in material terms. 'We must also remember how much they would profit, by adopting our ideas of a regular and well-ordered society; their minds would be opened, and formed, their savage manners softened: In short, those nations would become men, who have just now nothing human but their figure.' For Europe the obvious benefits would be commercial, but there was also a subtler aspect which appealed to the scholarly de Brosses and was taken over into the pages of Callender, for 'Here, if anywhere, we may expect to find a faithful picture of the innocence and simplicity of the first ages.'[8]

The hint of scepticism in this comment perhaps came from the Frenchman's awareness that there was a mystifying diversity of races scattered across the ocean. The Dutch explorer, Roggeveen, as he struggled to explain the widespread dispersion of|Polynesians|through the islands of the south Pacific, concluded in his journal of 1722 that it 'must be placed among those questions which exceed the understanding, and therefore are to be heard, but answered with silence'.[9] Of the inhabitants of the three great island groups of the Pacific – Melanesia, Micronesia and Polynesia – a modern authority has written, 'The Melanesians, as their name suggests, were Negroid in origin, the Polynesians and the Micronesians a hybrid race, descended in the main from at least four originally distinct stocks, Negroid, Mongoloid and the two so-called primitive "white" groups, usually referred to as Caucasoids.'[10] These divisions were not clear-cut; there was a mingling of peoples after successive migrations, and a seeping of cultural influences from one island group to another. Europeans were entering a region where societies were organized in a series of baffling, overlapping layers; and the tools the explorers possessed to probe these tessellated areas of humanity were crude and poorly adapted to the task. Imbued with more in the way of prejudice than knowledge, and linguistically inadequate, the first European expeditions into the Pacific after 1763 were not equipped to present any systematic account of the peoples they encountered. Though more serious in intent than their predecessors they had no methodological basis on which to operate. Simple stereotypes of noble savagery, hazy ideas of Rousseauite philosophy, a nodding acquaintanceship with some of the deist literature of the period, some experience of American Indians or African slaves, had little relevance to the problems of understanding which confronted the explorers. These were the more difficult to solve because of the strained nature of the contact. The Pacific navigators of the period were for the most part moderate and humane commanders, by earlier standards remarkably so. The ruthless exploiters of men and souls were missing: there was no Pizarro to view with equanimity the slaughter of all in his way, no Winthrop to glory in the destruction of heathen villages and their inhabitants. Even so, the Europeans were intruders, emerging by the hundred from their great vessels anchored in some island bay, appearing and disappearing without warning, and often violating sacred customs and ground. Over the encounters between voyagers and islanders hung an inescapable tension, sometimes dissipated by individual contacts and trade which offered benefits to both sides, but on other occasions erupting into violence.

The first discovery expedition to the Pacific in the new era of oceanic exploration which followed the Treaty of Paris was that of Commodore John Byron in 1764. His secret instructions had much on commercial and strategic objectives in both the south and north Pacific, but gave no directives on noting the characteristics of the peoples in the lands he reached. It was a sign of growing European interest in the Pacific that although an authorized account of the voyage had to wait for Hawkesworth's collection in 1773, an unofficial, anonymous narrative published in 1767 was translated into French, Italian, Spanish and German before the end of the decade. Hawkesworth, that 'self-appointed expert in anthropology', as the voyage's modern editor has put it,[11] tampered vigorously with Byron's journal, a disappointing record of the voyage which shows the advance that is to come with Cook, Bougainville, and the new generation of explorers. Byron was in years and outlook of a different age. A quarter-century earlier he had sailed with Anson, he had served in the navy in war and peace, in the Caribbean and off West Africa as well as in home waters. His attitude towards the Pacific islanders was incurious, at times contemptuous. Active, naked and nimble is about as far as his journal takes us in describing them.

Byron's voyage was to be followed by another, in fact by two separate expeditions, for not only was the British Admiralty determined on a new venture to the south Pacific, but in France the bookish interest in the South Seas displayed by Maupertuis and de Brosses had hardened into plans to forestall the English. In August 1766 Captain Samuel Wallis in the *Dolphin* and Lieutenant Philip Carteret in the *Swallow* left England for the South Seas; a few months later the *Boudeuse* and the *Etoile* sailed from France under the command of Louis Antoine de Bougainville, bound first for the Falklands and then the Pacific. The officers of the British expedition were little known outside professional circles. Wallis had been a naval officer since 1748, but had no experience of exploration. Carteret, on the other hand, had sailed with Byron on his recent voyage, and was to prove an enterprising commander. Again, there were no scientists, no civilian observers or artists on the voyage, a sure sign that the Admiralty was more interested in new lands than in new peoples, in tangible returns for British trade than in scholarly investigation. The French expedition was a far more brilliant affair. The nobility was well represented among the officers, the astronomer Véron and the naturalist Commerson were on board, and Bougainville himself was a figure of European renown. Aristocrat, soldier, diplomat, he was truly a man of the Enlightenment, a friend of de Brosses, well-read in Montesquieu, Voltaire, Rousseau and Buffon. The tracks of the two expeditions crossed at several points, although there was no direct contact until February 1769 when one of Bougainville's officers boarded Carteret's vessel in the south Atlantic for a brief visit. Wallis and the *Dolphin* arrived back in England in May 1768 after a voyage as unenterprising as Byron's; Bougainville was home by March 1769; and Carteret, after a heroic voyage in the ill-found *Swallow*, was back last of all in May 1769. The authorized account of the discoveries of the two English vessels appeared in Hawkesworth's *Voyages*, but so outraged was Carteret by its alterations that he wrote his own narrative for publication, while on the *Dolphin* the master, George Robertson, kept a good journal. Neither was to be published until the present century, when they have given us two seamen's reactions to the Pacific islands, unhindered by the swaddling-clothes of Hawkesworth's 'sentiments and observations'. In publication, if not in exploration, the French forestalled the English; for brief accounts of uncertain accuracy but lively public appeal were printed before the end of 1769, and in 1771 appeared Bougainville's own account, which was translated into English in 1772. Placed together, the British and French accounts form the background to Cook's first circumnavigation, for the great explorer was in the Pacific while the narratives of his predecessors' voyages were going through the press.

Before reaching the Pacific both expeditions had to overcome the dangers of the Strait of Magellan, where their sight of the dismal situation of the Fuegans gave them food for thought on the lot of man in a state of nature. The form that 'nature' took could obviously be a decisive factor, and the harsh environment of the Strait region, where man struggled to keep alive, was made a standard test for the advocates of primitivism. It was during the passage through the Strait that Wallis became separated from Carteret. He showed little initiative in his track across the Pacific, but it was marked by a chance discovery whose intellectual and emotional impact was out of all proportion to its geographical significance, for in June 1767 the *Dolphin*'s crew sighted late one afternoon the high peak of Tahiti. First reactions to the discovery were of a different order from those which were to swell in the published accounts; as Robertson entered in his journal, 'We now suposd we saw the long wishd for Southern Continent, which has been often talkd of, but neaver before seen by any Europeans'. That shimmering vision may have lent enchantment to the prospect, but no preconceptions can explain the exuberant description given by Robertson the next day as the vessel drew nearer. 'The most beautiful appearance its posable to imagin . . . a fine leavel country that appears to be all laid out in plantations . . . great numbers of cocoa nut trees . . . beautiful valeys between the mountains . . . tall trees . . . the most populoss country I ever saw, the whole shore side was lined with men women and children all the way that we saild along.'[12]

The very number of the islanders led to uneasy discussion on board as to whether a landing to obtain much-needed refreshment and rest should be risked. Nightmare prospects of being attacked by hundreds of canoes, and wiped out to the last man, loomed large, but the decision to anchor was taken. Almost inevitably, it seemed, thieving began, stones were thrown, muskets and then cannon fired, and Tahitians killed. Robertson wrote of the reaction of the islanders to the carnage in words which showed him more sensitive than most: 'How terrible must they be shockd, to see their nearest and dearest of friends dead, and toar to peces in such a manner as I am certain they neaver beheald before – to attempt to say what this poor ignorant creatures thought of us, would be taking more upon me than I am able to perform.' After further encounters, relations between the crew and the islanders quietened, and trade began. Provisions were plentiful, and so it seemed were accommodating women. In laconic fashion Robertson described the events of 27 June, the first of those meetings between European sailors and Polynesian women which were to stamp an erotic imprint on Europe's image of the South Seas. To the breaking surf, the palm-fringed beaches, the dramatic volcanic peaks, were added sensuous overtones – of women and girls, nubile, garlanded and welcoming. The boat crew went ashore, Robertson wrote, for water and provisions, but were soon distracted by the offer of beautiful, soft-skinned girls by the older men on the beach who lined them up in rows for the seamen to take their choice: 'this piece of news made all our men madly fond of the shore, even the sicke who hade been on the Doctors list for some weeks before, now declard they would be happy if they were permited to go ashore'.[13]

On less personal matters Robertson, unsophisticated seaman though he no doubt regarded himself, showed some inquisitiveness about those general problems which were soon to perplex scientists and philosophers. He speculated about the origin of the islanders, guessing that they had come from Asia, but ran into the same difficulty which had worried earlier voyagers: 'there is three distink colours of people here, which is a thing most difficult to account for of anything we have yet seen'. Equally interesting to men of an age when Rousseau's writings on primitivism seem to have reached even the unlettered was the realization that concepts of property existed on the island. Nails had to be offered before a tree could be cut down, and offered to the rightful owner if an unseemly squabble was to be avoided. After one such dispute the matter was resolved in a way which, wrote Robertson, 'in my oppinion plainly demonstrats, that their is both justice, and property in this happy island'.[14] The search by the British for a ruler produced not a king but a 'queen', Purea (the 'Oberea' of Cook and Banks), 'a tall woman, who seemed to be about five and forty years of age, of a pleasing countenance and majestic deportment', Wallis wrote in the pages of Hawkesworth. She was helpful, too helpful for the good of Wallis's reputation, for he was not allowed to forget quickly the passage in which he described how, because of his illness, 'whenever we came to a plash of water, or dirt, she lifted me over with as little trouble as it would cost me to have lifted over a child if I had been well'.[15] Before Europe could hear of Purea in the Hawkesworth volumes she had been overthrown in an inter-island quarrel, for the harmony which Wallis and Robertson praised was more fragile than they realized.

Ten months later, in April 1768, Bougainville's ships reached Tahiti, and the French reaction to the island was theatrical in its intensity and extravagance. Commerson sent back to France a fulsome account of the island which was printed in November 1768, though it had been anticipated by another bizarre description issued as a newsletter in July.[16] In his fuller narrative, published in 1771, Bougainville described the first sighting of Tahiti, the distant beauty of its mountains and cascades, and the lush fertility of the island which was revealed as the ships drew nearer. The more Bougainville saw of Tahiti during his short stay the more he was enchanted by its beauty and by the innocent happiness of its people. A walk into the interior seemed to take him into a veritable garden of Eden. Wherever he went Bougainville found 'hospitality, ease, innocent joy, and every appearance of happiness' among a people who were healthy, lived long, and refused alcohol and tobacco. Disillusionment came slowly, and only after the French sailed for home. With them went a Tahitian, Ahu-toru, and conversation with him on the voyage and in Paris, though difficult at the best of times, led Bougainville to introduce some drastic revisions into the second edition of his book. He withdrew his claims of equality and freedom among the Tahitians: 'I was mistaken; the distinction of ranks is very great at Taiti and the disproportion very tyrannical. The kings and grandees have power of life and death over their servants and slaves, and I am inclined to believe, they have the same barbarous prerogatives with regard to the common people.'[17]

These second thoughts came too late to have any immediate dampening effect on the effusive reaction of the French literary world to the descriptions of Tahiti provided in the original accounts. Ahu-toru, bored, unable to cope with the strange consonants of the French tongue, was displayed in the fashionable *salons* and presented to Louis

XV. He became a convenient tool for the satirists who made him comment in their writings with predictable disdain on the lack of dignity, sincerity and constancy of his French hosts. A more substantial contribution to the pamphlets, letters and verses which swirled about Paris in the wake of Bougainville's expedition was Diderot's celebrated *Supplément au Voyage de Bougainville*. It is best remembered for its advocacy of free love, Tahitian-style, but its weightiest theme was its rejection of European political and religious institutions – 'examine them deeply; and unless I am much mistaken, you will see the human race bent, age after age, under the yoke which a handful of scoundrels have planned to impose on it'.[18] Although the *Supplément* was not published until 1796, much of Diderot's thinking, and particularly his expressions of anti-colonialism, were set out in Raynal's *Histoire des Deux Indes*, first published in English translation in 1777. Large sections of the *Histoire* were written by Diderot, who, when his work as editor and contributor to the *Encyclopédie* in the 1750s and 1760s is also taken into account, made a massive contribution to the intellectual life of mid-century Europe. Like many of the *philosophes*, Diderot had little doubt of the superiority of the savage state over the civilized. The savage suffered only the ills of nature, the civilized man the miseries of an unjust social order and of degrading and brutalizing work. In his later writings there is an attempt to establish some sort of halfway stage between the savage and civilized states, where the freedom of the one could be joined to the practical advantages of the other – a middle way, as he put it, 'entre l'état sauvage et notre merveilleux état policé . . . entre l'enfance du sauvage et notre décrépitude'.[19]

Altogether the discussion in France at this time was a heavier, more sombre affair than in England, where the main debating point of the first Pacific voyages of George III's reign was a squabble about the Patagonian 'giants' – a subject which, if we must take it seriously, was more biological than political, and more American than Pacific.[20] Cook was back from his first circumnavigation in 1771 and so, more noisily, was Joseph Banks. But if the first voyage was to be associated by the public with the irrepressible naturalist rather than with the dour naval officer, the second voyage and, still more, the fateful third were to be Cook's both in name and reality. His three voyages, following each other in quick succession, revealed the Pacific to Europe in a way no previous explorations had done. As the books, maps and views came off the presses – not only in England, but in France, Holland, Germany and Italy as well – Cook became a figure of European fame. Other explorers were in the Pacific during the years that Cook's ships were out, but attention was focused on the methodical, comprehensive explorations of the remarkable Englishman. The public saw the first voyage mainly through the eyes of Hawkesworth, who joined the accounts of Cook and Banks to make the *Endeavour* expedition the climax to his *Voyages* of 1773; the second voyage through Cook's own journal, published in 1777 with a minimum of amendment, and accompanied by engravings based, sometimes rather loosely, on Hodges' magnificent pai tings; and the third voyage through a combination of the journals of Cook, King and Anderson, edited by Douglas, and published in 1784 with illustrations by Webber.

Scientific investigation loomed larger now than in the earlier voyages: the role of the Royal Society, the observation of the transit of Venus from Tahiti in 1769, the activity of Banks and his little retinue of scientists and artists, all pointed to this. Cook's instructions of 1768 – more detailed than those of Byron or Wallis – to report on all aspects of new lands discovered, and to bring back specimens, drawings and surveys, were in the tradition of the 'Directions for Seamen, bound for far voyages', issued by the Royal Society a hundred years earlier. It was the Society's intention, so the preface ran, 'to study nature rather than books, and from the observations, made of the phenomena and effects she presents, to compose such a history of her, as may hereafter serve to build a solid and useful philosophy upon.'[21] Shortly before the *Endeavour* sailed, the President of the Royal Society, Lord Morton, drew up a collection of 'Hints' for Cook and Banks which began by appealing for 'the utmost patience and forbearance with respect to the natives of the several lands where the ship may touch', and went on to advise them 'to observe the genius, temper, disposition and number of the natives.'[22] Even Dr Johnson, no friend of savages or of their admirers, had called for voyagers with a scientific turn of mind – 'not intent, like merchants, only on the acts of commerce, the value of commodities, and the probabilities of gain, nor engaged, like military officers, in the care of subsisting armies, securing passes, obviating stratagems, and defeating opposition, but vacant to every object of curiosity, and at leisure for the most minute remarks'.[23] Banks, for his part, established the precedent (at his own expense) that artists and scientists should accompany the discovery expeditions, and his influence on Cook was considerable. With him Banks took a library, much scientific equipment, and four assistants – the Swedish naturalist Solander, secretary and learned factotum Spöring, and the artists Buchan and Parkinson. The atmosphere of intellectual enquiry which Banks brought to the *Endeavour* is illuminated by a journal entry as the vessel was heading south from Tahiti to New Zealand.

> Now do I wish that our freinds in England could by the assistance of some magical spying glass take a peep at our situation: Dr Solander setts at the cabbin table describing, myself at the bureau journalizing,

between us hangs a large bunch of sea weed, upon the table lays the wood and barnacles; they would see that notwithstanding our different occupations our lips move very often, and without being conjurors might guess that we were talking about what we should see upon the land which there is now no doubt we shall see very soon.[24]

In addition to Cook's own accounts there were the other narratives – Banks and Sydney Parkinson on the first voyage, the Forsters on the second, and a whole flurry of unauthorized books on the third. Despite their deficiencies they combined to give a fuller picture of the Pacific within a dozen years than had emerged during the previous two centuries and more of sporadic, often secretive exploration. Understandably, Cook felt more at ease in describing the geography of the Pacific than its peoples. However difficult to follow an intricate coastline might be, it could be traced, surveyed, pinned down on a chart – and there it would remain, unvarying in outline over the years, only changing imperceptibly with the centuries. To the practised navigator a stretch of coast was the same whether it lay within the coral reefs of a Pacific island or was lapped by the fog-shrouded waters of Newfoundland; as Cook's own career showed it remained susceptible to the same precise methods of survey and representation. Investigation of the human population of these areas had no such firm basis; not only was there among the different peoples of the Pacific no fundamental similarity of culture and language, there was no known method of categorization and classification. Neither Cook nor his companions had any training in anthropological investigation because there was none to be had. It was their voyages which helped in the long run to give birth to anthropology and ethnology, for the earnest enquiry by the explorers into the exotic life styles which confronted them, and their careful if often uninformed collection of detail, brought a new urgency to the need for a more systematic approach to the study of man. As the younger Forster noted, 'What Cook has added to the mass of our knowledge is such that it will strike deep roots and will long have the most decisive influence on the activity of men.'[25]

Cook's first voyage took him to Tahiti, New Zealand and the east coast of Australia. His journal owed much to Banks, but as the voyage progressed it became a more independent, reflective account and by the end Cook was to equal if not outdo Banks in his observations of primitive peoples. But first there was Tahiti, and inevitably we compare Cook and Banks with Bougainville and Commerson, sometimes forgetting that the Englishmen at this time knew nothing of the French visit, and so their journals were in no way a riposte to the French effusions on Tahiti. The resemblances are there, of course. Just as Bougainville wrote about Hercules and Mars, Venus and the Phrygian shepherd, so Banks launched into a disquisition on Homer and Arcadia, and named Tahitian chiefs after Greek heroes. In general the English approach was more level-headed, and the length of Cook's stay of four months taught him much about Tahiti that Bougainville in his nine days had missed. As they explored the interior Cook's men came across skeletons left from the warfare which had swept the island since the French visit, and Banks wrote uneasily of the jawbones hanging up in the dwellings that 'they had been carried away as trophies and are usd by the Indians here in exactly the same manner as the North Americans do scalps'.[26] The Englishmen found a darker side to the free love of the *ario'i* on which Commerson had discoursed so lyrically, and were shocked to find that 'the children who are so unfortunate as to be thus begot are smother'd at the moment of their birth'.[27] There was little in the English journals on the carefree equality which the French thought that they had found; instead there were references to 'the better sort' and 'the inferior sort', even (inaccurately) to slaves. Excited by this, Hawkesworth finally toppled over into absurdity. He concocted parallels between Tahiti and feudal Europe which had him searching the journals for the equivalents of king, baron, vassal and villein in Tahiti, and did nothing to advance understanding.

It is true that Cook, like Byron and Wallis before him, looked for familiar political forms – for kings, queens, priests, chiefs – but the political and religious patterns of Polynesia refused to conform to European shapes, and it is a mark of Cook's discernment that, unpractised though he was in such matters, he came to realize and accept this. Banks too was readier than his French counterpart to recognize the limitations which ignorance of language and custom brought. He made attempts to learn Tahitian, but finally gave up his efforts to discuss religion since 'the language in which it is conveyed, at least many words of it, are different from those usd in common conversation'.[28] Cook was to return to Tahiti and its perplexing ways on his second and third voyages, Banks not, and his long journal entry on the beauty of the island, its mild climate and languorous inhabitants, was in the nature of a regretful farewell. Parkinson, who relied on drawings rather than words to express his sentiments, also enthused about the virtues of the primitive life, where 'Ambition, and the love of luxurious banquets, and other superfluities, are but little known'. The islanders lived close to nature; robust, healthy and carefree, they showed how Europeans were before the excesses and demands of civilized life weakened them.[29] The feelings of the majority of the crew can only be guessed. Perhaps they were represented in a newspaper report on the expedition's return: 'We continued here [Tahiti] three months, and became as easy and familiar in the time as the natives of the climate; who are a kind, hospitable, active, sensible people. We married with their women, and enjoyed a felicity amongst them peculiar to the salubrity of so sweet a clime. As for my part, I never relinquished a situation with so much grief and dissatisfaction.'[30]

New Zealand and its inhabitants presented Cook and Banks with a series of harsher challenges, not least an initial clash of arms which left several New Zealanders dead, and the two Englishmen sorrowing over the melancholy affair with self-lacerating journal entries. They saw much to admire in the natives of New Zealand: their strength and courage, their moderation in diet and avoidance of intoxicating liquors, their general honesty. But there were other aspects which were incomprehensible. Once more Cook and Banks set off to discover a European-style monarch or chief, and in November 1769 they seemed to have found one. Banks wrote in some triumph at the Bay of Plenty: 'As far as we have yet gone along the coast from Cape Turnagain to this place the people have acknowledged only one chief *Teratu*: if his dominion is really so large he may have princes or governors under him capable of drawing together a vast many people.'[31] In reality, the eagerness to find a king had entangled Cook and Banks in a maze of misunderstanding: they seem, J. C. Beaglehole drily pointed out, to have 'confused a personal name and a direction' – Te Ratu, a minor chief, and *te ra to*, the westward.[32] Nor were they more successful in determining the religious beliefs of the New Zealanders, and this area of investigation was even more difficult to probe than in Tahiti since there seemed to be no ceremonies or places of worship as in the Society Islands.

But dominating all investigation of the New Zealanders was the question of cannibalism. Although the warlike disposition of the Maoris, their bravery, the fearsome *haka*, were accepted by Cook and Banks, they needed much convincing, and the production of some gruesome evidence, before they could bring themselves to accept the probability of cannibalism. As he struggled to reconcile the discovery of cannibalism with his conventional eighteenth-century ideas on the Chain of Being, Banks could come to terms with the shock only by insisting that it must be of a ritualistic nature. Since nature provided no example of 'any species preying upon itself', there was no possibility that the New Zealanders ate human flesh 'as a dainty or even look upon it as part of common food'. As Banks brooded over the natural order of things, listing the animal world in ascending order from oyster to 'the half reasoning elephant' and 'the sagacious dog', he was more than ever convinced that 'the admirable chain of nature in which Man, alone endowed with reason, justly claims the highest rank', made such an aberration impossible.[33]

The Australian Aborigines presented a different test again. The voyagers' predisposition was a critical one, based on Dampier's strictures. This Banks readily admitted as he described how on their first distant sight of the Australians they were taken to be 'enormously black: so far did the prejudices which we had built on Dampiers account influence us that we fancied we could see their colour when we could scarce distinguish whether or not they were men'.[34] Closer acquaintance confirmed much of this unfavourable initial impression – the Aborigines were stunted, naked and filthy – but it is a sign of the relative sophistication of Cook's approach in particular that these people, so unprepossessing in European terms, were not dismissed out of hand. Whatever the eccentricities of many aspects of primitivist writing, it taught some observers to assess indigenous peoples against their own background, not by the standards of contemporary Europe. Apathy could be mistaken for contentment, mere survival for a deliberate eschewing of material goods. Even so, Banks showed more than a little inkling of the harmony between man and his natural environment when he concluded his description of the Aborigines: 'Thus live these I had almost said happy people, content with little nay almost nothing, far enough removd from the anxieties attending upon riches, or even the possession of what we Europeans call common necessaries.'[35] Rather more unexpected is Cook's emphatic agreement with this. One could understand a plain sailor mellowing under the ‌influence of Tahiti, or respecting the hardihood of the Maoris, but there seemed little in the Aborigine to catch the untutored eye. But then Cook was no longer, if he had ever been, simply a plain sailor, and certainly he was no longer untutored. He had come a long way since the first months of the voyage, both in distance and in thought processes, as he wrote:

> From what I have said of the natives of New-Holland they may appear to some to be the most wretched people upon Earth, but in reality they are far more happier than we Europeans; being wholy unacquainted not only with the superfluous but the necessary conveniences so much sought after in Europe, they are happy in not knowing the use of them. They live in a tranquillity which is not disturb'd by the inequality of condition: the earth and sea of their own accord furnishes them with all the things necessary for life, they covet not magnificent houses, household-stuff & cᵃ, they live in a warm and fine climate and enjoy a very wholsome air, so that they have very little need of clothing . . . In short they seem'd to set no value upon any thing we gave them, nor would they ever part with any thing of their own for any one article we could offer them.[36]

There is little of the sentimentality of Bougainville or Commerson here; it is a deliberate analysis of a primitive life-style which proceeds on the basis that the competitive, materialistic culture is to be avoided rather than imitated. In parenthesis, Cook's description of aboriginal life, however superficial, was an indictment of the society from which he came. It was turned into nonsense by Hawkesworth who, ignoring its link with the Australian climate, inexplicably transferred it to the situation of the Fuegans encountered early in the voyage.

In the lack of a full account of the expedition before 1773, public reaction to Cook's achievement was muted. Banks gained most attention, and when the Hawkesworth volumes and Parkinson's journal were published it was Banks and his amorous exploits in Tahiti which held the stage. A scattering of mediocre verses commented on the business,[37] and Hawkesworth came in for criticism on several counts: his editorial meddling with the voyagers' journals, his lack of conventional religious expression, and his pretentiousness. Horace Walpole grumbled at the dullness of the navigational material in the accounts, and added, 'Doctor Hawkesworth is still more provoking – an old black gentlewoman of forty carried Capt. Wallis cross a river, when he was too weak to walk, and the man represents them as a new edition of Dido and Aeneas.'[38] There was no literary equivalent in England of Diderot's *Supplément*, but the year of Hawkesworth and Parkinson saw the beginning of publication of a work which had much bearing on the new discoveries in the Pacific. Lord Monboddo's *Origins and Progress of Language*, whose first volume was published in 1773, was noted for its provoking identification of man and the orang-outang, but this made up only a minor if long-winded part of the theories of the Scottish judge and peer on the origins and development of man. Monboddo showed how far much current thought was moving from the primitivist thinkers of the Enlightenment who postulated a state of nature, uniform in all parts of the world, in which the eternal truths of the universe were evident to men before they became sophisticated and corrupt. Monboddo agreed on the need to study primitive peoples – 'Whoever, therefore, would trace human nature up to its source, must study very diligently the manners of barbarous nations, instead of forming theories of man from what he observes among civilized nations' – but he saw man's departure from his earliest state as being a progression, not a decline or degeneration. The capacity for rational thought was not inbred and natural; it was developed by application and hard work like any art or science. To make the point plain, Monboddo continued: 'There cannot be virtue, properly so called, until man is become a rational and political animal; then he shows true courage, very different from the ferocity of the brute or savage . . . with all the other virtues which so much exalt human nature, but which we can as little expect to find in the mere savage as in the brute, or infant of our species.'[39]

Lord Kames was typical of the Scottish writers of the period in his acceptance of the 'four stages' theory of socio-economic development which (as we have explained earlier) relied on the mode of subsistence as the crucial identifying element of human societies. His *Sketches of the History of Man*, published in 1774, took into account the volumes of Bougainville and Hawkesworth. Again, there is the insistence on development and progress. 'The moral sense is born with us; and so is taste; yet both of them require much cultivation. Among savages, the moral sense is faint and obscure; and taste still more so.' Tahiti provided an example of society based on hunting and fishing, with weak concepts of property, and therefore little internal strife. The balmy climate praised by the explorers hindered rather than stimulated man's progress, and Kames' exposition of the effects of climate on society was a running commentary on the passage in Banks where he noted that one hour's digging and planting by a Tahitian would produce enough breadfruit for his own lifetime and for that of his descendants.

> The many difficulties that men encounter, and their objects of pursuit, rouse the understanding, and set the reasoning faculty at work for means to accomplish desire . . . The wants of those who inhabit the torrid zone are easily supplied: they need no cloathing, scarce any habitation; and fruits, which ripen there to perfection, give them food without labouring for it. Need we any other cause for their inferiority of understanding, compared with the inhabitants of other climates, where the mind, as well as the body, are constantly at work for procuring necessaries?[40]

The linking of climate and human development, much invoked in debates about Asia, was now standard practice; as Antonelli Gerbi has written, the hygrometer and thermometer almost became a standard part of a scholar's equipment.[41] Adam Ferguson was among those who had concluded that extremes of hot and cold were equally unfavourable to progress, and that one looked for the most advanced societies in environments which introduced 'some intermediate degree of inconvenience'. He was writing just before the surge of Pacific exploration which provided Kames, Forster and Herder with much evidence on this matter, but anticipated their conclusions when he asserted that 'the shade of the barren oak and the pine are more favourable to the genius of mankind, than that of the palm or the tamarind'.[42] The same insistence on the importance of the environment came from James Steuart, writing in 1770: 'If the soil be vastly rich, situated in a warm climate, and naturally watered, the productions of the earth will be almost spontaneous: this will make the inhabitants lazy . . . It is in climates less favoured by nature, and where the soil produces to those only who labour, and in proportion to the industry of every one, where we may expect to find great multitudes.'[43] Much of this heavy environmental emphasis was to be used against the African Negro. John Millar, in the first edition in 1771 of his *Observations concerning the Distinction of Ranks in Society*, moved on to reflect on the connection between economic progress and political liberty. He accepted that because primitive peoples such as the American Indians produced little wealth, they experienced none of the ills of authoritarian government; but this was a negative feature, simply a lack of development in all directions. More positive and exciting, Millar argued, were recent economic and political advances. 'In those European nations which have made the greatest improvements in commerce and manufactures, the highest liberty is usually enjoyed . . . The laws and customs of the modern European nations have carried the advantages of liberty to a height which was never known in any other age or country.'[44]

Cook was to read (and be irritated by) Hawkesworth, and was to hear of Monboddo and his theories, but not for two years after the publication of their volumes, for in July 1772 he had left on his second Pacific expedition, arguably the greatest, most perfect, of all seaborne voyages of exploration. In his three years away he disposed of the theory of a great southern continent, reached closer to the South Pole than any other man, and touched on a multitude of lands – New Zealand and Tahiti again, and for the first time Easter Island, the Marquesas, the New Hebrides and New Caledonia. With him sailed the painter William Hodges, whose luminous, sun-drenched Pacific landscapes evoked the South Seas as no artist had done before; William Wales as astronomer and meteorologist, who in addition to his professional duties kept an acerbic journal; and, after Banks' intemperate withdrawal from the expedition, that awkward, prickly but learned man, Johann Reinhold Forster, and his son George. The written records from the voyage are overwhelming in their richness and profusion. First, there was Cook's own journal, this time polished by Cook himself before publication, and then issued in 1777 as his *Voyage towards the South Pole*, a mighty affair of more than 700 pages. Several of the officers kept good journals, Clerke and Pickersgill in particular. And then there were the Forsters. Johann Reinhold kept a detailed daily journal which has only recently been unearthed;[45] against the immediacy of that record we have his more reflective, sometimes portentous *Observations made during a Voyage round the World*, published in 1778; and the lively account by George, *A Voyage round the World*, published in two volumes in March 1777, six weeks before the appearance of Cook's narrative.

Cook on the second voyage was a more experienced and mature observer than on the first. Because of this and because of differences of temperament, he owed less to the Forsters than he had done to Banks. His journal reflects a determination to reconsider some of the problems he had noted on his first voyage, to look for example at Polynesian societies in the light of Bougainville's narrative. J. R. Forster, whose son had been responsible for the English translation of Bougainville's book, was intent on providing a careful account of the scientific implications of the voyage. With his knowledge of philology, botany, geology, geography and history, not to speak of a love of the classics which studded the pages of his journal with quotations from Virgil and Horace, he was for all his quirky ways a valuable man to have on the voyage. Almost 400 pages of his *Observations* of 1778 were devoted to 'Remarks on the Human Species in the South-Sea Isles', and he began with a resounding, capitalized quotation from Pope: 'The proper study of mankind is MAN.' Ten years later he explained that he had wanted 'to investigate closely the habits, rites, ceremonies, religious beliefs, way of life, clothing, agriculture, commerce, arts, weapons, words of warfare, political organisation, and the language of the people we met'.[46] He took with him a large collection of books of science and travel, a reputed knowledge of seventeen languages, and a determination to settle some of the questions about the Pacific which were perplexing the scholars of Europe. Rarely had philosophers been willing to emerge from their closets, and provide in person, under the most arduous circumstances, the information necessary for the pursuit of their studies. Herder may have been overdoing it when he termed the ungainly, accident-prone Johann Reinhold 'the Ulysses' of the Pacific, but there was much substance in his accompanying statement that Forster 'has given us such a learned and intelligent account of the species and varieties of the human race in them, that we cannot but wish we had similar materials for a *philosophico-physical geography* of other parts of the world, as foundations for a history of man'.[47]

Tahiti was bound to be the focal point of interest and investigation: the writings of Commerson and Bougainville, and the forthcoming Hawkesworth volumes, had made it so. To the newcomers the island still had a breathtaking impact, though William Wales derided Bougainville's description of it which he thought 'suits much better with Mahomet's Paradise', and after agreeing that it was 'a very beautiful island', pointed out that it 'appears, no doubt, to great advantage after a long voyage. I remember well that England does so . . .'[48]. Others were more impressionable. George Forster wrote of his first sighting, on 15 August 1773, how 'In the evening, about sun-set, we plainly saw the mountains of that desirable island, lying before us, half emerging from the gilded clouds on the horizon.'[49] Once ashore, the old hands found that there had been changes. Parts of the island had been further ravaged by war since Cook's first visit, and some familiar faces were missing. There was a new chief – or could he, Cook enquired, be called a king? If so, then Tu seemed to embody much that was desirable in a man of authority: he was affable, approachable, had even been seen working his own canoe. Cook's concern with chiefs and monarchs was often to mislead him in an area where political and religious systems were intertwined in a way which defied easy comprehension, but in most matters he remained a percipient observer. Bougainville's book in hand, he sternly corrected the Frenchman's errors about Tahiti. It was wrong, he pointed out, to maintain that property was held in common; cultivation was bound to result in private possession, and the crews had long since found that every productive tree on the island belonged to an individual owner.[50] On his next voyage Cook was to come across an even sharper sense of proprietorship when he tried to cut grass at Nootka Cove and found to his cost that 'there was not a blade of grass that had not a separated owner'.[51]

The elder Forster meanwhile was contemplating matters in more global terms. Agreeing with Cook's point about the moderate nature of Tahitian government, he speculated that the islanders had come from Asia, and that as they journeyed southward they gradually lost the 'formality and humiliating respect' they had given chiefs in their old homeland. Tahiti was the spot where the Pacific peoples had 'arrived at that happy mean which assigns the just bounds of prerogative to each rank of people, and thus places the true principles of happiness on a firm and solid basis'.[52] By and large, he was convinced that the obvious benefits of superior civilization would outweigh any harm that might be done in the islands by the presence of Europeans. George Forster was less sanguine. He wrote at length about the 'good and simple' Tahitians living in 'one of the happiest spots on the globe', where one could find only a single villain for every fifty in Europe, though his radical instincts noted the person of Tu with marked disapproval – 'a luxurious individual spending his life in the most sluggish inactivity, and without one benefit to society, like the privileged parasites of more civilized climates, fattening on the superfluous produce of the soil, of which he robbed the labouring multitude'. But generally the latter were better off than their European counterparts, and like other visitors George Forster contrasted the idyllic scenes he saw with the noisome realities of life for the poor at home. A little labour, he pointed out, provided the necessities of life for a Tahitian, and the difference in living standards between the highest and lowest in Tahiti was less than that between a tradesman and a labourer in England. What to Ferguson and Kames was a sluggish tropical backwater, where mankind stagnated without hope of improvement and progress, provided in Forster's eyes a setting for contented, unambitious living which knew neither the 'absolute want' nor the 'unbounded voluptuousness' of European society. This state of affairs he thought doomed. The indolent chief on the one hand, the European intruders with their goods and alien ways on the other, were only the first signs of the disintegration to come. Like Diderot a few years earlier, the younger Forster stood appalled and helpless at the prospect he could see opening before the Pacific islanders, and concluded that 'if the knowledge of a few individuals can only be acquired at such a price as the happiness of nations, it were better for the discoverers, and the discovered, that the South Sea had remained unknown to Europe and its restless inhabitants'.[53]

From Tahiti, Cook reached the Tongan islands to the southwest, discovered by Tasman in 1643 and occasionally touched at since, but neither explored nor charted. If anything, the two islands visited, Tongatapu and Eua, and their inhabitants, were thought to be even lovelier than Tahiti. Eua, wrote Gilbert, was 'one intire garden laid out with great design'. Even Wales was charmed – it was 'the most beautiful & variegated prospect I ever beheld'.[54] As the ships prepared to leave the islands, the elder Forster launched into a lengthy disquisition on the state of the Tongan and Society islands. Though their inhabitants did not approach the 'high refined civilization' of Europe, he thought that they had 'a rank among the civilized nations', and set out his reasons for this assertion. First, they had religions which were neither idolatrous nor animistic, and distinguishable political structures with various regulations and laws. In behaviour they were charitable and hospitable, and though they had no knowledge of letters or formal science they were expert navigators and shipbuilders, they cultivated the land, they loved music and dancing. Unlike the Aborigines, they were clothed, and in a manner 'varied to the seasons & the time of the day, & the ranks of people, which is still a greater proof of their civilization'.[55] Others also drew a connection between nakedness and savagery, and this was indicated in an entry by Charles Clerke after he spotted an albino native in New Caledonia: |'It had a most singular and striking appearance to see a white fellow naked running about among these dark colour'd gentry, it really appear'd to me highly unnatural and disgusting'.[56]

New Zealand was used as Cook's base between his sweeps towards the Antarctic in one direction and Polynesia in the other. This time the menace of violence, never far removed, flared into ugly life with the massacre of an entire boat-crew from Cook's consort vessel. James Burney, who found the remains, was sickened by it all, and in his private journal wrote of the Maoris, 'they are at present in a state very

279

little, if any thing, superior to the brute part of the creation'.[57] Cook
heard definite news of the affair only when he reached the Cape on the
homeward voyage, and his comment was surprisingly calm: 'I must
however observe in favour of the New Zealanders that I allways found
them of a brave, noble, open and benevolent disposition, but they are a
people who will never put up with an insult.' He reserved his most
outraged remarks for a different business altogether, the New Zealanders' prostitution of their women to the ships' crews:

> such are the concequence of a commerce with Europeans and what is
> still more to our shame civilized Christians, we debauch their morals
> already too prone to vice and we interduce among them wants and
> perhaps diseases which they never before knew and which serves only
> to disturb that happy tranquillity they and their fore fathers had
> injoy'd. If any one denies the truth of this assertion let him tell me what
> the natives of the whole extent of America have gained by the com-
> merce they have had with the Europeans.[58]

George Forster echoed Cook's remarks when he wrote that not only had
the discovery voyages meant a loss of innocent lives, but also a corrupt-
ing effect on the morals of 'little uncivilized communities'. The cannibalism of the New Zealanders he tried to put into perspective in a way
reminiscent of Montaigne: 'But though we are too much polished to be
cannibals, we do not find it unnaturally and savagely cruel to take the
field, and to cut one another's throats by thousands, without a single
motive, besides the ambition of a prince, or the caprice of his mistress!
Is it not from prejudice that we are disgusted with the idea of eating a
dead man, when we feel no remorse in depriving him of life?'[59]

Though both Forsters showed much sympathy with and understanding of the Pacific peoples they encountered, neither was a blind advocate
of primitivism. One of the most revealing entries in the elder Forster's
journal came in April 1773 when he contemplated the bustling scene at
Dusky Bay, and wrote of buildings and improvements completed by
the crew in a few days which 500 New Zealanders could not have
accomplished in three months. This was proof to him of 'the superiority
& advantages, which the use of sciences, arts & mechanical improved
trades, & the use of convenient tools give to civilized nations over those
that live in a more pure state of nature'.[60] George in turn could easily
lose patience with the more sentimental aspects of the primitivist school
of thinking. An encounter with the wretched, shivering inhabitants of
Tierra del Fuego provoked him into saying that 'Till it can be proved,
that a man in continual pain, from the rigour of climate, is happy, I
shall not give credit to the eloquence of philosophers, who have either
had no opportunity of contemplating human nature under all its
modifications, or who have not felt what they have seen.'[61]

In his *Observations* of 1778 Johann Reinhold made a comprehensive effort, based on first-hand experience as well as wide reading, to come to terms with the great variety of peoples he had encountered on the voyage. Even at his most verbose and ponderous there is a certain astringency about Forster, a determination to test matters scientifically and empirically. He was aware of the difficulties, particularly of language, and often noted in his journal that ignorance of a people's language prevented him from gaining a proper knowledge of their beliefs and customs. If this held good for Forster, with his linguistic capabilities, it was still more of a handicap for the others. Wales wrote of the stay at Tahiti that so limited was their acquaintance with the language that there were misunderstandings even in simple barter transactions. Cook was also aware of the problem, and it seems to have weighed on him, for Boswell reported a dinner conversation with the explorer after the return in which 'he candidly confessed to me that he and his companions who visited the south sea islands could not be certain of any information they got, or supposed they got, except as objects falling under the observation of the senses; their knowledge of the language was so imperfect they required the aid of their senses, and anything which they learnt about religion, government, or traditions might be quite erroneous.'[62]

Despite all uncertainties, Forster remained committed to a monogenetic interpretation of the peopling of the world, explaining the 'remarkable differences' between races by environmental factors – exposure to heat or cold, type of diet and activity. In a different way, the paintings of Hodges were making the same point. Bernard Smith has written of Hodges' marvellous depiction of 'A View taken in the Bay of Oaitepeha, Otaheite', that it asserts 'the existence of the Tahitian paradise not by pointing to classical parallels of dress, physique, and customs with their idealistic associations but by seeking for an explanation and a unifying factor in the salubrity of the climate'.[63] Forster could be less impressionistic, more precise. He related the two extremes of the human condition, civilization and barbarism, to the fact that the first was to be found in the temperate zones, the second in the 'frozen' zones. The Fuegans fitted into the last category, the South Sea islanders on the other hand lived betwixt and between, and so were 'more improved', but still ranked in Forster's estimation only 'one remove above barbarians'.[64] His fellow botanist on the voyage, Anders Sparrman, showed the practical application of Forster's theory when he wrote, 'If I were asked the reason why the New Zealander seems to have developed harsher sentiments than the other South Sea natives, my answer would be the severity of the climate, and probably the gnawing hunger caused by the scarcity of vegetable and animal food;

also the preponderance of small and independent communities or households which entail disputes over fishing grounds, fern-plants, and other vital needs.'[65] Diversity, comparative customs, the climatic environment – these were the new catchphrases, bandied around as much in literary London as in the discussions of the philosopher-travellers. It was at this time that Dr Johnson's friend, Mrs Thrale, wrote to him: '*My* great delight like yours would be to see how life is carried on in other countries, how various climates produce various effects, and how different notions of religion & government operate upon the human manners & the human mind.'[66]

Characterization according to latitude left Forster with a number of problems, not least that of explaining why the Pacific islanders seemed to many to live in a more just and equitable society than the 'highly civilized nations' of the northern temperate zone. He explained, rather defensively, that the defects of European societies sprang from the excesses of 'a few profligate individuals', together with a more general indulgence in 'luxury and vice'. Complicating factors cut across this climatic determinism, notably the maturity of particular societies. They resembled individuals in that a savage people was akin to childhood, a civilized state to responsible adulthood. Other problems arose, for as Forster admitted, there were islands in the Pacific in the same latitude, with the same climate, which were very different in character. Suddenly, almost any consideration one could think of seemed relevant: 'All the ideas, all the improvements of mankind relative to sciences, arts, manufactures, social life, and even morality, ought to be considered as the *sum total of the efforts of mankind ever since its existence*.'[67] This was not so much a despairing opening of the flood-gates as a plea for open-mindedness, for a non-dogmatic approach. It was a long way from the global uniformity preached by some primitivist thinkers; instead it approached the position of Buffon with his insistence on the importance of diet and custom as well as climate, and of Herder who insisted that mankind existed in different forms according to circumstance – 'the law of necessity and congruity, which is composed of potencies of place and time, everywhere brings forth different fruits'.[68]

In the various journals and books on Cook's voyage some consensus of opinion seemed to be emerging. Advanced civilizations were not necessarily equated with happiness, simply with technical development. 'Felicity' might be more apparent in Tahiti than in England or France. As societies had moved forward, so they had become perverted. Chronological progression had somehow been overtaken by chronological deterioration; 'our civilized communities', asserted George Forster, 'are stained with vices and enormities'.[69] The ravages of venereal disease were symbolic of this. Many of Cook's journal entries were tinged with sadness, almost with despair, as he wrote of this, and he was not alone. Soon after the return of the *Resolution* in 1775, one of its officers wrote (anonymously) to a periodical about Tahiti, where 'we have established a disease which will ever prove fatal to these unhappy innocents, who seem to have enjoyed a perfect state of simplicity and nature till we, a more refined race of monsters, contaminated all their bliss by an introduction of our vices'.[70] And there were vices more insidious and threatening than those of the body. Although most writers of the period followed Hume's argument in his essay 'Of Luxury' (printed in the *Political Discourses* of 1752) which stressed the importance of property, industry and consumption in the development of society, some felt a sense of foreboding as they viewed the material progress of European nations. The year 1776 saw the publication of the first volume of Gibbon's *Decline and Fall of the Roman Empire*, a work which was to linger long in the European memory with its eloquent warning of the dangers of decadence. But it did not need Gibbon's imaginative and literary powers to sense the threat. Cook and Banks had expressed it in 1770 as they contemplated the austere lifestyle of the Australian Aborigines – 'far more happier than we Europeans'. Kames put it in more portentous terms in his *Sketches* of 1774 as he argued that 'luxury, the never failing concomitant of wealth is a slow poison that debilitates men and renders them incapable of any great effort . . . In other words, man by constant prosperity and peace degenerates into a mean, impotent and selfish animal. An American savage who treasures up the scalps of his enemy as trophies of his prowess is a being far superior.'[71]

If seamen and philosophers alike realized the dangers of contamination, physical and moral, which the European presence was bringing to the Pacific, their conclusions had little in common with the traditional school of primitivist thinking in England, which greeted the arrival of Omai in 1774 (on Cook's consort vessel) with uncritical acclaim.[72] He became as familiar a figure in London society as Ahutoru had been in Paris a few years earlier. Dressed in the latest fashion, patronised by the famous, Omai stayed in the great country houses, was presented to George III, and as a final accolade had his portrait painted by Joshua Reynolds, who by refining a facial feature here and adding a toga-like drape there produced an elegant and striking young man. Possessed of considerable innate dignity, Omai made a good impression. His dexterity in bowing, manipulating knives and forks and so on was much admired; lapses from the conventions of polite society were greeted with equal rapture as the behaviour of natural man. Unwarlike (at least in London), deferential, light-skinned, Omai was an immensely reassuring primitive. Only the occasional dissident voice pointed out that Omai, and perhaps even his fellow-islanders on Ulaietea, might have profited more from his stay in England if he had been given some useful instruction in practical things.[73] To those who had seen the islands, Tahiti and its neighbours might be nearer an earthly paradise than any other region known to man, but they realized now that there was shade as well as light; there was war, infanticide, distinction of rank and property. As Sparrman wrote, 'That is why, with its wars of conquest and its human sacrifices, the beautiful land of Otaheite presented such a sad spectacle.'[74] In the beauty of Polynesia much was redeemed by the physical setting, balmy climate and fertile soil, but the finely-balanced island societies at the moment of the European intrusion were increasingly recognized as the product of a fortuitous combination of circumstances – of migration, location, climate and isolation. The life-style of the islands might be envied while it remained, but it could not in any realistic way be transported to Europe.

Scepticism about the alleged perfection of the South Sea islands, and concern about the effect on them of the European arrival – the two coincidental if often divergent sentiments of the mid-1770s – were strengthened by the happenings of Cook's third voyage. The main aim of the expedition was a precise geographical object, the Northwest Passage. All else – new and old islands, reports on peoples and products – was subsidiary. But the need to return Omai, and Cook's own inclination to use familiar stopping-places, meant that the approach to the northwest coast of America was to take the ships through the south Pacific once more. And if there were no 'scientific gentlemen' of independent means and uncertain temperament this time, no Banks, no Forster, in compensation there was ample knowledge of the Pacific among Cook's officers. Two of them, Charles Clerke, commanding the consort vessel, *Discovery*, and John Gore, first lieutenant on the *Resolution*, outdid Cook in Pacific experience, for they were on their fourth navigation. James Burney, first lieutenant on the *Discovery*, had sailed on Cook's second voyage, as had William Anderson whose interests far outran his official duties as surgeon on the *Resolution*. He was, one of his shipmates wrote after his death on the voyage, 'by far the most accurate & inquisitive person on board'.[75] Devoted to natural history, philology and much else, he kept a journal second in interest only to Cook's. James King, second lieutenant on the *Resolution*, was on his first Pacific voyage, and his journal has a stimulating freshness about it as he viewed the lands and peoples now becoming familiar to his fellow officers. He was an intelligent and sensitive man who had studied science at Oxford and Paris, was friendly with Edmund Burke and his family, and was said to have 'a true genius for politics'.[76] And there was

John Webber, not in the same class as a landscape painter as Hodges, but a careful artist whose work forms the fullest visual record of all Cook's voyages. His sixty-one engravings which accompanied the official account of the voyage in 1784 helped to give that three-volume edition, made up of the journals of Cook, Anderson and King, some of its great public appeal.

The killing of Cook at Kealakekua Bay in February 1779 overshadowed all else. Sandwich wrote to Banks on hearing the news, 'what is uppermost in our mind allways must come out first, poor captain Cooke is no more'.[77] Cook's death, following as it did the massacre of the *Adventure*'s boat crew in 'a shocking scene of carnage and barbarity' in New Zealand in 1773 during the second voyage, and the gruesome killing of the French navigator Marion du Fresne and two dozen of his men not far away a year earlier, was proof to many of the treacherous and murderous disposition of the Pacific peoples. Marion's second-in-command, Crozet, bitterly criticized the image of the 'affable, humane and hospitable' islander depicted by the philosophers, and insisted rather that 'there is amongst all the animals of creation none more ferocious and dangerous for human beings than the primitive and savage man . . . I have traversed the greater part of the globe, and I have seen everywhere that when reason is not assisted and perfectioned by good laws, or by a good education,\ it becomes the prey of force or of treachery, equally as much so among primitive men as amongst animals, and I conclude that reason without culture is but a brutal instinct.'[78]

Signs of this new feeling were evident as soon as Cook's vessels reached New Zealand in 1777. It was not only Cook and the officers who, remembering the fate of the *Adventure*'s men, were apprehensive – for once, the seamen failed to respond to the offers of the New Zealand women. 'They had taken a kind of dislike to these people', Cook wrote, 'and were either unwilling or afraid to associate with them.'[79] More than ever Cook and his men noted the endemic violence of the New Zealanders, and were especially repelled by the way in which the inhabitants of Queen Charlotte Sound tried to turn the *Adventure* massacre to their own advantage by blaming it on nearby groups who should, they urged, be struck down. As Cook remarked in his journal, 'if I had followed the advice of all our pretended friends, I might have extirpated the whole race'. To many there was a striking difference between Cook's forbearance and the New Zealanders' insistence on *utu* or remorseless revenge, and little now to admire in a Hobbesian state of nature in which 'the New Zealanders must live under perpetual apprehinsions of being distroyed by each other'.[80] If we can believe Crozet, Rousseau himself was staggered by the French navigator's account of the behaviour of the New Zealanders, and responded – 'Is it possible that the good Children of Nature can really be so wicked?'[81] Nor could Cook and his officers find much sign of that quest for knowledge and advancement which they regarded as desirable, and the lack of which made the Fuegans, for example, such pitiful objects in their eyes. The New Zealanders, Cook wrote with disapproval, 'seem to be a people perfectly satisfied with the little knowledge they are masters of without attempting in the least to improve it, nor are they remarkably curious either in their observations or enquir[i]es'. Anderson agreed, and doubted the much-vaunted bravery of the New Zealanders, for he thought that it was in evidence only when there was no fear of retribution. In general, their way of life seemed to Anderson quite intolerable. They were 'clamorous and disorderly' even when not actually fighting, and when intent on war were 'more like infernal daemons than men' as they prepared themselves for the shedding of blood and the eating of flesh.[82]

It was with relief that Cook left New Zealand in February 1777, heading first for Tahiti but then, realizing that he had lost any chance of reaching northwest America that year, turning towards the Tongan islands. In 1773 and 1774 his visits to the group had totalled only eleven days; this time he stayed as many weeks, long enough to be doubly perplexed by the intricacies of a system in which secular and religious authority were at once separated and linked. As always, Cook looked hopefully for the supreme ruler, no simple matter as he came to realize. Having met Finau, introduced to him as 'King of all the Friendly Isles', Cook found after treating him with due deference for some days that he lived in the shadow of a superior, Paulaho. Cook accepted this discovery philosophically, 'As it was my intrest as well as inclination to pay my court to all these great men, without enquiring into the legality of their titles'. The aura of authority which surrounded Paulaho soon convinced Cook that if indeed there was a king of Tonga, then here was he; and the submissiveness which all others, even Finau, showed him, had its attractions for Cook who was, one suspects, tiring of noisy throngs. But of kings and chiefs there were more to come, for having paid his respects first to Finau and then to Paulaho, Cook was told of one even more powerful, Maealiuaki, and it is he who appears in Cook's journal henceforth as 'the king'. There was, in some ways, too much of the king about him for the sensibilities of some of Cook's officers, and Clerke grumbled that with his request to the ships' officers to strip to the waist as a sign of submissiveness, and his reluctance to enter Cook's cabin because the men on deck would be higher than he was, Maealiuaki was demanding more respect than the king of England.[83]

Cook was prepared to leave off his shirt if the occasion demanded, despite the disapproval of at least one of his officers, who wrote, 'I cannot help thinking he rather let himself down'.[84] One of the most remarkable passages in Cook's journal described how he stripped to the waist and wore his hair down, thus conforming to local customs, so that he could watch the *inasi* ceremony on Tongatapu. Of this he gave a long, detailed description, finishing with an admission that he could not discover the meaning either of the occasion or of the various rituals observed. His queries simply drew the reply *tabu* which, as Cook noted, 'is applied to many other things'.[85] Among the information which he did seem to gather was that in three months' time another ceremony would be held, this time with the sacrifice of ten human victims, a reminder that the state of bliss which some earlier accounts had assumed to be normal in the islands proved on closer acquaintance to have its flaws. The report of human sacrifice was treated with some reserve, for by now the more perceptive of the observers on Cook's ships were aware of the problems involved in investigating the island societies, and the dangers of hasty judgments. Anderson had referred to these problems a little earlier when he remarked of the clamorous reception at Atiu in the Cook Islands that 'We regretted much that their behaviour prevented us making any observations on the country, for we were seldom a hundred yards from the place where we were introduc'd to the chiefs on landing and consequently were confind only to the objects that surrounded us. It was an oppurtunity I had long wish'd for, to see a people following the dictates of nature without being bias'd by education or corrupted at leisure, but was here disappointed.'[86] Even on Tonga, where Omai served as interpreter, and Cook penetrated the outer layers of custom and ceremony, the difficulties of describing, let alone explaining, the culture of the Tongans hung heavily over the journal-keepers. Cook warned that although two or three months in the area might be expected to give a good insight into the customs of the inhabitants, this was far from being the case. Few were willing to take his questions seriously, and when they did misunderstanding resulted in 'a hundred mistakes'. Finally, and fatally to the cause of scholarship, the arrival of the ships halted the normal processes of living. 'It was always holyday', reflected Cook gloomily.[87] Later in the voyage King added his views when he stressed the fallacy of believing that men from a sophisticated culture could easily understand 'the workings of the human mind in its rude state'. There was real difficulty in distinguishing the permanent from the transient, and a danger of misunderstanding not only speech but action.[88]

From the Tongan Islands the ships headed for Tahiti, where Cook discovered that Spaniards had been and gone, that Purea was dead, but that Tu was still alive. The grim centrepiece of Cook's stay was his presence at a ceremony of human sacrifice. Webber drew the scene, and managed to capture some of the horror of the occasion missing from Cook's rather detached account (evidence perhaps of his increasing sense of how to conduct scientific investigations); for only after he had carefully observed the whole ceremony did Cook make his protest, and even then was overtaken by Omai. Not content with interpreting Cook's expressions of disapproval, he burst out with some sentiments of his own to the effect that 'if he a Cheif in England had put a man to death as he had done he would be hanged for it'.[89] Webber's depiction has a scene of barbaric activity near a *marai* festooned with human skulls, with drums beating, and in the centre a forlorn human figure bound to a pole – and one would have to read the text to realize that the victim was already dead, and so spared the agony of anticipation. Away to the right is a passive group of onlookers, including Cook and some of his officers. The latters' accounts add details not in Cook. Anderson, for example, was especially shocked by the lack of solemnity about the occasion, counted at least fifty skulls at the *marai*, and remembering Tongan claims about occasions when ten victims at a time were sacrificed, feared that 'the practice is extended all over the islands of these seas'.[90]

In other ways, too, disillusionment was setting in. It is there in an entry where Cook is ruminating on Omai's lack of application, and continues: 'This kind of indifferency is the true character of his nation. Europeans have visited them at times for these ten years past, yet we find neither new arts nor improvements in the old, nor have they copied after us in any one thing.'[91] This had become crucial. The expeditions were setting out from a Europe where as we have seen in earlier chapters the capacity and desire for improvement had become the touchstone by which human societies were measured; and whether the discoverers looked at the silent, apathetic Fuegans or the gregarious, boisterous Tahitians, they seemed to find few Pacific peoples which conformed to western ideals of progress and development. It is significant that when Herder was illustrating his 'progressive scale, from the man who borders on the brute to the purest genius', it was to the southern hemisphere that he turned for examples of the former – 'the New-Zealand cannibal and a Fenelon, a Newton and a wretched persheray'.[92]

For King it was the first visit to Tahiti, and his expectations were high. Inevitably, perhaps, they were disappointed. He was less than enchanted with the greeting given to the ships' officers by the notables on the island – 'no strong symptoms of affection; they were very inquisitive in finding the diff^t rank of the gentlemen, & proportioned their caresses accordingly'. The men (though not the women, as beguiling as ever) he compared unfavourably with those of Tonga 'in shape, air, sweetness, & manliness', and indeed 'in most things that give one set of people the preference over another'. Omai's future he thought bleak since the rigidity of Tahitian society was such 'that there is not perhaps a single instance where merit or abilities have rais'd a low man to a high rank among them'. The island itself, though undeniably beautiful, 'instead of being a delightful garden, is a rich wilderness'. As the ships headed north from the Society Islands, King fired a parting shot: 'I rather think that whoever goes to this country will be mistaken in his expectations of finding it that Elysium which warm imaginations have paint'd it to be.'[93]

In sailing on the unfrequented route from Tahiti to the northwest coast of America the expedition made the major, and for Cook himself fatal, discovery of the Sandwich (Hawaiian) Islands in January 1778. Cook quickly noted, and wondered at, the resemblance between the inhabitants and those of Tahiti; but if in some ways this farthest north of the Polynesian island groups seemed familiar, a new and unexpected development was the reverential respect paid to Cook, with people on Kauai lying prone as he approached. When the ships returned at the end of 1778 after a wearing, frustrating season of exploration on the northwest coast of America, this had turned into something altogether more elaborate and significant, for on the largest island, Hawaii, Cook was now undoubtedly regarded as a god, probably Lono, bringer of light, plenty and peace.[94] We hear nothing of Cook's reaction to this, since his journal ends on 17 January 1779, the day he landed in Hawaii; but elsewhere we read much of the extraordinary happenings of the next month – Cook's escort of priests, the abasement before him of the populace, the offering of food, the protection of the expedition's store places by the imposition of a *tabu*. As Clerke informed the Admiralty later, Cook's treatment 'more resembled that due to a Deity than a human being'.[95] Whatever reservations Cook may have had, the practical convenience of priestly support and popular submission was undoubted. King wrote at the end of January that they could put 'entire confidence' in the people, and it was because of this atmosphere of respect and helpfulness that the change of mood when the ships returned to Kealakekua Bay for repairs was not only unwelcome but unexpected. Cook certainly showed less than his usual judgment and care in the events leading up to his death in a fracas on the beach on 14 February. Writing two days later, Clerke was still mystified by it all: 'The extraordinary friendship and attention of these priests since our first arrival among them has been such as we never before met with nor could expect from any Indians, or indeed I believe I may say any nation of people in the world, they abound in the riches of the country which they deal out with a most liberal hand.' The next month Clerke returned to the subject again as he explained that the islanders had seemed to compete with each other in helping the crews. But then came the return of the ships, and the inexplicable transformation of the islanders, in Clerke's eyes, from a friendly, hospitable people to a menacing mob. He concluded, 'How they will stand in the eyes of the world now I cannot presume to say.'[96] The answer to this was that the world, or at least that part of it interested in Cook's doings, was shocked and revolted by the news of his death; and the reaction began with Cook's men. Even after the first impulse to wreak bloody retribution among the Hawaiians had died down, the change of mood was unmistakeable. As the ships reached Kauai once more, Clerke noted that all efforts by the inhabitants to persuade crew members to desert were unavailing, that a life in the islands, for which men had been willing to risk everything, was now regarded by them with horror.

The death of Cook brought into sharper focus the conflict of attitudes which had accompanied the Pacific voyages from the beginning. There were still those who discerned in the islands traces of the golden age of man's past, and feared that European influences would corrupt and contaminate. James Dunbar lamented in 1780 that the discovery expeditions 'have never yet been happy for any of the tribes of mankind visited by us. The vices of Europe have already contaminated the Otaheitan blood . . . the natives of that happy island, so cruelly abused, will have cause to lament for ages, that any European vessel ever touched their shores.'[97] Horace Walpole used more extravagant language when he wrote in the same year, 'How I abominate Mr Banks and Dr Solander who routed the poor Otaheitians out of the centre of the ocean, and carried our abominable passions amongst them! Not even that poor little speck could escape European restlessness.'[98] Others could see only ignorance, backwardness and villainy among the islanders. A versifier expressed this view in his *Ode to the Memory of the late Captain Cook*:

> Here did th'inglorious native wear away
> The blissful night, the prowling day . . .
>
> Whose darken'd mind in mercy found no joy,
> Who vengeful – conquer'd only to destroy![99]

These represented the extremes; less committed observers considered the problem in a more piecemeal and empirical way. The primitivists, now looking rather old-fashioned, had found support for their ideas in the lucubrations of Bougainville, Commerson and Hawkesworth. The swing away from these came with Cook's second voyage, with its more critical and detached writings, its violent deaths, and the attempts by the Forsters to match theory with observation. At home the works of writers ranging from Monboddo to Millar were placing the new discoveries, along with the older reports on the American Indian and the African Negro, firmly in a context of socio-economic evolution. They demanded, not selective examples to support arguments of universal validity, but a massing of observations which would surely show the infinite variety of mankind. They did not all regard primitive peoples as degenerate and inferior, but Herder expressed an increasingly common sentiment when he wrote in 1773 that 'the human race is destined for a progress of scenes, of education, of manners'.[100]

On his three voyages Cook had established the salient features of the Pacific. Much remained to be done, but in the way of defining detail rather than in solving major geographical problems. The tasks and achievements of his successors inevitably appeared more mundane, and their voyages were rivalled by the appearance of trading, missionary and settlement enterprises. By the end of the century there was British settlement in Australia; Nootka had taken on a new significance – no longer simply Cook's watering place on the northwest coast of America, but a centre of international dispute; the first missionaries had reached Tahiti; and everywhere the vessels of the traders and whalers were beginning to follow the explorers' tracks. As the freshness and novelty of the first, ecstatic discoveries faded, so did the earlier conviction that Europe could learn much from the Pacific. The South Seas retained their allure, but as a remote haven for the few, far removed from the conventions of civilized society. Tahiti, in particular, still cast its spell. As Bligh wrote of the *Bounty* mutineers: 'They imagined it in their power to fix themselves in the midst of plenty, on one of the finest islands in the world, where they need not labour, and where the allurements of dissipation are beyond any thing that can be conceived.'[101] In England Robert Southey sympathized with the decision of the *Bounty* mutineers:

> Why is there not some corner of the world where wealth is useless! Is humanity so very vicious that society cannot exist without so many artificial distinctions linked together as we are in the great chain. Why should the extremity of that chain be neglected? At this moment I could form the delightful theory of an island . . . Otaheitia independent of its women had many inducements not only for the sailor but the philosopher . . . He might introduce the advantages and yet avoid the vices of cultivated society.[102]

There were still new arrivals to the islands who were entranced by what they saw. The *Pandora*'s surgeon, George Hamilton, on the vessel's eventful search for the *Bounty* mutineers, wrote of Tahiti in terms so extravagant as to recall memories of Bougainville and Hawkesworth: '. . . the Cytheria of the southern hemisphere . . . where the earth without tillage produces both food and cloathing, the trees loaded with the most odoriferous flowers, and the fair ones ever willing to fill your arms with love.'[103] A little earlier, in the north Pacific, the experiences of a shipwrecked crew among the hospitable Palau islanders prompted the narrator of their adventures to draw a conventional distinction between the two cultures: 'The people of PELEW, tutored in the school of Nature, acted from her impulse alone, they were open and undisguised; unconscious of deceit themselves, they neither feared nor looked for it in others. Our countrymen – born and brought up in a civilized nation, where Art assumes every form and colouring of life, and is even perfectioned into a science, were fashioned by education to suspicion and distrust.'[104]

More experienced observers of the Pacific scene generally held different opinions. George Vancouver, who had sailed with Cook on his second and third voyages, and commanded a notable surveying expedition in the 1790s, noted with foreboding the changes which had taken place in Tahiti over the preceding two decades. European implements and supplies were now in common use and great demand, to an extent which had made the islanders 'regardless of their former tools and manufactures, which are now growing fast out of use, and, I may add, equally out of remembrance'.[105] As he wrote of this new vulnerability he reflected the opinion of the editor of Cook's second voyage who had expressed similar concern: 'It would have been far better for these poor people, never to have known our superiority in the accommodation and arts that make life comfortable, than, after once knowing it, to be again abandoned to their original incapacity of improvement.'[106] De Pauw, though writing of the Americas at the time of the Spanish conquest rather than of the Pacific in the late eighteenth century, had postulated these ominous possibilities in direct and precise form when he noted 'l'extrême fragilité d'un équilibre, qui s'est trouvé brusquement rompu par l'invasion des Européens'.[107] Herder stressed the potentially destructive effects of European overseas expansion on both the discoverers and the discovered, the exploiters and the exploited: 'The modern conquerors of savage nations, full of European arrogance when they arrived, ended by being swallowed up by the illnesses of the new climate . . . The conquered, too, forced to bend themselves to the way of life of the conquerors, did violence to their own genius and fell into decadence.'[108]

To the implications of European material superiority other observers added more general considerations in the aftermath of Cook's voyages. The published account of the disastrous expedition by La

Pérouse in 1785–88 had numerous comments by the commander on what he saw to be the brutish nature of the peoples of the Pacific. The preface to the English edition set the tone for much that followed: 'In reading the narratives of those who have visited savage nations, it is impossible to avoid contemplating with self-exultation, the superiority of civilized man over a state of nature, which if it means any thing, signifies a state of ignorance, where cunning and treachery almost universally prevail.' With rather more authority, if equal prejudice, La Pérouse, soured by violent clashes and the killing of some of his men, insisted that man in a state of nature was 'cruel, base, and deceitful'. He appealed to his 'sad experience' for support. 'In vain may philosophers exclaim against this picture. While they are making books by the fire-side, I have been traversing the globe for thirty years, and have actually witnessed the cunning and injustice of nations which they portray as necessarily simple and virtuous, because little removed from a state of nature.'[109] Similar sentiments were expressed about the Aborigines by British officers involved in establishing the convict settlement in New South Wales in 1788. The European arrival, Governor Phillip wrote, brought 'order and useful arrangement' to a scene of 'tumult and confusion'; for there was a general consensus of opinion that the Aborigines of the area, 'shivering savages . . . ready to perish for one half of the year with hunger' must 'rank very low, even in the scale of savages'. Captain Tench of the Marine detachment with the First Fleet, went on to wish 'a thousand times' that 'those European philosophers, whose closet speculations exalt a state of nature above a state of civilization, could survey the phantom, which their heated imaginations have raised: possibly they might then learn, that a state of nature is, of all others, least adapted to promote the happiness of a being'.[110]

Then there was also, as Bernard Smith has written, 'the austere religious temper of evangelical thought growing more powerful among all classes of English society year by year, a temper that was disposed to take neither a lenient view of cannibalism, infanticide, and what appeared to be the licentious dances and sexual orgies of native savages . . . English society was slowly but surely ceasing to be diverted, instructed, and amused by savages.'[111] Instead, they were being regarded as degenerate (or backward) and certainly licentious beings, but worthy of redemption. To that end was directed the first sermon delivered by Thomas Haweis to the London Missionary Society soon after its founding in 1795: 'A new world hath lately opened to our view, call it island or continent, that exceeds Europe in size: New Holland; and now become the receptacles of our outcasts of society – New Zealand, and the innumerable islands, which spot the bosom of the

Pacific Ocean . . . which seem to realise the fabled Gardens of the Hesperides . . . But amidst these enchanting scenes, savage nature still feasts on the flesh of its prisoners – appeases its Gods with human sacrifices – whole societies of men and women live promiscuously, and murder every infant born among them.'[112] The next year the missionary vessel *Duff* left for Tahiti; and soon the accounts of the explorers were being supplemented by the reports of devoted missionaries whose task it was to save the Pacific islanders from eternal hellfire. Chateaubriand reflected on the change: 'Tahiti has lost her dances, her choirs, her voluptuous customs. The beautiful girls of New Cythera perhaps praised too much by Bougainville, are today under their breadfruit trees and their elegant palmtrees, puritans who go to the service, read the Scripture with Methodist missionaries, discuss from morning to night and atone in great boredom for the excessive gaiety of their mothers.'[113]

Alongside the new spirit of missionary endeavour went a continuation of the insistence which the Forsters, Herder and others had expressed that the fleeting, subjective impressions of the explorers should be replaced by an intensive, scientific investigation of the Pacific peoples. Only thus could the confused, contradictory medley of impressions be reconciled. The dissatisfaction of scholars at the explorers' accounts and the more precise instructions given to the later expeditions showed this mood. It was summed up in a percipient memorandum written for Baudin's expedition to the south Pacific of 1800–3 by a young French scholar, Joseph-Marie Degérando. His basic premise was a familiar one. In scrutinizing the peoples of the Pacific, 'we shall in a way be taken back to the first periods of our own history; we shall be able to set up secure experiments on the origin and generation of ideas, on the formation and development of language, and on the relations between these two processes. The philosophical traveller, sailing to the ends of the earth, is in fact travelling in time; he is exploring the past; every step he makes is the passage of an age. Those unknown islands that he reaches are for him the passage of human society.' The detailed instructions which he suggested for the expedition's guidance were those which anthropologists would adopt later, much later, in the century. The stay should be lengthy and unobtrusive; the inward life as well as the external forms of a society should be examined; the language should be mastered; European standards and parallels should be ignored.[114] Degérando's 'philosophical traveller' was not to be found on Baudin's expedition, nor indeed on any other for several decades. Anthropology and ethnology did not emerge as recognizable disciplines until the mid-nineteenth century, and by then the Pacific was to a large extent explored, settled and administered. No anthropologist would ever investigate the culture of the Tahitians, the Maoris or the Aborigines in their pre-contact setting, for that had long been contaminated and changed by European influences. By the time that scholars trained in the new sciences reached the Pacific they had to probe its remotest, most inaccessible regions before they could determine how the peoples of the great ocean might have lived before the coming of the Europeans.

NOTES

1 John Douglas, Introduction to James Cook and James King, *A Voyage to the Pacific Ocean*. . . . (1784), I, lxvii.
2 See Michèle Duchet, *Anthropologie et histoire au siècle des lumières* (Paris, 1971), pp. 60, 108.
3 John Callender, *Terra Australis Cognita* (1766–68), I, 77–8; II, 308.
4 References in this paragraph from *ibid.*, I, 85, 278; II, 152, 157–8, 160, 166–7.
5 *Ibid.*, II, 242, 362.
6 *The Voyages of Abel Janszoon Tasman*, ed. Andrew Sharp (Oxford, 1968), pp. 124, 136.
7 The original passages are in Charles le Gobien, *Histoire des Isles Marianes* (Paris, 1700), pp. 43–8, 140–3; via de Brosses they were taken into Callender, III, 41–6.
8 Callender, I, 11; III, 736.
9 *The Journal of Jacob Roggeveen*, ed. Andrew Sharp (Oxford, 1970), p. 153.
10 See *La Austrialia del Espiritu Santo*, ed. Celsus Kelly (The Hakluyt Society. Cambridge, 1966), I, 63–4. The whole of this section, 'The islands and their peoples', by G. S. Parsonson, forms an admirable summary.
11 *Byron's Journal of his Circumnavigation 1764–1766*, ed. R. E. Gallagher (The Hakluyt Society, Cambridge, 1964), p. lxxvii.
12 *The Discovery of Tahiti* . . . , ed. Hugh Carrington (The Hakluyt Society, 1948), pp. 135, 140.
13 *Ibid.*, pp. 166–7.
14 *Ibid.*, pp. 179, 187.
15 John Hawkesworth, *An Account of the Voyages undertaken by the Order of His Present Majesty for making Discoveries in the Southern Hemisphere* (1773), I, 461, 463–4.
16 The reports are printed in *The Quest and Occupation of Tahiti* . . . *1772–76*, ed. B. G. Corney (The Hakluyt Society, 1913–19), II, 461–6; *News from New Cythera: A Report of Bougainville's Voyage 1766–1769*, ed. L. Davis Hammond (Minneapolis, 1970).
17 'Lewis' de Bougainville, *A Voyage round the World* . . . trans. J. R. Forster (1772), p. 269. For a recent scholarly edition which at last does justice to the journals kept on the voyage see *Bougainville et ses compagnons autour du monde 1766–1769*, ed. Etienne Taillemite (Paris, 1977).
18 The best scholarly edition is that by Gilbert Chinard (Paris, 1935); the summary and extract here are taken from the English translation by Wilfrid Jackson (1926), pp. 155–6.
19 See Duchet, *Anthropologie et histoire*, p. 462.

20 For this dispute, which involved among others Matthew Maty, Horace Walpole, de Pauw and Dom Pernety, and in the end centred around the question of the virility of the American, see the appendix on 'The Patagonian Giants' by Helen Wallis in Gallagher, *Byron's Journal*, pp. 185–96.

21 Quoted Bernard Smith, *European Vision and the South Pacific 1768–1850* (Oxford, 1960), p. 8.

22 See *The Journals of Captain James Cook: The Voyage of the Endeavour 1768–1771*, ed. J. C. Beaglehole (The Hakluyt Society, Cambridge, 1955), p. 514.

23 Quoted T. M. Curley, *Samuel Johnson and the Age of Travel* (Athens, Ga., 1976), p. 66.

24 *The Endeavour Journal of Joseph Banks 1768–1771*, ed. J. C. Beaglehole (Sydney, 1962), p. 396.

25 Quoted Michael E. Hoare, 'The Forsters and Cook's Second Voyage 1772–1775', in *Captain Cook: Image and Impact*, ed. Walter Veit (Melbourne, 1972), p. 114.

26 Banks, *Endeavour Journal*, p. 305.

27 Cook, *Journal 1768–1771*, p. 128; Banks, *Endeavour Journal*, p. 351.

28 *Ibid.*, p. 379.

29 Sydney Parkinson, *A Journal of a Voyage to the South Seas* (1773), p. 23.

30 Quoted Alan Frost, 'The Pacific ocean: the eighteenth century's "new world" ', in *Studies on Voltaire and the eighteenth century*, CLI-CLV (1976), 797.

31 Banks, *Endeavour Journal*, p. 424.

32 *Ibid.*, p. 424 n.

33 *Ibid.*, II, 19–20.

34 *Ibid.*, II, 50.

35 *Ibid.*, II, 130.

36 Cook, *Journal 1768–1771*, p. 399. For further comment on this see Glyndwr Williams, ' "Far more happier than we Europeans ": Reactions to the Australian Aborigines on Cook's Voyage', *Historical Studies*, XX (1981).

37 See Colin Roderick, 'Sir Joseph Banks, Queen Oberea and the Satirists', in Veit, *Cook: Image and Impact*, pp. 67–89.

38 *The Yale Edition of Horace Walpole's Correspondence*, ed. W. S. Lewis (New Haven, 1937–), XXXII, 127–8. Several scholars have recently defended Hawkesworth's editorial methods; see, for example, W. H. Pearson, 'Hawkesworth's Voyages', in *Studies in the Eighteenth Century*, ed. R. F. Brissenden, II (Canberra, 1973), 239–58.

39 James Burnet (Lord Monboddo), *Origin and Progress of Language*, I (Edinburgh, 1773), 133, 440.

40 Henry Home (Lord Kames), *Sketches of the History of Man* (Edinburgh, 1774), pp. 106, 384–5.

41 Antonelli Gerbi, *The Dispute of the New World: the History of a Polemic, 1750–1900* (Pittsburgh, 1973), p. 74.

42 Adam Ferguson, *An Essay on the History of Civil Society* (Edinburgh, 1767), pp. 384–5.

43 James Denham Steuart, *Works* (1804), I, 44.

44 John Millar, *Observations concerning the Distinction of Ranks in Society* (London, 1771), especially pp. 112, 143, 232.

45 Edited by Michael E. Hoare, it is being published by the Hakluyt Society in four volumes as *The Resolution Journal of Johann Reinhold Forster 1772–1775*. I am much indebted to Dr Hoare for his permission to consult this edition when it was in typescript form.

46 J. R. Forster, *Enchiridion historiae naturali inserviens* (Halle, 1788). I am grateful to Dr Hoare for this reference.

47 J. G. Herder, *Outlines of a Philosophy of the History of Man*, trans. T. Churchill (1800), p. 153.

48 *The Journals of Captain James Cook: The Voyage of the Resolution and Adventure 1772–1775*, ed. J. C. Beaglehole (The Hakluyt Society, Cambridge, 1961), p. 795.

49 George Forster, *A Voyage round the World* . . . (London, 1777), p. 14 (all references are to the 1968 edition published in Berlin as Volume I of *Georg Forsters Werke*).

50 Cook, *Journal 1772–1775*, p. 235.

51 *The Journals of Captain James Cook: The Voyage of the Resolution and Discovery 1776–1780*, ed. J. C. Beaglehole (The Hakluyt Society, Cambridge, 1967), p. 306.

52 J. R. Forster, *Observations made during a Voyage round the World* (1778), p. 361.

53 George Forster, *Voyage*, pp. 178, 182, 216, 217.

54 Cook, *Journal 1772–1775*, p. 260 n.

55 *The Resolution Journal of Johann Reinhold Forster 1772–1775*, ed. Michael E. Hoare (typescript) entry for 7 October 1773.

56 Cook, *Journal 1772–1775*, p. 536 n.

57 *With Captain James Cook in the Antarctic and Pacific: the private journal of James Burney* (Canberra, 1975), p. 51.

58 Cook, *Journal 1772–1775*, p. 175.

59 George Forster, *Voyage*, pp. 133, 298.

60 *Resolution Journal of Forster* (typescript) entry for 24 April 1773.

61 George Forster, *Voyage*, p. 618.

62 Cook, *Journal 1772–1775*, p. 234 n.

63 Smith, *European Vision and the South Pacific*, pp. 46–7.

64 J. R. Forster, *Observations*, p. 421.

65 A. Sparrman, *A Voyage round the World*, transl. H. Beamish and A. Mackenzie-Grieve (1953), p. 38.

66 Quoted Curley, *Johnson and the Age of Travel*, p. 69.

67 J. R. Forster, *Observations*, p. 295.

68 See A. O. Lovejoy, 'Herder and the Enlightenment Philosophy of History', *Essays in the History of Ideas* (Baltimore, 1948), p. 171. Also above p. 139.

69 George Forster, *Voyage*, p. 618.

70 *The London Magazine*, XLIV (1775), 497.

71 Kames, *Sketches*, II, 296. Kames was one of several who saw the ultimate dangers of decadence in 'commercial' societies embodied in China or India; see above, pp. 150–1.

72 There is a considerable literature on Omai: two recent books are Michael Alexander, *Omai: 'Noble Savage'* (1977) and E. H. McCormick, *Omai: Pacific Envoy* (Auckland, 1977).

73 See Anon., *Omiah's Farewell* (1776), p. ii.

74 Sparrman, *Voyage*, p. 123.

75 Cook, *Journal 1776–1780*, p. lxxxiv n.

76 *Ibid.*, p. lxxvi n.

77 J. C. Beaglehole, *The Life of Captain James Cook* (1974), p. 689.

78 *Crozet's Voyage in the Years 1771–1772*, transl. H. Ling Roth (1891), pp. 49, 63.

79 Cook, *Journal 1776–1780*, p. 60.

80 *Ibid.*, pp. 62, 71.

81 *Crozet's Voyage*, p. 184.

82 Cook, *Journal 1776–1780*, pp. 73, 184.

83 *Ibid.*, pp. 115, 117, 1304.

84 *Ibid.*, p. 151 n.

85 *Ibid.*, p. 153.

86 *Ibid.*, pp. 839–40.

87 *Ibid.*, p. 166.

88 *Ibid.*, pp. 1406–7.

89 *Ibid.*, p. 206.

90 *Ibid.*, p. 983.

91 *Ibid.*, p. 241.
92 Herder, *Outlines*, p. 93. A 'persheray' was a Percherais or Fuegan.
93 Cook, *Journal 1776–1780*, pp. 1373, 1374, 1386, 1390, 1391.
94 For some brief remarks on a large, and contentious, subject see Beaglehole, *Life of Cook*, pp. 657–60.
95 Cook, *Journal 1776–1780*, p. 1536.
96 *Ibid.*, pp. 543, 593.
97 James Dunbar, *Essays on the History of Mankind* (1780), pp. 356–7.
98 *Walpole's Correspondence*, II, 225.
99 Quoted Smith, *European Vision and South Pacific*, p. 86.
100 Quoted Lovejoy, *Essays*, p. 170.
101 William Bligh, *A Voyage to the South Sea* (1792), p. 162.
102 Quoted Frost, 'The Pacific ocean', pp. 805–6.
103 George Hamilton, *A Voyage round the World in His Majesty's Frigate Pandora* (Berwick, 1793), pp. 37–8.
104 George Keate, *An Account of the Pelew Islands* (1788), p. 250.
105 George Vancouver, *A Voyage of Discovery to the North Pacific Ocean* (1798), I, 37.
106 James Cook, *A Voyage towards the South Pole* (1777), II, 136.
107 Duchet, *Anthropologie et histoire*, p. 203.
108 Quoted Frank E. Manuel, *The Eighteenth Century Confronts the Gods* (Cambridge, Mass., 1959), p. 293.
109 *The Voyage of La Pérouse round the World*, ed. M. L. A. Milet Mureau (1798), I, preface, and pp. 152–3.
110 See *The Voyage of Governor Phillip to Botany Bay*, ed. James J. Auchmuty (Sydney, 1970), especially p. 79; and *Sydney's First Four Years . . . by Captain Watkin Tench of the Marines*, ed. L. F. Fitzhardinge (Sydney, 1961), especially pp. 281, 291.
111 Smith, *European Vision and South Pacific*, p. 100. See also above pp. 121, 123.
112 Quoted *ibid.*, pp. 106–7.
113 Quoted J. K. Dowling, 'Bougainville and Cook', in Veit, *Cook: Image and Impact*, p. 38.
114 *The Observations of Savage Peoples by Joseph-Marie Degérando*, ed. F. C. T. Moore (1969), pp. 63–5.

Conclusion

This book has been concerned with the efforts of Englishmen for more than a century to make sense of a world outside Europe. Travellers and explorers had written about it in their letters, journals and sometimes in published books. At home students of all sorts had assessed this material and tried to shape it into convincing patterns. Painters and illustrators of books had depicted it. A few playwrights, poets or novelists had tried to re-create it in their work. Craftsmen and designers had sometimes drawn upon it for new motifs.

At the end of our period, around 1800, those who were engaged in these very diverse attempts to explain the world to themselves or to their European contemporaries were generally confident about their success. They contrasted their efforts with those of previous generations who, they believed, had either been credulous of myth or prone to excessive generalization on insubstantial foundations. Specialization and the accumulation of apparently exact knowledge had become matters for pride. Although at the end of the eighteenth century there were still men of colossal intellectual range, such as Joseph Banks or William Jones, who tried to study all aspects of human activity as well as the physical sciences, the age of the men of universal knowledge, Adam Smith or Dr Johnson, Montesquieu or Voltaire, was passing. The Natural History of Man was breaking down into separate disciplines: geography, history, political economy, the study of language, and even what has come to be seen with hindsight as the origins of anthropology.[1] Regional specializations, Egyptology, Indology and Sinology were developing. No single mind could perhaps hope to comprehend all that was now known of man, but the division of labour had, it was thought, produced a great corpus of verifiable certainties. The world was better mapped; a sure chronology of man's past was emerging; non-European languages were being studied systematically; and, however presumptuous such claims may now seem, the workings of human societies of all kinds were considered to be well understood and their future development predictable.

The march of exact knowledge and the dispelling of myth and

illusion about Asia were thought to have been gathering speed even at the end of the seventeenth century.[2] Few then, for instance, believed in a rich, bountiful, golden India. Ideas of a rational, tolerant Islam, postulated by a few free thinkers, had never gained many adherents. The enchanted world of the *Arabian Nights* was shown to have no present existence. Hopes for what was exotic or astonishing still, however, survived for parts of Asia to which European access had so far been relatively restricted. During the eighteenth century such hopes were shown to be groundless. Assessments of China were radically changed. It could no longer be regarded as a prodigy of serene paternal government and flourishing agriculture. There was no Arabia the Happy worthy of the name. No mighty Khan lived in Tartary. Gibbon and Ferguson asked themselves whether another great invading horde could arise in Central Asia and sweep into Europe. They were now sure that this could not happen. Tartary, 'the nursery of nations is itself gone to decay', Ferguson commented.[3]

As far as the world of 'savagery' was concerned, there was by 1800 a growing European demand for more dispassionate, scientific investigation. The Pacific expeditions of Cook and his contemporaries had set a new standard against which most of the books of travel and exploration looked insubstantial indeed. The complaints of scholars in the last years of the eighteenth century show their dissatisfaction with much of what existed. The American Presbyterian minister and Princeton professor, Samuel Stanhope Smith, thought that 'ordinary travellers' were no longer to be trusted with the task: 'Countries are described from a single spot, manners from a single action, and men from the first man that is seen on a foreign shore.'[4] Archibald Dalzel's editor stressed the difficulty of deciphering the history of peoples who did not keep written records, and criticized those books of travel based on brief glimpses of an alien scene: 'Scraps hastily picked up and ill understood, put into form by a fertile imagination, constitute most of those works that are offered under such names.'[5] Degérando was concerned that explorers were 'divided by other concerns, and with a greater impetus to discover new countries than to study them, constantly moving when they should have stayed at rest, biased perhaps by those unjust prejudices that cast a slur in our eyes on savage societies.'[6] Herder despaired of finding realistic delineations of exotic peoples, and wished for 'a magic wand, which, at once transforming into faithful pictures all the vague verbal descriptions that hath hitherto been given, might present man with a gallery of figures of his fellow-creatures'.[7]

The demand for more detailed and impartial observations was not matched by any reluctance to generalize and evaluate on the basis of what was available. The process of Britain's expansion overseas in this period was encouraged and justified by increasingly confident assumptions of intellectual, moral and practical superiority. Less was heard now of those primitivist interpretations which had revealed self-doubt and hesitancy on the part of earlier writers about their own culture. There was instead a general acceptance that to relate primitive lifestyles to the European environment was misleading and unscholarly, and this stern insistence cut deeply into those philosophical notions which had seen in the carefree existence of the savage an implied condemnation of western society. Institutions and customs at home might still come under critical fire, but they were no longer likely to be seriously compared with those of the American Indian or the Pacific islander. The emphasis which Montesquieu, Buffon and the writers of the Scottish Enlightenment placed both on physical and cultural environment, and on historical evolution does much to explain this. The life of the savage was not an alternative to that of the European: it was enforced backwardness produced by adverse circumstances. Furthermore, there was a growing practical realization that societies across the world varied greatly in strength and resilience. Scholars did not need to indulge in Hume's denigration of 'all the other species' to reflect that most primitive societies which had come into contact with Europeans had changed and crumbled before the impact. Their alarming fragility raised doubts about their integrity, and the concern shown by many observers in the second half of the century about the dangers of European pressures indicated contemporary assumptions about the weakness of primitive cultures.

The analogy of the savage as an infant was a popular and influential concept; it explained existing backwardness and allowed for future improvement. So George Vancouver saw his Pacific surveys as part of 'that expansive arch over which the arts and sciences should pass to the furthermost corners of the earth, for the instruction and happiness of the most lowly children of nature . . . the untutored parts of the human race.'[8] The identity and nationality of any future tutor no doubt varied from country to country in Europe, but certainly in Britain William Guthrie expressed sentiments which were becoming commonplace when he insisted that 'Great Britain, though she cannot boast of a more luxuriant soil or a happier climate than many other countries, has advantages of another and superior kind, which make her the delight, the envy, and the mistress of the world: these are, the equity of her laws, the freedom of her political constitution, and the moderation of her religious system.'[9] This was a claim which could be directed against Britain's continental neighbours, or deployed on a more global scale. The elder Stephen, stalwart of the early abolition movement, linked the two areas when he wrote that British involvement in the slave-trade was the more deplorable because 'Science shines upon us with her meridian beams . . . morals and manners have happily distinguished us from the other nations of Europe.'[10]

The humanitarianism of the period, shown in the abolitionist movement, and in the founding of the new missionary societies, was not an inhibiting force as far as the extension of British influence was concerned. It represented an important dimension in the growing concern for indigenous peoples, but also revealed that attitudes towards them, sometimes critical, sometimes protective, were now rarely admiring. To John Leyden, putting together his history of Africa for publication in 1799, the real damage inflicted by European contact on Africans was that it had turned their energies to the slave-trade, 'Instead of converting to purposes of utility that admiration and unbounded curiosity, which European refinement excited in their simple minds; instead of availing themselves of that propensity to imitation which rude tribes exhibit, for introducing the arts, sciences, and legitimate commerce.'[11] To Wilberforce, the savage world appeared imperfect in all respects: it knew neither the blessings of the Christian religion, nor the practical advantages of western civilization. The one would serve to introduce the other.[12] How precisely this might be done would vary according to situation, and presumably according to the strength of the indigenous culture. The Aborigines of Australia were adjudged to have no political or social existence, and so New South Wales was regarded as *terra nullius*, open to occupation and dominion by Britain through virtue of Cook's discoveries.[13] In West Africa, on the other hand, there were recognizable institutions and government, but Banks in 1799 had no hesitation in recommending 'conquest' to the government as one of the possible ways of extending British influence in the region.[14]

At the end of the eighteenth century, despite general complacency about Britain's role in India, a world-wide British empire of conquest was still a forbidding prospect for some. The costs involved and the likely stimulus to militaristic and authoritarian tendencies at home aroused some misgivings. Nevertheless, the ultimate inevitability and desirability of expansion by Britain throughout the world in some form or other, trade, influence and missions as well as conquest, seemed not to be at issue. Few now seriously argued that apparently simple societies, such as those of the Pacific islands, should be left uncontaminated by European contact. To replace disorder with order, to end the atrophy of ages, to encourage regularity of cultivation and moderation of rule, were obviously beneficent objectives. That they might also coincide with Britain's material interests should not be interpreted too cynically. As trade with indigenous peoples expanded, so would they be encouraged to produce and consume more, thus achieving a higher standard of life. Religious enlightenment and secular knowledge would be propagated from Britain by missionaries and school masters. As a contributor to the *Edinburgh Review* put it in 1802, 'Europe is the light of the world, and the ark of knowledge: upon the welfare of Europe, hangs the destiny of the most remote and savage people.'[15]

The processes of ordering the world both in the minds and by the actions of Englishmen were not necessarily connected. Scholars could work on areas where British influence was negligible, and men of action could be largely oblivious of the peoples among whom they conducted their operations. But in most cases the two activities clearly did have connections with one another. It was, for instance, no coincidence that Britain became the main interpreter of India to Europe at the time when her conquests began, nor that the world's leading naval power should have been the most assiduous explorer of the Pacific. Yet if there are connections between assumed knowledge of the world and the growth of British power and influence, they are not simple ones. On the one hand, it would be hard to make a convincing general case that knowledge preceded expansion and provided a blueprint for it; on the other, it would be a serious distortion to depict late eighteenth-century British views of the peoples of the world as no more than *ex post facto* rationalizations of Britain's material interests. There is probably some substance in both propositions. The relationship of idea and action is in our view a confused mixture of cause and effect. What we have tried to do in this book is to examine this relationship in specific instances and to show how views about the world's peoples and an increasingly active British role in their lives went together. By the end of the eighteenth century, educated Englishmen and some wider sections of British society had come to believe both that the workings of non-European societies were comprehensible to them, and that what was being revealed were societies inferior to their own and capable of being changed for the better by outside intervention. This was a view of the world appropriate to a nation which was already exercising considerable influence beyond its shores and in the years ahead was to acquire the greatest of all the European overseas empires.

NOTES

1 M. Duchet, *Anthropologie et histoire au siècle des lumières* (Paris, 1971), pp. 12–13.
2 See above, p. 245.
3 *An Essay on the History of Civil Society*, ed. D. Forbes (Edinburgh, 1966), p. 104.
4 S. S. Smith, *An Essay on the Causes of the Variety of Complexion and Figure in the Human Species* (Edinburgh, 1788), p. 138 *n*.
5 Archibald Dalzel, *The History of Dahomy, an Inland Kingdom of Africa* (1793), pp. v–vi.
6 *The Observations of Savage Peoples by Joseph-Marie Degérando*, ed. F. C. T. Moore (1969), pp. 64–5.
7 J. G. Herder, *Outlines of a Philosophy of the History of Man*, trans. T. Churchill (1800), p. 161.
8 George Vancouver, *A Voyage of Discovery to the North Pacific Ocean* (1798), I, 37.
9 William Guthrie, *A New Geographical, Historical and Commercial Grammar* (9th edn. 1785), preface.
10 Quoted D. B. Davis, *The Problem of Slavery in the Age of Revolution 1770–1823* (Ithaca, 1975), pp. 366–7.
11 [John Leyden], *A Historical and Philosophical Sketch of the Discoveries and Settlements of the Europeans in Northern & Western Africa* (Edinburgh, 1799), p. 90.
12 See Howard Temperley, 'Anti-Slavery as a form of cultural Imperialism', in *Anti-Slavery, Religion and Reform*, ed. Christine Bolt and Seymour Drescher (Folkestone, 1980), p. 346.
13 See Alan Frost, *Convicts and Empire: A Naval Question 1776–1811* (Melbourne, 1980), pp. 122–3, 140.
14 See above, p. 254.
15 *Edinburgh Review*, II (1802), 64.

Index